Multicore
Application
Programming

Multicore Application Programming

For Windows, Linux, and Oracle® Solaris

Darryl Gove

✦✦ Addison-Wesley

Upper Saddle River, NJ • Boston • Indianapolis • San Francisco
New York • Toronto • Montreal • London • Munich • Paris • Madrid
Capetown • Sydney • Tokyo • Singapore • Mexico City

Many of the designations used by manufacturers and sellers to distinguish their products are claimed as trademarks. Where those designations appear in this book, and the publisher was aware of a trademark claim, the designations have been printed with initial capital letters or in all capitals.

The author and publisher have taken care in the preparation of this book, but make no expressed or implied warranty of any kind and assume no responsibility for errors or omissions. No liability is assumed for incidental or consequential damages in connection with or arising out of the use of the information or programs contained herein.

The publisher offers excellent discounts on this book when ordered in quantity for bulk purchases or special sales, which may include electronic versions and/or custom covers and content particular to your business, training goals, marketing focus, and branding interests. For more information, please contact:

U.S. Corporate and Government Sales
(800) 382-3419
corpsales@pearsontechgroup.com

For sales outside the United States please contact:

International Sales
international@pearson.com

Visit us on the Web: informit.com/aw

Library of Congress Cataloging-in-Publication Data

Gove, Darryl.
 Multicore application programming : for Windows, Linux, and Oracle Solaris / Darryl Gove.
     p.   cm.
 Includes bibliographical references and index.
 ISBN 978-0-321-71137-3 (pbk. : alk. paper)
 1. Parallel programming (Computer science) I. Title.
 QA76.642.G68 2011
 005.2'75–dc22
                                            2010033284

ISBN-13: 978-0-321-71137-3
ISBN-10:   0-321-71137-8
Text printed in the United States on recycled paper at RR Donnelley in Crawfordsville, IN.
First printing, October 2010

Editor-in-Chief
Mark Taub

Acquisitions Editor
Greg Doench

Managing Editor
John Fuller

Project Editor
Anna Popick

Copy Editor
Kim Wimpsett

Indexer
Ted Laux

Proofreader
Lori Newhouse

Editorial Assistant
Michelle Housley

Cover Designer
Gary Adair

Cover Photograph
Jenny Gove

Compositor
Rob Mauhar

Contents at a Glance

Contents

Preface

For a number of years, home computers have given the illusion of doing multiple tasks simultaneously. This has been achieved by switching between the running tasks many times per second. This gives the appearance of simultaneous activity, but it is only an appearance. While the computer has been working on one task, the others have made no progress. An old computer that can execute only a single task at a time might be referred to as having a single processor, a single CPU, or a single "core." The core is the part of the processor that actually does the work.

Recently, even home PCs have had *multicore* processors. It is now hard, if not impossible, to buy a machine that is not a multicore machine. On a multicore machine, each core can make progress on a task, so multiple tasks really do make progress at the same time.

The best way of illustrating what this means is to consider a computer that is used for converting film from a camcorder to the appropriate format for burning onto a DVD. This is a compute-intensive operation—a lot of data is fetched from disk, a lot of data is written to disk—but most of the time is spent by the processor decompressing the input video and converting that into compressed output video to be burned to disk.

On a single-core system, it might be possible to have two movies being converted at the same time while ignoring any issues that there might be with disk or memory requirements. The two tasks could be set off at the same time, and the processor in the computer would spend some time converting one video and then some time converting the other. Because the processor can execute only a single task at a time, only one video is actually being compressed at any one time. If the two videos show progress meters, the two meters will both head toward 100% completed, but it will take (roughly) twice as long to convert two videos as it would to convert a single video.

On a multicore system, there are two or more available cores that can perform the video conversion. Each core can work on one task. So, having the system work on two films at the same time will utilize two cores, and the conversion will take the same time as converting a single film. Twice as much work will have been achieved in the same time.

Multicore systems have the capability to do more work per unit time than single-core systems—two films can be converted in the same time that one can be converted on a single-core system. However, it's possible to split the work in a different way. Perhaps the multiple cores can work together to convert the same film. In this way, a system with two cores could convert a single film twice as fast as a system with only one core.

This book is about using and developing for multicore systems. This is a topic that is often described as complex or hard to understand. In some way, this reputation is justified. Like any programming technique, multicore programming can be hard to do both correctly and with high performance. On the other hand, there are many ways that multicore systems can be used to significantly improve the performance of an application or the amount of work performed per unit time; some of these approaches will be more difficult than others.

Perhaps saying "multicore programming is easy" is too optimistic, but a realistic way of thinking about it is that multicore programming is perhaps no more complex or no more difficult than the step from procedural to object-oriented programming. This book will help you understand the challenges involved in writing applications that fully utilize multicore systems, and it will enable you to produce applications that are functionally correct, that are high performance, and that scale well to many cores.

Who Is This Book For?

If you have read this far, then this book is likely to be for you. The book is a practical guide to writing applications that are able to exploit multicore systems to their full advantage. It is not a book about a particular approach to parallelization. Instead, it covers various approaches. It is also not a book wedded to a particular platform. Instead, it pulls examples from various operating systems and various processor types. Although the book does cover advanced topics, these are covered in a context that will enable all readers to become familiar with them.

The book has been written for a reader who is familiar with the C programming language and has a fair ability at programming. The objective of the book is not to teach programming languages, but it deals with the higher-level considerations of writing code that is correct, has good performance, and scales to many cores.

The book includes a few examples that use SPARC or x86 assembly language. Readers are not expected to be familiar with assembly language, and the examples are straightforward, are clearly commented, and illustrate particular points.

Objectives of the Book

By the end of the book, the reader will understand the options available for writing programs that use multiple cores on UNIX-like operating systems (Linux, Oracle Solaris, OS X) and Windows. They will have an understanding of how the hardware implementation of multiple cores will affect the performance of the application running on the system (both in good and bad ways). The reader will also know the potential problems to avoid when writing parallel applications. Finally, they will understand how to write applications that scale up to large numbers of parallel threads.

Structure of This Book

This book is divided into the following chapters.

Chapter 1 introduces the hardware and software concepts that will be encountered in the rest of the book. The chapter gives an overview of the internals of processors. It is not necessarily critical for the reader to understand how hardware works before they can write programs that utilize multicore systems. However, an understanding of the basics of processor architecture will enable the reader to better understand some of the concepts relating to application correctness, performance, and scaling that are presented later in the book. The chapter also discusses the concepts of threads and processes.

Chapter 2 discusses profiling and optimizing applications. One of the book's premises is that it is vital to understand where the application currently spends its time before work is spent on modifying the application to use multiple cores. The chapter covers all the leading contributors to performance over the application development cycle and discusses how performance can be improved.

Chapter 3 describes ways that multicore systems can be used to perform more work per unit time or reduce the amount of time it takes to complete a single unit of work. It starts with a discussion of virtualization where one new system can be used to replace multiple older systems. This consolidation can be achieved with no change in the software. It is important to realize that multicore systems represent an opportunity to change the way an application works; they do not require that the application be changed. The chapter continues with describing various patterns that can be used to write parallel applications and discusses the situations when these patterns might be useful.

Chapter 4 describes sharing data safely between multiple threads. The chapter leads with a discussion of data races, the most common type of correctness problem encountered in multithreaded codes. This chapter covers how to safely share data and synchronize threads at an abstract level of detail. The subsequent chapters describe the operating system–specific details.

Chapter 5 describes writing parallel applications using POSIX threads. This is the standard implemented by UNIX-like operating systems, such as Linux, Apple's OS X, and Oracle's Solaris. The POSIX threading library provides a number of useful building blocks for writing parallel applications. It offers great flexibility and ease of development.

Chapter 6 describes writing parallel applications for Microsoft Windows using Windows native threading. Windows provides similar synchronization and data sharing primitives to those provided by POSIX. The differences are in the interfaces and requirements of these functions.

Chapter 7 describes opportunities and limitations of automatic parallelization provided by compilers. The chapter also covers the OpenMP specification, which makes it relatively straightforward to write applications that take advantage of multicore processors.

Chapter 8 discusses how to write parallel applications without using the functionality in libraries provided by the operating system or compiler. There are some good reasons for writing custom code for synchronization or sharing of data. These might be for finer control or potentially better performance. However, there are a number of pitfalls that need to be avoided in producing code that functions correctly.

Chapter 9 discusses how applications can be improved to scale in such a way as to maximize the work performed by a multicore system. The chapter describes the common areas where scaling might be limited and also describes ways that these scaling limitations can be identified. It is in the scaling that developing for a multicore system is differentiated from developing for a multiprocessor system; this chapter discusses the areas where the implementation of the hardware will make a difference.

Chapter 10 covers a number of alternative approaches to writing parallel applications. As multicore processors become mainstream, other approaches are being tried to overcome some of the hurdles of writing correct, fast, and scalable parallel code.

Chapter 11 concludes the book.

Acknowledgments

A number of people have contributed to this book, both in discussing some of the issues that are covered in these pages and in reviewing these pages for correctness and coherence. In particular, I would like to thank Miriam Blatt, Steve Clamage, Mat Colgrove, Duncan Coutts, Harry Foxwell, Karsten Guthridge, David Lindt, Jim Mauro, Xavier Palathingal, Rob Penland, Steve Schalkhauser, Sukhdeep Sidhu, Peter Strazdins, Ruud van der Pas, and Rick Weisner for proofreading the drafts of chapters, reviewing sections of the text, and providing helpful feedback. I would like to particularly call out Richard Friedman who provided me with both extensive and detailed feedback.

I'd like to thank the team at Addison-Wesley, including Greg Doench, Michelle Housley, Anna Popick, and Michael Thurston, and freelance copy editor Kim Wimpsett for providing guidance, proofreading, suggestions, edits, and support.

I'd also like to express my gratitude for the help and encouragement I've received from family and friends in making this book happen. It's impossible to find the time to write without the support and understanding of a whole network of people, and it's wonderful to have folks interested in hearing how the writing is going. I'm particularly grateful for the enthusiasm and support of my parents, Tony and Maggie, and my wife's parents, Geoff and Lucy.

Finally, and most importantly, I want thank my wife, Jenny; our sons, Aaron and Timothy; and our daughter, Emma. I couldn't wish for a more supportive and enthusiastic family. You inspire my desire to understand how things work and to pass on that knowledge.

About the Author

Darryl Gove is a senior principal software engineer in the Oracle Solaris Studio compiler team. He works on the analysis, parallelization, and optimization of both applications and benchmarks. Darryl has a master's degree as well as a doctorate degree in operational research from the University of Southampton, UK. He is the author of the books *Solaris Application Programming* (Prentice Hall, 2008) and *The Developer's Edge* (Sun Microsystems, 2009), as well as a contributor to the book *OpenSPARC Internals* (lulu.com, 2008). He writes regularly about optimization and coding and maintains a blog at www.darrylgove.com.

Hardware, Processes, and Threads

It is not necessary to understand how hardware works in order to write serial or parallel applications. It is quite permissible to write code while treating the internals of a computer as a black box. However, a simple understanding of processor internals will make some of the later topics more obvious. A key difference between serial (or single-threaded) applications and parallel (or multithreaded) applications is that the presence of multiple threads causes more of the attributes of the system to become important to the application. For example, a single-threaded application does not have multiple threads contending for the same resource, whereas this can be a common occurrence for a multithreaded application. The resource might be space in the caches, memory bandwidth, or even just physical memory. In these instances, the characteristics of the hardware may manifest in changes in the behavior of the application. Some understanding of the way that the hardware works will make it easier to understand, diagnose, and fix any aberrant application behaviors.

Examining the Insides of a Computer

Fundamentally a computer comprises one or more processors and some memory. A number of chips and wires glue this together. There are also peripherals such as disk drives or network cards.

Figure 1.1 shows the internals of a personal computer. A number of components go into a computer. The processor and memory are plugged into a circuit board, called the *motherboard*. Wires lead from this to peripherals such as disk drives, DVD drives, and so on. Some functions such as video or network support either are integrated into the motherboard or are supplied as plug-in cards.

It is possibly easier to understand how the components of the system are related if the information is presented as a schematic, as in Figure 1.2. This schematic separates the compute side of the system from the peripherals.

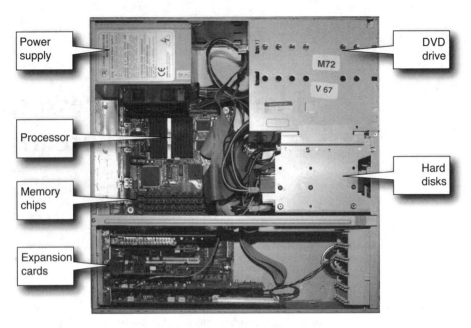

Figure 1.1 Insides of a PC

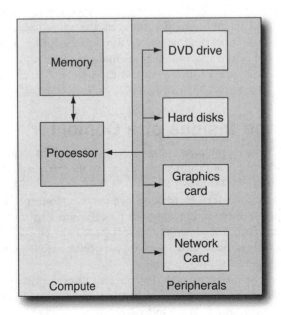

Figure 1.2 Schematic representation of a PC

The compute performance characteristics of the system are basically derived from the performance of the processor and memory. These will determine how quickly the machine is able to execute instructions.

The performance characteristics of peripherals tend to be of less interest because their performance is much lower than that of the memory and processor. The amount of data that the processor can transfer to memory in a second is measured in gigabytes. The amount of data that can be transferred to disk is more likely to be measured in megabytes per second. Similarly, the time it takes to get data from memory is measured in nanoseconds, and the time to fetch data from disk is measured in milliseconds.

These are order-of-magnitude differences in performance. So, the best approach to using these devices is to avoid depending upon them in a performance-critical part of the code. The techniques discussed in this book will enable a developer to write code so that accesses to peripherals can be placed off the critical path or so they can be scheduled so that the compute side of the system can be actively completing work while the peripheral is being accessed.

The Motivation for Multicore Processors

Microprocessors have been around for a long time. The x86 architecture has roots going back to the 8086, which was released in 1978. The SPARC architecture is more recent, with the first SPARC processor being available in 1987. Over much of that time performance gains have come from increases in processor clock speed (the original 8086 processor ran at about 5MHz, and the latest is greater than 3GHz, about a 600× increase in frequency) and architecture improvements (issuing multiple instructions at the same time, and so on). However, recent processors have increased the number of *cores* on the chip rather than emphasizing gains in the performance of a single thread running on the processor. The core of a processor is the part that executes the instructions in an application, so having multiple cores enables a single processor to simultaneously execute multiple applications.

The reason for the change to multicore processors is easy to understand. It has become increasingly hard to improve serial performance. It takes large amounts of area on the silicon to enable the processor to execute instructions faster, and doing so increases the amount of power consumed and heat generated. The performance gains obtained through this approach are sometimes impressive, but more often they are relatively modest gains of 10% to 20%. In contrast, rather than using this area of silicon to increase single-threaded performance, using it to add an additional core produces a processor that has the potential to do twice the amount of work; a processor that has four cores might achieve four times the work. So, the most effective way of improving overall performance is to increase the number of threads that the processor can support. Obviously, utilizing multiple cores becomes a software problem rather than a hardware problem, but as will be discussed in this book, this is a well-studied software problem.

The terminology around multicore processors can be rather confusing. Most people are familiar with the picture of a microprocessor as a black slab with many legs sticking out of it. A multiprocessor system is one where there are multiple microprocessors plugged into the system board. When each processor can run only a single thread, there is a relatively simple relationship between the number of processors, CPUs, chips, and cores in a system—they are all equal, so the terms could be used interchangeably. With multicore processors, this is no longer the case. In fact, it can be hard to find a consensus for the exact definition of each of these terms in the context of multicore processors.

This book will use the terms *processor* and *chip* to refer to that black slab with many legs. It's not unusual to also hear the word *socket* used for this. If you notice, these are all countable entities—you can take the lid off the case of a computer and count the number of sockets or processors.

A single multicore processor will present multiple *virtual CPUs* to the user and operating system. Virtual CPUs are not physically countable—you cannot open the box of a computer, inspect the motherboard, and tell how many virtual CPUs it is capable of supporting. However, virtual CPUs are visible to the operating system as entities where work can be scheduled.

It is also hard to determine how many cores a system might contain. If you were to take apart the microprocessor and look at the silicon, it might be possible to identify the number of cores, particularly if the documentation indicated how many cores to expect! Identifying cores is not a reliable science. Similarly, you cannot look at a core and identify how many software threads the core is capable of supporting. Since a single core can support multiple threads, it is arguable whether the concept of a core is that important since it corresponds to neither a physical countable entity nor a virtual entity to which the operating system allocates work. However, it is actually important for understanding the performance of a system, as will become clear in this book.

One further potential source of confusion is the term *threads*. This can refer to either hardware or software threads. A software thread is a stream of instructions that the processor executes; a hardware thread is the hardware resources that execute a single software thread. A multicore processor has multiple hardware threads—these are the virtual CPUs. Other sources might refer to hardware threads as *strands*. Each hardware thread can support a software thread.

A system will usually have many more software threads running on it than there are hardware threads to simultaneously support them all. Many of these threads will be inactive. When there are more active software threads than there are hardware threads to run them, the operating system will share the virtual CPUs between the software threads. Each thread will run for a short period of time, and then the operating system will swap that thread for another thread that is ready to work. The act of moving a thread onto or off the virtual CPU is called a *context switch*.

Supporting Multiple Threads on a Single Chip

The core of a processor is the part of the chip responsible for executing instructions. The core has many parts, and we will discuss some of those parts in detail later in this chapter. A simplified schematic of a processor might look like Figure 1.3.

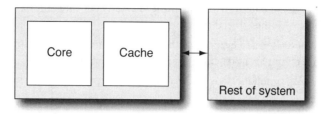

Figure 1.3 Single-core processor

Cache is an area of memory on the chip that holds recently used data and instructions. When you look at the piece of silicon inside a processor, such as that shown in Figure 1.7, the core and the cache are the two components that are identifiable to the eye. We will discuss cache in the "Caches" section later in this chapter.

The simplest way of enabling a chip to run multiple threads is to duplicate the core multiple times, as shown in Figure 1.4. The earliest processors capable of supporting multiple threads relied on this approach. This is the fundamental idea of multicore processors. It is an easy approach because it takes an existing processor design and replicates it. There are some complications involved in making the two cores communicate with each other and with the system, but the changes to the core (which is the most complex part of the processor) are minimal. The two cores share an interface to the rest of the system, which means that system access must be shared between the two cores.

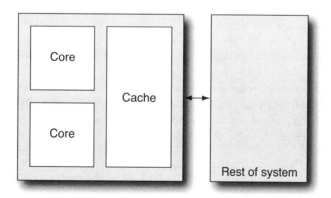

Figure 1.4 Dual-core processor capable of running two simultaneous
hardware threads

However, this is not the only approach. An alternative is to make a single core execute multiple threads of instructions, as shown in Figure 1.5. There are various refinements on this design:

- The core could execute instructions from one software thread for 100 cycles and then switch to another thread for the next 100.

- The core could alternate every cycle between fetching an instruction from one thread and fetching an instruction from the other thread.

- The core could simultaneously fetch an instruction from each of multiple threads every cycle.

- The core could switch software threads every time the stream that is currently executing hits a long latency event (such as a cache miss, where the data has to be fetched from memory).

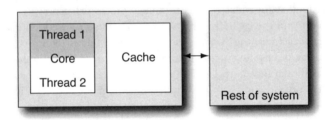

Figure 1.5 Single-core processor with two hardware threads

With two threads sharing a core, each thread will get a share of the resources. The size of the share will depend on the activity of the other thread and the number of resources available. For example, if one thread is stalled waiting on memory, then the other thread may have exclusive access to all the resources of the core. However, if both threads want to simultaneously issue the same type of instruction, then for some processors only one thread will be successful, and the other thread will have to retry on the next opportunity.

Most multicore processors use a combination of multiple cores and multiple threads per core. The simplest example of this would be a processor with two cores with each core being capable of supporting two threads, making a total of four threads for the entire processor. Figure 1.6 shows this configuration.

When this ability to handle multiple threads is exposed to the operating system, it usually appears that the system has many virtual CPUs. Therefore, from the perspective of the user, the system is capable of running multiple threads. One term used to describe this is *chip multithreading* (CMT)—one chip, many threads. This term places the emphasis on the fact that there are many threads, without stressing about the implementation details of how threads are assigned to cores.

The UltraSPARC T2 is a good example of a CMT processor. It has eight replicated cores, and each core is capable of running eight threads, making the processor capable of running 64 software threads simultaneously. Figure 1.7 shows the physical layout of the processor.

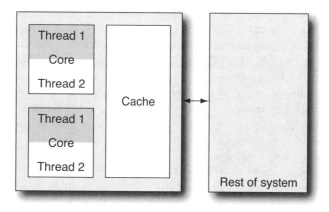

Figure 1.6 Dual-core processor with a total of four hardware threads

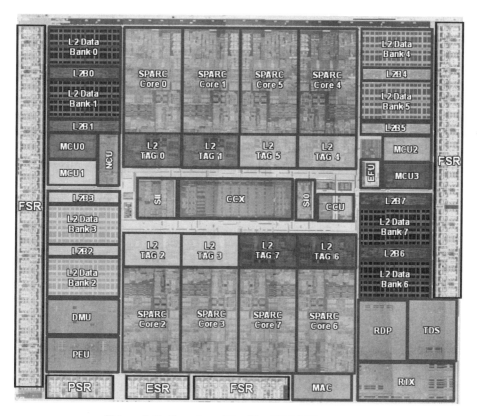

Figure 1.7 Floorplan of the UltraSPARC T2 processor

The UltraSPARC T2 floor plan has a number of different areas that offer support functionality to the cores of the processor; these are mainly located around the outside edge of the chip. The eight processor cores are readily identifiable because of their structural similarity. For example, SPARC Core 2 is the vertical reflection of SPARC Core 0, which is the horizontal reflection of SPARC Core 4. The other obvious structure is the crosshatch pattern that is caused by the regular structure elements that form the second-level cache area; this is an area of on-chip memory that is shared between all the cores. This memory holds recently used data and makes it less likely that data will have to be fetched from memory; it also enables data to be quickly shared between cores.

It is important to realize that the implementation details of CMT processors do have detectable effects, particularly when multiple threads are distributed over the system. But the hardware threads can usually be considered as all being equal. In current processor designs, there are not fast hardware threads and slow hardware threads; the performance of a thread depends on what else is currently executing on the system, not on some invariant property of the design.

For example, suppose the CPU in a system has two cores, and each core can support two threads. When two threads are running on that system, either they can be on the same core or they can be on different cores. It is probable that when the threads share a core, they run slower than if they were scheduled on different cores. This is an obvious result of having to share resources in one instance and not having to share resources in the other.

Fortunately, operating systems are evolving to include concepts of locality of memory and sharing of processor resources so that they can automatically assign work in the best possible way. An example of this is the *locality group* information used by the Solaris operating system to schedule work to processors. This information tells the operating system which virtual processors share resources. Best performance will probably be attained by scheduling work to virtual processors that do not share resources.

The other situation where it is useful for the operating system to understand the topology of the system is when a thread wakes up and is unable to be scheduled to exactly the same virtual CPU that was running it earlier. Then the thread can be scheduled to a virtual CPU that shares the same locality group. This is less of a disturbance than running it on a virtual processor that shares nothing with the original virtual processor. For example, Linux has the concept of *affinity*, which keeps threads local to where they were previously executing.

This kind of topological information becomes even more important in systems where there are multiple processors, with each processor capable of supporting multiple threads. The difference in performance between scheduling a thread on any of the cores of a single processor may be slight, but the difference in performance when a thread is migrated to a different processor can be significant, particularly if the data it is using is held in memory that is local to the original processor. Memory affinity will be discussed further in the section "The Characteristics of Multiprocessor Systems."

In the following sections, we will discuss the components of the processor core. A rough schematic of the critical parts of a processor core might look like Figure 1.8. This

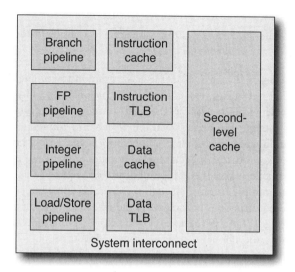

Figure 1.8 Block diagram of a processor core

shows the specialized pipelines for each instruction type, the on-chip memory (called *cache*), the translation look-aside buffers (TLBs) that are used for converting virtual memory addresses to physical, and the system interconnect (which is the layer that is responsible for communicating with the rest of the system).

The next section, "Increasing Instruction Issue Rate with Pipelined Processor Cores," explains the motivation for the various "pipelines" that are found in the cores of modern processors. Sections "Using Caches to Hold Recently Used Data," "Using Virtual Memory to Store Data," and "Translating from Virtual Addresses to Physical Addresses" in this chapter cover the purpose and functionality of the caches and TLBs.

Increasing Instruction Issue Rate with Pipelined Processor Cores

As we previously discussed, the *core* of a processor is the part of the processor responsible for executing instructions. Early processors would execute a single instruction every cycle, so a processor that ran at 4MHz could execute 4 million instructions every second. The logic to execute a single instruction could be quite complex, so the time it takes to execute the longest instruction determined how long a cycle had to take and therefore defined the maximum clock speed for the processor.

To improve this situation, processor designs became "pipelined." The operations necessary to complete a single instruction were broken down into multiple smaller steps. This was the simplest pipeline:

- **Fetch.** Fetch the next instruction from memory.
- **Decode.** Determine what type of instruction it is.

- **Execute.** Do the appropriate work.
- **Retire.** Make the state changes from the instruction visible to the rest of the system.

Assuming that the overall time it takes for an instruction to complete remains the same, each of the four steps takes one-quarter of the original time. However, once an instruction has completed the Fetch step, the next instruction can enter that stage. This means that four instructions can be in execution at the same time. The clock rate, which determines when an instruction completes a pipeline stage, can now be four times faster than it was. It now takes four clock cycles for an instruction to complete execution. This means that each instruction takes the same wall time to complete its execution. But there are now four instructions progressing through the processor pipeline, so the pipelined processor can execute instructions at four times the rate of the nonpipelined processor.

For example, Figure 1.9 shows the integer and floating-point pipelines from the UltraSPARC T2 processor. The integer pipeline has eight stages, and the floating-point pipeline has twelve stages.

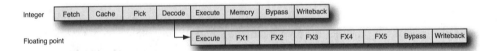

Figure 1.9 UltraSPARC T2 execution pipeline stages

The names given to the various stages are not of great importance, but several aspects of the pipeline are worthy of discussion. Four pipeline stages are performed regardless of whether the instruction is floating point or integer. Only at the Execute stage of the pipeline does the path diverge for the two instruction types.

For all instructions, the result of the operation can be made available to any subsequent instructions at the Bypass stage. The subsequent instruction needs the data at the Execute stage, so if the first instruction starts executing at cycle zero, a dependent instruction can start in cycle 3 and expect the data to be available by the time it is needed. This is shown in Figure 1.10 for integer instructions. An instruction that is fetched in cycle 0 will produce a result that can be bypassed to a following instruction seven cycles later when it reaches the Bypass stage. The dependent instruction would need this result as input when it reaches the Execute stage. If an instruction is fetched every cycle, then the fourth instruction will have reached the Execute stage by the time the first instruction has reached the Bypass stage.

The downside of long pipelines is correcting execution in the event of an error; the most common example of this is mispredicted branches.

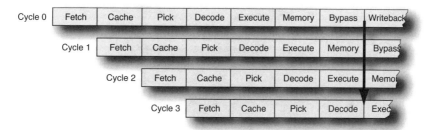

Figure 1.10 Pipelined instruction execution including bypassing of results

To keep fetching instructions, the processor needs to guess the next instruction that will be executed. Most of the time this will be the instruction at the following address in memory. However, a branch instruction might change the address where the instruction is to be fetched from—but the processor will know this only once all the conditions that the branch depends on have been resolved and once the actual branch instruction has been executed.

The usual approach to dealing with this is to predict whether branches are taken and then to start fetching instructions from the predicted address. If the processor predicts correctly, then there is no interruption to the instruction steam—and no cost to the branch. If the processor predicts incorrectly, all the instructions executed after the branch need to be flushed, and the correct instruction stream needs to be fetched from memory. These are called *branch mispredictions*, and their cost is proportional to the length of the pipeline. The longer the pipeline, the longer it takes to get the correct instructions through the pipeline in the event of a mispredicted branch.

Pipelining enabled higher clock speeds for processors, but they were still executing only a single instruction every cycle. The next improvement was "super-scalar execution," which means the ability to execute multiple instructions per cycle. The Intel Pentium was the first x86 processor that could execute multiple instructions on the same cycle; it had two pipelines, each of which could execute an instruction every cycle. Having two pipelines potentially doubled performance over the previous generation.

More recent processors have four or more pipelines. Each pipeline is specialized to handle a particular type of instruction. It is typical to have a memory pipeline that handles loads and stores, an integer pipeline that handles integer computations (integer addition, shifts, comparison, and so on), a floating-point pipeline (to handle floating-point computation), and a branch pipeline (for branch or call instructions). Schematically, this would look something like Figure 1.11.

The UltraSPARC T2 discussed earlier has four pipelines for each core: two for integer operations, one for memory operations, and one for floating-point operations. These four pipelines are shared between two groups of four threads, and every cycle one thread from both of the groups can issue an instruction.

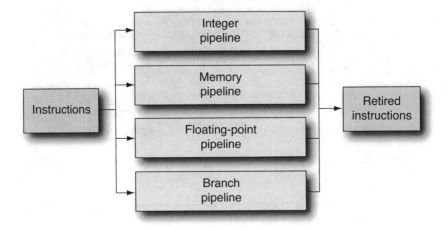

Figure 1.11 Multiple instruction pipelines

Using Caches to Hold Recently Used Data

When a processor requests a set of bytes from memory, it does not get only those bytes that it needs. When the data is fetched from memory, it is fetched together with the surrounding bytes as a *cache line*, as shown in Figure 1.12. Depending on the processor in a system, a cache line might be as small as 16 bytes, or it could be as large as 128 (or more) bytes. A typical value for cache line size is 64 bytes. Cache lines are always aligned, so a 64-byte cache line will start at an address that is a multiple of 64. This design decision simplifies the system because it enables the system to be optimized to pass around aligned data of this size; the alternative is a more complex memory interface that would have to handle chunks of memory of different sizes and differently aligned start addresses.

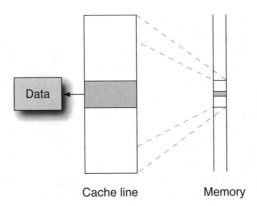

Figure 1.12 Fetching data and surrounding cache line from memory

When a line of data is fetched from memory, it is stored in a *cache*. Caches improve performance because the processor is very likely to either reuse the data or access data stored on the same cache line. There are usually caches for instructions and caches for data. There may also be multiple levels of cache.

The reason for having multiple levels of cache is that the larger the size of the cache, the longer it takes to determine whether an item of data is held in that cache. A processor might have a small first-level cache that it can access within a few clock cycles and then a second-level cache that is much larger but takes tens of cycles to access. Both of these are significantly faster than memory, which might take hundreds of cycles to access. The time it takes to fetch an item of data from memory or from a level of cache is referred to as its *latency*. Figure 1.13 shows a typical memory hierarchy.

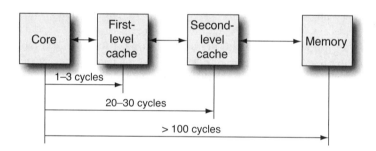

Figure 1.13 Latency to caches and memory

The greater the latency of accesses to main memory, the more benefit there is from multiple layers of cache. Some systems even benefit from having a third-level cache.

Caches have two very obvious characteristics: the size of the cache lines and the size of the cache. The number of lines in a cache can be calculated by dividing one by the other. For example, a 4KB cache that has a cache line size of 64 bytes will hold 64 lines.

Caches have other characteristics, which are less obviously visible and have less of a directly measurable impact on application performance. The one characteristic that it is worth mentioning is the associativity. In a simple cache, each cache line in memory would map to exactly one position in the cache; this is called a *direct mapped cache*. If we take the simple 4KB cache outlined earlier, then the cache line located at every 4KB interval in memory would map to the same line in the cache, as shown in Figure 1.14.

Obviously, a program that accessed memory in 4KB strides would end up just using a single entry in the cache and could suffer from poor performance if it needed to simultaneously use multiple cache lines.

The way around this problem is to increase the *associativity* of the cache—that is, make it possible for a single cache line to map into more positions in the cache and therefore reduce the possibility of there being a conflict in the cache. In a two-way associative

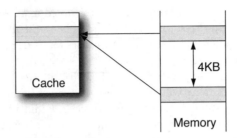

Figure 1.14 Mapping of memory to cache lines in a directed mapped cache

cache, each cache line can map into one of two locations. The location is chosen according to some replacement policy that could be random replacement, or it could depend on which of the two locations contains the oldest data (least recently used replacement). Doubling the number of potential locations for each cache line means that the interval between lines in memory that map onto the same cache line is halved, but overall this change will result in more effective utilization of the cache and a reduction in the number of cache misses. Figure 1.15 shows the change.

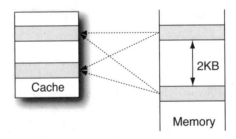

Figure 1.15 Mapping of memory to cache lines in a two-way set associative cache

A *fully associative cache* is one where any address in memory can map to any line in the cache. Although this represents the approach that is likely to result in the lowest cache miss rate, it is also the most complex approach to implement; hence, it is infrequently implemented.

On systems where multiple threads share a level of cache, it becomes more important for the cache to have higher associativity. To see why this is the case, imagine that two copies of the same application share a common direct-mapped cache. If each of them accesses the same virtual memory address, then they will both be attempting to use the same line in the cache, and only one will succeed. Unfortunately, this success will be short-lived because the other copy will immediately replace this line of data with the line of data that they need.

Using Virtual Memory to Store Data

Running applications use what is called *virtual* memory addresses to hold data. The data is still held in memory, but rather than the application storing the exact location in the memory chips where the data is held, the application uses a virtual address, which then gets translated into the actual address in physical memory. Figure 1.16 shows schematically the process of translating from virtual to physical memory.

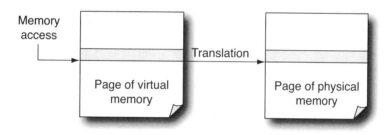

Figure 1.16 Mapping virtual to physical memory

This sounds like an unnecessarily complex way of using memory, but it does have some very significant benefits.

The original aim of virtual memory was to enable a processor to address a larger range of memory than it had physical memory attached to the system; at that point in time, physical memory was prohibitively expensive. The way it would work was that memory was allocated in pages, and each page could either be in physical memory or be stored on disk. When an address was accessed that was not in physical memory, the machine would write a page containing data that hadn't been used in a while to disk and then fetch the data that was needed into the physical memory that had just been freed. The same page of physical memory was therefore used to hold different pages of virtual memory.

Now, paging data to and from disk is not a fast thing to do, but it allowed an application to continue running on a system that had exhausted its supply of free physical memory.

There are other uses for paging from disk. One particularly useful feature is accessing files. The entire file can be mapped into memory—a range of virtual memory addresses can be reserved for it—but the individual pages in that file need only be read from disk when they are actually touched. In this case, the application is using the minimal amount of physical memory to hold a potentially much larger data set.

The other advantage to using virtual memory is that the same address can be reused by multiple applications. For example, assume that all applications are started by calling code at 0x10000. If we had only physical memory addresses, then only one application could reside at 0x10000, so we could run only a single application at a time. However, given virtual memory addressing, we can put as many applications as we need at the same virtual address and have this virtual address map to different physical addresses. So, to take the example of starting an application by calling 0x10000, all the applications could use this same virtual address, but for each application, this would correspond to a different physical address.

What is interesting about the earlier motivators for virtual memory is that they become even more important as the virtual CPU count increases. A system that has many active threads will have some applications that reserve lots of memory but make little actual use of that memory. Without virtual memory, this reservation of memory would stop other applications from attaining the memory size that they need. It is also much easier to produce a system that runs multiple applications if those applications do not need to be arranged into the one physical address space. Hence, virtual memory is almost a necessity for any system that can simultaneously run multiple threads.

Translating from Virtual Addresses to Physical Addresses

The critical step in using virtual memory is the translation of a virtual address, as used by an application, into a physical address, as used by the processor, to fetch the data from memory. This step is achieved using a part of the processor called the *translation look-aside buffer* (TLB). Typically, there will be one TLB for translating the address of instructions (the instruction TLB or ITLB) and a second TLB for translating the address of data (the data TLB, or DTLB).

Each TLB is a list of the virtual address range and corresponding physical address range of each page in memory. So when a processor needs to translate a virtual address to a physical address, it first splits the address into a virtual page (the high-order bits) and an offset from the start of that page (the low-order bits). It then looks up the address of this virtual page in the list of translations held in the TLB. It gets the physical address of the page and adds the offset to this to get the address of the data in physical memory. It can then use this to fetch the data. Figure 1.17 shows this process.

Unfortunately, a TLB can hold only a limited set of translations. So, sometimes a processor will need to find a physical address, but the translation does not reside in the TLB. In these cases, the translation is fetched from an in-memory data structure called a *page table*, and this structure can hold many more virtual to physical mappings. When a translation does not reside in the TLB, it is referred to as a *TLB miss*, and TLB misses have an impact on performance. The magnitude of the performance impact depends on whether the hardware fetches the TLB entry from the page table or whether this task is managed by software; most current processors handle this in hardware. It is also possible to have a page table miss, although this event is very rare for most applications. The page table is managed by software, so this typically is an expensive or slow event.

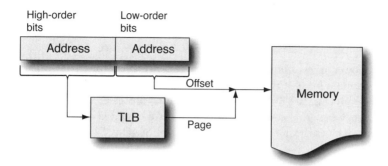

Figure 1.17 Virtual to physical memory address translation

TLBs share many characteristics with caches; consequently, they also share some of the same problems. TLBs can experience both capacity misses and conflict misses. A capacity miss is where the amount of memory being mapped by the application is greater than the amount of memory that can be mapped by the TLB. Conflict misses are the situation where multiple pages in memory map into the same TLB entry; adding a new mapping causes the old mapping to be evicted from the TLB. The miss rate for TLBs can be reduced using the same techniques as caches do. However, for TLBs, there is one further characteristic that can be changed—the size of the page that is mapped.

On SPARC architectures, the default page size is 8KB; on x86, it is 4KB. Each TLB entry provides a mapping for this range of physical or virtual memory. Modern processors can handle multiple page sizes, so a single TLB entry might be able to provide a mapping for a page that is 64KB, 256KB, megabytes, or even gigabytes in size. The obvious benefit to larger page sizes is that fewer TLB entries are needed to map the virtual address space that an application uses. Using fewer TLB entries means less chance of them being knocked out of the TLB when a new entry is loaded. This results in a lower TLB miss rate. For example, mapping a 1GB address space with 4MB pages requires 256 entries, whereas mapping the same memory with 8KB pages would require 131,072. It might be possible for 256 entries to fit into a TLB, but 131,072 would not.

The following are some disadvantages to using larger page sizes:

- Allocation of a large page requires a contiguous block of physical memory to allocate the page. If there is not sufficient contiguous memory, then it is not possible to allocate the large page. This problem introduces challenges for the operating system in handling and making large pages available. If it is not possible to provide a large page to an application, the operating system has the option of either moving other allocated physical memory around or providing the application with multiple smaller pages.

- An application that uses large pages will reserve that much physical memory even if the application does not require the memory. This can lead to memory being used inefficiently. Even a small application may end up reserving large amounts of physical memory.

- A problem particular to multiprocessor systems is that pages in memory will often have a lower access latency from one processor than another. The larger the page size, the more likely it is that the page will be shared between threads running on different processors. The threads running on the processor with the higher memory latency may run slower. This issue will be discussed in more detail in the next section, "The Characteristics of Multiprocessor Systems."

For most applications, using large page sizes will lead to a performance improvement, although there will be instances where other factors will outweigh these benefits.

The Characteristics of Multiprocessor Systems

Although processors with multiple cores are now prevalent, it is also becoming more common to encounter systems with multiple processors. As soon as there are multiple processors in a system, accessing memory becomes more complex. Not only can data be held in memory, but it can also be held in the caches of one of the other processors. For code to execute correctly, there should be only a single up-to-date version of each item of data; this feature is called *cache coherence*.

The common approach to providing cache coherence is called *snooping*. Each processor broadcasts the address that it wants to either read or write. The other processors watch for these broadcasts. When they see that the address of data they hold can take one of two actions, they can return the data if the other processor wants to read the data and they have the most recent copy. If the other processor wants to store a new value for the data, they can invalidate their copy.

However, this is not the only issue that appears when dealing with multiple processors. Other concerns are memory layout and latency.

Imagine a system with two processors. The system could be configured with all the memory attached to one processor or the memory evenly shared between the two processors. Figure 1.18 shows these two alternatives.

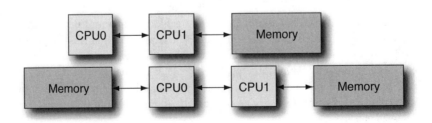

Figure 1.18 Two alternative memory configurations

Each link between processor and memory will increase the latency of any memory access by that processor. So if only one processor has memory attached, then that processor will see low memory latency, and the other processor will see higher memory latency. In the situation where both processors have memory attached, then they will have both local memory that is low cost to access and remote memory that is higher cost to access.

For systems where memory is attached to multiple processors, there are two options for reducing the performance impact. One approach is to interleave memory, often at a cache line boundary, so that for most applications, half the memory accesses will see the short memory access, and half will see the long memory access; so, on average, applications will record memory latency that is the average of the two extremes. This approach typifies what is known as a *uniform memory architecture* (UMA), where all the processors see the same memory latency.

The other approach is to accept that different regions of memory will have different access costs for the processors in a system and then to make the operating system aware of this hardware characteristic. With operating system support, this can lead to applications usually seeing the lower memory cost of accessing local memory. A system with this architecture is often referred to as having *cache coherent nonuniform memory architecture* (ccNUMA).

For the operating system to manage ccNUMA memory characteristics effectively, it has to do a number of things. First, it needs to be aware of the locality structure of the system so that for each processor it is able to allocate memory with low access latencies. The second challenge is that once a process has been run on a particular processor, the operating system needs to keep scheduling that process to that processor. If the operating system fails to achieve this second requirement, then all the locally allocated memory will become remote memory when the process gets migrated.

Consider an application running on the first processor of a two-processor system. The operating system may have allocated memory to be local to this first processor. Figure 1.19 shows this configuration of an application running on a processor and using local memory. The shading in this figure illustrates the application running on processor 1 and accessing memory directly attached to that processor. Hence, the process sees local memory latency for all memory accesses.

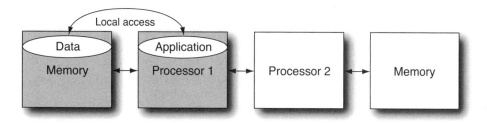

Figure 1.19 Process running with local memory

The application will get good performance because the data that it frequently accesses will be held in the memory with the lowest access latency. However, if that application then gets migrated to the second processor, the application will be accessing data that is remotely held and will see a corresponding drop in performance. Figure 1.20 shows an application using remote memory. The shading in the figure shows the application running on processor 2 but accessing data held on memory that is attached to processor 1. Hence, all memory accesses for the application will fetch remote data; the fetches of data will take longer to complete, and the application will run more slowly.

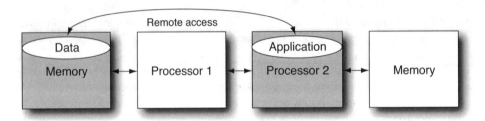

Figure 1.20 Process running using remote memory

How Latency and Bandwidth Impact Performance

Memory latency is the time between a processor requesting an item of data and that item of data arriving from memory. The more processors there are in a system, the longer the memory latency. A system with a single processor can have memory latency of less than 100ns; with two processors this can double, and when the system gets large and comprises multiple boards, the memory latency can become very high. Memory latency is a problem because there is little that a processor can do while it is waiting for data that it needs to be returned from memory. There are techniques, such as out-of-order (OoO) execution, which enable the processor to make some forward progress while waiting for data from memory. However, it is unlikely that these techniques will hide the entire cost of a memory miss, although they may manage to cover the time it takes to get data from the second-level cache. These techniques also add significant complexity and implementation area to the design of the processor core.

Cores that support multiple hardware threads are an alternative solution to the problem of memory latency. When one thread is stalled waiting for data to be returned from memory, the other threads can still make forward progress. So although having multiple hardware threads does not improve the performance of the stalled thread, it improves the utilization of the core and consequently improves the throughput of the core (that is, there are threads completing work even if one thread is stalled).

The other measurement that is relevant to discussions of memory is *bandwidth*. The bandwidth measures how much data can be returned from memory per second. For example, imagine that in one second a virtual CPU issues 10 million load instructions and each request misses cache. Each cache miss will fetch a 64-byte cache line from memory so that a single virtual CPU has consumed a bandwidth of 640MB in a second.

A CMT chip can make large demands of memory bandwidth since, at any one time, each thread could possibly have one or more outstanding memory requests. Suppose that there are 64 threads on a processor, the memory latency is 100 cycles, and the processor is clocked at a modest rate of 1GHz. If each thread is constantly issuing requests for new cache lines from memory, then each thread will issue one such request every 100 cycles (100 cycles being the time it takes for the previous request to complete). This makes 1 billion / 100 * 64 = 640 million memory requests per second. If each request is for a fresh 64-byte cache line, then this represents an aggregate bandwidth of approximately 41GB/s.

The Translation of Source Code to Assembly Language

Processors execute instructions. Instructions are the basic building blocks of all computation; they perform tasks such as add numbers together, fetch data from memory, or store data back to memory. The instructions operate on registers that hold the current values of variables and other machine state. Consider the snippet of code shown in Listing 1.1, which increments an integer variable pointed to by the pointer `ptr`.

Listing 1.1 **Code to Increment Variable at Address**

```
void func( int * ptr )
{
   ( *ptr )++;
}
```

Listing 1.2 shows this snippet of code compiled to SPARC assembly code.

Listing 1.2 **SPARC Assembly Code to Increment a Variable at an Address**

```
ld      [%o0], %o5   // Load value from address %o0 in to register %o5
add     %o5, 1, %o5   // Add one to value in register %o5
st      %o5, [%o0]    // Store value in register %o5 into address %o0
retl                  // Return from routine
```

The SPARC code[1] has the pointer `ptr` passed in through register %o0. The load instruction loads from this address into register %o5. Register %o5 is incremented. The store instruction stores the new value of the integer held in register %o5 into the memory location pointed to by %o0, and then the return instruction exits the routine.

1. This is a slightly simplified SPARC assembly that neglects to include the effect of the branch delay slot on instruction ordering. The true order would exchange the store and return instructions.

Listing 1.3 shows the same source code compiled for 32-bit x86. The x86 code is somewhat different. The first difference is that the x86 in 32-bit mode has a stack-based calling convention. This means that all the parameters that are passed into a function are stored onto the stack, and then the first thing that the function does is to retrieve these stored parameters. Hence, the first thing that the code does is to load the value of the pointer from the stack—in this case, at the address `%esp+4`—and then it places this value into the register `%eax`.

Listing 1.3 32-Bit x86 Assembly Code to Increment a Variable at an Address

```
movl     4(%esp), %eax    // Load value from address %esp + 4 into %eax
addl     $1, (%eax)       // Add one to value at address %eax
ret                       // Return from routine
```

We then encounter a second difference between x86 and and SPARC assembly language. SPARC is a *reduced instruction set computer* (RISC), meaning it has a small number of simple instructions, and all operations must be made up from these simple building blocks. x86 is a *complex instruction set computer* (CISC), so it has instructions that perform more complex operations. The x86 instruction set has a single instruction that adds an increment to a value at a memory location. In the example, the instruction is used to add 1 to the value held at the address held in register `%eax`. This is a single CISC instruction, which contrasts with three RISC instructions on the SPARC side to achieve the same result.

Both snippets of code used two registers for the computation. The SPARC code used registers `%o0` and `%o5`, and the x86 code used `%esp` and `%eax`. However, the two snippets of code used the registers for different purposes. The x86 code used `%esp` as the stack pointer, which points to the region of memory where the parameters to the function call are held. In contrast, the SPARC code passed the parameters to functions in registers. The method of passing parameters is called the *calling convention*, and it is part of the *application binary interface* (ABI) for the platform. This specification covers how programs should be written in order to run correctly on a particular platform.

Both the code snippets use a single register to hold the address of the memory being accessed. The SPARC code used `%o0`, and the x86 code used `%eax`. The other difference between the two code snippets is that the SPARC code used the register `%o1` to hold the value of the variable. The SPARC code had to take three instructions to load this value, add 1 to it, and then store the result back to memory. In contrast, the x86 code took a single instruction.

A further difference between the two processors is the number of registers available. SPARC actually has 32 general-purpose registers, whereas the x86 processor has eight general-purpose registers. Some of these general-purpose registers have special functions. The SPARC processor ends up with about 24 registers available for an application to use, while in 32-bit mode the x86 processor has only six. However, because of its CISC instruction set, the x86 processor does not need to use registers to hold values that are only transiently needed—in the example, the current value of the variable in memory was not even loaded into a register. So although the x86 processor has many fewer registers, it is possible to write code so that this does not cause an issue.

However, there is a definite advantage to having more registers. If there are insufficient registers available, a register has to be freed by storing its contents to memory and then reloading them later. This is called register *spilling* and *filling*, and it takes both additional instructions and uses space in the caches.

The two performance advantages introduced with the 64-bit instruction set extensions for x86 were a significant increase in the number of registers and a much improved calling convention.

The Performance of 32-Bit versus 64-Bit Code

A 64-bit processor can, theoretically, address up to 16 exabytes (EB), which is 4GB squared, of physical memory. In contrast, a 32-bit processor can address a maximum of 4GB of memory. Some applications find only being able to address 4GB of memory to be a limitation—a particular example is databases that can easily exceed 4GB in size. Hence, a change to 64-bit addresses enables the manipulation of much larger data sets.

The 64-bit instruction set extensions for the x86 processor are referred to as AMD64, EMT64, x86-64, or just x64. Not only did these increase the memory that the processor could address, but they also improved performance by eliminating or reducing two problems.

The first issue addressed is the stack-based calling convention. This convention leads to the code using lots of store and load instructions to pass parameters into functions. In 32-bit code when a function is called, all the parameters to that function needed to be stored onto the stack. The first action that the function takes is to load those parameters back off the stack and into registers. In 64-bit code, the parameters are kept in registers, avoiding all the load and store operations.

We can see this when the earlier code is compiled to use the 64-bit x86 instruction set, as is shown in Listing 1.4.

Listing 1.4 **64-Bit x86 Assembly Code to Increment a Variable at an Address**

```
addl      $1, (%rdi) // Increment value at address %rdi
ret                  // Return from routine
```

In this example, we are down to two instructions, as opposed to the three instructions used in Listing 1.3. The two instructions are the increment instruction that adds 1 to the value pointed to by the register %rdi and the return instruction.

The second issue addressed by the 64-bit transition was increasing the number of general-purpose registers from about 6 in 32-bit code to about 14 in 64-bit code. Increasing the number of registers reduces the number of register spills and fills.

Because of these two changes, it is very tempting to view the change to 64-bit code as a performance gain. However, this is not strictly true. The changes to the number of registers and the calling convention occurred at the same time as the transition to 64-bit but could have occurred without this particular transition—they could have been introduced on the 32-bit x86 processor. The change to 64-bit was an opportunity to reevaluate the architecture and to make these fundamental improvements.

The actual change to a 64-bit address space is a performance loss. Pointers change from being a 4-byte structure into an 8-byte structure. In Unix-like operating systems, long-type variables also go from 4 to 8 bytes. When the size of a variable increases, the memory footprint of the application increases, and consequently performance decreases. For example, consider the C data structure shown in Listing 1.5.

Listing 1.5 **Data Structure Containing an Array of Pointers to Integers**

```
struct s
{
  int *ptr[8];
};
```

When compiled for 32-bits, the structure occupies 8 * 4 bytes = 32 bytes. So, every 64-byte cache line can contain two structures. When compiled for 64-bit addresses, the pointers double in size, so the structure takes 64 bytes. So when compiled for 64-bit, a single structure completely fills a single cache line.

Imagine an array of these structures in a 32-bit version of an application; when one of these structures is fetched from memory, the next would also be fetched. In a 64-bit version of the same code, only a single structure would be fetched. Another way of looking at this is that for the same computation, the 64-bit version requires that up to twice the data needs to be fetched from memory. For some applications, this increase in memory footprint can lead to a measurable drop in application performance. However, on x86, most applications will see a net performance gain from the other improvements. Some compilers can produce binaries that use the EMT64 instruction set extensions and ABI but that restrict the application to a 32-bit address space. This provides the performance gains from the instruction set improvements without incurring the performance loss from the increased memory footprint.

It is worth quickly contrasting this situation with that of the SPARC processor. The SPARC processor will also see the performance loss from the increase in size of pointers and longs. The SPARC calling convention for 32-bit code was to pass values in registers, and there were already a large number of registers available. Hence, codes compiled for SPARC processors usually see a small decrease in performance because of the memory footprint.

Ensuring the Correct Order of Memory Operations

There is one more concern to discuss when dealing with systems that contain multiple processors or multiple cores: *memory ordering*. Memory ordering is the order in which memory operations are visible to the other processors in the system. Most of the time, the processor does the right thing without any need for the programmer to do anything.

However, there are situations where the programmer does need to step in. These can be either architecture specific (SPARC processors and x86 processors have different requirements) or implementation specific (one type of SPARC processor may have different needs than another type of SPARC processor). The good news is that the system libraries implement the appropriate mechanisms, so multithreaded applications that use system libraries should never encounter this.

On the other hand, there is some overhead from calling system libraries, so there could well be a performance motivation for writing custom synchronization code. This situation is covered in Chapter 8, "Hand-Coded Synchronization and Sharing."

The memory ordering instructions are given the name memory barriers (`membar`) on SPARC and memory fences (`mfence`) on x86. These instructions stop memory operations from becoming visible outside the thread in the wrong order. The following example will illustrate why this is important.

Suppose you have a variable, `count`, protected by a locking mechanism and you want to increment that variable. The lock works by having the value 1 stored into it when it is acquired and then the value 0 stored into it when the lock is released. The code for acquiring the lock is not relevant to this example, so the example starts with the assumption that the lock is already acquired, and therefore the variable `lock` contains the value 1. Now that the lock is acquired, the code can increment the variable `count`. Then, to release the lock, the code would store the value 0 into the variable `lock`. The process of incrementing the variable and then releasing the lock with a store of the value 0 would look something like the pseudocode shown in Listing 1.6.

Listing 1.6 **Incrementing a Variable and Freeing a Lock**

```
LOAD [&count], %A
INC %A
STORE %A, [&count]
STORE 0, [&lock]
```

As soon as the value 0 is stored into the variable `lock`, then another thread can come along to acquire the lock and modify the variable `count`. For performance reasons, some processors implement a weak ordering of memory operations, meaning that stores can be moved past other stores or loads can be moved past other loads. If the previous code is run on a machine with a weaker store ordering, then the code at execution time could look like the code shown in Listing 1.7.

Listing 1.7 **Incrementing and Freeing a Lock Under Weak Memory Ordering**

```
LOAD [&count], %A
INC %A
STORE 0, [&lock]
STORE %A, [&count]
```

At runtime, the processor has hoisted the store to the lock so that it becomes visible to the rest of the system before the store to the variable `count`. Hence, the lock is released before the new value of `count` is visible. Another processor could see that the lock was free and load up the old value of `count` rather than the new value.

The solution is to place a memory barrier between the two stores to tell the processor not to reorder them. Listing 1.8 shows the corrected code. In this example, the `membar` instruction ensures that all previous store operations have completed before the next store instruction is executed.

Listing 1.8 **Using a Memory Bar to Enforce Store Ordering**

```
LOAD [&count], %A
INC %A
STORE %A, [&count]
MEMBAR #store, #store
STORE 0, [&lock]
```

There are other types of memory barriers to enforce other orderings of load and store operations. Without these memory barriers, other memory ordering errors could occur. For example, a similar issue could occur when the lock is acquired. The load that fetches the value of count might be executed before the store that sets the lock to be acquired. In such a situation, it would be possible for another processor to modify the value of count between the time that the value was retrieved from memory and the point at which the lock was acquired.

The programmer's reference manual for each family of processors will give details about the exact circumstances when memory barriers may or may not be required, so it is essential to refer to these documents when writing custom locking code.

The Differences Between Processes and Threads

It is useful to discuss how software is made of both processes and threads and how these are mapped into memory. This section will introduce some of the concepts, which will become familiar over the next few chapters. An application comprises instructions and data. Before it starts running, these are just some instructions and data laid out on disk, as shown in Figure 1.21.

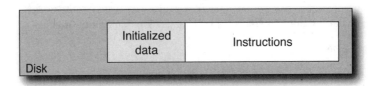

Figure 1.21 Application image stored on disk

An executing application is called a *process*. A process is a bit more than instructions and data, since it also has state. State is the set of values held in the processor registers, the address of the currently executing instruction, the values held in memory, and any other values that uniquely define what the process is doing at any moment in time. The important difference is that as a process runs, its state changes. Figure 1.22 shows the layout of an application running in memory.

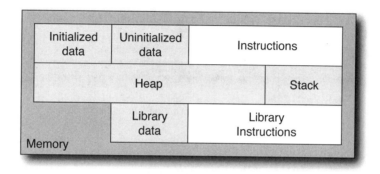

Figure 1.22 Single-threaded application loaded into memory

Processes are the fundamental building blocks of applications. Multiple applications running simultaneously are really just multiple processes. Support for multiple users is typically implemented using multiple processes with different permissions. Unless the process has been set up to explicitly share state with another process, all of its state is private to the process—no other process can see in. To take a more tangible example, if you run two copies of a text editor, they both might have a variable `current_line`, but neither could read the other one's value for this variable.

A particularly critical part of the state for an application is the memory that has been allocated to it. Recall that memory is allocated using virtual addresses, so both copies of the hypothetical text editor might have stored the document at virtual addresses 0x111000 to 0x11a000. Each application will maintain its own TLB mappings, so identical virtual addresses will map onto different physical addresses. If one core is running these two applications, then each application should expect on average to use half the TLB entries for its mappings—so multiple active processes will end up increasing the pressure on internal chip structures like the TLBs or caches so that the number of TLB or cache misses will increase.

Each process could run multiple threads. A thread has some state, like a process does, but its state is basically just the values held in its registers plus the data on its stack. Figure 1.23 shows the memory layout of a multithreaded application.

A thread shares a lot of state with other threads in the application. To go back to the text editor example, as an alternative implementation, there could be a single text editor application with two windows. Each window would show a different document, but the

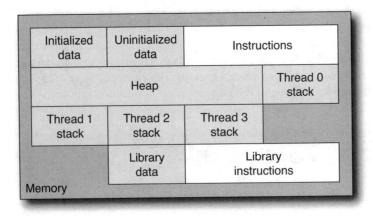

Figure 1.23 Multithreaded application loaded into memory

two documents could no longer both be held at the same virtual address; they would need different virtual addresses. If the editor application was poorly coded, activities in one window could cause changes to the data held in the other.

There are plenty of reasons why someone might choose to write an application that uses multiple threads. The primary one is that using multiple threads on a system with multiple hardware threads should produce results faster than a single thread doing the work. Another reason might be that the problem naturally decomposes into multiple threads. For example, a web server will have many simultaneous connections to remote machines, so it is a natural fit to code it using multiple threads. The other advantage of threads over using multiple processes is that threads share most of the machine state, in particular the TLB and cache entries. So if all the threads need to share some data, they can all read it from the same memory address.

What you should take away from this discussion is that threads and processes are ways of getting multiple streams of instructions to coordinate in delivering a solution to a problem. The advantage of processes is that each process is isolated—if one process dies, then it can have no impact on other running processes. The disadvantages of multiple processes is that each process requires its own TLB entries, which increases the TLB and cache miss rates. The other disadvantage of using multiple processes is that sharing data between processes requires explicit control, which can be a costly operation.

Multiple threads have advantages in low costs of sharing data between threads—one thread can store an item of data to memory, and that data becomes immediately visible to all the other threads in that process. The other advantage to sharing is that all threads share the same TLB and cache entries, so multithreaded applications can end up with lower cache miss rates. The disadvantage is that one thread failing will probably cause the entire application to fail.

The same application can be written either as a multithreaded application or as a multiprocess application. A good example is the recent changes in web browser design. Google's Chrome browser is multiprocess. The browser can use multiple tabs to display different web pages. Each tab is a separate process, so one tab failing will not bring down the entire browser. Historically, browsers have been multithreaded, so if one thread executes bad code, the whole browser crashes. Given the unconstrained nature of the Web, it seems a sensible design decision to aim for robustness rather than low sharing costs.

Summary

This chapter introduced some of the terminology of processor architecture. The important points to be aware of are how caches are used to improve the performance of applications and how TLBs are used to enable the use of virtual memory. The chapter introduced the various ways that multiple threads can be supported on a single processor. Although at a high level of abstraction the implementation details of this resource sharing are not important, we will discuss later how they do produce visible performance impacts. Finally, the chapter described how processes and software threads are mapped into memory and the important differences between multithreaded and multiprocess applications.

Coding for Performance

This chapter discusses how to design and write programs with performance in mind. Serial performance remains important even for parallel applications. There are two reasons for this. Each thread in a parallel application is a serial stream of instructions. Making these instructions execute as fast as possible will lead to better performance for the entire application. The second reason is that it is rare to find a parallel application that contains no serial code. As the number of threads increases, it is the performance of the serial sections of code that will ultimately determine how fast the application runs.

There are two approaches for improving the performance of an application. The first, which is unfortunately typical of many projects, is that performance is the problem to be solved once the program is functionally correct. The alternative approach is that performance is considered as one of the up-front specifications for the application. Taking performance into consideration in the initial phases of application design will lead to a better final product. This chapter discusses where performance can be gained (or lost) and how early consideration of performance can lead to an improved product.

Defining Performance

There are two common metrics for performance:

- **Items per unit time.** This might be transactions per second, jobs per hour, or some other combination of completed tasks and units of time. Essentially, this is a measure of bandwidth. It places the emphasis on the ability of the system to complete tasks rather than on the duration of each individual task. Many benchmarks are essentially a measure of bandwidth. If you examine the SPEC Java Application Server benchmark (SPEC jAppServer[1]), you'll find that final results are reported as transactions per second. Another example is the linpack benchmark used as a basis for the TOP500[2] list of supercomputers. The metric that is used to form the TOP500 list is the peak number of floating-point operations per second.

---

1. www.spec.org/jAppServer/
2. www.top500.org/

- **Time per item.** This is a measure of the time to complete a single task. It is basically a measure of latency or response time. Fewer benchmarks specifically target latency. The most obvious example of a latency-driven benchmark is the SPEC CPU benchmark suite, which has a speed metric as well as a rate metric.

Although these are both common expressions of performance, it can be specified as a more complex mix. For example, the results that e-commerce benchmark SPECweb publishes are the number of simultaneous users that a system can support, subject to meeting criteria on throughput and response time.

Many systems have a quality of service (QoS) metric that they must meet. The QoS metric will specify the expectations of the users of the system as well as penalties if the system fails to meet these expectations. These are two examples of alternative metrics:

- Number of transactions of latency greater than some threshold. This will probably be set together with an expectation for the average transaction. It is quite possible to have a system that exceeds the criteria for both the number of transactions per second that it supports and the average response time for a transaction yet have that same system fail due to the criteria for the number of responses taking longer than the threshold.

- The amount of time that the system is unavailable, typically called *downtime* or *availability*. This could be specified as a percentage of the time that the system is expected to be up or as a number of minutes per year that the system is allowed to be down.

The metrics that are used to specify and measure performance have many ramifications in the design of a system to meet those metrics. Consider a system that receives a nightly update. Applying this nightly update will make the system unavailable. Using the metrics that specify availability, it is possible to determine the maximum amount of time that the update can take while still meeting the availability criteria. If the designer knows that the system is allowed to be down for ten minutes per night, then they will make different design decisions than if the system has only a second to complete the update.

Knowing the available time for an update might influence the following decisions:

- How many threads should be used to process the update. A single thread may not be sufficient to complete the update within the time window. Using the data, it should be possible to estimate the number of threads that would be needed to complete the update within the time window. This will have ramifications for the design of the application, and it may even have ramifications for the method and format used to deliver the data to the application.

- If the update has to be stored to disk, then the write bandwidth of the disk storage becomes a consideration. This may be used to determine the number of drives necessary to deliver that bandwidth, the use of solid-state drives, or the use of a dedicated storage appliance.

- If the time it takes to handle the data, even with using multiple threads or multiple drives, exceeds the available time window, then the application might have to be structured so that the update can be completed in parallel with the application processing incoming transactions. Then the application can instantly switch between the old and new data. This kind of design might have some underlying complexities if there are pending transactions at the time of the swap. These transactions would need to either complete using the older data or be restarted to use the latest version.

In fact, defining the critical metrics and their expectations early in the design helps with three tasks:

- Clearly specified requirements can be used to drive design decisions, both for selecting appropriate hardware and in determining the structure of the software.

- Knowing what metrics are expected enables the developers to be confident that the system they deliver fulfills the criteria. Having the metrics defined up front makes it easy to declare a project a success or a failure.

- Defining the metrics should also define the expected inputs. Knowing what the inputs to the system are likely to look like will enable the generation of appropriate test cases. These test cases will be used by the designers and developers to test the program as it evolves.

Understanding Algorithmic Complexity

Algorithmic complexity is a measure of how much computation a program will perform when using a particular algorithm. It is a measure of its efficiency and estimate of operation count. It is not a measure of the complexity of the code necessary to implement a particular algorithm. An algorithm with low algorithmic complexity is likely to be more difficult to implement than an algorithm with higher algorithmic complexity. The most important fact is that the algorithmic complexity is not a model of the execution time but a model of the way execution time changes as the size of the input changes. It is probably best to illustrate this through some examples.

Examples of Algorithmic Complexity

Suppose you want to write a program that sums the first N numbers. You would probably write something like the code shown in Listing 2.1.

Listing 2.1 **Sum of the First N Numbers**

```
void sum(int N)
{
  int total=0;
  for (int i=1; i<=N; i++)
  {
```

```
    total += i;
  }
  printf( "Sum of first %i integers is %i\n", N, total );
}
```

For a given input value N, the code will take N trips around the loop and do N additions. The algorithmic complexity focuses on the number of operations, which in this case are the N additions. It assumes that any additional costs are proportional to this number. The time it would take to complete this calculation is some cost per addition, k, multiplied by the number of additions, N. So, the time would be k * N. The algorithmic complexity is a measure of how this time will change as the size of the input changes, so it is quite acceptable to ignore the (constant) scaling factor and say that the calculation will take of the *order* of N computations. This is typically written O(N). It is a very useful measure of the time it will take to complete the program as the size of the input changes. If N is doubled in value, then it will take twice as long for the program to complete.

Another example will probably clarify how this can be useful. Assume that you want to sum the total of the first N factorials (a factorial is N * (N-1) * (N-2) * ... * 1); you might write a program similar to the one shown in Listing 2.2.

Listing 2.2 **Sum of the First N Factorials**

```
int factorial(int F)
{
  int f = 1;
  for (int i=1; i<=F; i++)
  {
     f = f*i;
  }
  return f;
}

void fsum(int N)
{
  int total = 0;
  for (int i=1; i<N; i++)
  {
    total+=factorial(i);
  }
}
```

This program contains a doubly nested loop. The outer loop will do N iterations, and the inner loop will do an average (over the run) of N/2 iterations. Consequently, there will be about N * N/2 multiply operations and N additions. The algorithmic complexity is concerned only with the dominant factor, which is N * N. So, the entire calcula-tion is $O(N^2)$. If N doubles in size, the time that this algorithm takes will go up by a factor of 4.

The complexity is represented by the dominant term in the function. If the complex-ity turned out to be $(N+1)^2$, then as N increased, there would eventually be little differ-ence between this and N^2. In the limit, as N becomes larger, $O(N^2)$ will dominate the complexity of $O(N)$.

The previous examples are somewhat contrived, and in both cases there are more efficient ways to provide the required result.

A more common programming problem is sorting data. The domain of sorting has many different algorithms, of which the two most famous are probably *bubble sort* and *quicksort*.

Bubble sort iterates through a list of numbers, comparing adjacent pairs of numbers. If the pair is not in the correct sort order, the pair is swapped. Listing 2.3 shows a simple implementation.

Listing 2.3 **Implementation of Bubble Sort**

```
void bubble_sort(int*array, int N)
{
  int sorted =0;
  while ( !sorted )
  {
    sorted=1;
    for ( int i=0; i < N-1; i++ )
    {
      if (array[i] > array[i+1])
      {
        int temp   = array[i+1];
        array[i+1] = array[i];
        array[i]   = temp;
        sorted=0;
      }
    }
  }
}
```

The smallest elements "bubble" to the top of the array, which is why it's called a *bub-ble* sort. It also leads to the optimization, omitted from this implementation, that it is not necessary to sort the bottom of the list, because it will gradually fill with previously sorted largest elements.

Using the algorithm as written, it will take N comparisons to get each element into the correct place. There are N elements, so it will take N * N comparisons to sort the entire list. For unsorted data, this leads to an algorithmic complexity of $O(N^2)$.

On the other hand, *quicksort*, as might be expected by its name, is a much faster algorithm. It relies on splitting the list of elements into two: a list of elements that are smaller than a "pivot" element and elements that are larger. Once the list has been split, the algorithm repeats on each of the smaller lists. An implementation of the quicksort algorithm might look like the code shown in Listing 2.4.

Listing 2.4 **Implementation of Quicksort**

```
void quick_sort(int * array, int lower, int upper)
{
  int tmp;
  int mid    = (upper+lower)/2;
  int pivot  = array[mid];
  int tlower = lower
  int tupper = upper;
  while (tlower <= tupper)
  {
    while ( array[tlower] < pivot ) { tlower++; }
    while ( array[tupper] > pivot ) { tupper--; }
    if ( tlower <= tupper )
    {
      tmp           = array[tlower];
      array[tlower] = array[tupper];
      array[tupper] = tmp;
      tupper--;
      tlower++;
    }
  }
  if (lower<tupper) { quick_sort(array,  lower, tupper); }
  if (tlower<upper) { quick_sort(array, tlower,  upper); }
}
```

The algorithmic complexity of quicksort is hard to calculate. For the average case, it is possible to prove that the complexity is $O(N*\log_2(N))$. This can be explained using the following reasoning. Assume a uniform distribution of items, and that every time the array is split, it will result in two equal halves. For a given N, it will take $\log_2(N)$ splits before the array is split into a sequence of N individual elements and the sort is complete. Each time the array splits, there are two function calls, one to sort the lower half and one to sort the upper half. So, at every split, the entire array of N elements will be iterated through. Therefore, the algorithmic complexity is $O(N*\log_2(N))$.

To see the practical impact of this difference in the complexity of sorting operations, consider sorting a list of 10 items. The bubble sort algorithm will perform about 10 * 10 = 100 operations, whereas quicksort will perform about 10 * $\log_2(10)$ = 30 operations, which is about three times fewer operations. However, the time taken to sort a 10-element list is unlikely to be a significant factor in the runtime of an application. It is more interesting to consider a list of 1,000 elements. The bubble sort will take about 1,000,000 operations, while quicksort will take about 3,000 operations—a ratio of about 300×.

Why Algorithmic Complexity Is Important

Algorithmic complexity represents the expected performance of a section of code as the number of elements being processed increases. In the limit, the code with the greatest algorithmic complexity will dominate the runtime of the application.

Assume that your application has two regions of code, one that is O(N) and another that is $O(N^2)$. If you run a test workload of 100 elements, you may find that the O(N) code takes longer to execute, because there may be more instructions associated with the computation on each element. However, if you were to run a workload of 10,000 elements, then the more complex routine would start to show up as important, assuming it did not completely dominate the runtime of the application.

Picking a small workload will mislead you as to which parts of the code need to be optimized. You may have spent time optimizing the algorithmically simpler part of the code, when the performance of the application in a real-world situation will be dominated by the algorithmically complex part of the code. This emphasizes why it is important to select appropriate workloads for developing and testing the application. Different parts of the application will scale differently as the workload size changes, and regions that appear to take no time can suddenly become dominant.

Another important point to realize is that a change of algorithm is one of the few things that can make an order of magnitude difference to performance. If 80% of the application's runtime was spent sorting a 1,000-element array, then switching from a bubble sort to a quicksort could make a 300× difference to the performance of that function, making the time spent sorting 300× smaller than it previously was. The 80% of the runtime spent sorting would largely disappear, and the application would end up running about five times faster.

Table 2.1 shows the completion time of a task with different algorithmic complexities as the number of elements grows. It is assumed that the time to complete a single unit of work is 100ns. As the table illustrates, it takes remarkably few elements for an $O(N^2)$ algorithm to start consuming significant amounts of time.

Table 2.1 **Execution Duration at Different Algorithm Complexities**

Elements	O(1)	O(N)	O(N $\log_2$ N)	O(N^2)
1	100ns	100ns	100ns	100ns
10	100ns	1,000ns	3,322ns	10,000ns
100	100ns	10,000ns	66,439ns	1,000,000ns
1,000	100ns	100,000ns	996,578ns	100,000,000ns
10,000	100ns	1,000,000ns	13,287,712ns	10,000,000,000ns

The same information can be presented as a chart of runtimes versus the number of elements. Figure 2.1 makes the same point rather more dramatically. It quickly becomes apparent that the runtime for an $O(N^2)$ algorithm will be far greater than one that is linear or logarithmic with respect to the number of elements.

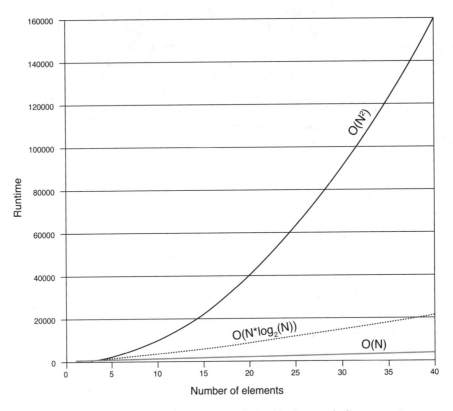

Figure 2.1 Different orders of algorithmic complexity

Using Algorithmic Complexity with Care

Although algorithmic complexity is a very good guide to where time could be spent, several issues need to be considered.

It may be tempting to select the most efficient algorithms for every aspect of the code. Compare the lines of code necessary to implement the quicksort with those required for the bubble sort as well as how easy it is to read those lines of code and understand how the algorithm works. Algorithms with lower algorithmic complexity are usually more difficult to implement and more difficult to understand. Both of these factors will lead to more developer time needed for the implementation, and the code may potentially need a more experienced developer to maintain it. The point is that using more complex algorithms can have an impact on developer time and cost. A simpler algorithm might be easier to implement and result in lower development costs. It may also be possible that the code does not need a more complex algorithm for typical workloads.

A second point to consider is that algorithmic complexity is concerned with the operation count. It does not consider the cost of those instructions. It may weigh the cost of an add operation the same as a multiply yet be possible to have algorithms that perform the same task with very different numbers of add and multiply operations. At another level, the algorithms don't consider implementation details such as caches. One algorithm might be very cache friendly, whereas another could incur many cache misses. In any code, stall time because of cache misses can easily dominate the performance. Therefore, it is necessary to both look at the algorithmic complexity and evaluate the actual implementation of the algorithm to determine whether the implementation is likely to achieve good performance.

It is possible to look at an algorithm in the context of the number of loads that it will take and how likely each load is to miss cache. This would give an estimate of the amount of time spent waiting for data to arrive from memory. Of course, changing the algorithm will impact both the complexity and the probability of events. In the example of load misses, one algorithm might have higher miss rates but a lower-order complexity versus another algorithm.

One final consideration in the selection of algorithms may be whether the algorithms scale to multiple processors. If the algorithm has low algorithmic complexity but does not scale beyond a single thread, it could be slower than an algorithm of higher complexity that can be parallelized to run over multiple threads.

How Structure Impacts Performance

Three attributes of the construction of an application can be considered as "structure." The first of these is the build structure, such as how the source code is distributed between the source files. The second structure is how the source files are combined into applications and supporting libraries. Finally, and probably the most obvious, is that way data is organized in the application. How these three structures influence performance is the subject of the following sections.

Performance and Convenience Trade-Offs in Source Code and Build Structures

The structure of the source code for an application can cause differences to its performance. Source code is often distributed across source files for the convenience of the developers. It is appropriate that the developers' convenience is one of the main criteria for structuring the sources, but care needs to be taken that it does not cause inconvenience to the user of an application.

Performance opportunities are lost when the compiler sees only a single file at a time. The single file may not present the compiler with all the opportunities for optimizations that it might have had if it were to see more of the source code. This kind of limitation is visible when a program uses an accessor function—a short function that returns the value of some variable. A trivial optimization is for the compiler to replace this function call with a direct load of the value of the variable. Consider the code sequence shown in Listing 2.5 for an example of accessor functions.

Listing 2.5 **Accessor Functions**

```
#include <stdio.h>

int a;

void setvalue( int v ) { a = v; }

int  getvalue() { return a; }

void main()
{
  setvalue( 3 );
  printf( "The value of a is %i\n", getvalue() );
}
```

The code in Listing 2.5 can be replaced with the equivalent but faster code shown in Listing 2.6. This is an example of inlining within a source file. The calls to the routines `getvalue()` and `setvalue()` are replaced by the actual code from the functions.

Listing 2.6 **Pseudosource Code After Inlining Optimization**

```
#include <stdio.h>

int a;

void main()
{
  a = 3;
  printf( "The value of a is %i\n", a );
}
```

At some optimization level, most compilers support inlining within the same source file. Hence, the transformation in Listing 2.6 is relatively straightforward for the compiler to perform. The problem is when the functions are distributed across multiple source files.

Fortunately, most compilers support cross-file optimization where they take all the source code and examine whether it is possible to further improve performance by inlining a routine from one source file into the place where it's called in another source file. This can negate much of any performance loss incurred by the structure used to store the source code. Cross-file optimization will be discussed in more detail in the section "How Cross-File Optimization Can Be Used to Improve Performance."

Some build methodologies reduce the ability of the compiler to perform optimizations across source files. One common approach to building is to use either static or archive libraries as part of the build process. These libraries combine a number of object files into a single library, and at link time, the linker extracts the relevant code from the library.

Listing 2.7 shows the steps in this process. In this case, two source files are combined into a single archive, and that archive is used to produce the application.

Listing 2.7 **Creating an Archive Library**

```
$ cc -c a.c
$ cc -c b.c
$ ar -r lib.a a.o b.o
ar: creating lib.a
$ cc main.c lib.a
```

There are three common reasons for using static libraries as part of the build process:

- For "aesthetic" purposes, in that the final linking of the application requires fewer objects. The build process appears to be cleaner because many individual object files are combined into static libraries, and the smaller set appears on the link line. The libraries might also represent bundles of functionality provided to the executable.

- To produce a similar build process whether the application is built to use static or dynamic libraries. Each library can be provided as either a static or a dynamic version, and it is up to the developer to decide which they will use. This is common when the library is distributed as a product for developers to use.

- To hide build issues, but this is the least satisfactory reason. For example, an archive library can contain multiple versions of the same routine. At link time, the linker will extract the first version of this routine that it encounters, but it will not warn that there are multiple versions present. If the same code was linked using individual object files without having first combined the object files into an archive, then the linker would fail to link the executable.

Listing 2.8 demonstrates how using static libraries can hide problems with multiply defined functions. The source files a.c and b.c both contain a function status(). When they are combined into an archive and linked into an executable, the linker will extract one of the two definitions of the function. In the example, the linker selects the definition from a.c. However, the build fails with a multiply defined symbol error if an attempt is made to directly link the object files into an executable.

Listing 2.8 Example of a Static Library Hiding Build Issues

```
$ more a.c
#include <stdio.h>
void status()
{
  printf("In status of A\n");
}

$ more b.c
#include <stdio.h>
void status()
{
    printf("In status of B\n");
}

$ cc -c a.c
$ cc -c b.c
$ ar -r lib.a a.o b.o
ar: creating lib.a

$ more main.c
void status();
void main()
{
 status();
}

$ cc main.c lib.a
$ a.out
In status of A

$ cc main.c a.o b.o
ld: fatal: symbol 'status' is multiply-defined:
        (file a.o type=FUNC; file b.o type=FUNC);
ld: fatal: File processing errors. No output written to a.out
```

An unfortunate side effect of using static libraries is that some compilers are unable to perform cross-file optimization of code contained in the static libraries. This may mean that functions are not inlined from the static library into the executable or that the code held in the static library does not take any part in cross-file optimization.

Using Libraries to Structure Applications

Libraries are the usual mechanism for structuring applications as they become larger. There are some good technical reasons to use libraries:

- Common functionality can be extracted into a library that can be shared between different projects or applications. This can lead to better code reuse, more efficient use of developer time, and more effective use of memory and disk space.

- Placing functionality into libraries can lead to more convenient upgrades where only the library is upgraded instead of replacing all the executables that use the library.

- Libraries can provide better separation between interface and implementation. The implementation details of the library can be hidden from the users, allowing the implementation of the library to evolve while maintaining a consistent interface.

- Stratifying functionality into libraries according to frequency of use can improve application start-up time and memory footprint by loading only the libraries that are needed. Functionality can be loaded on demand rather than setting up all possible features when the application starts.

- Libraries can be used as a mechanism to dynamically provide enhanced functionality. The functionality can be made available without having to change or even restart the application.

- Libraries can enable functionality to be selected based on the runtime environment or characteristics of the system. For instance, an application may load different optimized libraries depending on the underlying hardware or select libraries at runtime depending on the type of work it is being asked to perform.

On the other hand, there are some nontechnical reasons why functionality gets placed into libraries. These reasons may represent the wrong choice for the user.

- Libraries often represent a convenient product for an organizational unit. One group of developers might be responsible for a particular library of code, but that does not automatically imply that a single library represents the best way for that code to be delivered to the end users.

- Libraries are also used to group related functionality. For example, an application might contain a library of string-handling functions. Such a library might be appropriate if it contains a large body of code. On the other hand, if it contains only a few small routines, it might be more appropriate to combine it with another library.

There is a strong attraction to breaking applications down into a set of libraries. Libraries make sense for all the reasons outlined previously, but it is quite possible to have either inappropriate splits of functionality or libraries that implement too little functionality.

There are costs associated with libraries. A call into a function provided by a library will typically be more costly than a call into a function that is in the main executable. Code provided in a library may also have more overhead than code provided in the executable. There are a few contributors to cost:

- Library calls may be implemented using a table of function addresses. This table may be a list of addresses for the routines included in a library. A library routine calls into this table, which then jumps to the actual code for the routine.

- Each library and its data are typically placed onto new TLB entries. Calls into a library will usually also result in an ITLB miss and possibly a DTLB miss if the code accesses library-specific data.

- If the library is being lazy loaded (that is, loaded into memory on demand), there will be costs associated with disk access and setting up the addresses of the library functions in memory.

- Unix platforms typically provide libraries as position-independent code. This enables the same library to be shared in memory between multiple running applications. The cost of this is an increase in code length. Windows makes the opposite trade-off; it uses position-dependent code in libraries, reducing the opportunity of sharing libraries between running applications but producing slightly faster code.

Listing 2.9 shows code for two trivial libraries that can be used to examine how memory is laid out at runtime.

Listing 2.9 **Defining Two Libraries**

```
$ more liba.c
#include <stdio.h>

void ina()
{
  printf( "In library A\n" );
}

$ more libb.c
#include <stdio.h>

void inb()
{
    printf( "In library B\n" );
}
```

Listing 2.10 shows the process of compiling these two libraries on Solaris.

Listing 2.10 **Compiling Two Libraries**

```
$ cc -G -Kpic -o liba.so liba.c
$ cc -G -Kpic -o libb.so libb.c
```

The compiler flag -G tells the compiler to make a library, while the flag -Kpic tells the compiler to use position-independent code. The advantage of position-independent code is that the library can reside at any location in memory. The same library can even be shared between multiple applications and have each application map it at a different address.

The main program shown in Listing 2.11 will call the code in liba.so and then pause so we can examine the memory layout of the application.

Listing 2.11 **Calling Library Code**

```
$ more libmain.c
#include <unistd.h>

void ina();
void inb();

void main()
{
  ina();
  sleep(20);
}
$ cc libmain.c -L. -R. -la -lb
```

The compile command in Listing 2.11 builds the main executable. The flag -L tells the linker where to find the library at link time. The flag -R tells the runtime linker where to locate the file at runtime. In the example, these two flags are set to the current directory. The application will link and execute only if the current directory does contain the library. However, other approaches are more resilient. Running this application enables us to look at the memory map using the utility **pmap**. Listing 2.12 shows the memory map.

Listing 2.12 **Memory Map of Application and Libraries on Solaris**

```
$ ./a.out&
In library A
[1] 1522
$ pmap -x 1522
1522:    ./a.out
Address  Kbytes    RSS   Anon  Locked Mode   Mapped File
08046000      8      8      8       - rwx--   [ stack ]
08050000      4      4      -       - r-x--   a.out
08060000      4      4      4       - rwx--   a.out
D29E0000     24     12     12       - rwx--   [ anon ]
D29F0000      4      4      4       - rwx--   [ anon ]
D2A00000   1276    936      -       - r-x--   libc_hwcap3.so.1
D2B4F000     32     32     32       - rwx--   libc_hwcap3.so.1
D2B57000      8      8      8       - rwx--   libc_hwcap3.so.1
D2B60000      4      4      -       - r-x--   libb.so
```

D2B70000	4	4	4	- rwx--	libb.so
D2B80000	4	4	-	- r-x--	liba.so
D2B90000	4	4	4	- rwx--	liba.so
D2BB0000	4	4	4	- rwx--	[anon]
D2BBE000	184	184	-	- r-x--	ld.so.1
D2BFC000	8	8	8	- rwx--	ld.so.1
D2BFE000	4	4	4	- rwx--	ld.so.1
--------	-------	-------	-------	-------	
total Kb	1576	1224	92	-	

In the memory map shown in Listing 2.12, each library has at least two mapped segments. The first is mapped with read and execute permissions that contain the code in the library. The second contains data and is mapped with read, write, and execute permissions. Both libraries are mapped in, even though the code does not contain any calls to libb.so and makes no use of the library. The RSS column indicates that the library has been loaded into memory. The x86 processor uses a 4KB default page size, so pages of memory are allocated in 4KB chunks. Although both liba.so and libb.so contain only a few bytes of code, both libraries are allocated 4KB of memory for instructions. The same is true for data. The concern is that each 4KB will require a single TLB entry for a virtual address to physical address mapping when a routine in that page is called. If liba.so and libb.so had been combined, the functions in the two libraries could have been placed into a single 4KB segment for each of the instructions and data.

It is possible to look at the sequence of events when the application is loaded by setting the environment variable LD_DEBUG=flags. Listing 2.13 shows an edited form of the output.

Listing 2.13 Output from Setting the Environment Variable LD_DEBUG=files

```
$ LD_DEBUG=files ./a.out

01615: file=/export/home/darryl/a.out  [ ELF ]; generating link map
01615: file=a.out;  analyzing

01615: file=liba.so;  needed by a.out
01615: file=./liba.so [ ELF ]; generating link map

01615: file=libb.so;  needed by a.out
01615: file=./libb.so [ ELF ]; generating link map

01615: file=libc.so.1;  needed by a.out
01615: file=/lib/libc.so.1  [ ELF ]; generating link map

01615: file=./liba.so;  analyzing

01615: file=./libb.so;  analyzing

01615: file=/lib/libc.so.1;  analyzing

01615: 1: transferring control: a.out
```

This shows the sequence of starting the application, having the runtime linker examine the application, and identifying the need for the libraries `liba.so`, `libb.so`, and `libc.so.1`. Once those libraries are loaded, it examines them for other libraries that might be needed.

The linker performs a sizable amount of work. However, the time spent processing the libraries is likely to be dominated by the time spent fetching them from disk. The more data and instructions a library contains, the more time it will take to read the library from disk. It is possible to use lazy loading to avoid loading libraries from disk until they are actually used. Listing 2.14 shows the application built with lazy loading enabled and the resulting runtime linking.

Listing 2.14 **Linking a Library to Use Lazy Loading**

```
$ cc libmain.c -L. -R. -z lazyload -la -lb

$ LD_DEBUG=files ./a.out

01712: file=/export/home/darryl/a.out  [ ELF ]; generating link map
01712: file=a.out;  analyzing

01712: file=libc.so.1;  needed by a.out

01712: file=/lib/libc.so.1;  analyzing
01712: 1: transferring control: a.out

01712: 1: file=liba.so;  lazy loading from file=a.out: symbol=ina
01712: 1: file=./liba.so  [ ELF ]; generating link map
01712: 1: file=./liba.so;  analyzing

In library A
```

In this instance, the application runs without loading either `liba.so` or `libb.so` up until the point where the symbol `ina()` is required from the library `liba.so`. At that point, the runtime linker loads and processes the library. The lazy loading of libraries has meant that the application did not need to load `libb.so` at all, thus reducing application start-up time.

One more thing to consider for the costs for libraries is the cost of calling code residing in libraries. The easiest way to demonstrate this is to modify the example code so it calls the routine `ina()` twice and then to use the debugger to examine what happens at runtime. The first call will load the library into memory, but that will happen only once and can be ignored. The second time the routine is called will be representative of all calls to all library routines. Listing 2.15 shows the output from the Solaris Studio debugger, `dbx`, showing execution up until the first call to the routine `ina()`.

Listing 2.15 **Execution Until the First Call to the Routine** `ina`

```
$ dbx a.out
Reading a.out
Reading ld.so.1
Reading libc.so.1
(dbx) stop in main
dbx: warning: 'main' has no debugger info
      -- will trigger on first instruction
(2) stop in main
(dbx) run
Running: a.out
(process id 1744)
stopped in main at 0x08050ab0
0x08050ab0: main : pushl %ebp
(dbx) nexti
stopped in main at 0x08050ab1
0x08050ab1: main+0x0001: movl %esp,%ebp
(dbx) nexti
stopped in main at 0x08050ab3
0x08050ab3: main+0x0003: call ina [PLT] [ 0x8050964, .-0x14f ]
```

At this stage, the application has reached the first call to the routine `ina()`. As can be seen from the disassembly, this call is actually a call to the procedure linkage table (PLT). This table contains a jump to the actual start address of the routine. However, the first time that the routine is called, the runtime linker will have to load the lazily loaded library from disk. Listing 2.15 earlier skips this first call. Listing 2.16 shows the code as it steps through the second call to the routine `ina()`.

Listing 2.16 **Jumping Through the PLT to the Routine** `ina`

```
(dbx) nexti
Reading liba.so
In library A
stopped in main at 0x08050ab8
0x08050ab8: main+0x0008: call ina [PLT] [ 0x8050964, .-0x154 ]
(dbx) stepi
stopped in (unknown) at 0x08050964
0x08050964: ina [PLT]: jmp *_GLOBAL_OFFSET_TABLE_+0x1c [ 0x8060b24 ]
(dbx) stepi
stopped in ina at 0xd2990510
0xd2990510: ina : pushl %ebp
```

By the second time the call to `ina()` is encountered, the library has already been loaded, and the call is again into the PLT. Using the debugger to step into the call, we can see that this time the target is a jump instruction to the start of the routine.

All calls to library functions, possibly even those within the library, will end up routed through the PLT. This imposes a small overhead on every call. There are ways to limit the scope of library functions so they are not visible outside the library and so calls within the library to those functions will not need to be routed through the PLT.

The same procedure can be followed on Linux. Listing 2.17 shows the steps necessary to compile the application on Linux.

Listing 2.17 **Compiling Libraries and Application on Linux**

```
$ gcc -shared -fpic -o liba.so liba.c
$ gcc -shared -fpic -o libb.so libb.c
$ gcc libmain.c `pwd`/liba.so `pwd`/libb.so
```

Listing 2.18 shows the steps to use the Linux debugger, gdb, to step through the process of calling the library function ina().

Listing 2.18 **Stepping Through Library Call on Linux**

```
$ gdb a.out
(gdb) display /i $eip

(gdb) break main
Breakpoint 1 at 0x8048502
(gdb) run
Starting program: /home/darryl/a.out
Breakpoint 1, 0x08048502 in main ()
0x8048502 <main+14>: sub $0x4,%esp
(gdb) nexti
0x8048505 <main+17>: call 0x804841c <ina@plt>
(gdb) nexti
In library A
0x804850a <main+22>: call 0x804841c <ina@plt>
(gdb) stepi
0x804841c <ina@plt>: jmp *0x804a008
(gdb) stepi
0xb7ede42c <ina>: push %ebp
```

The sequence for Linux shown in Listing 2.18 is basically the same as the sequence for Solaris shown in Listing 2.15 and Listing 2.16. The executable calls into the PLT, and then the application jumps from there into the routine.

The memory map for Linux shown in Listing 2.19 looks very similar to the memory map for Solaris shown in Listing 2.12. In the Linux memory map, both liba.so and libb.so are mapped onto three 4KB pages.

Listing 2.19 **Application Memory Map on Linux**

```
$ pmap 14392
14392:   ./a.out
08048000     4K r-x--  /home/darryl/a.out
08049000     4K r----  /home/darryl/a.out
0804a000     4K rw---  /home/darryl/a.out
b7e43000     4K rw---   [ anon ]
b7e44000  1392K r-x--  /lib/tls/i686/cmov/libc-2.9.so
b7fa0000     4K -----  /lib/tls/i686/cmov/libc-2.9.so
b7fa1000     8K r----  /lib/tls/i686/cmov/libc-2.9.so
b7fa3000     4K rw---  /lib/tls/i686/cmov/libc-2.9.so
b7fa4000    16K rw---   [ anon ]
b7fb4000     4K rw---   [ anon ]
b7fb5000     4K r-x--  /home/darryl/libb.so
b7fb6000     4K r----  /home/darryl/libb.so
b7fb7000     4K rw---  /home/darryl/libb.so
b7fb8000     4K r-x--  /home/darryl/liba.so
b7fb9000     4K r----  /home/darryl/liba.so
b7fba000     4K rw---  /home/darryl/liba.so
b7fbb000     8K rw---   [ anon ]
b7fbd000     4K r-x--   [ anon ]
b7fbe000   112K r-x--  /lib/ld-2.9.so
b7fda000     4K r----  /lib/ld-2.9.so
b7fdb000     4K rw---  /lib/ld-2.9.so
bfcc6000    84K rw---   [ stack ]
total      1684K
```

Therefore, there is a balance between the convenience of the developers of libraries and the convenience of the libraries' users. Rough guidelines for when to use libraries are as follows:

- Libraries make sense when they contain code that is rarely executed. If a substantial amount of code does not need to be loaded from disk for the general use of the application, then the load time of the application can be reduced if this functionality is placed in a library that is loaded only when needed.

- It is useful to place code that is common to multiple applications into shared libraries, particularly if the applications are out of the control of the developers of the libraries. This is the situation with most operating systems, where the applications that use the libraries will be developed separately from the core operating system. Most applications use libc, the C standard library, so it makes sense to deliver this library as a shared library that all applications can use. If the internals of the operating system change or if a bug is fixed, then the libraries can be modified without needing to change the applications that use those libraries. This is a form of encapsulation.

- Device drivers are usually packaged as libraries. There is a temptation to produce multiple libraries, some of which are core and some of which are device specific. If there is likely to only ever be a single device of a specific type attached to a system, then it is better to provide a single library. If there are likely to be multiple types of devices attached that all share the common core, then it might be appropriate to split the code into device-specific and common code.
- Libraries can also provide dynamically loaded functionality. A library could be released to provide an existing application with new functionality. Placing as much functionality into as few libraries as possible is the most efficient approach, but in many instances the need to dynamically manage functionality will outweigh any overhead induced by packaging the functionality as libraries.

In general, it is best to make libraries lazy loaded when needed rather than have all the libraries load at start-up time. This will improve the application start-up time. Listing 2.20 shows code for a simple library that will be lazy loaded.

Listing 2.20 **Simple Library with Initialization Code**

```
#include <stdio.h>

void initialise()
{
  printf( "Initialisation code run\n" );
}
#pragma init (initialise)

void doStuff()
{
  printf( "Doing stuff\n" );
}
```

The application shown in Listing 2.21 uses the library from Listing 2.20.

Listing 2.21 **Application That Calls Library Code**

```
#include <stdio.h>
void doStuff();
void main()
{
  printf( "Application now running\n" );
  doStuff();
  printf( "Application now exiting\n" );
}
```

Listing 2.22 shows the results of compiling, linking, and running this application on Solaris without lazy loading.

Listing 2.22 **Using Library Code Without Lazy Loading**

```
$ cc -O -G -o liba.so liba.c
$ cc -O -o main main.c -L. -R. -la
$ ./main
Initialisation code run
Application now running
Doing stuff
Application now exiting
```

Listing 2.23 shows the same test but with the library being lazy loaded.

Listing 2.23 **Using Library Code with Lazy Loading**

```
$ cc -O -G -o liba.so liba.c
$ cc -O -o main main.c -L. -R. -zlazyload -la
$ ./main
Application now running
Initialisation code run
Doing stuff
Application now exiting
```

This change in the linking has enabled the library to be loaded after the application has started. Therefore, the start-up time of the application is not increased by having to load the library first. It is not a significant issue for the example code, which uses one small library, but can be a significant issue when multiple large libraries need to be loaded before the application can start.

There is one situation where libraries that are tagged as being lazy loaded are loaded anyway. If an application needs to find a symbol and the application was not explicitly linked with the library containing that object at compile time, then the application will load all the dependent libraries in order to resolve any unresolved symbols, undoing the usefulness of lazy loading. Suppose we add a second library that prints the message "Library B initializing" when it is loaded but contains no other code. Listing 2.24 shows the command line to compile this library to have a lazy-loaded dependence on `liba`.

Listing 2.24 **Compiling `libb` to Have a Lazy-Loaded Dependence on `liba`**

```
$ cc -O -G -o libb.so libb.c -zlazyload -R. -L. -la
```

The next step, shown in Listing 2.25, is to deliberately link the application so that it lazy loads `libb` but does not have a dependence on `liba`. This would usually cause the linker to fail with an unresolved symbol error, but we can switch that safety check off using the `-znodefs` flag.

Listing 2.25 **Compiling the Application to Only Recode the Dependence on** `libb`

```
$ cc -O -G -o main main.c -zlazyload -znodefs -R. -L. -lb
```

The resulting application contains an unresolved symbol for `ina()` but has a lazy-loaded dependence on `libb`. When the application is run, it will be unable to resolve the symbol `ina()`, so the runtime linker will start loading all the lazy-loaded libraries. Once it has loaded `libb`, it will then lazy load the dependencies of `libb`, where it will finally load `liba` and locate the routine `ina()`. Listing 2.26 shows the resulting output.

Listing 2.26 **Output Showing** `libb` **Being Lazy Loaded as Part of Search for** `doStuff()`

```
$ ./main
Application now running
Library B initialising
Initialisation code run
Doing stuff
Application now exiting
```

The other reason that lazy loading would be unsuccessful is if the code is not optimally distributed between the libraries. If each library requires code from another in order to work, then there is no way that a subset can be loaded without pulling them all into the application. Therefore, the distribution of code between the libraries is a critical factor in managing the start-up time of an application.

The Impact of Data Structures on Performance

Data structure is probably what most people think of first when they hear the word *structure* within the context of applications. Data structure is arguably the most critical structure in the program since each data structure will potentially be accessed millions of times during the run of an application. Even a slight gain in performance here can be magnified by the number of accesses and become significant.

When an application needs an item of data, it fetches it from memory and installs it in cache. The idea with caches is that data that is frequently accessed will become resident in the cache. The cost of fetching data from the cache is substantially lower than the cost of fetching it from memory. Hence, the application will spend less time waiting for frequently accessed data to be retrieved from memory. It is important to realize that each fetch of an item of data will also bring adjacent items into the caches. So, placing data that is likely to be used at nearly the same time in close proximity will mean that when one of the items of data is fetched, the related data is also fetched.

The amount of data loaded into each level of cache by a load instruction depends on the size of the cache line. As discussed in "Using Caches to Hold Recently Used Data" in Chapter 1, 64 bytes is a typical length for a cache line; however, some caches have longer lines than this, and some caches have shorter lines. Often the caches that are closer to the processor have shorter lines, and the lines further from the processor have longer lines. Figure 2.2 illustrates what happens when a line is fetched into cache from memory.

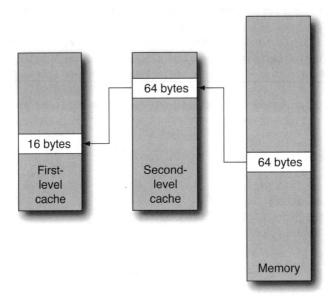

Figure 2.2 Fetching data from memory into caches

On a cache miss, a cache line will be fetched from memory and installed into the second-level cache. The portion of the cache line requested by the memory operation is installed into the first-level cache. In this scenario, accesses to data on the same 16-byte cache line as the original item will also be available from the first-level cache. Accesses to data that share the same 64-byte cache line will be fetched from the second-level cache. Accesses to data outside the 64-byte cache line will result in another fetch from memory.

If data is fetched from memory when it is needed, the processor will experience the entire latency of the memory operation. On a modern processor, the time taken to perform this fetch can be several hundred cycles. However, there are techniques that reduce this latency:

- *Out-of-order execution* is where the processor will search the instruction stream for future instructions that it can execute. If the processor detects a future load instruction, it can fetch the data for this instruction at the same time as fetching data for a previous load instruction. Both loads will be fetched simultaneously, and in the best case, the total cost of the loads can be potentially halved. If more than two loads can be simultaneously fetched, the cost is further reduced.

- *Hardware prefetching* of data streams is where part of the processor is dedicated to detecting streams of data being read from memory. When a stream of data is identified, the hardware starts fetching the data before it is requested by the processor. If the hardware prefetch is successful, the data might have become resident in the cache before it was actually needed. Hardware prefetching can be very effective in situations where data is fetched as a stream or through a strided access pattern. It is not able to prefetch data where the access pattern is less apparent.

- *Software prefetching* is the act of adding instructions to fetch data from memory before it is needed. Software prefetching has an advantage in that it does not need to guess where the data will be requested from in the memory, because the prefetch instruction can fetch from exactly the right address, even when the address is not a linear stride from the previous address. Software prefetch is an advantage when the access pattern is nonlinear. When the access pattern is predictable, hardware prefetching may be more efficient because it does not take up any space in the instruction stream.

Another approach to covering memory latency costs is with CMT processors. When one thread stalls because of a cache miss, the other running threads get to use the processor resources of the stalled thread. This approach, unlike those discussed earlier, does not improve the execution speed of a single thread. This can enable the processor to achieve more work by sustaining more active threads, improving throughput rather than single-threaded performance.

There are a number of common coding styles that can often result in suboptimal layout of data in memory. The following subsections describe each of these.

Improving Performance Through Data Density and Locality

Paying attention to the order in which variables are declared and laid out in memory can improve performance. As discussed earlier, when a load brings a variable in from memory, it also fetches the rest of the cache line in which the variable resides. Placing variables that are commonly accessed together into a structure so that they reside on the same cache line will lead to performance gains. Consider the structure shown in Listing 2.27.

Listing 2.27 **Data Structure**

```
struct s
{
  int var1;
  int padding1[15];
  int var2;
  int padding2[15];
}
```

When the structure member `var1` is accessed, the fetch will also bring in the surrounding 64 bytes. The size of an integer variable is 4 bytes, so the total size of `var1` plus `padding1` is 64 bytes. This ensures that the variable `var2` is located on the next cache line. Listing 2.28 shows the structure reordered so that `var1` and `var2` are adjacent. This will usually ensure that both are fetched at the same time.

Listing 2.28 **Reordered Data Structure So That Important Structure Members Are Likely to Share a Cache Line**

```
struct s
{
  int var1;
  int var2;
  int padding1[15];
  int padding2[15];
}
```

If the structure does not fit exactly into the length of the cache line, there will be situations when the adjacent `var1` and `var2` are split over two cache lines. This introduces a dilemma. Is it better to pack the structures as close as possible to fit as many of them as possible into the same cache line, or is it better to add padding to the structures to make them consistently align with the cache line boundaries? Figure 2.3 shows the two situations.

The answer will depend on various factors. In most cases, the best answer is probably to pack the structures as tightly as possible. This will mean that when one structure is accessed, the access will also fetch parts of the surrounding structures. The situation

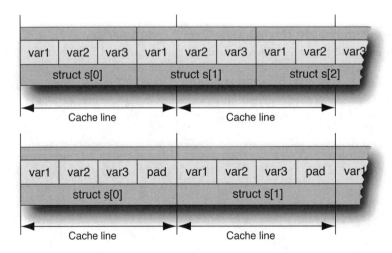

Figure 2.3 Using padding to align structures

where it is appropriate to add padding to the structure is when the structures are always accessed randomly, so it is more important to ensure that the critical data is not split across a cache line.

The performance impact of poorly ordered structures can be hard to detect. The cost is spread over all the accesses to the structure over the entire application. Reordering the structure members can improve the performance for all the routines that access the structures. Determining the optimal layout for the structure members can also be difficult. One guideline would be to order the structure members by access frequency or group them by those that are accessed in the hot regions of code. It is also worth considering that changing the order of structure members could introduce a performance regression if the existing ordering happens to have been optimal for a different frequently executed region of code.

A similar optimization is structure splitting, where an existing structure is split into members that are accessed frequently and members that are accessed infrequently. If the infrequently accessed structure members are removed and placed into another structure, then each fetch of data from memory will result in more of the critical structures being fetched in one action. Taking the previous example, where we assume that `var3` is rarely needed, we would end up with a resulting pair of structures, as shown in Figure 2.4.

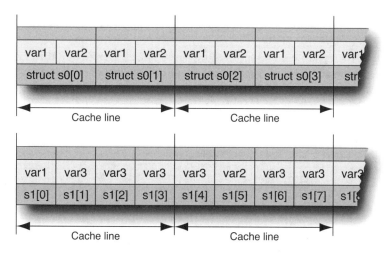

Figure 2.4 Using structure splitting to improve memory locality

In this instance, the original structure `s` has been split into two, with `s0` containing all the frequently accessed data and `s1` containing all the infrequently accessed data. In the limit, this optimization is converting what might be an array of structures into a set of arrays, one for each of the original structure members.

Selecting the Appropriate Array Access Pattern

One common data access pattern is striding through elements of an array. The performance of the application would be better if the array could be arranged so that the selected elements were contiguous. Listing 2.29 shows an example of code accessing an array with a stride.

Listing 2.29 **Noncontiguous Memory Access Pattern**

```
{
   double ** array;
   double total=0;
   …
   for (int i=0; i<cols; i++)
     for (int j=0; j<rows; j++)
       total += array[j][i];
   …
}
```

C/C++ arrays are laid out in memory so that the adjacent elements of the final index (in this case indexed by the variable i) are adjacent in memory; this is called *row-major* order. However, the inner loop within the loop nest is striding over the first index into the matrix and accessing the ith element of that array. These elements will not be located in contiguous memory.

In Fortran, the opposite ordering is followed, so adjacent elements of the first index are adjacent in memory. This is called *column-major* order. Accessing elements by a stride is a common error in codes translated from Fortran into C. Figure 2.5 shows how memory is addressed in C, where adjacent elements in a row are adjacent in memory.

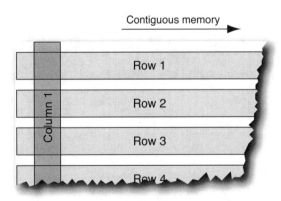

Figure 2.5 Row major memory ordering

Fortunately, most compilers are often able to correctly interchange the loops and improve the memory access patterns. However, there are many situations where the compiler is unable to make the necessary transformations because of aliasing or the order in which the elements are accessed in the loop. In these cases, it is necessary for the developer to determine the appropriate layout and then restructure the code appropriately.

Choosing Appropriate Data Structures

Choosing the best structure to hold data, such as choosing an algorithm of the appropriate complexity, can have a major impact on overall performance. This harks back to the discussions of algorithmic complexity earlier in this chapter. Some structures will be efficient when data is accessed in one pattern, while other structures will be more efficient if the access pattern is changed.

Consider a simple example. Suppose you have a dictionary of words for a spell-checker application. You don't know at compile time how many words will be in the dictionary, so the easiest way to cope with this might be to read in the words and place them onto a linked list, as shown in Figure 2.6.

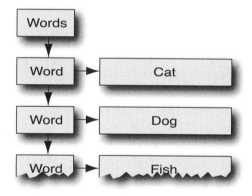

Figure 2.6 Using a linked list to hold an ordered list of words

Every time the application needs to check whether a word is in the dictionary, it traverses the linked list of words, so a spell-check of the entire document is an $O(N^2)$ activity.

An alternative implementation might be to allocate an array of known length to hold pointers to the various words, as shown in Figure 2.7.

Although there might be some complications in getting the array to be the right length to hold all the elements, the benefit comes from being able to do a binary search on the sorted list of words held in the array. A binary search is an $O(\log_2(N))$ activity, so performing a spell-check on an entire document would be an $O(N*\log_2(N))$ activity, which, as indicated earlier, would be a significantly faster approach.

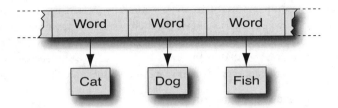

Figure 2.7 Using an array to hold an ordered list of words

As in any example, there are undoubtedly better structures to choose for holding a dictionary of words. Choosing the appropriate one for a particular application is a case of balancing the following factors:

- Programmer time to implement the algorithm. There will probably be constraints on the amount of time that a developer can spend on implementing a single part of the application.

- User sensitivity to application performance. Some features are rarely used, so a user might accept that, for example, performing a spell-check on an entire document will take time. It may also be the case that the compute part of the task is not time critical; in the case of a spell-check, if a spelling error is reported, the user may spend time reading the text to determine the appropriate word to use, during which the application could continue and complete the spell-check of the rest of the document.

- The problem size is not large enough to justify the more complex algorithm. If the application is limited to documents of only a few hundred words, it is unlikely that a spell-check of the entire document would ever take more than about half a second. Any performance gains from the use of an improved algorithm would be unnoticeable.

In many situations, there are preexisting libraries of code that implement different data management structures. For C++, the Standard Template Library provides a wealth of data structures. Careful coding to encapsulate the use of the data structures can minimize developer time by allowing the original structures to be easily replaced with more efficient ones should that prove necessary.

The Role of the Compiler

The purpose of the compiler is to take the source code and produce a functionally correct implementation, using only the information that the developer provides either in the source code or as part of the compilation process. It is important to recognize the constraints that the compiler is working under—something that is obvious to the developer may not be obvious to the compiler.

Most applications have execution paths that are rarely executed. A developer inspecting the code will probably be able to identify the paths that are likely to be executed infrequently. However, the compiler will be rarely able to extract additional contextual information from the source code to determine which path is most common. Consider the code shown in Listing 2.30, which has variable names that might indicate the developers' expectations of the frequency of execution of the two code paths.

Listing 2.30 **Code Where a Developer Might Guess Common Path**

```
...
  if (error) { value=0.001; }
  else       { value=numerator/denominator; }
...
```

The use of pointer variables raises a common problem. To the compiler, a pointer can point to any location in memory, including the address of other variables or the addresses held by other pointers. Hence, any memory location accessed through a pointer may modify or have been modified by a different memory access.

If two pointers hold the address of the same memory location, they are said to *alias*. The safe assumption is for the compiler to assume that any pointer may alias with any other data. In some cases, the compiler is able to prove that a particular memory location was not accessed through the pointer, and then the compiler can avoid reloading or storing data. However, the presence of a pointer may mean that the compiler cannot safely perform many optimizations. In Listing 2.31, the compiler has to assume that the two pointers passed into the functions might alias the same location in memory.

Listing 2.31 **Code Containing Potential Aliasing**

```
void func(int * a, int *b)
{
  *b = *b + *a;
  *a = *a + 2;
}
```

If pointers a and b do not alias, then the value of a needs to be loaded only a single time. If they do, then the store to b will change the value of a. In the absence of further information, the compiler must assume that the two pointers do alias and that the variable a needs to be loaded twice.

The compiler can sometimes determine from the source code that two pointers do not alias. In other cases, the compiler may be able to produce multiversion code that, at runtime, selects either the variant of the code where it is assumed that aliasing occurs or another variant where it is assumed that aliasing does not occur. However, the compiler should never produce code that will generate a wrong answer; optimizations that the compiler performs must either be provably safe or be specifically enabled, either implicitly or explicitly, by the user.

If the compiler is able to inspect more of the code, it is usually able to make better decisions. Cross-file optimization allows the compiler to combine all the source code for an executable. If the compiler can see all the source code, it knows how functions are called and sees the code that gets executed in the function call so it can make better inlining decisions. It can also see all the uses of a variable or memory region and can better optimize the use of that variable. Allowing the compiler visibility into more of the application will enable it to produce better-performing code.

The Two Types of Compiler Optimization

There are two fundamental types of optimization: elimination of work or restructuring of work. Although there is a huge list of optimizations that can be performed by compilers, all of them resolve to either not doing something or doing something in a more efficient way. Consider the snippet of code shown in Listing 2.32.

Listing 2.32 **Empty Loop**

```
for (int i=0; i<1000; i++) { }
```

It quite clearly does not perform any useful work; a programmer might have included it as a naïve delay. An optimizing compiler will eliminate the entire loop. Consider the variant of the code shown in Listing 2.33.

Listing 2.33 **Loop Containing Function Call**

```
for (int i=0; i<1000; i++) { do_nothing(); }
```

Unless the compiler can inspect the body of the function do_nothing() or the programmer has used some other mechanism to indicate to the compiler that the code does nothing, then the compiler will have to leave this loop in the code.

Listing 2.34 shows another code snippet.

Listing 2.34 **Loop Containing Floating-Point Arithmetic**

```
double total=0.0;
for (int i=0; i<1000; i++) { total = total + 1.0;}
```

Although a human would determine that the code is equivalent to adding 1,000 to the floating-point variable total, a compiler may perform all the individual additions. This is in case there is some side effect from the floating-point computation that a different part of the code is watching for. For example, there might be a floating-point exception handler that gets triggered by the computation of this loop. By default, some compilers cannot eliminate this code, but when given suitable compiler flags, the compiler will remove the loop. This is a demonstration that the compiler needs to be given appropriate instructions by the user in order for it to perform all the optimizations that it is capable of.

The other fundamental type of optimization is an improvement in the efficiency of the operations. In the section "Array Access Patterns," we saw a potential example where the compiler could interchange two loops in order to improve the pattern of memory accesses. This improved the performance of the code by reducing the memory access costs. Another example of this improvement in the efficiency of the code is where one operation can be replaced by a less expensive one. This is called *strength reduction*. A good demonstration of strength reduction is replacing integer division by a power of two with a shift operation. The code in Listing 2.35 contains an integer division by two.

Listing 2.35 **Code with Opportunity for Optimization**

```
unsigned int b;
...
unsigned int a = b/2;
```

An integer division by two can be replaced by a shift right operation, as shown in Listing 2.36.

Listing 2.36 **Code After Optimization**

```
unsigned int b;
...
unsigned int a = b>>1;
```

Another common optimization is to replace conditional code with logical operations. The performance gains come from the ease with which the processor is able to execute the resulting code. The improved sequence may eliminate branch instructions, therefore eliminating branch misprediction stalls, or maybe the new sequence needs fewer instructions. Listing 2.37 shows code with an opportunity for the replacement of conditional code with logical operations.

Listing 2.37 **Conditional Code**

```
if ( (value & 1) == 1 )
{
  odd = 1;
}
else
```

```
{
  odd = 0;
}
```

The code shown in Listing 2.37 can be replaced by the equivalent code shown in Listing 2.38.

Listing 2.38 **Logical Operations**

```
odd = value & 1;
```

Selecting Appropriate Compiler Options

Compilers tend to have many possible command-line options, or *flags*. The programmer's task is to identify the smallest subset of flags that will provide the most appropriate set of optimizations. Usually this falls into a set of three objectives for the build:

- The basic optimization level is the debug level. These are the flags necessary to generate code that can be effectively debugged. This kind of build is useful for debugging logical errors in the code. If the code dies with a null-pointer exception, running the debug version of the code will allow the developer to determine whether that exception is a result of optimization or an intrinsic property of the code. It will also allow the developer to step through the code in the smallest possible steps to see exactly how the application gets into that state. However, this capability usually comes at the cost of the reduced runtime performance.

- An optimized build of an application builds quickly and runs at a reasonable speed. A developer will build and run the application many times over the development cycle, so it is important that the compiler does not take long to compile the application and that the application executes with reasonable performance. Typically, compilers indicate an optimized compilation with the flag -O. The optimizations performed by this flag typically represent a good trade-off between attaining fast runtime performance and spending large amounts of time compiling.

- Higher optimizations levels may also be appropriate. The developer first needs to evaluate whether a more aggressive compilation of the application provides further gains. If a more highly optimized build of the application delivers no further performance gains, then it is unnecessary to use higher levels of optimization. The build with the lower level of optimization but identical performance can be delivered as the production version of the application. On the other hand, if higher optimization levels deliver greater performance, a production build of the application may get better performance at the expense of a longer build cycle. If more aggressive compiler options deliver enhanced performance, it is recommended that these options be investigated to determine exactly which options provide the performance and whether they are appropriate to the application before being used on the production build.

Most compilers have a set of flags that match this philosophy. A debug build of an application is performed with either no optimization flags or a low optimization level flag, together with the flags that generate debug information. As the optimization level is increased, the compiler will examine the code, testing for an increasing range optimization opportunities. The more opportunities that the compiler checks for, the longer it takes to complete the compilation. Most compilers provide a flag, often –O, that selects a level of optimization that will deliver a good proportion of the maximum possible performance, without taking an unreasonable amount of compile time. Most compilers also provide a macro-flag, such as –fast, that enables a selection of more advanced optimizations. These additional optimizations may result in the highest performance but at the cost of a further increase in compile time.

There are two general optimizations worth exploring in some detail: cross-file optimization and profile feedback.

How Cross-File Optimization Can Be Used to Improve Performance

We have already discussed how the source structure of an application can impact the performance of an application. In Figure 2.8, function A() calls function B(), but function B() is defined in the file b.c, and function A() is defined in the file a.c.

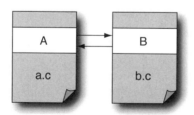

Figure 2.8 Function calls

There are a number of costs to making this call:

- There will be a branch and return instruction to make the call.

- Registers might be stored to memory before the call and restored from memory after the call because the called routine might use or modify the variables that they currently hold.

- Registers might be spilled to memory to provide empty registers for the called routine to use.

- Both routine A() and routine B() might perform computations that could be identified as unnecessary if the source for the combination of the two routines were evaluated.

One way to overcome these limitations is by using cross-file optimization. This is typically a final step after the compiler has produced object files for all the source files in an application. At this step, the compiler reads all the object files and looks for optimizations it can perform using full knowledge of the entire application. For inlining, the compiler will determine that there is a call from A() to B() and rewrite routine A() with a new version that combines the code from A() with the code from B(). This new version is the one that appears in the final executable.

Inlining is a very good optimization to enable because it should have no impact on the correctness of the application (the executed code should be equivalent to the original code), but it reduces the execution costs and also introduces further opportunities for optimization. Listing 2.39 shows code with an opportunity for an inlining optimization.

Listing 2.39 **Code with an Inlining Opportunity**

```
int B( int p, int q )
{
  if ( q == 1 )
  {
    return p;
  }
  else
  {
    return p * B( p, q-1 );
  }
}

int A( int p )
{
    return B( p, 1 );
}
```

In this example, the function B() is an inefficient way of calculating p^q. However, it is called by routine A() with the value of q as a constant 1, so the return value of the function will always be the value of the variable p. With inlining, the compiler can choose to inline function B() into function A(), and it will discover that q is always 1 for this call and can eliminate both the conditional code and the untaken recursive branch of the conditional code. In fact, the whole of routine A will collapse down to a statement that returns the value of the variable p, as shown in Listing 2.40.

Listing 2.40 **Code After Inlining Optimization**

```
int A( int p )
{
    return p;
}
```

This new version of the routine `A( )` is also a very good candidate for inlining since it only returns the value of the variable passed into it. Although this might appear to be an unlikely example, there is a more generally occurring code pattern, as shown in Listing 2.41.

Listing 2.41 **Accessor Pattern**

```
static int count;

int get_count()
{
  return count;
}
```

It is very common to have routines that exist only to get and set the value of variables. These routines are very strong candidates for inlining since they contribute only one useful instruction (the load of the variable) and at least two overhead instructions (the call and return).

Another situation where inlining improves performance is where it can eliminate loads and stores of variables to memory. Listing 2.42 shows code where inlining will reduce the number of memory operations.

Listing 2.42 **Code with Potential for Optimization by Function Inlining**

```
int number_of_elements;
int max;

void calculate_max(int* elements)
{
  max=elements[0];
  for (int i=1; i<number_of_elements; i++)
  {
    if ( elements[i] > max )
    {
      max=elements[i];
    }
  }
}
```

```
void doWork()
{
   ....
   number_of_elements = ....;
   calculate_max(elements);
   ....
}
```

The routine `calculate_max()` needs the variable `number_of_elements` to be updated before it is called. In the general case, the compiler needs to store all visible variables to memory before calling the routine. This is necessary in case the routine reads any of the variables. The variables need to be reloaded after the call in case the routine has modified any of them. After inlining, the compiler does not need to include these loads and stores because it can hold the necessary values in registers and execute only the loads and stores that are necessary.

Cross-file optimization has a benefit in that it enables the compiler to generate optimal code regardless of how the source code is distributed between source files. The only limitation involves static or dynamic libraries, in which case the compiler may not be able to perform the necessary cross-file inlining.

Using Profile Feedback

Most compilers support profile feedback, which is a mechanism that enables the compiler to gather information about the runtime behavior of the application. Consider the snippet of code shown in Listing 2.43.

Listing 2.43 **Code Where the Runtime Behavior of the Code Is Uncertain**

```
if ( a != 0 )
  { d++; }
else
  { d--; }
```

In this situation, the compiler has no idea whether the general case is to increment or decrement the variable d. The usual solution is for the compiler to either guess one is more likely than the other or produce code that favors neither assumption. However, if the code is in the frequently executed part of the application, the appropriate choice may lead to an observable improvement in performance.

Another case where knowledge of the runtime behavior of the application is useful is in determining which routines to inline. As discussed in the previous section, picking the correct routine to inline can lead to significant performance benefits. However, every time a called routine gets inlined, it increases the number of instructions in the calling routine. This code size increase is likely to cause the instruction cache to be less efficiently utilized, leading to a drop in performance. Hence, it can be quite important to inline routines that will benefit performance and avoid inlining those that will only increase the instruction cache footprint.

Profile feedback, or feedback-directed optimization, allows the compiler the opportunity to gather runtime information on the behavior of the application. It is a three-step process. The first step is to build an instrumented version of the application to collect runtime metrics. The next step is to run this application on a data set, which is "typical" of the one that the application will really run on but whose runtime is much shorter. The final step is to recompile the application using this profile information. Listing 2.44 shows the steps using the Solaris Studio compiler.

Listing 2.44 **Steps for Using Profile Feedback with the Sun Studio Compiler**

```
$ cc -O -xprofile=collect:./profile -o a.out prog.c
$ a.out
$ cc -O -xprofile=use:./profile -o a.out prog.c
```

The benefit of profile feedback depends on the application. Some applications will see no benefit, while some may see a significant gain. As outlined earlier, the gains typically come from either getting the compiler to lay out a performance-critical section of code in an optimal way or inlining a performance-critical routine.

It is interesting to observe that profile feedback tends to give the greatest benefit to codes where there are lots of branches or calls rather than codes where there are a lot of loops. The compiler can predict that loops will be iterated many times but has a harder job correctly guessing for codes where there are plenty of control flow instructions. Codes that have significant control flow instructions also tend to have few instructions between control flow, so there are not many opportunities for the compiler to extract performance in other ways. Hence, profile feedback can be the most effective way of improving performance in a class of codes that is otherwise hard to optimize.

There are two concerns with using profile feedback. The first is that using profile feedback complicates the build process and increases its duration. This can be controlled by using profile feedback only on the release builds and not as part of the regular developer builds. It can also be managed by ensuring that the build process is as efficient as possible. For instance, the build process can be parallelized so that it takes advantage of multiple cores.

The other concern is that using profile feedback optimizes the application for one particular scenario at the expense of the performance in other scenarios. This is the zero-sum view of performance; a gain on one workload has to be compensated by a loss of performance in another. In general, this concern is misplaced. Profile feedback helps the compiler make decisions about the frequently executed paths and frequently called functions. In most instances, the behavior of the application is only weakly dependent on the input data set. For example, the same routines get called (although with a different frequency), the same branches get taken, and so forth. This does not mean that every control transfer instruction has the same profile, but the majority of the control transfers in the code have the same direction.

The exception is an application that has different "modes": explicit modes where the application is requested to perform different tasks or implicit modes where some characteristic of the input data causes the application to behave in a particular way.

An explicit mode might appear in the code as a `switch/case` statement that calls entirely different code sections depending on an input condition. An implicit mode might be an application that has multiple ways of solving a problem, and the problem-solving approach used at each stage in the solution depends on the results of the previous steps.

If the application has modes of operation, then it is necessary to provide training inputs that capture all the different modes of operation. The profile of the application and the code coverage data for the particular training data used provide the best indication of whether the application has these modes. Input data sets that do not cover significant parts of the code base are a strong indicator for the existence of these modes and definitely indicate that more input data sets should be used in providing training data for the application's build.

The performance benefit from compiling with profile feedback is variable. Codes where the time is spent in loops tend to benefit less from profile feedback, whereas codes containing high numbers of control transfer instructions tend to see a much greater benefit. The typical gain is probably around 5% to 10%, but gains can be much greater if the profile feedback happens to lead to other opportunities for further performance gains. The developer's choice to use profile feedback should be taken in light of whether using it gets performance gains.

How Potential Pointer Aliasing Can Inhibit Compiler Optimizations

One of the most common barriers to optimization with C and C++ codes is pointer aliasing. In most situations, a compiler cannot tell whether two (or more) pointers point to the same address in memory or to different addresses. The compiler needs to make the safe choice, so it will often default to assuming that the pointers do alias, even when the programmer knows that the pointers do not. In some cases, the compiler is able to work around this problem by producing multiple versions of the code and using runtime checking to determine which version is appropriate. Consider the code shown in Listing 2.45.

Listing 2.45 **Code with Potential Pointer Aliasing**

```
void sum( double * total, double * array, int len )
{
  for (i=0; i<len; i++)
  {
    *total += array[i];
  }
}
```

The compiler cannot determine whether the memory location where the variable `total` is stored is part of the array. It has to make the safe assumption that the variable is part of the array, which results in code that stores the value of the variable `total` back to memory in every iteration. The loop shown in Listing 2.46 comes from the code compiled at a low level of optimization.

Listing 2.46 **Loop Containing Store Operation Because of Potential Aliasing**

```
top:
  ldd       [%o1],%f0      ! Load of array[i]
  add       %o4,1,%o4      ! Increment i
  add       %o1,8,%o1      ! Increment pointer to array[i];
  cmp       %o4,%o5        ! Check for end of loop
  faddd     %f2,%f0,%f4    ! Perform addition
  std       %f4,[%o0]      ! Store of the variable total
  bl,a,pt %icc,top         ! Loop to top
  ldd       [%o0],%f2      ! Reload of the variable total
```

At higher levels of optimization, the compiler can version the loop so that the version that performs the store to memory can be avoided if the loop contains no alias. Listing 2.47 shows the equivalent source code.

Listing 2.47 **Source Code Showing Two Versions of Loop with Potential Pointer Aliasing**

```
void sum( double * total, double * array, int len )
{
  if ( (total < array) || (total > array + len) )
  {
    double tmp = *total;
    for (int i=0; i<len; i++)
    {
       tmp += array[i];
    }
    *total = tmp;
  }
  else
  for ( int i=0; i<len; i++ )
  {
     *total += array[i];
  }
}
```

The modified source code uses a temporary variable to hold the calculated value so that the compiler knows that no aliasing is possible. This is a good technique to use in order to avoid possible aliasing issues with pointers to global data.

There are two fundamental performance issues in the presence of potential aliasing. The first is illustrated in the example disassembly in Listing 2.46. Aliasing requires the compiler to include unnecessary stores or loads of variables. It is possible to identify this problem by counting the generated memory operations and confirming that they correspond to the expected number from the source code.

The second issue is more subtle and involves the ability of the compiler to reorder instructions. Often, a compiler will move loads earlier in the instruction stream to give them more time to complete and move stores to later in the instruction stream to give more time for the instruction feeding data to them to complete. Unfortunately, aliasing issues limit the ability of the compiler to do this. When the disassembly is viewed, the problem appears as a store instruction followed immediately by a load instruction. This schedule ensures the correct memory ordering, but it may not be optimal for performance. Listing 2.48 shows this problem.

Listing 2.48 **Code with Potential Aliasing Issues**

```
void func(int * a, int * b)
{
  (*a)++;
  (*b)++;
}
```

When compiled, this code produces the SPARC assembly code shown in Listing 2.49.

Listing 2.49 **SPARC Assembly Code Produced in the Presence of Possible
            Pointer Aliasing**

```
    ld    [%o0],%o5   ! Load *a
    add   %o5,1,%o5   ! Increment
    st    %o5,[%o0]   ! Store *a    // Store of first variable
    ld    [%o1],%o4   ! Load *b     // Load of second variable
    add   %o4,1,%o3   ! Increment
    st    %o3,[%o1]   ! Store *b
```

The store of the variable a needs to be completed before the load of the variable b is issued. The code shown in Listing 2.50 has no pointer aliasing problems.

Listing 2.50 **Code with No Aliasing Problems**

```
void func(int * a)
{
  a[0]++;
  a[1]++;
}
```

Compiling the code shown in Listing 2.50 produces the SPARC assembly code shown in Listing 2.51.

Listing 2.51 **SPARC Assembly Code Produced in the Absence of Pointer Aliasing**

```
ld   [%o0],%o5     ! Load a[0]
ld   [%o0+4],%o4   ! Load a[1]  // Load of second variable
add  %o5,1,%o5     ! Increment
st   %o5,[%o0]     ! Store a[0] // Store of first variable
add  %o4,1,%o3     ! Increment
st   %o3,[%o1]     ! Store a[1]
```

Because the compiler is able to tell that there is no aliasing between the two operations, it can reorder the instructions to ensure that both loads start as early as possible.

A bigger problem with aliasing is that it often inhibits the compiler's ability to perform complex transformations of the code. Once a code has more than two streams of input data, it becomes very difficult to produce runtime code that dynamically checks for aliasing issues. For instance, the compiler would find runtime checking for aliasing difficult for the code shown in Listing 2.52. In this code, the matrix a is accessed contiguously so the compiler has knowledge of the range of memory that will be modified. The matrix b is accessed through the first index, which is a pointer into multiple arrays. Any of these arrays might overlap with the one pointed to by a.

Listing 2.52 **Code Where Code Runtime Checking of Aliasing Is Difficult**

```
void add(double **a, double **b)
{
  for( int i=0; i<100; i++ )
    for( int j=0; j<100; j++ )
      a[i][j] += b[j][i];
}
```

There are multiple ways to avoid aliasing issues. The first is to use local or stack-based variables. The compiler knows that these variables cannot alias with global variables; therefore, it can produce code based on this knowledge. For scalar variables with aliasing problems, this can often be the simplest solution.

Another approach is to advise the compiler what assumptions it is allowed to make about the code. The Solaris Studio compiler supports the flag -xalias_level=<level>, which allows the developer to specify, per file, the degree of aliasing that the code uses. The compiler also supports the flag -xrestrict, which tells the compiler that pointers passed into functions do not alias. Incidentally, this is the default for the Fortran standard. The gcc compiler supports the flag -fansi_alias, which tells the compiler that the code has aliasing that conforms to the C standard. The biggest issue with these flags is that they specify aliasing at the file or whole application level, and for large applications it can be difficult or impossible to prove that applying the flags is safe.

Compilers often support pragmas or directives that can be added to the source code to indicate the degree of aliasing at a function level. The finer level of control means that the directives can be added in places (a) where the biggest performance impact is seen and (b) where the developer can be certain that aliasing does not occur. However, compiler pragmas or directives are rarely the same across multiple compilers, so using them may lead to code that only compiles with a particular compiler and is not portable to others.

The most effective solution to the aliasing problem for C-language programs may be the `restrict` keyword. This enables the developer to use *restrict*-qualified pointers. These tell the compiler that no other pointers point to the same memory at the position in the code where the pointer is assigned. This is most useful for when pointers are passed into functions. Listing 2.53 shows the code from Listing 2.52 modified to use the `restrict` keyword.

Listing 2.53 **Code Modified to Use the `restrict` Keyword**

```
void add( double ** restrict a, double ** restrict b )
{
  for( int i=0; i<100; i++ )
    for( int j=0; j<100; j++ )
      a[i][j] += b[j][i];
}
```

The fact that either array a or b is restrict-qualified means that there is no aliasing between the arrays and means the compiler can generate more efficient code.

Identifying Where Time Is Spent Using Profiling

As soon as it is possible to run the application with meaningful results, a runtime profile of the application should be collected. Profiling is important for multiple reasons, the most fundamental of which is that *what is not measured is not managed*. If the performance of the application is not monitored as it develops, then there is no mechanism to identify changes that impact the performance of the application. However, there are other reasons for doing this:

- Verifying that the time is mainly spent in the functionally critical part of the code. Applications will go through multiple states at runtime, some concerned with start-up or teardown, but there will be a critical core of functionality that actually defines the purpose of the application. The time should be spent in the critical sections of the code and not in the parts of the code that facilitate the critical code. Imagine an application that loads data from a database, performs some analysis of that data, and then produces a chart as output. Time spent doing the analysis is probably the critical purpose of the application, and the bulk of the time should be spent there. The other sections of code should be completed as quickly as possible. If this is not the case, then you might question the code used in those stages.

Depending on where the time is spent, this might be the method of retrieving the data or the complexity of the charts being printed.

- Avoid time spent in noncritical or error-handling code. A frequent performance sink for applications is code that shouldn't be executed. This might be exception-handling code, writing error messages to `stderr`, or code that was meant to only handle corner cases. Once an application is profiled, it is relatively easy to identify sections of the code that were not expected to be visible in the profile.

- Checking the distribution of time between user, system, and other program states. Some applications will spend significant time in system code or some kind of waiting. System time might be necessary for the application to perform its task, but it can be an indication of something either going wrong or being poorly coded. An application might spend system time calling a heavyweight function to get the data for a time stamp when a lighter-weight alternative exists. Similarly, an application might spend significant time waiting for data to be returned across the network or waiting for the screen to be redrawn; performance might be improved by having a second thread carry on with computation while the main thread is in the wait state.

- Detecting time spent in exceptional conditions. These might be software traps to handle floating-point calculations involving subnormal numbers, or they could be something as mundane as TLB misses. These conditions are often hard to detect because they may not cause additional system time, but they are detectable either through observation using hardware counters or by careful examination of the exact assembly language instruction where the time is attributed.

Profiling applications as they are written and used is probably the most effective way of managing the performance of the application and should be routinely done during the development cycle as well as after any changes are made to the application.

Commonly Available Profiling Tools

Most modern profiling tools do not require you to do anything special to the application. However, it is often beneficial to build the application with debug information. The debug information can enable the tools to aggregate runtime at the level of individual lines of source code. There are also two common approaches to profiling.

The first approach is system-wide profiling. This is the approach taken by tools such as Intel's VTune, AMD's CodeAnalyst, and the open source profiling tool `oprofile`. The entire system is inspected, and timing information is gathered for all the processes running on the system. This is a very useful approach when there are a number of coordinating applications running on the system. During the analysis of the data, it is normal to focus on a single application.

Figure 2.9 shows the output from the AMD CodeAnalyst listing all the active processes on the system.

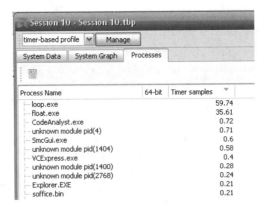

Figure 2.9 AMD CodeAnalyst's list of amount of time consumed by each running application

In this instance, there are two applications using up almost all of the CPU resources between them.

The second common approach is to profile just the application of interest. This approach is exemplified by the Solaris Studio Performance Analyzer. Profiling a single application enables the user to focus entirely on that application and not be distracted by the other activity on the system.

Regardless of the tool used, there are a common set of necessary and useful features. The most critical feature is probably the profile of the time spent in each function. Figure 2.10 shows the time spent in each function as reported by the Solaris Studio Performance Analyzer.

The profile for this code shows that about 70% of the user time is spent in the routine `calc()` with the remainder spent in the routine `__write()`.

Profile data at the function level can be useful for confirming that time is being spent in the expected routines. However, more detail is usually necessary in order to improve the application. Figure 2.11 shows time attributed to lines of source in the AMD CodeAnalyzer.

Functions	Callers–Callees	Source	Disassembly	Timeline	Experiments

User CPU ∇ (sec.)	User CPU (sec.)	Name
2.200	2.200	`<Total>`
1.320	1.320	`calc`
0.880	0.880	`__write`
0.	2.200	`main`
0.	0.880	`_ndoprnt`
0.	0.880	`printf`
0.	2.200	`_start`
0.	0.880	`write`
0.	0.880	`_xflsbuf`

Figure 2.10 Solaris Studio Performance Analyzer showing hot functions

Address	Line	Trace	Source	Code Bytes	Timer samples
0x4113c0			calc		100
	1		// float.cpp : Defines the entry po...		0
	2		//		0
	3				0
	4		#include "stdafx.h"		0
	5				0
	6		double calc(double d)		0
0x4113c0	7		{		0
0x4113de	8		double total=0.0;		0
0x4113e3	9		for (int i=0; i<10000000;...		9.41
	10		{		0
0x4113fe	11		total+=d;		75.15
0x411407	12		}		15.44
0x411409	13		return d;		0
0x41140c	14		}		0
0x411430			doWork		0
	15				0
	16		void doWork()		0

Figure 2.11 AMD's CodeAnalyzer showing time attributed to
lines of source

Using the source-level profile, most developers can make decisions about how to
restructure their code to improve performance. It can also be reassuring to drop down
into assembly code level to examine the quality of the code produced by the compiler
and to identify the particular operations that are taking up the time. At the assembly
code level, it is possible to identify problems such as pointer aliasing producing suboptimal code, memory operations taking excessive amounts of time, or other instructions
that are contributing significant time. Figure 2.12 shows the disassembly view from the
AMD CodeAnalyst.

Address	Line	Trace	Source	Code Bytes	Timer samples
	6		double calc(double d)		0
0x4113c0	7		{		0
0x4113de	8		double total=0.0;		0
0x4113e3	9		for (int i=0; i<10000000;...		9.41
0x4113e3			mov [ebp-18h],00000000h	C7 45 E8 00 00 0...	0
0x4113ea			jmp $+0bh (0x4113f5)	EB 09	0
0x4113ec			mov eax,[ebp-18h]	8B 45 E8	0
0x4113ef			add eax,01h	83 C0 01	4.04
0x4113f2			mov [ebp-18h],eax	89 45 E8	1.25
0x4113f5			cmp [ebp-18h],00989680h	81 7D E8 80 96 9...	0
0x4113fc			jnl $+0dh (0x411409)	7D 0B	4.12
	10		{		0
0x4113fe	11		total+=d;		75.15
0x4113fe			fld qword [ebp-0ch]	DD 45 F4	0.94
0x411401			fadd qword [ebp+08h]	DC 45 08	65.27
0x411404			fstp qword [ebp-0ch]	DD 5D F4	8.95
0x411407	12		}		15.44
0x411407			jmp $-1bh (0x1004113ec)	EB E3	15.44
0x411409	13		return d;		0
0x41140c	14		}		0
0x411430			doWork		0

Figure 2.12 AMD's CodeAnalyst showing time attributed to individual
instructions

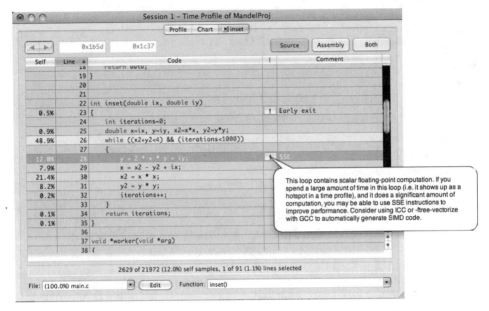

Figure 2.13 Apple's Shark profiling tool offering suggestions for
performance improvement

Some tools are able to provide suggestions on how to improve the performance of
the application. Figure 2.13 shows output from Apple's Shark tool, which suggests
improving performance by recompiling the application to use SSE instructions.

Many performance problems can be analyzed and solved at the level of lines of source
code. However, in some instances, the problem is related to how the routine is used. In
this situation, it becomes important to see the call stack for a routine. Figure 2.14 shows
a call chart from Intel's Vtune tool. The figure shows two threads in the application and
indicates the caller-callee relationship between the functions called by the two threads.

An alternative way of presenting caller-callee data is from the Oracle Solaris Studio
Performance Analyzer, as shown in Figure 2.15. This hierarchical view allows the user to
drill down into the hottest regions of code.

Another view of the data that can be particularly useful is the time line view. This
shows program activity over time. Figure 2.16 shows the time live view from the Solaris
Studio Performance Analyzer. In this case, the time line view shows both thread activity,
which corresponds to the shaded region of the horizontal bars, together with call stack
information, indicated by the different colors used to shade the bars. Examining the run
of an application over time can highlight issues when the behavior of an application
changes during the run. An example of this might be an application that develops a great
demand for memory at some point in its execution and consequently spends a period of
its runtime exclusively in memory allocation code.

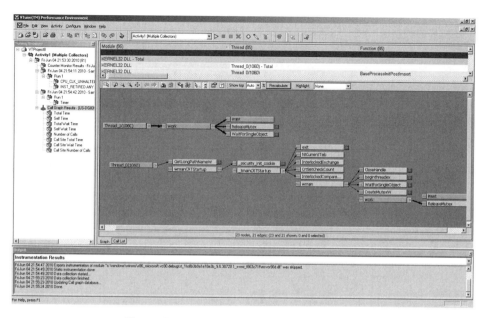

Figure 2.14 Call graph information from Vtune

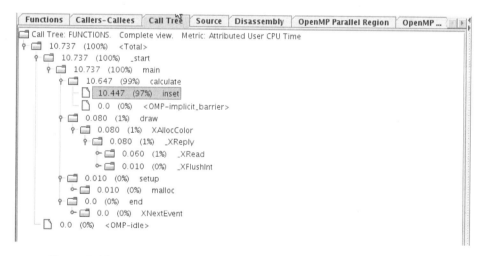

Figure 2.15 Call tree shown in the Oracle Solaris Studio Performance Analyzer

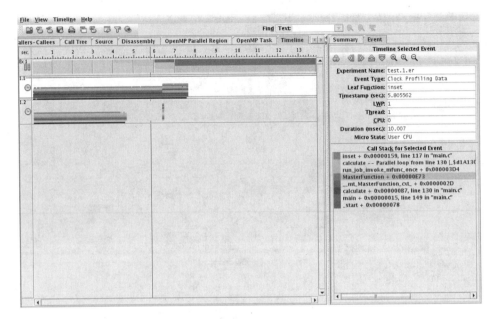

Figure 2.16 Time line view of thread activity from the Oracle
Performance Analyzer

A similar view is available from Apple's Instruments tool, as shown in Figure 2.17. An *instrument* is the name given to a tool that gathers data about processor, disk, network, and memory usage over the run of an application. This particular example shows processor utilization by the two threads over the run of the application. The time line view is particularly useful for multithreaded applications. To get the best performance, the work needs to be evenly divided between all threads. The time line view is a quick way of telling whether some threads are more active than others. It can also be useful for codes where a synchronization event, such as garbage collection in the case of Java, causes most of the threads in an application to pause.

Performance analysis tools are critical in producing optimal serial and parallel codes. Consequently, it is important to become familiar with the tools available on your system. For serial codes, a performance analysis tool will identify the region of code that needs to be improved to increase the performance of an application. For parallel codes, they will allow you to identify regions of code where the parallelization could be improved or where the work could be better distributed across the available processors or threads.

How Not to Optimize

When people talk about optimizing an application, there is a temptation to immediately think of recoding the hot routines in assembly language or of reaching for one of the

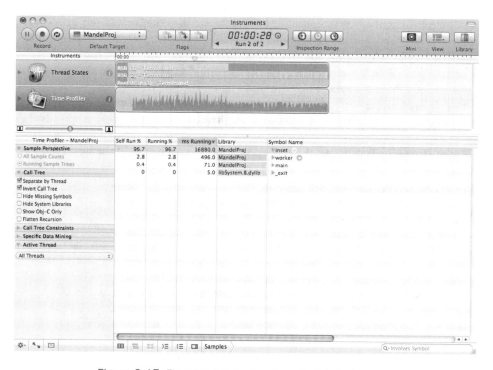

Figure 2.17 Time line information from Apple's Instruments

many books about performance optimization that talk about loop unrolling, invariant hoisting, and so on.

These do not represent the best place to start. In general, it is best to avoid optimizations that make the code less easy to read. The best approach is to make minimal changes to the source code or to select improved compiler flags.

It used to be the case that optimization did mean writing in assembly language or manually applying loop transformations in the source. That is why books on optimizations typically have extensive coverage of these topics. However, these optimizations are usually trivial for any modern compiler to do, given the right flags. Using the compiler to do the optimization has several benefits:

- First, the compiler will get the optimization correct. Manually undertaking complex instructions can potentially lead to bugs.

- The second benefit is that the code remains manageable. If the details of algorithm change, it will require only the minimal number of modifications to the source code, and the compiler will reapply the same optimization.

- There is a third benefit—that the compiler will do the optimization only if it is likely to result in a performance gain. Some optimizations might be a help on one processor but result in performance loss on a different processor.

Therefore, the important steps are to identify where the time is spent and then determine why the compiler isn't performing an optimization. Often, solving the problem is simply a minor change to the source code or the addition of a compiler flag.

Having said all that, there will be situations where it is impossible to coax optimal code out of the compiler and where manually optimizing the code is unavoidable. However, even before doing this, consider the gain that the optimization will provide. Doubling the performance of part of the code where 10% of the runtime is spent will result in a 5% gain in performance. This gain needs to be considered in light of the time spent rewriting the code to get the gain and the maintenance costs of the new code.

Performance by Design

This chapter has outlined a number of different places in the design process that impact performance. One way of visualizing this is to realize that there is a maximum possible performance for a given combination of system and problem to be solved. The choices made during design and implementation will either lead to the system meeting this maximum upper bound or cause the performance to be below this.

Decisions made early in the design process potentially have the largest impact on the performance of the application. The choice of algorithm can completely change the way the application behaves as the size of the problem increases. Similarly, a poor choice of algorithm can limit the scaling of the application as the number of available cores increases.

In many cases, it is possible to write the application in such a way as to encapsulate the choice of algorithm for critical parts of the code so that if it becomes critical to performance, it can be replaced at a later point. With careful consideration, the code can be structured so that the compiler can optimize away any inefficiencies introduced by this encapsulation.

With all design processes, it is usually easy to make significant changes early in the design process rather than later. Change introduced earlier takes less effort to implement and is cheaper than late-introduced fixes. Hence, early consideration given to appropriate workloads and use cases will lead to better choices during design and implementation.

All too often, performance tuning is considered at the point just before the application ships or at the point that it becomes obvious that the application is too slow. At this stage, it can be hard, and costly, to make the changes that are necessary to improve performance. Figure 2.18 shows the traditional view of the impact of change over the development cycle of an application.

Some program modifications are relatively easy to do at the end of the development cycle, such as changing the compiler flags, but the impact is likely to be small. Other actions, such as implementing a new algorithm, will have much higher costs if performed at the end of the project but could have a much greater impact. Ideally, such high-impact work should be completed early where it incurs less cost.

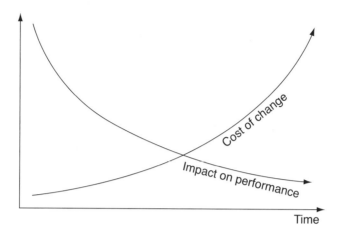

Figure 2.18 Cost of change and impact on performance over project life cycle

Summary

From this chapter you should have gained an understanding of how performance needs to be engineered into an application. Understanding the desirable performance characteristics of the solution to the problem will help guide development of a product that will meet those characteristics. That performance can be reduced by a poor choice of algorithms, data structures, compiler flags, or other decisions made during the process of design and implementation. Rectifying these decisions has engineering costs, and the later fixes have greater cost.

You should have gained an appreciation of how a compiler can be used to produce the best code possible and how good development practices can enable the compiler to do a better job.

One important point to take away from this chapter is that it is important to profile an application during the development process to ensure both that it is fast enough to meet the acceptance criteria and that it is spending its runtime in useful work and not suboptimal code.

3

Identifying Opportunities for Parallelism

This chapter discusses parallelism, from the use of virtualization to support multiple operating systems to the use of multiple threads within a single application. It also covers the concepts involved in writing parallel programs, some ways of visualizing parallel tasks, and ways of architecting parallel applications. The chapter continues with a discussion of various parallelization strategies, or patterns. It concludes by examining some of the limitations to parallelization. By the end of the chapter, you should be in a position to understand some of the ways that a system can support multiple applications and that an existing application might be modified to utilize multiple threads. You will also be able to identify places in the code where parallelization might be applicable.

Using Multiple Processes to Improve System Productivity

Consider a home computer system. This will probably have only one active user at a time, but that user might be running a number of applications simultaneously. A system where there is a single core produces the illusion of simultaneous execution of multiple applications by switching between the active applications many times every second. A multicore system has the advantage of being able to truly run multiple applications at the same time.

A typical example of this happens when surfing the Web and checking e-mail. You may have an e-mail client downloading your e-mail while at the same time your browser is rendering a web page in the background. Although these applications will utilize multiple threads, they do not tend to require much processor time; their performance is typically dominated by the time it takes to download mail or web pages from remote machines. For these applications, even a single-core processor often provides sufficient processing power to produce a good user experience. However, a single-core processor can get saturated if the e-mail client is indexing mail while an animation-heavy web page is being displayed.

In fact, these applications will probably already take advantage of multiple threads. Figure 3.1 shows a newly opened instance of Mozilla Firefox launching 20 threads. A consequence of this is that just by having a multicore processor, the performance of the system will improve because multiples of those threads can be executed simultaneously— and this requires no change to the existing applications.

Alternatively, there are a number of tasks we perform on our personal computer systems that are inherently compute intensive, such as playing computer games, encoding audio for an MP3 player, transforming one video format into another suitable for burning to DVD, and so on. In these instances, having multiple cores can enable the work to take less time by utilizing additional cores or can keep the system responsive while the task is completed in the background.

Figure 3.2 shows the system stack when a single user runs multiple applications on a system.

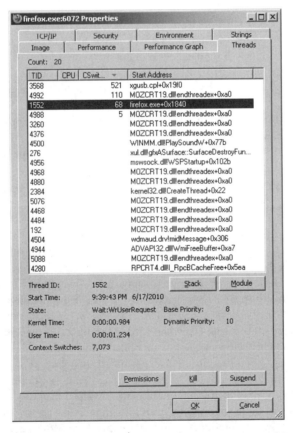

Figure 3.1 Windows Process Explorer showing thread activity in
Mozilla Firefox

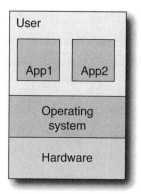

Figure 3.2 Single user on system

It is also possible to have multiple users in a home environment. For example, on Windows, it is quite possible for one user to be logged in and using the computer while another user, having logged in earlier, has set some other applications running. For example, you may have left some DVD-authoring package running in the background while another user logs into their account to check their e-mail.

Multiple Users Utilizing a Single System

In business and enterprise computing, it is much more common to encounter systems with multiple simultaneous users. This is often because the computer and software being shared are more powerful and more costly than the typical consumer system. To maximize efficiency, a business might maintain a database on a single shared system. Multiple users can simultaneously access this system to add or retrieve data. These users might just as easily be other applications as well as humans.

For many years, multiuser operating systems like UNIX and Linux have enabled sharing of compute resources between multiple users. Each user gets a "slice" of the available compute resources. In this way, multicore systems provide more compute resources for the users to share.

Figure 3.3 illustrates the situation with multiple users of the same system.

Multicore systems can be very well utilized running multiple applications, running multiple copies of the same application, and supporting multiple simultaneous users. To the OS, these are all just multiple processes, and they will all benefit from the capabilities of a multicore system.

Multiuser operating systems enforce separation between the applications run by different users. If a program one user was running were to cause other applications to crash or to write randomly to disk, the damage is limited to only those applications owned by that user or the disk space they have permission to change.

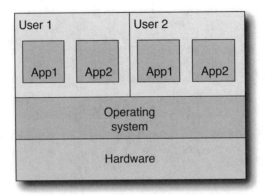

Figure 3.3 A single system supporting multiple users

Such containment and security is critical for supporting multiple simultaneous users. As the number of users increases, so does the chance that one of them will do something that could "damage" the rest of the system. This could be something as simple as deleting critical files or enabling someone to get unauthorized access to the system.

Improving Machine Efficiency Through Consolidation

Multicore computing is really just the continuing development of more powerful system architectures. Tasks that used to require a dedicated machine can now be performed using a single core of a multicore machine. This is a new opportunity to consolidate multiple tasks from multiple separate machines down to a single multicore machine. An example might be using a single machine for both a web server and e-mail where previously these functions would be running on their own dedicated machines.

There are many ways to achieve this. The simplest would be to log into the machine and start both the e-mail and web server. However, for security reasons, it is often necessary to keep these functions separated. It would be unfortunate if it were possible to send a suitably formed request to the web server allowing it to retrieve someone's e-mail archive.

The obvious solution would be to run both servers as different users. This could use the default access control system to stop the web server from getting access to the e-mail server's file. This would work, but it does not guard against user error. For example, someone might accidentally put one of the mail server's files under the wrong permissions, leaving the mail open to reading or perhaps leaving it possible to install a back door into the system. For this reason, smarter technologies have evolved to provide better separation between processes running on the same machine.

Using Containers to Isolate Applications Sharing a Single System

One such technology is containerization. The implementations depend on the particular operating system, for example, Solaris has Zones, whereas FreeBSD has Jails, but the concept is the same. A control container manages the host operating system, along with a multitude of guest containers. Each guest container appears to be a complete operating system instance in its own right, and an application running in a guest container cannot see other applications on the system either in other guest containers or in the control container. The guests do not even share disk space; each guest container can appear to have its own root directory system.

The implementation of the technology is really a single instance of the operating system, and the illusion of containers is maintained by hiding applications or resources that are outside of the guest container. The advantage of this implementation is very low overhead, so performance comes very close to that of the full system. The disadvantage is that the single operating system image represents a single point of failure. If the operating system crashes, then all the guests also crash, since they also share the same image. Figure 3.4 illustrates containerization.

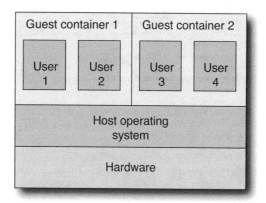

Figure 3.4 Using containers to host multiple guest operating systems in one system

Hosting Multiple Operating Systems Using Hypervisors

Two other approaches that enforce better isolation between guests' operating systems also remove the restriction that the guests run the same operating system as the host. These approaches are known as *type 1* and *type 2* hypervisors.

Type 1 hypervisors replace the host operating system with a very lightweight but high-level system supervisor system, or *hypervisor*, that can load and initiate multiple operating system instances on its own. Each operating system instance is entirely isolated from the others while sharing the same hardware.

Each operating system appears to have access to its own machine. It is not apparent, from within the operating system, that the hardware is being shared. The hardware has effectively been *virtualized*, in that the guest operating system will believe it is running on whatever type of hardware the hypervisor indicates.

This provides the isolation that is needed for ensuring both security and robustness, while at the same time making it possible to run multiple copies of different operating systems as guests on the same host. Each guest believes that the entire hardware resources of the machine are available. Examples of this kind of hypervisor are the Logical Domains provided on the Sun UltraSPARC T1 and T2 product lines or the Xen hypervisor software on x86. Figure 3.5 illustrates a type 1 hypervisor.

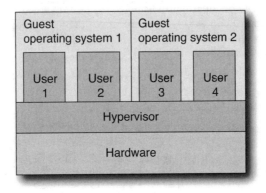

Figure 3.5 Type 1 hypervisor

A type 2 hypervisor is actually a normal user application running on top of a host operating system. The hypervisor software is architected to host other operating systems. Good examples of type 2 hypervisors are the open source VirtualBox software, VMware, or the Parallels software for the Apple Macintosh. Figure 3.6 illustrates a type 2 hypervisor.

Clearly, it is also possible to combine these strategies and have a system that supports multiple levels of virtualization, although this might not be good for overall performance.

Even though these strategies are complex, it is worth exploring why virtualization is an appealing technology.

- **Security.** In a virtualized or containerized environment, it is very hard for an application in one virtualized operating system to obtain access to data held in a different one. This also applies to operating systems being hacked; the damage that a hacker can do is constrained by what is visible to them from the operating system that they hacked into.
- **Robustness.** With virtualization, a fault in a guest operating system can affect only those applications running on that operating system, not other applications running in other guest operating systems.

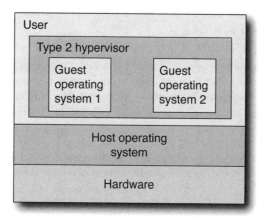

Figure 3.6 Type 2 hypervisor

- **Configuration isolation**. Some applications expect to be configured in particular ways: They might always expect to be installed in the same place or find their configuration parameters in the same place. With virtualization, each instance believes it has the entire system to itself, so it can be installed in one place and not interfere with another instance running on the same host system in a different virtualized container.

- **Restricted control**. A user or application can be given root access to an instance of a virtualized operating system, but this does not give them absolute control over the entire system.

- **Replication**. There are situations, such as running a computer lab, where it is necessary to be able to quickly reproduce multiple instances of an identical configuration. Virtualization can save the effort of performing clean reinstalls of an operating system. A new guest operating system can be started, providing a new instance of the operating system. This new instance can even use a preconfigured image, so it can be up and running easily.

- **Experimentation**. It is very easy to distribute a virtualized image of an operating system. This means a user can try a new operating system without doing any damage to their existing configuration.

- **Hardware isolation**. In some cases, it is possible to take the running image of a virtualized operating system and move that to a new machine. This means that old or broken hardware can be switched out without having to make changes to the software running on it.

- **Scaling**. It is possible to dynamically respond to increased requests for work by starting up more virtual images. For example, a company might provide a web-hosted computation on-demand service. Demand for the service might peak on weekday evenings but be very low the rest of the time. Using virtualization, it would be possible to start up new virtual machines to handle the load at the times when the demand increases.

- **Consolidation.** One of the biggest plays for virtualization is that of consolidating multiple old machines down to fewer new machines. Virtualization can take the existing applications, and their host operating systems can move them to a new host. Since the application is moved with its host operating system, the transition is more likely to be smooth than if the application had to be reconfigured for a new environment.

All these characteristics of virtualization make it a good fit for *cloud computing*. Cloud computing is a service provided by a remote farm of machines. Using virtualization, each user can be presented with root access to an unshared virtual machine. The number of machines can be scaled to match the demand for their service, and new machines can quickly be brought into service by replicating an existing setup. Finally, the software is isolated from the physical hardware that it is running on, so it can easily be moved to new hardware as the farm evolves.

Using Parallelism to Improve the Performance of a Single Task

Virtualization provides one way of utilizing a multicore or multiprocessor system by extracting parallelism at the highest level: running multiple tasks or applications simultaneously. For a user, a compelling feature of virtualization is that utilizing this level of parallelism becomes largely an administrative task.

But the deeper question for software developers is how multiple cores can be employed to improve the throughput or computational speed of a single application. The next section discusses a more tightly integrated parallelism for enabling such performance gains.

One Approach to Visualizing Parallel Applications

One way to visualize parallelization conceptually is to imagine that there are two of you; each thinks the same thoughts and behaves in the same way. Potentially, you could achieve twice as much as one of you currently does, but there are definitely some issues that the two of you will have to face.

You might imagine that your double could go out to work while you stay at home and read books. In this situation, you are implicitly controlling your double: You tell them what to do.

However, if you're both identical, then your double would also prefer to stay home and read while you go out to work. So, perhaps you would have to devise a way to determine which of you goes to work today—maybe splitting the work so that one would go one week, and the other the next week.

Of course, there would also be problems on the weekend, when you both would want to read the same newspaper at the same time. So, perhaps you would need two copies of the paper or work out some way of sharing it so only one of you had the paper at a time.

On the other hand, there would be plenty of benefits. You could be painting one wall, while your double is painting another. One of you could mow the lawn while the other washes the dishes. You could even work together cooking the dinner; one of you could be chopping vegetables while the other is frying them.

Although the idea of this kind of double person is fanciful, these examples represent very real issues that arise when writing parallel applications. As a thought experiment, imagining two people collaborating on a particular task should help you identify ways to divide the task and should also indicate some of the issues that result.

The rest of the chapter will explore some of these opportunities and issues in more detail. However, it will help in visualizing the later parts of the chapter if you can take some of these more "human" examples and draw the parallels to the computational problems.

Parallelism provides an opportunity to get more work done. This work might be independent tasks, such as mowing the lawn and washing the dishes. These could correspond to different processes or perhaps even different users utilizing the same system. Painting the walls of a house requires a little more communication—you might need to identify which wall to paint next—but generally the two tasks can proceed independently. However, when it comes to cooking a meal, the tasks are much more tightly coupled. The order in which the vegetables are chopped should correspond to the order in which they are needed. You might even need messages like "Stop what you're doing and get me more olive oil, now!" Preparing a meal requires a high amount of communication between the two workers.

The more communication is required, the more likely it is that the effect of the two workers will not be a doubling of performance. An example of communication might be to indicate which order the vegetables should be prepared in. Inefficiencies might arise when the person cooking is waiting for the other person to complete chopping the next needed vegetable.

The issue of accessing resources, for example, both wanting to read the same newspaper, is another important concern. It can sometimes be avoided by duplicating resources— both of you having your own copies—but sometimes if there is only a single resource, we will need to establish a way to share that resource.

In the next section, we will explore this thought experiment further and observe how the algorithm we use to solve a problem determines how efficiently the problem can be solved.

How Parallelism Can Change the Choice of Algorithms

Algorithms have characteristics that make them more or less appropriate for a multi-threaded implementation. For example, suppose you have a deck of playing cards that are in a random order but you would like to sort them in order. One way to do this would be to hold the unsorted cards in one hand and place each card into its appropriate place in the other hand. There are N cards, and a binary search is needed to locate each card into its proper place. So, going back to the earlier discussion on algorithmic complexity, this is an O(n*log(n)) algorithm.

However, suppose you have someone to help, and you each decide to sort half the pack. If you did that, you would end up with two piles of sorted cards, which you would then have to combine. To combine them, you could each start with a pile of cards, and then whoever had the next card could place it onto the single sorted stack. The complexity of the sort part of this algorithm would be O(n*log(n)) (for a value of n that was half the original), and the combination would be O(n). So although we have increased the number of "threads," we do not guarantee a doubling of performance.

An alternative way of doing this would be to take advantage of the fact that playing cards have an existing and easily discernible order. If instead of sorting the cards, you just place them at the correct place on a grid. The grid could have the "value" of the card as the x-axis and the "suit" of the card as the y-axis. This would be an O(n) operation since the time it takes to place a single card does not depend on the number of cards that are present in the deck. This method is likely to be slightly slower than keeping the cards in your hands because you will have to physically reach to place the cards into the appropriate places in the grid. However, if you have the benefit of another person helping, then the deck can again be split into two, and each person would have to sort only half the cards. Assuming you don't obstruct each other, you should be able to attain a near doubling of performance. So, comparing the two algorithms, using the grid method might be slower for a single person but would scale better with multiple people.

The point here is to demonstrate that the best algorithm for a single thread may not necessarily correspond to the best parallel algorithm. Further, the best parallel algorithm may be slower in the serial case than the best serial algorithm.

Proving the complexity of a parallel algorithm is hard in the general case and is typically handled using approximations. The most common approximation to parallel performance is Amdahl's law.

Amdahl's Law

Amdahl's law is the simplest form of a scaling law. The underlying assumption is that the performance of the parallel code scales with the number of threads. This is unrealistic, as we will discuss later, but does provide a basic starting point. If we assume that S represents the time spent in serial code that cannot be parallelized and P represents the time spent in code that can be parallelized, then the runtime of the serial application is as follows:

$$Runtime = S + P$$

The runtime of a parallel version of the application that used N processors would take the following:

$$\text{Runtime} = S + \frac{P}{N}$$

It is probably easiest to see the scaling diagrammatically. In Figure 3.7, we represent the runtime of the serial portion of the code and the portion of the code that can be made to run in parallel as rectangles.

Figure 3.7 Single-threaded runtime

If we use two threads for the parallel portion of the code, then the runtime of that part of the code will halve, and Figure 3.8 represents the resulting processor activity.

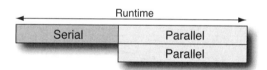

Figure 3.8 Runtime with two threads

If we were to use four threads to run this code, then the resulting processor activity would resemble Figure 3.9.

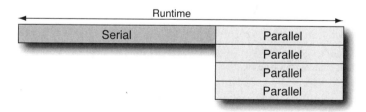

Figure 3.9 Runtime with four threads

There are a couple of things that follow from Amdahl's law. As the processor count increases, performance becomes dominated by the serial portion of the application. In the limit, the program can run no faster than the duration of the serial part, S. Another observation is that there are diminishing returns as the number of threads increases: At some point adding more threads does not make a discernible difference to the total runtime.

These two observations are probably best illustrated using the chart in Figure 3.10, which shows the parallel speedup over the serial case for applications that have various amounts of code that can be parallelized.

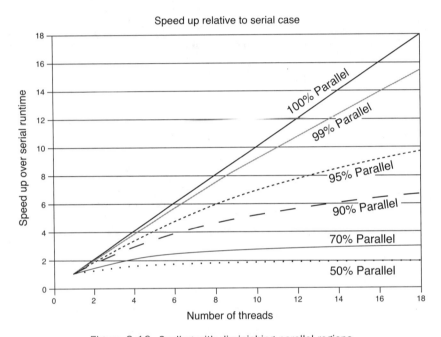

Figure 3.10 Scaling with diminishing parallel regions

If all the code can be made to run in parallel, the scaling is perfect; a code run with 18 threads will be 18x faster than the serial version of the code. However, it is surprising to see how fast scaling declines as the proportion of code that can be made to run in parallel drops. If 99% of the application can be converted to parallel code, the application would scale to about 15x the serial performance with 18 threads. At 95% serial, this would drop to about 10x the serial performance. If only half the application can be run in parallel, then the best that can be expected is for performance to double, and the code would pretty much attain that at a thread count of about 8.

There is another way of using Amdahl's law, and that is to look at how many threads an application can scale to given the amount of time it spends in code that can be parallelized.

Determining the Maximum Practical Threads

If we take Amdahl's law as a reasonable approximation to application scaling, it becomes an interesting question to ask how many threads we should expect an application to scale to.

If we have an application that spends only 10% of its time in code that can be parallelized, it is unlikely that we'll see much noticeable gain when using eight threads over using four threads. If we assume it took 100 seconds to start with, then four threads would complete the task in 92.5 seconds, whereas eight threads would take 91.25 seconds. This is just over a second out of a total duration of a minute and a half. In case the use of seconds might be seen as a way of trivializing the difference, imagine that the original code took 100 days; then the difference is equivalent to a single day out of a total duration of three months.

There will be some applications where every last second is critical and it makes sense to use as many resources as possible to increase the performance to as high as possible. However, there are probably a large number of applications where a small gain in performance is not worth the effort.

We can analyze this issue assuming that a person has a tolerance, T, within which they cease to care about a difference in performance. For many people this is probably 10%; if the performance that they get is within 10% of the best possible, then it is acceptable. Other groups might have stronger or weaker constraints.

Returning to Amdahl's law, recall that the runtime of an application that has a proportion P of parallelizable code and S of serial code and that is run with N threads is as follows:

$$\text{Runtime}_N = S + \frac{P}{N}$$

The optimal runtime, when there are an infinite number of threads, is S. So, a runtime within T percent of the optimal would be as follows:

$$\text{Acceptable runtime} = S * (1 + T)$$

We can compare the acceptable runtime with the runtime with N threads:

$$S * (1 + T) = \left(S + \frac{P}{N} \right)$$

We can then rearrange and solve for N to get the following relationship for N:

$$N = \frac{P}{ST} = \frac{P}{(1 - P)T}$$

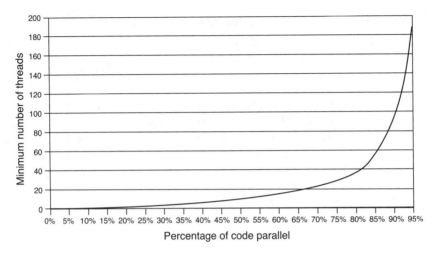

Figure 3.11 Minimum number of threads required to get 90% of
peak performance

Using this equation, Figure 3.11 shows the number of threads necessary to get a run-time that is within 10% of the best possible.

Reading this chart, it is clear that an application will have only limited scalability until it spends at least half of its runtime in code that can be parallelized. For an application to scale to large numbers of cores, it requires that 80%+ of the serial runtime is spent in parallelizable code.

If Amdahl's law were the only constraint to scaling, then it is apparent that there is lit-tle benefit to using huge thread counts on any but the most embarrassingly parallel applications. If performance is measured as throughput (or the amount of work done), it is probable that for a system capable of running many threads, those threads may be bet-ter allocated to a number of processes rather than all being utilized by a single process.

However, Amdahl's law is a simplification of the scaling situation. The next section will discuss a more realistic model.

How Synchronization Costs Reduce Scaling

Unfortunately, there are overhead costs associated with parallelizing applications. These are associated with making the code run in parallel, with managing all the threads, and with the communication between threads. You can find a more detailed discussion in Chapter 9, "Scaling on Multicore Systems."

In the model discussed here, as with Amdahl's law, we will ignore any costs intro-duced by the implementation of parallelization in the application and focus entirely on the costs of synchronization between the multiple threads. When there are multiple threads cooperating to solve a problem, there is a communication cost between all the threads. The communication might be the command for all the threads to start, or it might represent each thread notifying the main thread that it has completed its work.

We can denote this synchronization cost as some function F(N), since it will increase as the number of threads increases. In the best case, F(N) would be a constant, indicating that the cost of synchronization does not change as the number of threads increases. In the worst case, it could be linear or even exponential with the number threads. A fair estimate for the cost might be that it is proportional to the logarithm of the number of threads (F(N)=K*ln(N)); this is relatively easy to argue for since the logarithm represents the cost of communication if those threads communicated using a balanced tree. Taking this approximation, then the cost of scaling to N threads would be as follows:

$$\text{Runtime} = S + \frac{P}{N} + K \ln(N)$$

The value of K would be some constant that represents the communication latency between two threads together with the number of times a synchronization point is encountered (assuming that the number of synchronization points for a particular application and workload is a constant). K will be proportional to memory latency for those systems that communicate through memory, or perhaps cache latency if all the communicating threads share a common level of cache. Figure 3.12 shows the curves resulting from an unrealistically large value for the constant K, demonstrating that at some thread count the performance gain over the serial case will start decreasing because of the synchronization costs.

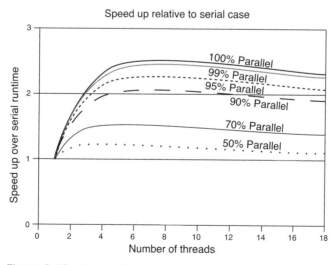

Figure 3.12 Scaling with exaggerated synchronization overheads

It is relatively straightforward to calculate the point at which this will happen:

$$\frac{d\ \text{runtime}}{dN} = \frac{-P}{N^2} + \frac{K}{N}$$

Solving this for N indicates that the minimal value for the runtime occurs when

$$N = \frac{P}{K}$$

This tells us that the number of threads that a code can scale to is proportional to the ratio of the amount of work that can be parallelized and the cost of synchronization. So, the scaling of the application can be increased either by making more of the code run in parallel (increasing the value of P) or by reducing the synchronization costs (reducing the value of K). Alternatively, if the number of threads is held constant, then reducing the synchronization cost (making K smaller) will enable smaller sections of code to be made parallel (P can also be made smaller).

What makes this interesting is that a multicore processor will often have threads sharing data through a shared level of cache. The shared level of cache will have lower latency than if the two threads had to communicate through memory. Synchronization costs are usually proportional to the latency of the memory through which the threads communicate, so communication through a shared level of cache will result in much lower synchronization costs. This means that multicore processors have the opportunity to be used for either parallelizing regions of code where the synchronization costs were previously prohibitive or, alternatively, scaling the existing code to higher thread counts than were previously possible.

So far, this chapter has discussed the expectations that a developer should have when scaling their code to multiple threads. However, a bigger issue is how to identify work that can be completed in parallel, as well as the patterns to use to perform this work. The next section discusses common parallelization patterns and how to identify when to use them.

Parallelization Patterns

There are many ways that work can be divided among multiple threads. The objective of this section is to provide an overview of the most common approaches and to indicate when these might be appropriate.

Broadly speaking, there are two categories of parallelization, often referred to as *data parallel* and *task parallel*.

A data parallel application has multiple threads performing the same operation on separate items of data. For example, multiple threads could each take a chunk of iterations from a single loop and perform those iterations on different elements in a single array. All the threads would perform the same task but to different array indexes.

A task parallel application would have separate threads performing different operations on different items of data. For example, an animated film could be produced having one process render each frame and then a separate process take each rendered frame and incorporate it into a compressed version of the entire film.

Data Parallelism Using SIMD Instructions

Although this book discusses data parallelism in the context of multiple threads cooperating on processing the same item of data, the concept also extends into instruction sets. There are instructions, called *single instruction multiple data* (SIMD) instructions, that load a vector of data and perform an operation on all the items in the vector. Most processors have these instructions: the SSE instruction set extensions for x86 processors, the VIS instructions for SPARC processors, and the AltiVec instructions on Power/PowerPC processors.

The loop shown in Listing 3.1 is ideal for conversion into SIMD instructions.

Listing 3.1 **Loop Adding Two Vectors**

```
void vadd(double * restrict a, double * restrict b , int count)
{
 for (int i=0; i < count; i++)
 {
   a[i] += b[i];
 }
}
```

Compiling this on an x86 box without enabling SIMD instructions generates the assembly language loop shown in Listing 3.2.

Listing 3.2 **Assembly Language Code to Add Two Vectors Using x87 Instructions**

```
loop:
    fldl    (%edx)      // Load the value of a[i]
    faddl   (%ecx)      // Add the value of b[i]
    fstpl   (%edx)      // Store the result back to a[i]
    addl    8,%edx      // Increment the pointer to a
    addl    8,%ecx      // Increment the pointer to b
    addl    1,%esi      // Increment the loop counter
    cmp     %eax,%esi   // Test for the end of the loop
    jle     loop        // Branch back to start of loop if not complete
```

Compiling with SIMD instructions produces code similar to that shown in Listing 3.3.

Listing 3.3 **Assembly Language Code to Add Two Vectors Using SSE Instructions**

```
loop:
    movupd (%edx),%xmm0 // Load a[i] and a[i+1] into vector register
    movupd ($ecx),%xmm1 // Load b[i] and b[i+1] into vector register
    addpd  %xmm1,%xmm0  // Add vector registers
    movpd  %xmm0,(%edx) // Store a[i] and a[i+1] back to memory
    addl   16,%edx      // Increment pointer to a
    addl   16,%ecx      // Increment pointer to b
    addl   2,%esi       // Increment loop counter
    cmp    %eax,%esi    // Test for the end of the loop
    jle    loop         // Branch back to start of loop if not complete
```

Since two double-precision values are computed at the same time, the trip count around the loop is halved, so the number of instructions is halved. The move to SIMD instructions also enables the compiler to avoid the inefficiencies of the stack-based x87 floating-point architecture.

SIMD and parallelization are very complementary technologies. SIMD is often useful in situations where loops perform operations over vectors of data. These same loops could also be parallelized. Simultaneously using both approaches enables a multicore chip to achieve high throughput. However, SIMD instructions have an additional advantage in that they can also be useful in situations where the amount of work is too small to be effectively parallelized.

Parallelization Using Processes or Threads

The rest of the discussion of parallelization strategies in this chapter will use the word *tasks* to describe the work being performed and the word *thread* to describe the instruction stream performing that work. The use of the word *thread* is purely a convenience. These strategies are applicable to a multithreaded application where there would be a single application with multiple cooperating threads and to a multiprocess application where there would be an application made up of multiple independent processes (with some of the processes potentially having multiple threads).

The trade-offs between the two approaches are discussed in Chapter 1, "Hardware, Processes, and Threads." Similarly, these patterns do not need to be restricted to a single system. They are just as applicable to situations where the work is spread over multiple systems.

Multiple Independent Tasks

As discussed earlier in the chapter, the easiest way of utilizing a CMT system is to perform many independent tasks. In this case, the limit to the number of independent tasks is determined by resources that are external to those tasks. A web server might require a large memory footprint for caching recently used web pages in memory. A database server might require large amounts of disk I/O. These requirements would place load on the system and on the operating system, but there would be no synchronization constraints between the applications running on the system.

A system running multiple tasks could be represented as a single system running three independent tasks, A, B, and C, as shown in Figure 3.13.

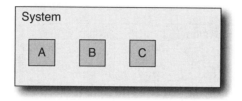

Figure 3.13 Three independent tasks

An example of this kind of usage would be consolidation of multiple machines down to a single machine. This consolidation might just be running the web server, e-mail server, and so on, on the same machine or might involve some form of virtualization where different tasks are isolated from each other.

This approach is very common but not terribly interesting from a parallelization strategy since there is no communication between the components. Such an approach would increase the utilization of the machine and could result in space or power savings but should not be expected to lead to a performance change (except that which is attained from the intrinsic differences in system performance).

One place where this strategy is common is in cluster, grid, or cloud computing. Each individual *node* (that is, *system*) in the cloud might be running a different task, and the tasks are independent. If a task fails (or a node fails while completing a task), the task can be retried on a different node. The performance of the cloud is the aggregate throughput of all the nodes.

What is interesting about this strategy is that because the tasks are independent, performance (measured as throughput) should increase nearly linearly with the number of available threads.

Multiple Loosely Coupled Tasks

A slight variation on the theme of multiple independent tasks would be where the tasks are different, but they work together to form a single *application*. Some applications do need to have multiple independent tasks running simultaneously, with each task generally independent and often different from the other running tasks. However, the reason this is an application rather than just a collection of tasks is that there is some element of communication within the system. The communication might be from the tasks to a central task controller, or the tasks might report some status back to a status monitor.

In this instance, the tasks themselves are largely independent. They may occasionally communicate, but that communication is likely to be asynchronous or perhaps limited to exceptional situations.

Figure 3.14 shows a single system running three tasks. Task A is a control or supervisor, and tasks B and C are reporting status to task A.

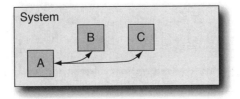

Figure 3.14 Loosely coupled tasks

The performance of the application depends on the activity of these individual tasks. If the CPU-consuming part of the "application" has been split off into a separate task, then the rest of the components may become more responsive. For an example of this improved responsiveness, assume that a single-threaded application is responsible for receiving and forwarding packets across the network and for maintaining a log of packet activity on disk. This could be split into two loosely coupled tasks—one receives and forwards the packets while the other is responsible for maintaining the log. With the original code, there might be a delay in processing an incoming packet if the application is busy writing status to the log. If the application is split into separate tasks, the packet can be received and forwarded immediately, and the log writer will record this event at a convenient point in the future.

The performance gain arises in this case because we have shared the work between two threads. The packet-forwarding task only has to process packets and does not get delayed by disk activity. The disk-writing task does not get stalled reading or writing packets. If we assume that it takes 1ms to read and forward the packet and another 1ms to write status to disk, then with the original code, we can process a new packet every 2ms (this represents a rate of 5,000 packets per second). Figure 3.15 shows this situation.

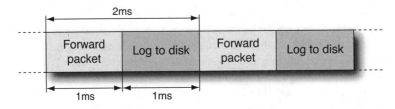

Figure 3.15 Single thread performing packet forwarding and log writing

If we split these into separate tasks, then we can handle a packet every 1ms, so throughput will have doubled. It will also improve the responsiveness because we will handle each packet within 1ms of arrival, rather than within 2ms. However, it still takes 2ms for the handling of each packet to complete, so the throughput of the system has doubled, but the response time has remained the same. Figure 3.16 shows this situation.

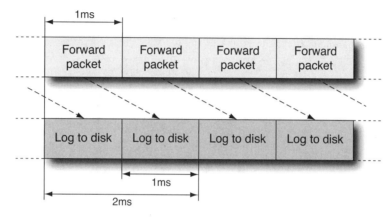

Figure 3.16   Using two threads to perform packet forwarding and log writing

Multiple Copies of the Same Task

An easy way to complete more work is to employ multiple copies of the same task. Each individual task will take the same time to complete, but because multiple tasks are completed in parallel, the throughput of the system will increase.

This is a very common strategy. For example, one system might be running multiple copies of a rendering application in order to render multiple animations. Each application is independent and requires no synchronization with any other.

Figure 3.17 shows this situation, with a single system running three copies of task A.

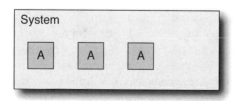

Figure 3.17   Multiple copies of a single task

Once again, the performance of the system is an increase in throughput, not an improvement in the rate at which work is completed.

Single Task Split Over Multiple Threads

Splitting a single task over multiple threads is often what people think of as parallelization. The typical scenario is distributing a loop's iterations among multiple threads so that each thread gets to compute a discrete range of the iterations.

This scenario is represented in Figure 3.18 as a system running three threads and each of the threads handling a separate chunk of the work.

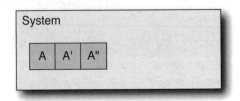

Figure 3.18 Multiple threads working on a single task

In this instance, a single unit of work is being divided between the threads, so the time taken for the unit of work to complete should diminish in proportion to the number of threads working on it. This is a reduction in completion time and would also represent an increase in throughput. In contrast, the previous examples in this section have represented increases in the amount of work completed (the throughput), but not a reduction in the completion time for each unit of work.

This pattern can also be considered a fork-join pattern, where the fork is the division of work between the threads, and the join is the point at which all the threads synchronize, having completed their individual assignments.

Another variation on this theme is the divide-and-conquer approach where a problem is recursively divided as it is divided among multiple threads.

Using a Pipeline of Tasks to Work on a Single Item

A pipeline of tasks is perhaps a less obvious strategy for parallelization. Here, a single unit of work is split into multiple stages and is passed from one stage to the next rather like an assembly line.

Figure 3.19 represents this situation. A system has three separate threads; when a unit of work comes in, the first thread completes task A and passes the work on to task B, which is performed by the second thread. The work is completed by the third thread performing task C. As each thread completes its task, it is ready to accept new work.

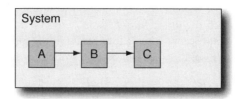

Figure 3.19 Pipeline of tasks

There are various motivations for using a pipeline approach. A pipeline has some amount of flexibility, in that the flow of work can be dynamically changed at runtime. It also has some implicit scalability because an implementation could use multiple copies of a particular time-consuming stage in the pipeline (combining the pipeline pattern with the multiple copies of a single task pattern), although the basic pipeline model would have a single copy of each stage.

This pattern is most critical in situations where it represents the most effective way the problem can be scaled to multiple threads. Consider a situation where packets come in for processing, are processed, and then are retransmitted. A single thread can cope only with a certain limit of packets per second. More threads are needed in order to improve performance. One way of doing this would be to increase the number of threads doing the receiving, processing, and forwarding. However, that might introduce additional complexity in keeping the packets in the same order and synchronizing the multiple processing threads.

In this situation, a pipeline looks attractive because each stage can be working on a separate packet, which means that the performance gain is proportional to the number of active threads. The way to view this is to assume that the original processing of a packet took three seconds. So, every three seconds a new packet could be dealt with. When the processing is split into three equal pipeline stages, each stage will take a second. More specifically, task A will take one second before it passes the packet of work on to task B, and this will leave the first thread able to take on a new packet of work. So, every second there will be a packet starting processing. A three-stage pipeline has improved performance by a factor of three. The issues of ordering and synchronization can be dealt with by placing the items in a queue between the stages so that order is maintained.

Notice that the pipeline does not reduce the time taken to process each unit of work. In fact, the queuing steps may slightly increase it. So, once again, it is a throughput improvement rather than a reduction in unit processing time.

One disadvantage to pipelines is that the rate that new work can go through the pipeline is limited by the time that it takes for the work of the slowest stage in the pipeline to complete. As an example, consider the case where task B takes two seconds. The second thread can accept work only every other second, so regardless of how much faster tasks A and C are to complete, task B limits the throughput of the pipeline to one task every two seconds. Of course, it might be possible to rectify this bottleneck by having two threads performing task B. Here the combination would complete one task every second, which would match the throughput of tasks A and C. It is also worth considering that the best throughput occurs when all the stages in the pipeline take the same amount of time. Otherwise, some stages will be idle waiting for more work.

Division of Work into a Client and a Server

With a *client-server* configuration, one thread (the *client*) communicates requests to another thread (the *server*), and the other thread responds. The split into client and server might provide a performance improvement, because while the server is performing some calculation, the client can be responding to the user; the client might be the visible UI to the application, and the server might be the compute engine that is performing the task in the background. There are plenty of examples of this approach, such as having one thread to manage the redraw of the screen while other threads handle the activities of the application. Another example is when the client is a thread running on one system while the server is a thread running on a remote system; web browsers and web servers are obvious, everyday examples.

A big advantage of this approach is the sharing of resources between multiple clients. For example, a machine might have a single Ethernet port but have multiple applications that need to communicate through that port. The client threads would send requests to a server thread. The server thread would have exclusive access to the Ethernet device and would be responsible for sending out the packets from the clients and directing incoming packets to the appropriate client in an orderly fashion.

This client-server relationship can be represented as multiple clients: A, communicating with a server, B, as shown in Figure 3.20. Server B might also control access to a set of resources, which are not explicitly included in the diagram.

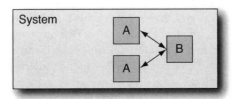

Figure 3.20 Client-server division of work

Implicit in the client-server pattern is the notion that there will be multiple clients seeking the attention of a single server. The single server could, of course, be implemented using multiple threads.

The client-server pattern does not improve responsiveness but represents a way of sharing the work between multiple threads, especially where the server thread actually does some work. Alternatively, it represents a way of sharing a common resource between multiple clients (in which case any gains in throughput are a fortunate by-product rather than a design goal).

Splitting Responsibility into a Producer and a Consumer

A *producer-consumer model* is similar to both the pipeline model and the client-server. Here, the producer is generating units of work, and the consumer is taking those units of work and performing some kind of process on them.

For example, the movie-rendering problem described earlier might have a set of producers generating rendered frames of a movie. The consumer might be the task that has the work of ordering these frames correctly and then saving them to disk.

This can be represented as multiple copies of task A sending results to a single copy of task B, as shown in Figure 3.21. Alternatively, there could be multiple producers and a single consumer or multiple producers and consumers.

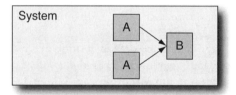

Figure 3.21 Producer-consumer division of work

Again, this approach does not necessarily reduce the latency of the tasks but provides an improvement in throughput by allowing multiple tasks to progress simultaneously. In common with the client-server task, it may also provide a way of reducing the complexity of combining the output from multiple producers of data.

Combining Parallelization Strategies

In many situations, a single parallelization strategy might be all that is required to produce a parallel solution for a problem. However, in other situations, there is no single strategy sufficient to solve the problem effectively, and it is necessary to select a combination of approaches.

The pipeline strategy represents a good starting point for a combination of approaches. The various stages in the pipeline can be further parallelized. For example, one stage might use multiple threads to perform a calculation on one item of data. A different stage might have multiple threads working on separate items of data.

When mapping a process to an implementation, it is important to consider all the ways that it is possible to exploit parallelism and to avoid limiting yourself to the first approach that comes to mind. Consider a situation where a task takes 100 seconds to complete. Suppose that it's possible to take 80 of those seconds and use four threads to complete the work. Now the runtime for the task is 20 serial seconds, plus 20 seconds when four threads are active, for a total of 40 seconds. Suppose that it is possible to use a different strategy to spread the serial 20 seconds over two threads, leading to a performance gain of 10 seconds, so the total runtime is now 30 seconds: 10 seconds with two threads and 20 seconds with four threads. The first parallelization made the application two and a half times faster. The second parallelization made it 1.3x faster, which is not nearly as great but is still a significant gain. However, if the second optimization had been the only one performed, it would have resulted in only a 1.1x performance gain, not nearly as dramatic a pay-off as the 1.3x gain that it obtained when other parts of the code had already been made parallel.

How Dependencies Influence the Ability Run Code in Parallel

Dependencies within an application (or the calculation it performs) define whether the application can possibly run in parallel. There are two types of dependency: *loop-* or *data-carried dependencies* and *memory-carried dependencies*.

With a loop-carried dependency, the next calculation in a loop cannot be performed until the results of the previous iteration are known. A good example of this is the loop to calculate whether a point is in the Mandelbrot set. Listing 3.4 shows this loop.

Listing 3.4 **Code to Determine Whether a Point Is in the Mandelbrot Set**

```
int inSet(double ix, double iy)
{
   int iterations=0;
   double x = ix, y = iy, x2 = x*x, y2 = y*y;
   while ( (x2+y2 < 4) && (iterations < 1000) )
   {
     y  = 2 * x * y + iy;
     x  = x2 - y2 + ix;
     x2 = x * x;
     y2 = y * y;
     iterations++;
   }
   return iterations;
}
```

Each iteration of the loop depends on the results of the previous iteration. The loop terminates either when 1,000 iterations have been completed or when the point escapes a circle centered on the origin of radius two. It is not possible to predict how many iterations this loop will complete. There is also insufficient work for each iteration of the loop to be split over multiple threads. Hence, this loop must be performed serially.

Memory-carried dependencies are more subtle. These represent the situation where a memory access must be ordered with respect to another memory access to the same location. Consider the snippet of code shown in Listing 3.5.

Listing 3.5 **Code Demonstrating Ordering Constraints**

```
int val=0;

void g()
{
   val = 1;
}

void h()
{
   val = val + 2;
}
```

If the routines `g()` and `h()` are executed by different threads, then the result depends on the order in which the two routines are executed. If `g()` is executed followed by `h()`, then the `val` will hold the result 3. If they are executed in the opposite order, then `val` will contain the result 1. This is an example of a memory-carried dependence because to produce the correct answer, the operations need to be performed in the correct order.

Antidependencies and Output Dependencies

Suppose one task, A, needs the data produced by another task, B; A depends on B and cannot start until B completes and releases the data needed by A. This is often referred to as *true dependency*. Typically, B writes some data, and A needs to read that data. There are other combinations of two threads reading and writing data. Table 3.1 illustrates the four ways that tasks might have a dependency.

Table 3.1 **Possible Ordering Constraints**

| | | Second task | |
		Read	Write
First task	**Read**	Read after read (RAR) No dependency	Write after read (WAR) Antidependency
	Write	Read after write (RAW) True dependency	Write after write (WAW) Output dependency

When both threads perform read operations, there is no dependency between them, and the same result is produced regardless of the order the threads run in.

With an antidependency, or write after read, one task has to read the data before the second task can overwrite it. With an output dependency, or write after write, one of the two tasks has to provide the final result, and the order in which the two tasks write their results is critical. These two types of dependency can be most clearly illustrated using serial code.

In the code shown in Listing 3.6, there is an antidependency on the variable `data1`. The first statement needs to complete before the second statement because the second statement reuses the variable `data1`.

Listing 3.6 **An Example of an Antidependency**

```
void anti-dependency()
{
    result1 = calculation( data1 );  // Needs to complete first
    data1   = result2 + 1;           // Will overwrite data1
}
```

If one of the statements was modified to use an alternative or temporary variable, for example, `data1_prime`, then both statements could proceed in any order. Listing 3.7 shows this modified code.

Listing 3.7 **Fixing an Antidependency**

```
void anti-dependency()
{
    data1_prime = data1;       // Local copy of data1
    result1 = calculation( data1_prime );
    data1   = result2 + 1;     // No longer has antidependence
}
```

The code shown in Listing 3.8 demonstrates an output dependency on the variable `data1`. The second statement needs to complete after the first statement only because they both write to the same variable.

Listing 3.8 **An Output Dependency**

```
void output-dependency()
{
    data1 = result1 + 2;
    data1 = result2 + 2; // Overwrites same variable
}
```

If the first target variable was renamed `data1_prime`, then both statements could proceed in any order. Listing 3.9 shows this fix.

Listing 3.9 **Fixing an Output Dependency**

```
void output-dependency()
{
   data1_prime = result1 + 2;
   data1       = result2 + 2; // No longer has output-dependence
}
```

What is important about these two situations is that both output and antidependencies can be avoided by *renaming* the data being written, so the final write operation goes to a different place. This might involve taking a copy of the object and having each task work on their own copy, or it might be a matter of duplicating a subset of the active variables. In the worst case, it could be resolved by both tasks working independently and then having a short bit of code that sets the variables to the correct state.

Using Speculation to Break Dependencies

In some instances, there is a clear potential dependency between different tasks. This dependency means it is impossible to use a traditional parallelization approach where the work is split between the two threads. Even in these situations, it can be possible to extract some parallelism at the expense of performing some unnecessary work. Consider the code shown in Listing 3.10.

Listing 3.10 **Code with Potential for Speculative Execution**

```
void doWork( int x, int y )
{
  int value = longCalculation( x, y );
  if (value > threshold)
  {
    return value + secondLongCalculation( x, y );
  }
  else
  {
    return value;
  }
}
```

In this example, it is not known whether the second long calculation will be performed until the first one has completed. However, it would be possible to speculatively compute the value of the second long calculation at the same time as the first calculation is performed. Then depending on the return value, either discard the second value or use it. Listing 3.11 shows the resulting code parallelized using pseudoparallelization directives.

Listing 3.11 **Speculatively Parallelized Code**

```
void doWork(int x, int y)
{
  int value1, value2;
  #pragma start parallel region
  {
    #pragma perform parallel task
    {
      value1 = longCalculation( x, y );
    }
    #pragma perform parallel task
    {
      value2 = secondLongCalculation( x, y );
    }
  }
  #pragma wait for parallel tasks to complete
  if (value1 > threshold)
  {
    return value1 + value2;
  }
  else
  {
    return value1;
  }
}
```

The #pragma directives in the previous code are very similar to those that are actually used in OpenMP, which we will discuss in Chapter 7, "OpenMP and Automatic Parallelization." The first directive tells the compiler that the following block of code contains statements that will be executed in parallel. The two #pragma directives in the parallel region indicate the two tasks to be performed in parallel. A final directive indicates that the code cannot exit the parallel region until both tasks have completed.

Of course, it is important to consider whether the parallelization will slow performance down more than it will improve performance. There are two key reasons why the parallel implementation could be slower than the serial code.

- The overhead from performing the work and synchronizing after the work is close in magnitude to the time taken by the parallel code.
- The second long calculation takes longer than the first long calculation, and the results of it are rarely used.

It is possible to put together an approximate model of this situation. Suppose the first calculation takes T1 seconds and the second calculation takes T2 seconds; also suppose that the probability that the second calculation is actually needed is P. Then the total runtime for the serial code would be T1 + P * T2.

For the parallel code, assume that the calculations take the same time as they do in the serial case and the probability remains unchanged, but there is also an overhead from synchronization, S. Then the time taken by the parallel code is S + max (T1,T2).

Figure 3.22 shows the two situations.

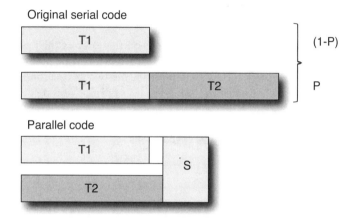

Figure 3.22 Parallelization using speculative execution

We can further deconstruct this to identify the constraints on the two situations where the parallel version is faster than the serial version:

- If T1 > T2, then for the speculation to be profitable, S+T1 < T1+P*T2, or S < P*T2. In other words, the synchronization cost needs to be less than the average amount of time contributed by the second calculation. This makes sense if the second calculation is rarely performed, because then the additional overhead of synchronization needed to speculatively calculate it must be very small.

- If T2 > T1 (as shown in Figure 3.21), then for speculation to be profitable, S+T2 < T1+P*T2 or P > (T2 +S −T1)/T2. This is a more complex result because the second task takes longer than the first task, so the speculation starts off with a longer runtime than the original serial code. Because T2 > T1, T2 + S −T1 is always >0. T2 + S −T1 represents the overhead introduced by parallelization. For the parallel code to be profitable, this has to be lower than the cost contributed by executing T2. Hence, the probability of executing T2 has to be greater than the ratio of the additional cost to the original cost. As the additional cost introduced by the parallel code gets closer to the cost of executing T2, then T2 needs to be executed increasingly frequently in order to make the parallelization profitable.

The previous approach is *speculative execution*, and the results are thrown away if they are not needed. There is also *value speculation* where execution is performed, speculating on the value of the input. Consider the code shown in Listing 3.12.

Listing 3.12 **Code with Opportunity for Value Speculation**

```
void doWork(int x, int y)
{
  int value = longCalculation( x, y );
  return secondLongCalculation( value );
}
```

In this instance, the second calculation depends on the value of the first calculation. If the value of the first calculation was predictable, then it might be profitable to speculate on the value of the first calculation and perform the two calculations in parallel. Listing 3.13 shows the code parallelized using value speculation and pseudoparallelization directives.

Listing 3.13 **Parallelization Using Value Speculations**

```
void doWork(int x, int y)
{
  int value1, value2;
  static int last_value;
  #pragma start parallel region
  {
    #pragma perform parallel task
    {
      value1 = longCalculation( x, y );
    }
    #pragma perform parallel task
    {
      value2 = secondLongCalculation( lastValue );
    }
  }
  #pragma wait for parallel tasks to complete
  if (value1 == lastvalue)
  {
    return value2;
  }
  else
  {
    lastValue = value1;
    return secondLongCalculation( value1 );
  }
}
```

The value calculation for this speculation is very similar to the calculation performed for the speculative execution example. Once again, assume that T1 and T2 represent the

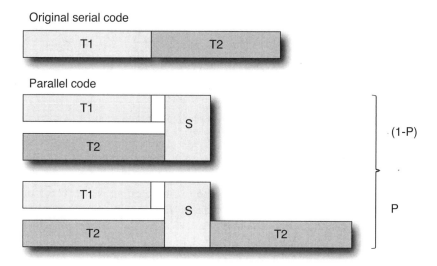

Figure 3.23 Parallelization using value speculation

costs of the two routines. In this instance, P represents the probability that the speculation is incorrect. S represents the synchronization overheads. Figure 3.23 shows the costs of value speculation.

The original code takes T1+T2 seconds to complete. The parallel code takes max(T1,T2)+S+P*T2. For the parallelization to be profitable, one of the following conditions needs to be true:

- If T1 > T2, then for the speculation to be profitable, T1 + S + P*T2 < T1 +T2. So, S < (1-P) * T2. If the speculation is mostly correct, the synchronization costs just need to be less than the costs of performing T2. If the synchronization is often wrong, then the synchronization costs need to be much smaller than T2 since T2 will be frequently executed to correct the misspeculation.

- If T2 > T1, then for the speculation to be profitable, T2 + S + P*T2 < T1 +T2. So, S <T1 − P*T2. The synchronization costs need to be less than the cost of T1 after the overhead of recomputing T2 is included.

As can be seen from the preceding discussion, speculative computation can lead to a performance gain but can also lead to a slowdown; hence, care needs to be taken in using it only where it is appropriate and likely to provide a performance gain.

Critical Paths

One way of looking at parallelization is by examining the *critical paths* in the application. A critical path is the set of steps that determine the minimum time that the task can

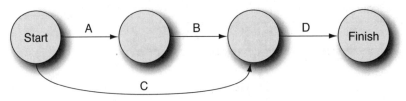

Figure 3.24 Critical paths

complete in. A serial program might complete tasks A, B, C, and D. Not all of the tasks need to have dependencies. B might depend on the results of A, and D might depend on the results of B and C, but C might not depend on any previous results. This kind of data can be displayed on a graph such as the one in Figure 3.24.

It is relatively straightforward to identify the critical path in a process once the dependencies and durations have been identified. From this graph, it is apparent that task C could be performed in parallel with tasks A and B. Given timing data, it would be possible to estimate the expected performance of this parallelization strategy.

Identifying Parallelization Opportunities

The steps necessary to identify parallelization opportunities in codes are as follows:

1. Gather a representative runtime profile of the application, and identify the regions of code where the most time is currently being spent.

2. For these regions, examine the code for dependencies, and determine whether the dependencies can be broken so that the code can be performed either as multiple parallel tasks or as a loop over multiple parallel iterations. At this point, it may also be worth investigating whether a different algorithm or approach would give code that could be more easily made parallel.

3. Estimate the overheads and likely performance gains from this parallelization strategy. If the approach promises close to linear scaling with the number of threads, then it is probably a good approach; if the scaling does not look very efficient, it may be worth broadening the scope of the analysis.

4. Broaden the scope of the analysis by considering the routine that calls the region of interest. Is it possible to make this routine parallel?

The important point to remember is that parallelization incurs synchronization costs, so the more work that each thread performs before it needs synchronization, the better the code will scale. Consequently, it is always worth looking further up the call stack of a region of code to determine whether there is a more effective parallelization point. For example, consider the pseudocode shown in Listing 3.14.

Listing 3.14 **Opportunities for Parallelization at Different Granularities**

```
void handlePacket(packet_t *packet)
{
   doOneTask(packet);
   doSecondTask(packet);
}

void handleStream( stream_t* stream )
{
  for( int i=0; i < stream->number_of_packets; i++)
  {
    handlePacket( stream->packets[i] );
  }
}
```

In this example, there are two long-running tasks; each performs some manipulation of a packet of data. It is quite possible that the two tasks, doOneTask() and doSecondTask(), could be performed in parallel. However, that would introduce one synchronization point after every packet that is processed. So, the synchronization cost would be O(N) where N is the number of packets.

Looking further up the stack, the calling routine, handleStream(), iterates over a stream of packets. So, it would probably be more appropriate to explore whether this loop could be made to run in parallel. If this was successful, then there would be a synchronization point only after an entire stream of packets had been handled, which could represent a significant reduction in the total synchronization costs.

Summary

This chapter has discussed the various strategies that can be used to utilize systems more efficiently. These range from virtualization, which increases the productivity of the system through increasing the number of active applications, to the use of parallelization techniques that enable developers to improve the throughput or speed of applications.

It is important to be aware of how the amount of code that is made to run in parallel impacts the scaling of the application as the number of threads increases. Consideration of this will enable you to estimate the possible performance gains that might be attained from parallelization and determine what constraints need to be met for the parallelization to be profitable.

The chapter introduces various parallelization strategies, and these should provide you with insights into the appropriate strategy for the situations you encounter. Successful parallelization of applications requires identification of the dependencies present in code. This chapter demonstrates ways that the codes can be made parallel even in the presence of dependencies.

This chapter has focused on the strategies that might be employed in producing parallel applications. There is another aspect to this, and that is the handling of data in parallel applications. The individual threads need to coordinate work and share information. The appropriate method of sharing information or synchronizing will depend on the implementation of the parallelization strategy. The next chapter will discuss the various mechanisms that are available to support sharing data between threads and the ways that threads can be synchronized.

Synchronization and Data Sharing

For a multithreaded application to do useful work, it is usually necessary for some kind of common state to be shared between the threads. The degree of sharing that is necessary depends on the task. At one extreme, the only sharing necessary may be a single number that indicates the task to be performed. For example, a thread in a web server might be told only the port number to respond to. At the other extreme, a pool of threads might be passing information constantly among themselves to indicate what tasks are complete and what work is still to be completed. Beyond sharing to coordinate work, there is sharing common data. For example, all threads might be updating a database, or all threads might be responsible for updating counters to indicate the amount of work completed.

This chapter discusses the various methods for sharing data between threads and the costs of these approaches. It starts with a discussion of *data races*, which are situations where multiple threads are updating the same data in an unsafe way. One way to avoid data races is by utilizing proper synchronization between threads. This chapter provides an overview of the common approaches to data sharing supported by most operating systems. This discussion focuses, as much as possible, on the abstract methods of synchronization and coordination. The following chapters will provide implementation-specific details for the POSIX and Windows environments.

Data Races

Data races are the most common programming error found in parallel code. A data race occurs when multiple threads use the same data item and one or more of those threads are updating it. It is best illustrated by an example. Suppose you have the code shown in Listing 4.1, where a pointer to an integer variable is passed in and the function increments the value of this variable by 4.

Listing 4.1 **Updating the Value at an Address**

```
void update(int * a)
{
    *a = *a + 4;
}
```

The SPARC disassembly for this code would look something like the code shown in Listing 4.2.

Listing 4.2 **SPARC Disassembly for Incrementing a Variable Held in Memory**

```
ld  [%o0], %o1   // Load *a
add %o1, 4, %o1  // Add 4
st  %o1, [%o0]   // Store *a
```

Suppose this code occurs in a multithreaded application and two threads try to increment the same variable at the same time. Table 4.1 shows the resulting instruction stream.

Table 4.1 **Two Threads Updating the Same Variable**

Value of variable a = 10	
Thread 1	**Thread 2**

`ld  [%o0], %o1   // Load %o1 = 10`
`add %o1, 4, %o1 // Add    %o1 = 14`
`st  %o1, [%o0]   // Store %o1`
	`ld  [%o0], %o1   // Load %o1 = 10`
	`add %o1, 4, %o1 // Add %o1 = 14`
	`st  %o1, [%o0]   // Store %o1`

Value of variable a = 14	

In the example, each thread adds 4 to the variable, but because they do it at exactly the same time, the value 14 ends up being stored into the variable. If the two threads had executed the code at different times, then the variable would have ended up with the value of 18.

This is the situation where both threads are running simultaneously. This illustrates a common kind of data race and possibly the easiest one to visualize.

Another situation might be when one thread is running, but the other thread has been context switched off of the processor. Imagine that the first thread has loaded the value of the variable a and then gets context switched off the processor. When it eventually runs again, the value of the variable a will have changed, and the final store of the restored thread will cause the value of the variable a to regress to an old value.

Consider the situation where one thread holds the value of a variable in a register and a second thread comes in and modifies this variable in memory while the first thread is running through its code. The value held in the register is now out of sync with the value held in memory.

The point is that a data race situation is created whenever a variable is loaded and another thread stores a new value to the same variable: One of the threads is now working with "old" data.

Data races can be hard to find. Take the previous code example to increment a variable. It might reside in the context of a larger, more complex routine. It can be hard to identify the sequence of problem instructions just by inspecting the code. The sequence of instructions causing the data race is only three long, and it could be located within a whole region of code that could be hundreds of instructions in length.

Not only is the problem hard to see from inspection, but the problem would occur only when both threads happen to be executing the same small region of code. So even if the data race is readily obvious and can potentially happen every time, it is quite possible that an application with a data race may run for a long time before errors are observed. In the example, unless you were printing out every value of the variable a and actually saw the variable take the same value twice, the data race would be hard to detect.

The potential for data races is part of what makes parallel programming hard. It is a common error to introduce data races into a code, and it is hard to determine, by inspection, that one exists. Fortunately, there are tools to detect data races.

Using Tools to Detect Data Races

The code shown in Listing 4.3 contains a data race. The code uses POSIX threads, which will be introduced in Chapter 5, "Using POSIX Threads." The code creates two threads, both of which execute the routine func(). The main thread then waits for both the child threads to complete their work.

Listing 4.3 **Code Containing Data Race**

```
#include <pthread.h>

int counter = 0;

void * func(void * params)
{
    counter++;
}

void main()
{
  pthread_t thread1, thread2;
  pthread_create( &thread1, 0, func, 0);
  pthread_create( &thread2, 0, func, 0);
  pthread_join( thread1, 0 );
  pthread_join( thread2, 0 );
}
```

Both threads will attempt to increment the variable counter. We can compile this code with GNU gcc and then use Helgrind, which is part of the Valgrind[1] suite, to identify the data race. Valgrind is a tool that enables an application to be instrumented and its runtime behavior examined. The Helgrind tool uses this instrumentation to gather data about data races. Listing 4.4 shows the output from Helgrind.

Listing 4.4 **Using Helgrind to Detect Data Races**

```
$ gcc -g race.c -lpthread
$ valgrind --tool=helgrind ./a.out
...
==4742==
==4742== Possible data race during write of size 4
        at 0x804a020 by thread #3
==4742==   at 0x8048482: func (race.c:7)
==4742==   by 0x402A89B: mythread_wrapper (hg_intercepts.c:194)
==4742==   by 0x40414FE: start_thread
           (in /lib/tls/i686/cmov/libpthread-2.9.so)
==4742==   by 0x413849D: clone (in /lib/tls/i686/cmov/libc-2.9.so)
==4742== This conflicts with a previous write of size 4 by thread #2
==4742==   at 0x8048482: func (race.c:7)
==4742==   by 0x402A89B: mythread_wrapper (hg_intercepts.c:194)
==4742==   by 0x40414FE: start_thread
           (in /lib/tls/i686/cmov/libpthread-2.9.so)
==4742==   by 0x413849D: clone (in /lib/tls/i686/cmov/libc-2.9.so)
```

The output from Helgrind shows that there is a potential data race between two threads, both executing line 7 in the file race.c. This is the anticipated result, but it should be pointed out that the tools will find some false positives. The programmer may write code where different threads access the same variable, but the programmer may know that there is an enforced order that stops an actual data race. The tools, however, may not be able to detect the enforced order and will report the potential data race.

Another tool that is able to detect potential data races is the Thread Analyzer in Oracle Solaris Studio. This tool requires an instrumented build of the application, data collection is done by the collect tool, and the graphical interface is launched with the command tha. Listing 4.5 shows the steps to do this.

Listing 4.5 **Detecting Data Races Using the Sun Studio Thread Analyzer**

```
$ cc -g -xinstrument=datarace race.c
$ collect -r on ./a.out
Recording experiment tha.1.er ...
$ tha tha.1.er&
```

---

1. http://valgrind.org/

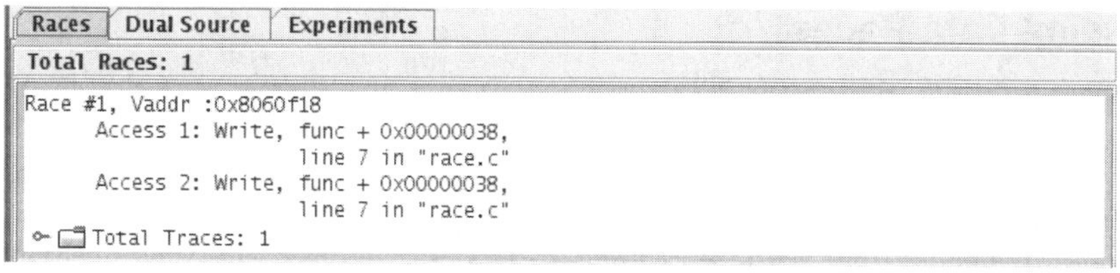

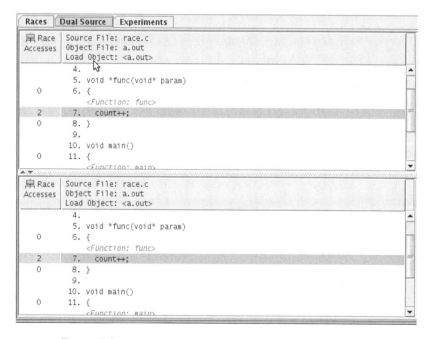

Figure 4.1 List of data races detected by the Solaris Studio
Thread Analyzer

The initial screen of the tool displays a list of data races, as shown in Figure 4.1.

Once the user has identified the data race they are interested in, they can view the source code for the two locations in the code where the problem occurs. In the example, shown in Figure 4.2, both threads are executing the same source line.

Figure 4.2 Source code with data race shown in Solaris Studio
Thread Analyzer

Avoiding Data Races

Although it can be hard to identify data races, avoiding them can be very simple: Make sure that only one thread can update the variable at a time. The easiest way to do this is to place a *synchronization lock* around all accesses to that variable and ensure that before referencing the variable, the thread must acquire the lock. Listing 4.6 shows a modified version of the code. This version uses a *mutex lock*, described in more detail in the next section, to protect accesses to the variable `counter`. Although this ensures the correctness of the code, it does not necessarily give the best performance, as will be discussed in later chapters.

Listing 4.6 **Code Modified to Avoid Data Races**

```
void * func( void * params )
{
  pthread_mutex_lock( &mutex );
  counter++;
  pthread_mutex_unlock( &mutex );
}
```

Synchronization Primitives

Synchronization is used to coordinate the activity of multiple threads. There are various situations where it is necessary; this might be to ensure that shared resources are not accessed by multiple threads simultaneously or that all work on those resources is complete before new work starts.

Most operating systems provide a rich set of synchronization primitives. It is usually most appropriate to use these rather than attempting to write custom methods of synchronization. There are two reasons for this. Synchronization primitives provided by the operating system will usually be recognized by the tools provided with that operating system. Hence, the tools will be able to do a better job of detecting data races or correctly labeling synchronization costs. The operating system will often provide support for sharing the primitives between threads or processes, which can be hard to do efficiently without operating system support. However, the most critical consideration is that the code provided by the operating system is unlikely to contain bugs. Discussion of writing custom synchronization primitives is covered in Chapter 8, "Hand-Coded Synchronization and Sharing."

Mutexes and Critical Regions

The simplest form of synchronization is a mutually exclusive (*mutex*) lock. Only one thread at a time can acquire a mutex lock, so they can be placed around a data structure to ensure that the data structure is modified by only one thread at a time. Listing 4.7 shows how a mutex lock could be used to protect access to a variable.

Listing 4.7 **Placing Mutex Locks Around Accesses to Variables**

```
int counter;

mutex_lock mutex;

void Increment()
{
    acquire( &mutex );
    counter++;
    release( &mutex );
}

void Decrement()
{
    acquire( &mutex );
    counter--;
    release( &mutex );
}
```

In the example, the two routines `Increment()` and `Decrement()` will either increment or decrement the variable counter. To modify the variable, a thread has to first acquire the mutex lock. Only one thread at a time can do this; all the other threads that want to acquire the lock need to wait until the thread holding the lock releases it. Both routines use the same mutex; consequently, only one thread at a time can either increment or decrement the variable `counter`.

If multiple threads are attempting to acquire the same mutex at the same time, then only one thread will succeed, and the other threads will have to wait. This situation is known as a *contended* mutex.

The region of code between the acquisition and release of a mutex lock is called a *critical section*, or *critical region*. Code in this region will be executed by only one thread at a time.

As an example of a critical section, imagine that an operating system does not have an implementation of `malloc()` that is *thread-safe*, or safe for multiple threads to call at the same time. One way to fix this is to place the call to `malloc()` in a critical section by surrounding it with a mutex lock, as shown in Listing 4.8.

Listing 4.8 **Placing a Mutex Lock Around a Region of Code**

```
void * threadSafeMalloc( size_t size )
{
    acquire( &mallocMutex );
    void * memory = malloc( size );
    release( &mallocMutex );
    return memory;
}
```

If all the calls to `malloc()` are replaced with the `threadSafeMalloc()` call, then only one thread at a time can be in the original `malloc()` code, and the calls to `malloc()` become thread-safe.

Threads *block* if they attempt to acquire a mutex lock that is already held by another thread. Blocking means that the threads are sent to sleep either immediately or after a few unsuccessful attempts to acquire the mutex.

One problem with this approach is that it can *serialize* a program. If multiple threads simultaneously call `threadSafeMalloc()`, only one thread at a time will make progress. This causes the multithreaded program to have only a single executing thread, which stops the program from taking advantage of multiple cores.

Spin Locks

Spin locks are essentially mutex locks. The difference between a mutex lock and a spin lock is that a thread waiting to acquire a spin lock will keep trying to acquire the lock without sleeping. In comparison, a mutex lock may sleep if it is unable to acquire the lock. The advantage of using spin locks is that they will acquire the lock as soon as it is released, whereas a mutex lock will need to be woken by the operating system before it can get the lock. The disadvantage is that a spin lock will spin on a virtual CPU monopolizing that resource. In comparison, a mutex lock will sleep and free the virtual CPU for another thread to use.

Often mutex locks are implemented to be a hybrid of spin locks and more traditional mutex locks. The thread attempting to acquire the mutex spins for a short while before blocking. There is a performance advantage to this. Since most mutex locks are held for only a short period of time, it is quite likely that the lock will quickly become free for the waiting thread to acquire. So, spinning for a short period of time makes it more likely that the waiting thread will acquire the mutex lock as soon as it is released. However, continuing to spin for a long period of time consumes hardware resources that could be better used in allowing other software threads to run.

Semaphores

Semaphores are counters that can be either incremented or decremented. They can be used in situations where there is a finite limit to a resource and a mechanism is needed to impose that limit. An example might be a buffer that has a fixed size. Every time an element is added to a buffer, the number of available positions is decreased. Every time an element is removed, the number available is increased.

Semaphores can also be used to mimic mutexes; if there is only one element in the semaphore, then it can be either acquired or available, exactly as a mutex can be either locked or unlocked.

Semaphores will also signal or wake up threads that are waiting on them to use available resources; hence, they can be used for signaling between threads. For example, a thread might set a semaphore once it has completed some initialization. Other threads could wait on the semaphore and be signaled to start work once the initialization is complete.

Depending on the implementation, the method that acquires a semaphore might be called *wait*, *down*, or *acquire*, and the method to release a semaphore might be called *post*, *up*, *signal*, or *release*. When the semaphore no longer has resources available, the threads requesting resources will block until resources are available.

Readers-Writer Locks

Data races are a concern only when shared data is modified. Multiple threads reading the shared data do not present a problem. Read-only data does not, therefore, need protection with some kind of lock.

However, sometimes data that is typically read-only needs to be updated. A *readers-writer lock* (or *multiple-reader lock*) allows many threads to read the shared data but can then lock the readers threads out to allow one thread to acquire a writer lock to modify the data.

A writer cannot acquire the write lock until all the readers have released their reader locks. For this reason, the locks tend to be biased toward writers; as soon as one is queued, the lock stops allowing further readers to enter. This action causes the number of readers holding the lock to diminish and will eventually allow the writer to get exclusive access to the lock.

The code snippet in Listing 4.9 shows how a readers-writer lock might be used. Most threads will be calling the routine `readData()` to return the value from a particular pair of cells. Once a thread has a reader lock, they can read the value of the pair of cells, before releasing the reader lock.

To modify the data, a thread needs to acquire a writer lock. This will stop any reader threads from acquiring a reader lock. Eventually all the reader threads will have released their lock, and only at that point does the writer thread actually acquire the lock and is allowed to update the data.

Listing 4.9 **Using a Readers-Writer Lock**

```
int readData( int cell1, int cell2 )
{
  acquireReaderLock( &lock );
  int result = data[cell] + data[cell2];
  releaseReaderLock( &lock );
  return result;
}

void writeData( int cell1, int cell2, int value )
{
  acquireWriterLock( &lock );
  data[cell1] += value;
  data[cell2] -= value;
  releaseWriterLock( &lock );
}
```

Barriers

There are situations where a number of threads have to all complete their work before any of the threads can start on the next task. In these situations, it is useful to have a barrier where the threads will wait until all are present.

One common example of using a barrier arises when there is a dependence between different sections of code. For example, suppose a number of threads compute the values stored in a matrix. The variable `total` needs to be calculated using the values stored in the matrix. A barrier can be used to ensure that all the threads complete their computation of the matrix before the variable `total` is calculated. Listing 4.10 shows a situation using a barrier to separate the calculation of a variable from its use.

Listing 4.10 **Using a Barrier to Order Computation**

```
Compute_values_held_in_matrix();
Barrier();
total = Calculate_value_from_matrix();
```

The variable `total` can be computed only when all threads have reached the barrier. This avoids the situation where one of the threads is still completing its computations while the other threads start using the results of the calculations. Notice that another barrier could well be needed after the computation of the value for `total` if that value is then used in further calculations. Listing 4.11 shows this use of multiple barriers.

Listing 4.11 **Use of Multiple Barriers**

```
Compute_values_held_in_matrix();
Barrier();
total = Calculate_value_from_matrix();
Barrier();
Perform_next_calculation( total );
```

Atomic Operations and Lock-Free Code

Using synchronization primitives can add a high overhead cost. This is particularly true if they are implemented as calls into the operating system rather than calls into a supporting library. These overheads lower the performance of the parallel application and can limit scalability. In some cases, either *atomic operations* or *lock-free code* can produce functionally equivalent code without introducing the same amount of overhead.

An *atomic operation* is one that will either successfully complete or fail; it is not possible for the operation to either result in a "bad" value or allow other threads on the system to observe a transient value. An example of this would be an atomic increment, which would mean that the calling thread would replace a variable that currently holds the value N with the value N+1. This might sound trivial, but bear in mind that the operation of incrementing a variable can involve multiple steps, as shown in Listing 4.12.

Listing 4.12 **Steps Involved in Incrementing a Variable**

```
LOAD   [%o0], %o1  // Load initial value
ADD    %o1, 1, %o1 // Increment value
STORE  %o1, [%o0]  // Store new value back to memory
```

During the execution of the three steps shown in Listing 4.12, another thread could have interfered and replaced the value of the variable held in memory with a new value, creating a data race.

An atomic increment operation would not allow another thread to modify the same variable and cause an erroneous value to be written to memory. Performing the increment operation atomically is logically equivalent to *implicitly* acquiring a mutex before the increment and releasing it afterward. The difference is that using a mutex relies on other threads using the same mutex to protect that variable. A thread that did not use the same mutex could cause an incorrect value to be written back to memory. With atomic operations, another thread cannot cause an incorrect value to be written to memory.

Most operating systems or compilers provide support for a range of atomic operations. However, hardware typically provides support only for a more limited range of operations; hence, the more complex atomic operations are usually made from the simple atomic instructions that the hardware provides.

Atomic operations are often used to enable the writing of *lock-free* code. Using a synchronization device such as a mutex lock solves the correctness problem; only one thread can access the protected memory location at a single time. However, it is not necessarily the approach with the best scaling, since threads that are waiting for access are blocked (sent to sleep). A lock-free implementation would not rely on a mutex lock to protect access; instead, it would use a sequence of operations that would perform the operation without having to acquire an explicit lock. This can be higher performance than controlling access with a lock. Lock-free does not imply that the other threads would not have to wait; it only indicates that they do not have to wait on a lock. A *wait-free* implementation would allow all the threads to simultaneously make forward progress.

Most of the more complex atomic operations are actually lock-free implementations. They use a low-level, hardware-provided atomic operation and wrap code around that to ensure that the required higher-level operation is actually atomic.

An example of a low-level atomic operation would be *compare and swap* (CAS), which atomically swaps the value held in a register with the value held in memory if and only if the value held in memory matches the expected value. As an example of using this hardware-provided atomic operation to produce a higher-level atomic operation, the CAS instruction could be used as the basis for an atomic increment operation. To do this, the CAS instruction would be executed in a loop. Each iteration, it would attempt to replace the value held in memory with the incremented value. The loop would exit when the CAS instruction successfully performed the increment operation.

Lock-free code can be used to achieve more complex operations; this will be discussed in Chapter 8, "Hand-Coding Synchronization and Sharing."

Deadlocks and Livelocks

So far, we've demonstrated some fundamental ways to share access to resources between threads. We now need to discuss the situations where strategies might go wrong.

First is the *deadlock*, where two or more threads cannot make progress because the resources that they need are held by the other threads. It is easiest to explain this with an example. Suppose two threads need to acquire mutex locks A and B to complete some task. If thread 1 has already acquired lock A and thread 2 has already acquired lock B, then A cannot make forward progress because it is waiting for lock B, and thread 2 cannot make progress because it is waiting for lock A. The two threads are *deadlocked*. Listing 4.13 shows this situation.

Listing 4.13 **Two Threads in a Deadlock**

Thread 1	Thread 2
| ```
void update1()
{
    acquire(A);
    acquire(B); <<< Thread 1
                    waits here
    variable1++;
    release(B);
    release(A);
}
``` | ```
void update2()
{
    acquire(B);
    acquire(A); <<< Thread 2
                    waits here
    variable1++;
    release(B);
    release(A);
}
``` |

The best way to avoid deadlocks is to ensure that threads always acquire the locks in the same order. So if thread 2 acquired the locks in the order A and then B, it would stall while waiting for lock A without having first acquired lock B. This would enable thread 1 to acquire B and then eventually release both locks, allowing thread 2 to make progress.

A *livelock* traps threads in an unending loop releasing and acquiring locks. Livelocks can be caused by code to back out of deadlocks. In Listing 4.14, the programmer has tried to implement a mechanism that avoids deadlocks. If the thread cannot obtain the second lock it requires, it releases the lock that it already holds.

The two routines `update1()` and `update2()` each have an outer loop. Routine `update1()` acquires lock A and then attempts to acquire lock B, whereas `update2()` does this in the opposite order. This is a classic deadlock opportunity, and to avoid it, the developer has written some code that causes the held lock to be released if it is not possible to acquire the second lock. The routine `canAquire()`, in this example, returns immediately either having acquired the lock or having failed to acquire the lock.

Listing 4.14 **Two Threads in a Livelock**

Thread 1	Thread 2
| ```
void update1()
{
``` | ```
void update2()
{
``` |

```
int done=0;                          int done=0;
while (!done)                        while (!done)
{                                    {
  acquire(A);                          acquire(B);
  if ( canAcquire(B) )                 if ( canAcquire(A) )
  {                                    {
    variable1++;                         variable2++;
    release(B);                          release(A);
    release(A);                          release(B);
    done=1;                              done=1;
  }                                    }
  else                                 else
  {                                    {
    release(A);                          release(B);
  }                                    }
}                                    }
}                                    }
```

If two threads encounter this code at the same time, they will be trapped in a livelock of constantly acquiring and releasing mutexes, but it is very unlikely that either will make progress. Each thread acquires a lock and then attempts to acquire the second lock that it needs. If it fails to acquire the second lock, it releases the lock it is holding, before attempting to acquire both locks again. The thread exits the loop when it manages to successfully acquire both locks, which will eventually happen, but until then, the application will make no forward progress.

Communication Between Threads and Processes

All parallel applications require some element of communication between either the threads or the processes. There is usually an implicit or explicit action of one thread sending data to another thread. For example, one thread might be signaling to another that work is ready for them. We have already seen an example of this where a semaphore might indicate to waiting threads that initialization has completed. The thread signaling the semaphore does not know whether there are other threads waiting for that signal. Alternatively, a thread might be placing a message on a queue, and the message would be received by the thread tasked with handling that queue.

These mechanisms usually require operating system support to mediate the sending of messages between threads or processes. Programmers can invent their own implementations, but it can be more efficient to rely on the operating system to put a thread to sleep until a condition is true or until a message is received.

The following sections outline various mechanisms to enable processes or threads to pass messages or share data.

Memory, Shared Memory, and Memory-Mapped Files

The easiest way for multiple threads to communicate is through memory. If two threads can access the same memory location, the cost of that access is little more than the memory latency of the system. Of course, memory accesses still need to be controlled to ensure that only one thread writes to the same memory location at a time. A multi-threaded application will share memory between the threads by default, so this can be a very low-cost approach. The only things that are not shared between threads are variables on the stack of each thread (local variables) and thread-local variables, which will be discussed later.

Sharing memory between multiple processes is more complicated. By default, all processes have independent address spaces, so it is necessary to preconfigure regions of memory that can be shared between different processes.

To set up shared memory between two processes, one process will make a library call to create a shared memory region. The call will use a unique descriptor for that shared memory. This descriptor is usually the name of a file in the file system. The create call returns a handle identifier that can then be used to map the shared memory region into the address space of the application. This mapping returns a pointer to the newly mapped memory. This pointer is exactly like the pointer that would be returned by `malloc()` and can be used to access memory within the shared region.

When each process exits, it detaches from the shared memory region, and then the last process to exit can delete it. Listing 4.15 shows the rough process of creating and deleting a region of shared memory.

Listing 4.15 **Creating and Deleting a Shared Memory Segment**

```
ID     = Open Shared Memory( Descriptor );
Memory = Map Shared Memory( ID );
...
Memory[100]++;
...
Close Shared Memory( ID );
Delete Shared Memory( Descriptor );
```

Listing 4.16 shows the process of attaching to an existing shared memory segment. In this instance, the shared region of memory is already created, so the same descriptor used to create it can be used to attach to the existing shared memory region. This will provide the process with an ID that can be used to map the region into the process.

Listing 4.16 **Attaching to an Existing Shared Memory Segment**

```
ID     = Open Shared Memory( Descriptor );
Memory = Map Shared Memory( ID );
...
Close Shared Memory( ID );
```

A shared memory segment may remain on the system until it is removed, so it is important to plan on which process has responsibility for creating and removing it.

Condition Variables

Condition variables communicate readiness between threads by enabling a thread to be woken up when a condition becomes true. Without condition variables, the waiting thread would have to use some form of polling to check whether the condition had become true.

Condition variables work in conjunction with a mutex. The mutex is there to ensure that only one thread at a time can access the variable. For example, the producer-consumer model can be implemented using condition variables. Suppose an application has one producer thread and one consumer thread. The producer adds data onto a queue, and the consumer removes data from the queue. If there is no data on the queue, then the consumer needs to sleep until it is signaled that an item of data has been placed on the queue. Listing 4.17 shows the pseudocode for a producer thread adding an item onto the queue.

Listing 4.17 **Producer Thread Adding an Item to the Queue**

```
Acquire Mutex();
Add Item to Queue();
If ( Only One Item on Queue )
{
   Signal Conditions Met();
}
Release Mutex();
```

The producer thread needs to signal a waiting consumer thread only if the queue was empty and it has just added a new item into that queue. If there were multiple items already on the queue, then the consumer thread must be busy processing those items and cannot be sleeping. If there were no items in the queue, then it is possible that the consumer thread is sleeping and needs to be woken up.

Listing 4.18 shows the pseudocode for the consumer thread.

Listing 4.18 **Code for Consumer Thread Removing Items from Queue**

```
Acquire Mutex();
Repeat
  Item = 0;
  If ( No Items on Queue() )
  {
    Wait on Condition Variable();
  }
```

```
    If (Item on Queue())
    {
        Item = remove from Queue();
    }
Until ( Item != 0 );
Release Mutex();
```

The consumer thread will wait on the condition variable if the queue is empty. When the producer thread signals it to wake up, it will first check to see whether there is anything on the queue. It is quite possible for the consumer thread to be woken only to find the queue empty; it is important to realize that the thread waking up does not imply that the condition is now true, which is why the code is in a repeat loop in the example. If there is an item on the queue, then the consumer thread can handle that item; otherwise, it returns to sleep.

The interaction with the mutex is interesting. The producer thread needs to acquire the mutex before adding an item to the queue. It needs to release the mutex after adding the item to the queue, but it still holds the mutex when signaling. The consumer thread cannot be woken until the mutex is released. The producer thread releases the mutex after the signaling has completed; releasing the mutex is necessary for the consumer thread to make progress.

The consumer thread acquires the mutex; it will need it to be able to safely modify the queue. If there are no items on the queue, then the consumer thread will wait for an item to be added. The call to wait on the condition variable will cause the mutex to be released, and the consumer thread will wait to be signaled. When the consumer thread wakes up, it will hold the mutex; either it will release the mutex when it has removed an item from the queue or, if there is still nothing in the queue, it will release the mutex with another call to wait on the condition variable.

The producer thread can use two types of wake-up calls: Either it can wake up a single thread or it can broadcast to all waiting threads. Which one to use depends on the context. If there are multiple items of data ready for processing, it makes sense to wake up multiple threads with a broadcast. On the other hand, if the producer thread has added only a single item to the queue, it is more appropriate to wake up only a single thread. If all the threads are woken, it can take some time for all the threads to wake up, execute, and return to waiting, placing an unnecessary burden on the system. Notice that because each thread has to own the mutex when it wakes up, the process of waking all the waiting threads is serial; only a single thread can be woken at a time.

The other point to observe is that when a wake-up call is broadcast to all threads, some of them may be woken when there is no work for them to do. This is one reason why it is necessary to place the wait on the condition variable in a loop.

The other problem to be aware of with condition variables is the *lost wake-up*. This occurs when the signal to wake up the waiting thread is sent before the thread is ready to receive it. Listing 4.19 shows a version of the consumer thread code. This version of the code can suffer from the lost wake-up problem.

Listing 4.19 **Consumer Thread Code with Potential Lost Wake-Up Problem**

```
Repeat
  Item = 0;
  If ( No Items on Queue() )
  {
     Acquire Mutex();
     Wait on Condition Variable();
     Release Mutex();
  }
  Acquire Mutex();
  If ( Item on Queue() )
  {
     Item = remove from Queue();
  }
  Release Mutex();
Until ( Item!=0 );
```

The problem with the code is the first `if` condition. If there are no items on the queue, then the mutex lock is acquired, and the thread waits on the condition variable. However, the producer thread could have placed an item and signaled the consumer thread between the consumer thread executing the `if` statement and acquiring the mutex. When this happens, the consumer thread waits on the condition variable indefinitely because the producer thread, in Listing 4.17, signals only when it places the first item into the queue.

Signals and Events

Signals are a UNIX mechanism where one process can send a signal to another process and have a handler in the receiving process perform some task upon the receipt of the message. Many features of UNIX are implemented using signals. Stopping a running application by pressing ^C causes a SIGKILL signal to be sent to the process.

Windows has a similar mechanism for *events*. The handling of keyboard presses and mouse moves are performed through the event mechanism. Pressing one of the buttons on the mouse will cause a click event to be sent to the target window.

Signals and events are really optimized for sending limited or no data along with the signal, and as such they are probably not the best mechanism for communication when compared to other options.

Listing 4.20 shows how a signal handler is typically installed and how a signal can be sent to that handler. Once the signal handler is installed, sending a signal to that thread will cause the signal handler to be executed.

Listing 4.20 **Installing and Using a Signal Handler**

```
void signalHandler(void *signal)
{
  ...
}

int main()
{
  installHandler( SIGNAL, signalHandler );
  sendSignal( SIGNAL );
}
```

Message Queues

A *message queue* is a structure that can be shared between multiple processes. Messages can be placed into the queue and will be removed in the same order in which they were added. Constructing a message queue looks rather like constructing a shared memory segment. The first thing needed is a descriptor, typically the location of a file in the file system. This descriptor can either be used to create the message queue or be used to attach to an existing message queue. Once the queue is configured, processes can place messages into it or remove messages from it. Once the queue is finished, it needs to be deleted.

Listing 4.21 shows code for creating and placing messages into a queue. This code is also responsible for removing the queue after use.

Listing 4.21 **Creating and Placing Messages into a Queue**

```
ID = Open Message Queue Queue( Descriptor );
Put Message in Queue( ID, Message );
...
Close Message Queue( ID );
Delete Message Queue( Description );
```

Listing 4.22 shows the process for receiving messages for a queue. Using the descriptor for an existing message queue enables two processes to communicate by sending and receiving messages through the queue.

Listing 4.22 **Opening a Queue and Receiving Messages**

```
ID=Open Message Queue ID(Descriptor);
Message=Remove Message from Queue(ID);
...
Close Message Queue(ID);
```

Named Pipes

UNIX uses *pipes* to pass data from one process to another. For example, the output from the command ls, which lists all the files in a directory, could be piped into the wc command, which counts the number of lines, words, and characters in the input. The combination of the two commands would be a count of the number of files in the directory. Named pipes provide a similar mechanism that can be controlled programmatically.

Named pipes are file-like objects that are given a specific name that can be shared between processes. Any process can write into the pipe or read from the pipe. There is no concept of a "message"; the data is treated as a stream of bytes. The method for using a named pipe is much like the method for using a file: The pipe is opened, data is written into it or read from it, and then the pipe is closed.

Listing 4.23 shows the steps necessary to set up and write data into a pipe, before closing and deleting the pipe. One process needs to actually make the pipe, and once it has been created, it can be opened and used for either reading or writing. Once the process has completed, the pipe can be closed, and one of the processes using it should also be responsible for deleting it.

Listing 4.23 **Setting Up and Writing into a Pipe**

```
Make Pipe( Descriptor );
ID = Open Pipe( Descriptor );
Write Pipe( ID, Message, sizeof(Message) );
...
Close Pipe( ID );
Delete Pipe( Descriptor );
```

Listing 4.24 shows the steps necessary to open an existing pipe and read messages from it. Processes using the same descriptor can open and use the same pipe for communication.

Listing 4.24 **Opening an Existing Pipe to Receive Messages**

```
ID=Open Pipe( Descriptor );
Read Pipe( ID, buffer, sizeof(buffer) );
...
Close Pipe( ID );
```

Communication Through the Network Stack

The *network stack* is a fairly complex set of layers that range from the network card up to the layer that provides the network packet communication used by applications like web browsers. Full coverage of it is outside the scope of this book. However, networking is available on most platforms, and as such it is a possible candidate for communication. An advantage to using networking to communicate is that applications can communicate between processes on a single system or processes on different systems connected by a network. The only changes necessary would be in the address where the packets of data were sent. Although communications across a network can be quite high latency, using networking to communicate between processes on the same machine will typically be lower cost, but not as low cost as some of the other methods of communication.

Communication across the network usually involves a client-server model. To set up a server, it is first necessary to open a socket and then bind that socket to the address on the local host before starting to listen for incoming connections. When a connection arrives, data can be read from it or written to it, until the connection is closed. Once the connection is closed, it is possible to close the socket. Listing 4.25 illustrates how the server thread of a client-server network connection can be set up.

Listing 4.25 **Setting Up Socket to Listen for Connections**

```
ID = Open Socket( Descriptor );
Bind Socket( ID, Address );
Listen( ID )
Conx = Wait for connection( ID );
Read( Conx, buffer, sizeof(buffer) );
...
Close( Conx );
Close Socket( ID );
```

Listing 4.26 shows the steps necessary to set up a client socket to connect to the server. Connecting to a remote server also requires initially setting up a socket. Once the socket is open, it can be used to connect to the server. After the communication is complete, the socket can be closed.

Listing 4.26 **Setting Up a Socket to Connect to a Remote Server**

```
ID=Open Socket( Descriptor );
Connect( ID, Address );
Write( ID, buffer, sizeof(buffer) );
...
Close( ID );
```

Other Approaches to Sharing Data Between Threads

There are several other approaches to sharing data. For example, data can be written to a file to be read by another process at a later point. This might be acceptable if the data needs to be stored persistently or if the data will be used at some later point. Still, writing to disk presents a long latency operation, which is not the best mechanism if the purpose is purely communication.

There are also operating system–specific approaches to sharing data between processes. Solaris *doors* allow one process to pass an item of data to another process and have the processed result returned. Doors are optimized for the round-trip and hence can be cheaper than using two different messages.

Storing Thread-Private Data

A single-threaded application might use global data to hold program state. For example, a single-threaded word processor might have global variables that hold the name of the document being edited or the current line number.

In a multithreaded application, it is sometimes necessary for each thread to hold some state. This state is private to the thread but can be accessed by all the code that the thread executes. Returning to the word processor example, if it opens multiple documents and each document is handled by a single thread, then each thread will want to have a separate variable to hold the name of the document and the current line number. This data would be private to each thread—no other thread could read it. The application may still have some global state—perhaps it records details of the person using it—and all threads would have access to this same information.

There are various approaches that a thread can use to store private data. The obvious way to do this would be to allocate an array to hold the thread-private data for all threads and then use the ID of the thread as an index into the array. This is a relatively straightforward approach that may suffice in a number of situations. Listing 4.27 shows how an array can be used to store data that is private, or local, to the thread. The array `MyData[]` is accessed by the ID of the currently executing thread. This allows each thread to store data at a unique location in the array.

Listing 4.27 **Using an Array to Store Thread-Local Data**

```
int MyData[20];

void ThreadedCode(int parameter)
{
   MyData[ GetMyThreadID() ] = parameter;
   ...
}
```

Another approach would be to store local thread data on the stack. Each thread has a stack that is private to the thread. Consequently, a thread can allocate data on the stack and have that data remain private to the thread. It is not advisable to pass pointers to that data across to other threads, since stack-based data is valid only while the thread is alive and while the stack frame containing the data exists. Listing 4.28 shows an example of using the stack to hold thread-local data.

Listing 4.28 **Holding Thread-Local Data on the Stack**

```
void ThreadedCode(int parameter)
{
   int MyData = parameter;
   ...
}
```

Yet another way of allocating data that is private to the thread is to use *thread-local storage*. As its name suggests, variables allocated to thread-local storage are private to the thread. Most compilers support the __thread keyword. For example, the code shown in Listing 4.29 would declare an integer variable named count that is local to each thread.

Listing 4.29 **Using the __thread Specifier to Identify Thread-Local Data**

```
__thread int count;

void ThreadedCode(int parameter)
{
   count = parameter;
   ...
}
```

Every time a thread referenced the variable count, it would access the value of the copy local to that thread.

Another approach to thread-local storage is to use support functions to allocate and deallocate local variables. Listing 4.30 shows the rough outline of the approach. First an identifier needs to be created to uniquely identify the thread-local variable. Using that identifier, the thread can then read data from or write data to that variable. When the thread has finished with the variable, the identifier needs to be deleted.

Listing 4.30 **Using an API to Manage Thread-Local Data**

```
ID = Create ID( );
Set Thread Local Data ( ID, Value );
Value = Get Thread Local Data ( ID );
Delete ID( ID );
```

Summary

This chapter discussed the different approaches that can be taken to synchronize threads and share data between them. Later chapters will discuss the implementation details of these approaches. You should now have an understanding of atomic operations and lock-free algorithms and have some knowledge of the various synchronization and data-sharing primitives offered by most operating systems.

5

Using POSIX Threads

The POSIX[1] standards specify the coding standards for portable UNIX applications. Most UNIX and UNIX-like operating systems adhere to the key features of these; hence, an application coded to the standards will be portable between UNIX implementations and UNIX-like operating systems, such as Linux and FreeBSD, and Mac OS X, which is also based on a UNIX-like kernel. Microsoft Windows does not implement the POSIX standards directly, although there are some solutions that enable programs written using POSIX interfaces to run on Windows platforms.

This chapter will discuss how to write multithreaded programs using the POSIX standard interfaces. These enable an application to create new threads and synchronize and share data between threads and processes.

Creating Threads

An application initially starts with a single thread, which is often referred to as the *main thread* or the *master thread*. Calling `pthread_create()` creates a new thread. It takes the following parameters:

- A pointer to a `pthread_t` structure. The call will return the handle to the thread in this structure.

- A pointer to a `pthread` attributes structure, which can be a null pointer if the default attributes are to be used. The details of this structure will be discussed later.

- The address of the routine to be executed.

- A value or pointer to be passed into the new thread as a parameter.

Listing 5.1 shows how this API call can be used.

---

1. www.unix.org

Listing 5.1 **Creating a New Thread**

```
#include <pthread.h>
#include <stdio.h>

void* thread_code( void * param )
{
  printf( "In thread code\n" );
}

int main()
{
  pthread_t thread;
  pthread_create( &thread, 0, &thread_code, 0 );
  printf( "In main thread\n" );
}
```

In this example, the main thread will create a second thread to execute the routine
thread_code(), which will print one message while the main thread prints another.
The call to create the thread has a value of zero for the attributes, which gives the thread
default attributes. The call also passes the address of a pthread_t variable for the function to store a handle to the thread.

The return value from the pthread_create() call is zero if the call is successful;
otherwise, it returns an error condition.

Thread Termination

Child threads terminate when they complete the routine they were assigned to run. In
Listing 5.2, the child thread will terminate when it completes the routine
thread_code(). The value returned by the routine executed by the child thread can be
made available to the main thread when the main thread calls the routine pthread_join().

The pthread_join() call takes two parameters. The first parameter is the handle of
the thread that is to be waited for. The second parameter is either zero or the address of
a pointer to a void, which will hold the value returned by the child thread.

The resources consumed by the thread will be recycled when the main thread calls
pthread_join(). If the thread has not yet terminated, this call will wait until the thread
terminates and then free the assigned resources. Listing 5.2 shows an expanded example
where the main thread waits for the child thread to complete.

Listing 5.2 **Creating a New Thread and Waiting for It to Complete**

```
#include <pthread.h>
#include <stdio.h>

void* thread_code( void * param )
{
```

```
    printf( "In thread code\n" );
}

int main()
{
    pthread_t thread;
    pthread_create( &thread, 0, &thread_code, 0 );
    printf( "In main thread\n" );
    pthread_join( thread, 0 );
}
```

Another way a thread can terminate is to call the routine `pthread_exit()`, which takes a single parameter—either zero or a pointer—to `void`. This routine does not return and instead terminates the thread. The parameter passed in to the `pthread_exit()` call is returned to the main thread through the `pthread_join()`. The child threads do not need to explicitly call `pthread_exit()` because it is implicitly called when the thread exits. Unless the thread is a detached thread, which will be covered later, the resources used by the thread are not freed until another thread calls `pthread_join()`, passing in the handle of the exited thread.

Passing Data to and from Child Threads

In many cases, it is important to pass data into the child thread and have the child thread return status information when it completes. To pass data into a child thread, it should be cast as a pointer to `void` and then passed as a parameter to `pthread_create()`. It is critical to realize that the child thread can start executing at any point after the call, so the pointer must point to something that still exists and still retains the same value. This rules out passing in pointers to changing variables as well as pointers to information held on the stack (unless the stack is certain to exist until after the child thread has read the value).

Listing 5.3 shows an acceptable way of passing the value of a variable into the child thread. The value is type cast to a `void*` and then passed as the parameter to the thread.

Listing 5.3 **Passing a Value into a Created Thread**

```
for ( int i=0; i<10; i++ )
pthread_create( &thread, 0, &thread_code, (void *)i );
```

Listing 5.4 shows an unacceptable way of passing the value of a variable into the child thread.

Listing 5.4 **Erroneous Way of Passing Data to a New Thread**

```
for ( int i=0; i<10; i++ )
pthread_create( &thread, 0, &thread_code, (void *)&i );
```

The code in Listing 5.4 code is unacceptable for two reasons: First, the variable i will almost certainly have changed value before the child thread starts executing, and second, the variable i is allocated on the stack, and there is no guarantee that the stack space will even be in scope when the child thread starts executing.

The child thread will receive the value passed by the main thread as a parameter, which usually will need to be type cast to an appropriate value. Listing 5.5 shows an example.

Listing 5.5 **Reading the Parameter Passed to the New Thread**

```
void* child_thread( void* value )
{
  int id = (int)value;
  ...
}
```

The return value from a child thread will be made available to the main thread through the second parameter of the pthread_join() function call, as shown in Listing 5.6.

Listing 5.6 **Reading the Return Value of an Exiting Child Thread**

```
#include <pthread.h>
#include <stdio.h>

void* child_thread( void * param )
{
  int id = (int)param;
  printf( "Start thread %i\n", id );
  return (void *)id;
}

int main()
{
  pthread_t thread[10];
  int return_value[10];
  for ( int i=0; i<10; i++ )
  {
    pthread_create( &thread[i], 0, &child_thread, (void*)i );
  }
  for ( int i=0; i<10; i++ )
  {
    pthread_join( thread[i], (void**)&return_value[i] );
    printf( "End thread %i\n", return_value[i] );
  }
}
```

This code will pass a unique number into each child thread, and then the child thread will return this number as its return code. The value is then made available to the main thread through the `pthread_join()` call.

Detached Threads

The previous discussion focused on *joinable* threads, threads that terminate and then wait for the main thread to read their return value before the resources that they consume are recycled.

It is also possible to create *detached* threads that do not wait around for another thread to call `pthread_join()` before the resources they consume are recycled. One way to do this is to set the appropriate attribute in the thread attributes structure; this will be discussed in the next section. Another way is to call `pthread_detach()` on an existing thread. Calling `pthread_join()` on detached threads is an error; they do not need the call, and making the call will return an error value.

The handle of the detached thread may be recycled when the thread exits, so any cached version of the handle may no longer refer to the original thread; hence, care needs to be taken when writing code that uses detached threads.

Listing 5.7 shows an example of detaching a thread. The child thread calls `pthread_self()` to get its own handle, which it can then use to convert itself into a detached thread.

Listing 5.7 **Detaching a Thread Using** `pthread_detach()` **Call**

```
#include <pthread.h>
#include <stdio.h>

void* child_routine( void * param )
{
  int id = (int)param;
  printf( "Detach thread %i\n", id );
  pthread_detach( pthread_self() );
}

int main()
{
  pthread_t thread[10];
  for ( int i=0; i<10; i++ )
  {
    pthread_create( &thread[i], 0, child_routine, (void*)i );
  }
}
```

Threads can also be created in the detached state. To do this, it is necessary to pass a set of attributes into the call to `pthread_create()`.

Setting the Attributes for Pthreads

The attributes for a thread are set when the thread is created. Some attributes, such as the detached state, can be modified once the thread exists, but others cannot be changed. To set the initial thread attributes, first create a thread attributes structure, and then set the appropriate attributes in that structure, before passing the structure into the `pthread_create()` call. Once the attributes have been used to set up a thread, they can be destroyed with `pthread_attr_destroy()`. Listing 5.8 shows the basic outline of this.

Listing 5.8 **Passing Attributes to** `pthread_create`

```
#include <pthread.h>

...

int main()
{
  pthread_t thread;
  pthread_attr_t attributes;
  pthread_attr_init( &attributes );
  pthread_create( &thread, &attributes, child_routine, 0 );
  pthread_attr_destroy( &attributes );
}
```

There are various attributes that can be set using API calls. The most useful ones determine whether the thread is created in the detached or joinable state, as well as the size of the stack allocated to the new thread.

A thread can be created as either a detached or a joinable thread. The default is to create a joinable thread. The code in Listing 5.9 sets the attributes to create a detached thread.

Listing 5.9 **Creating a Detached Thread**

```
#include <pthread.h>
#include <stdio.h>

void* child_routine( void * param )
{
  int id = (int)param;
  printf( "Thread %i\n", id );
}

int main()
{
  pthread_t thread;
```

```
  pthread_attr_t attributes;
  pthread_attr_init( &attributes );
  pthread_attr_setdetachstate( &attributes, PTHREAD_CREATE_DETACHED );
  pthread_create( &thread, &attributes, child_routine, 0 );
  pthread_attr_destroy( &attributes );
}
```

The default stack size is dependent upon the operating system. The code in Listing 5.10 will print out the default stack size.

Listing 5.10 **Reading the Stack Size Attribute for a New Thread**

```
#include <pthread.h>
#include <stdio.h>

int main()
{
  size_t stacksize;
  pthread_attr_t attributes;
  pthread_attr_init( &attributes );
  pthread_attr_getstacksize( &attributes, &stacksize );
  printf( "Stack Size = %i\n", stacksize);
  pthread_attr_destroy( &attributes );
}
```

Running it on Ubuntu produces the result shown in Listing 5.11, indicating that the default stack size is 8MB.

Listing 5.11 **Compiling and Running Code to Show Default Stack Size on Ubuntu**

```
$ gcc stack.c -lpthread
$ ./a.out
Stack Size = 8388608
```

However, running the same code on Solaris produces the result shown in Listing 5.12.

Listing 5.12 **Compiling and Running Code to Show Default Stack Size on Solaris**

```
$ cc stack.c
$ ./a.out
Stack Size = 0
```

Reading the man pages indicates that if zero is set for the stack size, the Solaris defaults to 1MB for 32-bit code and 2MB for 64-bit code.

Another command that controls stack size is `ulimit -s <stacksize>`. On Linux, this command is used to set the default stack size for both the initial thread created and for subsequent threads. On Solaris, this command controls only the stack size for the initial thread. Consequently, to write portable codes, it is best to explicitly control the size of the stack for any child threads, particularly if the code places large objects on the stack or uses recursion.

The obvious question to ask is, why not set the largest stack possible for all child threads? The answer to this question leads to a discussion on how stacks are created.

To allow the both the heap (where `malloc` obtains its memory from) and the stack to grow, the heap is usually placed after the application at the low end of the addressable memory, and the stack is usually placed at the upper end of memory, as in Figure 5.1. The heap grows upward, and the stack can grow downward.

Figure 5.1 Location of heap and stack in memory

This approach works for a single-threaded application, but each thread in a multi-threaded application needs its own stack. To do this, the application must have a limit to the size of the initial stack for the main thread. Each child thread must also have a limit to its stack size. The resulting layout in memory is rather like Figure 5.2.

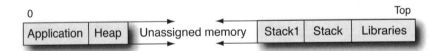

Figure 5.2 Memory layout for a multithreaded code

Each thread receives an adjacent block of memory of fixed size for its stack. There is a finite address space available, so memory used for stack space is taken from memory that can be used for the heap. For 64-bit applications, the address space is sufficiently large so that this is not a problem. For 32-bit applications, it is relatively easy to run out of address space. If each thread is allocated an 8MB stack, then there can be at most 512 simultaneous threads (512 * 8 MB = entire 4GB address space). Hence, for some applications, it can be a good idea to assess how much memory is actually required for the stack of each child thread. The absolute minimum acceptable memory to provide to a thread is stored in the variable `PTHREAD_STACK_MIN`. This size would provide no space on the stack for local variables or making function calls, so it would rarely be used without also including some additional space.

Compiling Multithreaded Code

Two potential problem areas that might arise when compiling multithreaded code are header files and libraries. Header files might require adaptations for multithreading, and multithreaded versions of supporting libraries might need to be linked. In general, the compiler will make the correct decisions, but it is important to be aware of these issues by reading the documentation when encountering a new platform for the first time.

One example of how the included header files might change in the presence of multiple threads is the `errno` variable on Solaris. Solaris provides different implementations of this variable for single-threaded and multithreaded applications. In a single-threaded application, there is only one `errno` variable, so this can be an integer value. In a multithreaded application, an `errno` variable needs to be defined for each thread. The compiler flag `-mt` passes the compiler flag `-D_REENTRANT`, which makes the `errno` variable a multithread-aware macro.

Listing 5.13 shows an example of a code that calls `errno` in a multithreaded context. Both the main and child threads call `fopen()` with invalid parameters; the child thread attempts to open the current directory for writing, and the main thread attempts to write to an unspecified file. Both of these actions will result in the value for `errno` being set to an error value.

Listing 5.13 **Example of Using** `errno` **in a Multithreaded Application**

```
#include <stdio.h>
#include <errno.h>
#include <pthread.h>

void * thread1( void* param )
{
  FILE *fhandle = fopen( ".", "w" );
  if ( !fhandle ) { printf( " thread1 %4i\n", errno ); }
    else { fclose( fhandle ); }
}

int main()
{
  pthread_t thread_data1;
  int i;
  pthread_create( &thread_data1, 0, thread1, 0 );
  FILE *fhandle = fopen( "", "r" );
  if ( !fhandle ) { printf( " main  %4i\n", errno ); }
    else { fclose( fhandle ); }
  pthread_join( thread_data1, 0 );
}
```

Using Solaris Studio compilers on Solaris, the -mt flag ensures the correct behavior in multithreaded contexts. Listing 5.14 shows the results of compiling and running the application both with and without the flag.

Listing 5.14 **Running a Multithreaded Code That Depends on errno on Solaris**

```
$ cc errno.c
$ ./a.out
 thread1    2
 main       2
$ cc -mt errno.c
$ ./a.out
 thread1    22
 main        2
```

When the code is correctly compiled, both of the calls to errno produce a value that is correct for the calling thread. When the –mt flag is omitted, the same value for errno is printed for both threads.

It is also necessary to ensure that the correct libraries are linked into an application. Some support libraries include both single-threaded and multithreaded versions, so selecting the appropriate one is important. Some operating systems will explicitly require the Pthread library to be linked into the application. For example, Solaris 9 would require an explicit –lpthread compiler flag; however, this changed in Solaris 10, when the threading library was combined with the C runtime library, and the compiler flag was no longer necessary.

The same situation is true when building with gcc. The compiler has the flag –pthread, which both passes the flag –D_REENTRANT and causes linking with the POSIX threading library. However, not all platforms need to define _REENTRANT; it makes no difference to the Linux header files, so the only benefit is that the compiler will include the POSIX threading library.

Some libraries are not multithread-safe; they do not guarantee the correct answer when called by a multithreaded application. For instance, the Solaris Studio compilers provide libfast, which is not multithread-safe but offers better performance than the default malloc(). It is easy to produce multithread-safe libraries using mutexes to ensure that only a single thread can have access at a time. However, this does not produce a library with performance that scales as the number of threads increases.

The other point to be aware of when compiling code that calls the POSIX API is that it may be necessary to define particular variables in order to get the correct versions of functions. These requirements are usually documented under man standards. Linux does not typically require this; however, Solaris does. For example, use of the define –D_POSIX_C_SOURCE=199309L will assert that the code is written to the POSIX.1b–1993 standard. Failure to set the appropriate feature test macro will usually cause warnings of undefined functions or of incompatible types being passed into functions.

Process Termination

When the main thread completes, all the child threads are terminated and their resources freed. We can see this demonstrated if we build and run the code shown in Listing 5.15.

Listing 5.15 **Code to Create a Child Thread**

```
#include <pthread.h>
#include <stdio.h>

void* thread_code( void * param )
{
  printf( "In thread code\n" );
}

int main()
{
  pthread_t thread;
  pthread_create( &thread, 0, &thread_code, 0 );
  printf( "In main thread\n" );
}
```

When the application works, we should see a message printed by both the main and child threads, as shown in Listing 5.16.

Listing 5.16 **Output from Both Original and Child Threads**

```
$ cc -mt t.c
$ ./a.out
In thread code
In main thread
```

However, sometimes the application will produce output only from the main thread, as shown in Listing 5.17.

Listing 5.17 **Output from Only the Original Thread**

```
$ ./a.out
In main thread
```

The reason for this behavior is that sometimes the main thread terminates before the child thread has had time to execute. To avoid this behavior, the main thread needs to call `pthread_exit()`, which, for the main thread, will wait until all the other threads have terminated before exiting. This is true, even if the child threads have been detached. Listing 5.18 shows a version of the code with this change.

Listing 5.18 **Main Thread Calls Waits for Child Threads to Complete**

```
#include <pthread.h>
#include <stdio.h>

void* thread_code( void * param )
{
  printf("In thread code\n");
}

int main()
{
  pthread_t thread;
  pthread_create( &thread, 0, &thread_code, 0 );
  pthread_detach( thread );
  printf( "In main thread\n" );
  pthread_exit( 0 );
}
```

After this change, all the child threads will print their output before the main thread exits.

Sharing Data Between Threads

A key advantage of multithreaded codes is that all threads see the same memory, so data is already shared between threads. However, it often important to coordinate access to this data, since failure to coordinate accesses could cause data races that lead to incorrect results. POSIX provides a large number of synchronization and data-sharing methods.

Protecting Access Using Mutex Locks

A *mutex lock* is a mechanism supported by the POSIX standard that can be acquired by only one thread at a time. Other threads that attempt to acquire the same mutex must wait until it is released by the thread that currently has it.

Before they can be used, mutex locks need to be initialized to the appropriate state by a call to pthread_mutex_init() or, for statically defined mutexes, by assignment with the value PTHREAD_MUTEX_INITIALIZER. The call to pthread_mutex_init() takes an optional parameter that points to attributes describing the type of mutex required. Initialization through static assignment uses default parameters, as does passing in a null pointer in the call to pthread_mutex_init().

Once a mutex is no longer needed, the resources it consumes can be freed with a call to pthread_mutex_destroy(). Listing 5.19 shows examples of initializing and destroying mutexes.

Listing 5.19 **Creating and Destroying Mutexes**

```
#include <pthread.h>

...
  pthread_mutex_t m1 = PTHREAD_MUTEX_INITIALIZER;
  pthread_mutex_t m2;

  pthread_mutex_init( &m2, 0 );

...
  pthread_mutex_destroy( &m1 );
  pthread_mutex_destroy( &m2 );
```

A thread can lock a mutex by calling `pthread_mutex_lock()`. Once it has finished with the mutex, the thread calls `pthread_mutex_unlock()`. If a thread calls `pthread_mutex_lock()` while another thread holds the mutex, the calling thread will wait, or *block*, until the other thread releases the mutex, allowing the calling thread to attempt to acquire the released mutex.

In many situations, it is not desirable for the calling thread to wait for the mutex to be available. The call `pthread_mutex_trylock()` will attempt to acquire the mutex. If it succeeds, the function will return the value of zero, and the calling thread will now be the owner of the mutex. If the mutex is already locked by another thread, the function will immediately return a nonzero value indicating the exact situation.

The code shown in Listing 5.20 shows a mutex lock protecting the variable `count` against simultaneous access by multiple threads. The variable `count` is declared as `volatile` to ensure that it is read from memory on each access and written back to memory after each access. Without the mutex lock, there would be a data race between the two threads. Hence, it is very unlikely that `count` would end up with the correct value.

Listing 5.20 **Mutex Lock Avoiding Data Race**

```
#include <pthread.h>
#include <stdio.h>

pthread_mutex_t mutex;
volatile int counter = 0;

void * count( void * param )
{
  for ( int i=0; i<100; i++ )
  {
    pthread_mutex_lock( &mutex );
    counter++;
    printf( "Count = %i\n", counter );
```

```
    pthread_mutex_unlock( &mutex );
  }
}

int main()
{
  pthread_t thread1, thread2;
  pthread_mutex_init( &mutex, 0 );
  pthread_create( &thread1, 0, count, 0 );
  pthread_create( &thread2, 0, count, 0 );
  pthread_join( thread1, 0 );
  pthread_join( thread2, 0 );
  pthread_mutex_destroy( &mutex );
  return 0;
}
```

Mutex Attributes

Mutexes can be shared between multiple processes. By default, mutexes are private to a process. To create a mutex that can be shared between processes, it is necessary to set up the attributes for `pthread_mutex_init()`, as shown in Listing 5.21.

Listing 5.21 **Creating a Mutex That Can Be Shared Between Processes**

```
#include <pthread.h>

int main()
{
  pthread_mutexattr_t attributes;
  pthread_mutex_t mutex;

  pthread_mutexattr_init( &attributes );
  pthread_mutexattr_setpshared( &attributes, PTHREAD_PROCESS_SHARED );
  pthread_mutex_init( &mutex, &attributes );
  pthread_mutexattr_destroy( &attributes );
  ...
}
```

The attributes structure `pthread_mutexattr_t` is initialized with default values by a call to `pthread_mutexattr_init()`. A call to `pthread_mutex_setpshared()` with a pointer to the attribute structure and the value `PTHREAD_PROCESS_SHARED` sets the attributes to cause a shared mutex to be created. By default, mutexes are not shared between processes; calling `pthread_mutex_setpshared()` with the value `PTHREAD_PROCESS_PRIVATE` restores the attribute to the default.

These attributes are passed into the call to `pthread_mutex_init()` to set the attributes of the initialized mutex. Once the attributes have been used, they can be disposed of by a call to `pthread_mutex_attr_destroy()`.

A mutex can have other attributes set using the same mechanism:

- The type of mutex. This can be a normal mutex, a mutex that detects errors such as multiple attempts to lock the mutex, or a recursive mutex that can be locked multiple times and then needs to be unlocked the same number of times.

- The protocol to follow when another thread is waiting for the mutex. This can be the default of no change to thread priority, that the thread holding the mutex inherits the priority of any higher-priority thread waiting for the mutex, or that the thread gets the highest priority associated with the mutexes held by it.

- The priority ceiling of the mutex. This is the priority that any lower-priority thread will be elevated to while it holds the mutex.

The attributes governing the priority of any thread holding the mutex are designed to avoid problems of priority inversion where a higher-priority thread is waiting for a lower-priority thread to release the mutex.

Using Spin Locks

The critical difference between *spin locks* and mutex locks is that a spin lock will keep spinning in a tight loop and consuming processor resources until it finally acquires the lock. Mutex locks will immediately put a thread to sleep when it cannot get the mutex, or an *adaptive mutex lock* will spin for a short time waiting for the lock to become free before going to sleep.

The interface for spin locks is very similar to that of mutex locks. The call `pthread_spin_init()` will initialize a spin lock. The spin lock can be created as shareable between processes or private to the process creating it. A spin lock that is private to a process is created by passing the value `PTHREAD_PROCESS_PRIVATE` as a parameter to the call to `pthead_spin_init()`, and passing the value `PTHREAD_PROCESS_SHARED` creates a spin lock that can be shared between processes.

Multiple threads in the process that created the lock will always be able to access it. However, if the spin lock is created to be private to a process, the behavior of the lock is not defined if it is used by other processes. The default is for the spin lock to be private to the creating process.

The call `pthread_spin_lock()` will spin until the lock is acquired, the call `pthread_spin_unlock()` will release the lock, and finally the call `pthread_spin_destroy()` will release any resources used by the lock. Listing 5.22 demonstrates the use of a spin lock. This example places access to a local variable under the control of the spin lock; however, in this example, the variable is not shared between threads, so it is not actually necessary to use any locking.

Listing 5.22 **Code Using a Spin Lock to Protect Access to a Variable**

```
#include <pthread.h>

pthread_spinlock_t lock;

void lockandunlock()
{
  int i = 10000;
  while ( i>0 )
  {
    pthread_spin_lock( &lock );
    i--;
    pthread_spin_unlock( &lock );
  }
}

int main()
{
  pthread_spin_init( &lock, PTHREAD_PROCESS_PRIVATE );
  lockandunlock();
  pthread_spin_destroy( &lock );
}
```

If the code is modified to create a spin lock that is shared between multiple processes, only one process should initialize and destroy the spin lock. The modification shown in Listing 5.23 will create a spin lock that can be shared between processes.

Listing 5.23 **Creating a Spin Lock That Can Be Shared Between Processes**

```
int main()
{
  pthread_spin_init(&lock,PTHREAD_PROCESS_SHARED);
  lockandunlock();
  pthread_spin_destroy(&lock);
}
```

In addition, the call `pthread_spin_trylock()` will attempt to acquire the lock but will immediately return whether or not the lock is successfully acquired. Since a spinning lock will be using processor resources, it might be more useful to attempt to acquire the lock and, if that fails, to complete some other task before repeating the test. This utilizes the processor in useful work rather than just spinning. Listing 5.24 shows the earlier code modified to use `pthread_spin_trylock()` and keep a count of the number of times the thread fails to get the lock.

Listing 5.24 **Counting the Number of Times That the Spin Lock Fails to Be Acquired**

```
void lockandunlock()
{
  int i = 0;
  int count = 0;
  while ( i == 0 )
  {
    if ( pthread_spin_trylock( &lock ) )
    {
      i++;
      pthread_spin_unlock( &lock );
    }
    else
    {
      count++;
    }
  }
  printf( "Failed tries = %i\n", count );
}
```

Read-Write Locks

Read-write locks allow multiple threads to simultaneously read a resource, but only a single thread may update that resource at any time. They share a similar initialization and destruction syntax to mutex locks in that they take a set of attributes and can be initialized either through a call to `pthread_rwlock_init()` or statically initialized by assignment of the value `PTHREAD_RWLOC_INITIALIZER`. Listing 5.25 shows the two methods.

Listing 5.25 **Initializing a Read-Write Lock**

```
pthread_rwlock_t lock1, lock2;

...
  pthread_rwlock_init( &lock1, 0 );
  lock2 = PTHREAD_RWLOCK_INITIALIZER;
...
```

If the attributes passed to the initialization routine are zero, then the lock is initialized with the default attribute of being private to the creating process. To create a read-write lock that is shared between processes, it is necessary to create and use a set of attributes. The call `pthread_rwlockattr_init()` initializes the attributes, while the call `pthread_rwlockattr_setpshared()` sets the shared attribute to the desired value. This set of attributes can then be passed into the `pthread_rwlock_init()` call to set the attributes for the read-write lock being created. Listing 5.26 demonstrates this.

Listing 5.26 **Creating a Read-Write Lock That Can Be Shared Between Processes**

```
pthread_rwlockattr_t attributes;
pthread_rwlock_t lock;
...
  pthread_rwlockattr_init( &attr );
  pthread_rwlockattr_setpshared( &attr, PTHREAD_PROCESS_SHARED );
  pthread_rwlock_init( &lock, &attr );
  pthread_rwlockattr_destroy( &attr );
...
  pthread_rwlock_destroy( &lock );
```

Once the lock has been created, it no longer references the attributes, so these can be either reused for a different lock or destroyed. The call to destroy the attributes is `pthread_rwlockattr_destroy()`. The resources consumed by the read-write lock are freed by the call to `pthread_rwlock_destroy()`.

Read-write locks have a more complex interface than mutex locks because they can be locked and unlocked for either reading or writing. Hence, there are two pairs of lock and unlock calls. The pairs `pthread_rwlock_rdlock()` and `pthread_rwlock_rdunlock()`lock and unlock for reading, and `pthread_rwlock_wrlock()` and `pthread_rwlock_wrunlock()`lock and unlock for writing. Listing 5.27 shows how the read-write lock might be used to protect access to a shared resource.

Listing 5.27 **Using a Read-Write Lock to Protect Access to a Shared Resource**

```
int readMatrix( int x,int y )
{
  int result;
  pthread_rwlock_rdlock( &lock );
  result = matrix[x,y];
  pthread_rwlock_rdunlock( &lock );
  return result;
}

void updateMatrix( int x,int y,int value );
{
  pthread_rwlock_wrlock( &lock );
  matrix[x,y] = value;
  pthread_rwlock_wrunlock( &lock );
}
```

The read-write lock is unnecessary in this short code snippet because load or store accesses to aligned integer variables are atomic. The lock would be critical if the updates and reads were of structures that required multiple writes.

The behavior of calls to acquire the lock is for the thread to block until the lock is acquired. However, there are also calls to try to acquire the lock. These calls return immediately either with or without having acquired the lock. To try to get a reader lock, the call is `pthread_rwlock_tryrwlock()`, and to try to acquire the lock as a writer, the call is `pthread_rwlock_trywrlock()`. Listing 5.28 shows an example of using these calls.

Listing 5.28 **Updating a Shared Value Only If the Read-Write Lock Is Acquired**

```
void typeUpdate( int value )
{
  if ( pthread_rwlock_trywrlock( &lock ) == 0 )
  {
    count += value;
    pthread_rwlock_wrunlock( &lock );
  }
}
```

There is a further option of using a timeout when acquiring the lock. The routines `pthread_rwlock_timedrdlock()` and `pthread_rwlock_timedwrlock()` return 0 if the lock is acquired or an error code if the lock has not been acquired by the absolute time specified. The routines `pthread_rwlock_timedrdlock_np()` and `pthread_rwlock_timedwrlock_np()` return an error code if the lock has not be acquired by the relative time specified.

A timespec structure is used to pass the timing information into the function. For relative timing, this structure needs to be initialized with the duration of the wait time; for absolute time, the structure can be initialized with the current time using a call to `clock_gettime()`. Listing 5.29 demonstrates how the timeout can be set to elapse in five seconds.

Listing 5.29 **Acquiring a Read-Write Lock with a Timeout**

```
#include <time.h>

void timeout_lock()
{
  struct timespec now;

  clock_gettime( CLOCK_REALTIME, &now );
  now.tv_sec += 5;
  if ( pthread_rwlock_timedrdlock( &lock, now ) == 0 )
  {
    ...
    pthread_rwlock_rdunlock( &lock );
  }
}
```

Alternatively, the code could directly call the relative timeout, as shown in Listing 5.30.

Listing 5.30 **Setting a Relative Timeout**

```
#include <time.h>

void timeout_lock()
{
  struct timespec now;

  now.tv_sec = 5;
  now.tv_nsec = 0;
  if ( pthread_rwlock_timedrdlock_np( &lock, now ) == 0 )
  {
    ...
    pthread_rwlock_rdunlock( &lock );
  }
}
```

Barriers

There are situations where a program needs to wait until an entire group of threads has completed its work before further progress can be made. This is a *barrier*.

A barrier is created by a call to `pthread_barrier_init()`. The call to initialize the barrier takes the following:

- A pointer to the barrier to be initialized.
- An optional attributes structure, this structure determines whether the barrier is private to a process or shared across processes.
- The number of threads that need to reach the barrier before any threads are released.

The resources consumed by a barrier can be released by a call to `pthread_barrier_destroy()`.

Each thread calls `pthread_barrier_wait()` when it reaches the barrier. This call will return when the appropriate number of threads has reached the barrier. The code in Listing 5.31 demonstrates using a barrier to cause the threads in an application to wait until all the threads have been created.

Listing 5.31 **Creating and Using a Barrier**

```
#include <pthread.h>
#include <stdio.h>

pthread_barrier_t barrier;
```

```
void * work( void* param)
{
  int id=(int)param;
  printf( "Thread arrived %i\n", id );
  pthread_barrier_wait( &barrier );
  printf( "Thread departed %i\n", id );
}

int main()
{
  pthread_t threads[10];
  pthread_barrier_init( &barrier, 0, 10 );
  for ( int i=0; i<10; i++ )
  {
    pthread_create( &threads[i], 0, work, (void*)i );
  }
  for ( int i=0; i<10; i++ )
  {
    pthread_join( threads[i], 0 );
  }
  pthread_barrier_destroy( &barrier );
}
```

The output from the program would show all the threads arriving at the barrier and then all the threads departing from the barrier. Without the barrier, the arrivals and departures of all the threads would be mixed.

Semaphores

A *semaphore* is a counting and signaling mechanism. One use for it is to allow threads access to a specified number of items. If there is a single item, then a semaphore is essentially the same as a mutex, but it is more commonly useful in a situation where there are multiple items to be managed. Semaphores can also be used to signal between threads or processes, for example, to tell another thread that there is data present in a queue. There are two types of semaphores: named and unnamed semaphores.

An *unnamed* semaphore is initialized with a call to sem_init(). This function takes three parameters. The first parameter is a pointer to the semaphore. The next is an integer to indicate whether the semaphore is shared between multiple processes or private to a single process. The final parameter is the value with which to initialize the semaphore. A semaphore created by a call to sem_init() is destroyed with a call to sem_destroy().

The code shown in Listing 5.32 initializes a semaphore with a count of 10. The middle parameter of the call to sem_init() is zero, and this makes the semaphore private to the thread; passing the value one rather than zero would enable the semaphore to be shared between multiple processes.

Listing 5.32 **Creating and Initializing a Semaphore**

```
#include <semaphore.h>

int main()
{
  sem_t semaphore;

  sem_init( &semaphore, 0, 10 );
...
  sem_destroy( &semaphore );
}
```

A *named* semaphore is opened rather than initialized. The process for doing this is similar to opening a file. The call to `sem_open()` returns a pointer to a semaphore. The first parameter to the call is the name of the semaphore. The name must conform to the naming conventions for files on the operating system and must start with a single slash sign and contain no further slash signs. The next parameter is the set of flags. There are three combinations of flags that can be passed to the `sem_open()` call. If no flags are passed, the function will return a pointer to the existing named semaphore if it exists and if the semaphore has the appropriate permissions to be shared with the calling process. If the `O_CREAT` flag is passed, the semaphore will be created; if it does not exist or if it does exist, a pointer will be returned to the existing version. The flag `O_EXCL` can be passed with the `O_CREAT` flag. This will successfully return a semaphore only if that semaphore does not already exist.

Creating a semaphore requires two additional parameters: the permissions that the semaphore should be created with and the initial value for the semaphore. Listing 5.33 shows an example of opening a semaphore with an initial value of 10, with read and write permissions for the user, the group, and all users.

Listing 5.33 **Opening a Named Semaphore**

```
#include <semaphore.h>

int main()
{
  sem_t * semaphore;
  semaphore = sem_open( "/my_semaphore", O_CREAT, 0777, 10 );
  ...
```

A named semaphore is closed by a call to `sem_close()`. This closes the connection to the semaphore but leaves the semaphore present on the machine. A call to `sem_unlink()` with the name of the semaphore will free the resources consumed by it but only once all the processes that have the semaphore open have closed their connection to it. The code shown in Listing 5.34 will close and unlink the previously opened semaphore.

Listing 5.34 Closing and Unlinking a Named Semaphore

```
  sem_close( semaphore );
  sem_unlink( "/my_semaphore" );
}
```

The semaphore is used through a combination of three methods. The function
`sem_wait()` will attempt to decrement the semaphore. If the semaphore is already zero,
the calling thread will wait until the semaphore becomes nonzero and then return, having decremented the semaphore. The call `sem_trywait()` will return immediately
either having decremented the semaphore or if the semaphore is already zero. The call to
`sem_post()` will increment the semaphore. One more call, `sem_getvalue()`, will write
the current value of the semaphore into an integer variable. The code in Listing 5.35
shows a semaphore used in the same way as a mutex might be, to protect the increment
of the variable `count`. On Solaris, the semaphore functions are defined in the real-time
library, so code needs to be linked with this library using `-lrt`.

Listing 5.35 Using a Semaphore as a Mutex

```
int main()
{
  sem_t semaphore;
  int count = 0;

  sem_init( &semaphore, 0, 1 );
  sem_wait( &semaphore );
  count++;
  sem_post( &semaphore );
  sem_destroy( &semaphore );
}
```

Another property of semaphores that is not fully exploited when using them as
mutex locks is *signaling* between threads. Semaphores can be used to signal that one task
has been completed or to ensure that two tasks will be executed in a predetermined
order. Consider the code shown in Listing 5.36.

Listing 5.36 Two Threads Executing Two Functions in a Nondeterministic Order

```
#include <pthread.h>
#include <stdio.h>

void *func1( void * param )
{
  printf( "Thread 1\n" );
}
```

```
void *func2( void * param )
{
  printf( "Thread 2\n" );
}


int main()
{
  pthread_t threads[2];
  pthread_create( &threads[0], 0, func1, 0 );
  pthread_create( &threads[1], 0, func2, 0 );
  pthread_join( threads[0], 0 );
  pthread_join( threads[1], 0 );
}
```

At runtime, the code can print either "Thread 1" or "Thread 2" first, depending on which thread gets to the printf() statement first. Semaphores can be used to ensure that the threads execute in a specific order. Suppose we want to ensure that the output is always "Thread 1" before "Thread 2"; then we need to make the second thread wait until the first thread completes before the second thread produces its output. Listing 5.37 shows how a semaphore can be used to ensure this ordering.

Listing 5.37　**Using a Semaphore to Enforce a Deterministic Ordering on Two Threads**

```
#include <pthread.h>
#include <stdio.h>
#include <semaphore.h>

sem_t semaphore;

void *func1( void * param )
{
  printf( "Thread 1\n" );
  sem_post( &semaphore );
}


void *func2( void * param )
{
  sem_wait( &semaphore );
  printf( "Thread 2\n" );
}

int main()
{
  pthread_t threads[2];
  sem_init( &semaphore, 0, 1 );
  pthread_create( &threads[0], 0, func1, 0 );
  pthread_create( &threads[1], 0, func2, 0 );
```

```
  pthread_join( threads[0], 0 );
  pthread_join( threads[1], 0 );
  sem_destroy( &semaphore );
}
```

The code creates a semaphore. Once the first thread completes its task, it signals the semaphore that the second thread can now perform its task. The logic of the second thread will cause it to wait at the semaphore until the first thread signals it, or if it does not reach the semaphore before the first thread completes its task, the second will not even wait at the semaphore. This use of a single semaphore ensures that the second thread always executes the `printf()` statement after the first thread has completed its `printf()` statement.

An extension of this ordering mechanism is the producer–consumer configuration of threads, as shown in Listing 5.38. The semaphore in this instance contains the number of items waiting in the queue to be processed. If there are no items in the queue, the consumer thread can sleep until an item is placed in the queue by the producer. The code uses the semaphore as a signaling mechanism between the two threads, not as a mechanism that ensures mutual exclusion to accesses to the queue. The code that manipulates the queue is omitted, but this code would ensure that multiple threads can safely simultaneously access the queue data structure.

Listing 5.38 Using a Semaphore in a Producer-Consumer System

```
#include <pthread.h>
#include <stdio.h>
#include <semaphore.h>

sem_t semaphore;
pthread_mutex_t mutex = PTHREAD_MUTEX_INITIALIZER;

int queue[200];
int queueLength;

void *producer( void * param)
{
  for ( int i=0; i<500; i++ )
  {
    // Add item to queue
    pthread_mutex_lock( &mutex );
    queue[ queueLength++ ] = i;
    pthread_mutex_unlock( &mutex );
    // Signal semaphore
    sem_post( &semaphore );
  }
}
```

```
void *consumer(void * param)
{
  for ( int i=0; i<500; i++ )
  {
    int item;
    // Wait if nothing in queue
    if (queueLength==0) { sem_wait(&semaphore); }

    pthread_mutex_lock( &mutex );
    item = queue[ --queueLength ];
    pthread_mutex_unlock( &mutex );
    printf( "Received %i\n", item);
  }
}

int main()
{
  pthread_t threads[2];
  sem_init( &semaphore, 0, 0 );
  pthread_create( &threads[0], 0, producer, 0 );
  pthread_create( &threads[1], 0, consumer, 0 );
  pthread_join( threads[0], 0 );
  pthread_join( threads[1], 0 );
  sem_destroy( &semaphore );
}
```

Controlling access to a finite number of elements is another situation where a semaphore is useful. This could be a real physical constraint, such as only sufficient spaces in a
list exist or only a finite amount of memory has been reserved. Or it could be a throt-
tling feature. For example, in the producer-consumer, we might want to limit the queue
length to avoid stacking up too much work for the consumer. Listing 5.39 shows the
modified version of the code.

Listing 5.39 **Producer-Consumer Modified So That the Producer Thread Can Be Throttled**

```
#include <pthread.h>
#include <stdio.h>
#include <semaphore.h>

sem_t semaphore;
sem_t limit;
pthread_mutex_t mutex = PTHREAD_MUTEX_INITIALIZER;

int queue[10];
int queueLength;
```

```
void *producer( void * param)
{
  for ( int i=0; i<500; i++ )
  {
    // Wait for space
    sem_wait( &limit );
    // Add item to queue
    pthread_mutex_lock( &mutex );
    queue[ queueLength++ ] = i;
    pthread_mutex_unlock( &mutex );
    // Signal semaphore
    sem_post( &semaphore );
  }
}

void *consumer(void * param)
{
  for ( int i=0; i<500; i++ )
  {
    int item;
    // Wait if nothing in queue
    if (queueLength==0) { sem_wait(&semaphore); }

    pthread_mutex_lock( &mutex );
    item = queue[ --queueLength ];
    pthread_mutex_unlock( &mutex );
    printf( "Received %i\n", item);
    sem_post( &limit );
  }
}

int main()
{
  pthread_t threads[2];
  sem_init( &semaphore, 0, 0 );
  sem_init( &limit, 0, 10 );
  pthread_create( &threads[0], 0, producer, 0 );
  pthread_create( &threads[1], 0, consumer, 0 );
  pthread_join( threads[0], 0 );
  pthread_join( threads[1], 0 );
  sem_destroy( &limit );
  sem_destroy( &semaphore );
}
```

The modifications introduce a second semaphore, `limit`. This semaphore is initialized with a value of 10. Before the producer threads adds an item to the queue, it calls `sem_wait()`, which will decrement the value of the semaphore. Every time the consumer thread removes an item from the queue, it calls `sem_post()`, which will increase the value of the semaphore. When the semaphore reaches zero, the producer thread will call `sem_wait()` and will not return from the call until the consumer thread has removed an item from the list. This will stop the producer thread from adding more items to the queue before the consumer thread has had the chance to deal with those items already there.

Condition Variables

Condition variables enable threads to communicate state changes. Using them requires both a mutex and a condition variable, together with the additional state that threads need to check.

A condition variable is initialized with a call to `pthread_cond_init()`, which takes the address of the condition variable together with any attributes. Condition variables are destroyed with a call to `pthread_cond_destroy()`, passing the address of the condition variable.

The default for condition variables is to be private to a process. Attributes can be used to produce a condition variable shared between processes. Listing 5.40 demonstrates using attributes to create a shared condition variable.

Listing 5.40 **Creating a Condition Variable That Can Be Shared Between Processes**

```
#include <pthread.h>

pthread_cond_t CV;

int main()
{
 pthread_condattr_t CVA;
 pthread_condattr_init( &CVA );
 pthread_condattr_setpshared( &CVA, PTHREAD_PROCESS_SHARED );

 pthread_cond_init( &CV, &CVA );

 pthread_condattr_destroy( &CVA );
 ...
 pthread_cond_destroy( &CV );
}
```

The condition variable requires an actual variable to be monitored. A producer-consumer is a good scenario to use for an example. We will use the variable `length` to denote the length of the queue. The condition variable is used to wake the consumer thread when the length of the queue is greater than zero. Listing 5.41 shows the initialization code.

Listing 5.41 **Creating Threads and Condition Variable for Producer-Consumer Example**

```
#include <pthread.h>
#include <stdio.h>

pthread_cond_t cv;
pthread_mutex_t mutex;
int length;
int queue[200];

...

int main()
{
 pthread_t threads[2];
 pthread_cond_init( &cv, 0 );
 pthread_mutex_init( &mutex, 0 );
 length = 0;
 pthread_create( &threads[0], 0, producer, 0 );
 pthread_create( &threads[1], 0, consumer, 0 );
 pthread_join( threads[1], 0 );
 pthread_join( threads[0], 0 );
 pthread_mutex_destroy( &mutex );
 pthread_cond_destroy( &cv );
}
```

Listing 5.42 shows the code for the producer thread. The producer thread will obtain the mutex and then increment the length of the queue before using the condition variable to signal to waiting threads that there is an item in the queue. This signal will wake one of the waiting threads. After the signal has completed, the mutex can be released.

Listing 5.42 **Code for Producer Thread**

```
void * producer( void* param )
{
  for (int i=0; i<200; i++)
  {
    pthread_mutex_lock( &mutex );
    queue[ length++ ] = i;
    pthread_cond_signal( &cv );
    pthread_mutex_unlock( &mutex );
  }
}
```

If there are no threads waiting on the condition variable, the call to `pthread_cond_signal()` has no effect. Hence, it is really necessary to make the call only if the queue was empty before the item was added. It is only in this situation where the consumer thread might have been waiting for items to be placed in the queue. In situations where there are already items in the queue, the consumer thread will not have stopped.

It is also possible to use a broadcast to signal to all waiting threads that there is an item in the queue. The function `pthread_cond_broadcast()` wakes all the threads waiting on the condition variable. This is illustrated in the version of the producer thread shown in Listing 5.43.

Listing 5.43 **Broadcasting the Arrival of a New Item to All Waiting Threads**

```
void * producer( void* param )
{
  item_t * item;
  for( int i=0; i<200; i++ )
  {
    pthread_mutex_lock( &mutex );
    queue[ length++ ] = i ;
    pthread_cond_broadcast( &cv );
    pthread_mutex_unlock( &mutex );
  }
}
```

There is no advantage to using broadcast in a situation where there is only a single task to perform, since it will incur the overhead of waking all the threads and then send all but one of them back to sleep. It is useful in the situation where there are multiple independent tasks to complete and each woken thread is able to identify an independent item of work.

Listing 5.44 shows the code for the consumer thread. This is slightly more complex than the code for the producer thread. The consumer thread is placed in a `while(true)` loop. In this loop, the first thing it needs to do is to acquire the mutex in order to get access to the variable `length`, which, in this example, is the proxy for the queue.

Listing 5.44 **Code for Consumer Thread**

```
void * consumer( void* param)
{
  for( int i=0; i<200; i++ )
  {
    pthread_mutex_lock(&mutex);
    while (length==0)
    {
      pthread_cond_wait( &cv, &mutex );
    }
```

```
      int item = queue[ --length ];
      pthread_mutex_unlock(&mutex);
      printf( "Received %i\n", item );
  }
}
```

The consumer thread needs to wait on the condition variable only when there are no items in the queue. If there are items in the queue, the consumer thread can immediately remove one and process it. Once the consumer thread has decremented the queue, it can release the mutex and process the item.

If the queue is empty, the consumer thread will need to wait to be signaled by the producer thread. It does this by calling `pthread_cond_wait()` while still holding the mutex. This call will release the mutex while the thread is waiting, but when signaled, the thread will wake up holding the mutex again. The call to `pthread_cond_wait()` needs to be placed in a loop. The thread will be woken when it is signaled that `length` is greater than zero, but it may also be signaled when `length` does not meet these criteria. Therefore, the thread needs to loop calling `pthread_cond_wait()` until the condition, in this instance the value of the variable `length`, is met.

An example of a thread being woken up when the condition is not true is when there are multiple threads waiting on the condition variable and all the threads are woken by a broadcast signal. If there is one item of work and two threads are woken, the first thread will get the item of work. When the second thread wakes, it will discover that there is no work for it. Hence, the second thread will appear to have suffered a spurious wake-up.

There is one problem that should be avoided when coding threads that wait on condition variables: the *lost wake-up* problem. Listing 5.45 shows an example.

Listing 5.45 **Potential "Lost Wake-Up" Issue**

```
void * consumer( void* param )
{
  for( int i=0; i<200; i++ )
  {
    int item;
    int go = 0;
    pthread_mutex_lock( &mutex );
    pthread_cond_wait( &cv, &mutex );
    if (length > 0)
    {
       item = queue[ --length ];
       go = 1;
    }
    pthread_mutex_unlock(&mutex);
    if (go)
    {
```

```
      printf( "Received %i\n", item );
    }
  }
}
```

In this version of the code, the consumer threads wait on the condition variable for each iteration of the loop. If the condition variable is signaled before the consumer thread reaches the wait call, then the signal is lost, and the consumer variable will wait until the next signal. If no further work is produced by the producer thread, the consumer thread will wait indefinitely, even though it has work waiting. This problem is compounded if the producer thread is set to signal only when new work was added to an empty queue; in this instance, the consumer thread will never get signaled, and the producer thread will keep adding work to the queue.

Condition variables have a method to provide a timeout when waiting to be signaled by the condition variable. The call is pthread_cond_timedwait(), which takes the timeout period, specified as an absolute time, as well as the condition variable and mutex. This call will return either holding the mutex lock or with an error code indicating the reason for the return. The code in Listing 5.46 illustrates using this function call to count the number of minutes waited until the condition variable was signaled.

Listing 5.46 **Using a Timeout to Count Elapsed Minutes**

```
#include <time.h>
#include <errno.h>

void * consumer( void* param )
{
  for( int i=0; i<200; i++ )
  {
    int seconds = 0;
    pthread_mutex_lock( &mutex );
    while ( length == 0 )
    {
      struct timespec now;
      now.tv_sec = time( 0 ) + 1;
      now.tv_nsec = 0;
      if ( pthread_cond_timedwait( &cv, &mutex, &now ) == ETIMEDOUT )
      {
        seconds++;
      }
    }
    int itcm = queue[ --length ];
    if ( seconds ) { printf( "%i seconds waited\n", seconds ); }
    pthread_mutex_unlock( &mutex );
```

```
    printf( "Received %i\n", item );
  }
}
```

The code uses `pthread_cond_timedwait()` to wait in units of one second. Every time the call fails to acquire the mutex, a count of seconds waited is incremented. If the producer thread is modified so that it sleeps between producing each item, then it is possible to see the timeout of the consumer thread.

Variables and Memory

Data can be shared either between threads or private to each thread. Examples of data that can be shared between threads are global variables and memory allocated on the heap. Listing 5.47 uses a global variable to hold the address of a region of memory allocated by a `malloc()` call. All the threads in an application would be able to access the global variable and therefore the allocated memory.

Listing 5.47 **Sharing Memory Using Global Variables**

```
#include <stdlib.h>

char * data;

int main()
{
   data = (char*) malloc( 1024*1024 );
...
```

As previously discussed, care needs to be taken with data shared between threads. If the data is modified by other threads, it might be necessary to declare that data as `volatile`. For example, the code in Listing 5.48 would become an infinite loop if the variable done were not declared volatile.

Listing 5.48 **Potential Infinite Loop**

```
volatile int done = 0;
void wait()
{
  while ( !done ) {}
}
```

Alternative approaches might be to cast the variable done to be a `volatile int`, which would mean that the variable would be reloaded in the code only where this behavior was desirable, as shown in Listing 5.49. However, not all compilers will honor the cast to volatile.

Listing 5.49 **Casting a Variable to Volatile**

```
int done =0;
void wait()
{
  while ( !(volatile int)done ) {}
}
```

Alternatively, it is possible to use a function call to force the reloading of the variable, as shown in Listing 5.50. The reloading is necessary because the called function might modify the global variable.

Listing 5.50 **Using a Function Call to Force the Reloading of a Variable**

```
int done = 0;

void pause()
{
}

void wait()
{
  while ( !done ) { pause(); }
}
```

Of course, some compiler optimizations such as inlining can cause code that relies on the side effects of function calls to enforce memory ordering to fail. Compilers often have directives or intrinsic functions that can be used to produce the desired behavior without risk of this breaking under inlining optimizations. This topic will be discussed in more detail in Chapter 8, "Hand-Coded Synchronization and Sharing."

Much of this chapter has dealt with the methods available through the POSIX standard that prevent multiple threads accessing the same data. But it is worth emphasizing that all accesses to shared data represent potential data races.

The other kind of data is *thread-private data*. Variables held on the stack are an example of thread-private data. Parameters passed into functions are another example. In the code shown in Listing 5.51, both variables a and b are private to a thread.

Listing 5.51 **Two Thread-Private Variables**

```
double func( double a )
{
  double b;
  ...
```

However, it is sometimes useful to have "global" data that is private to a thread—data that is visible to all the routines that a thread executes but with the restriction that each thread sees only its own private copy of the data; this is known as *thread-local storage*.

There are two ways of allocating thread-local data. The first is to declare globally variables with the __thread specifier. This prevents them being global variables and turns them into thread-local variables. In Listing 5.52, the variable mydata is local to the thread, so each thread can see a different value for the variable.

Listing 5.52 **Thread-Local Data Declared Using the __thread Specifier**

```
__thread void * mydata;

void * threadFunction( void * param )
{
  mydata = param;
...
```

POSIX also provides a set of function calls for declaring and using thread-local variables. These function calls are not as convenient as the __thread specifier, because they use a key to identify each item of shared data. The key is created with a call to pthread_key_create(). When the key is no longer needed, it can be deleted by a call to pthread_key_delete(). All the threads can now use this key to get and set a thread-local parameter. The call pthread_setspecific() takes the key plus a value for the thread-local variable. A call to pthread_getspecific() will return the previously set value when the same key is passed in. Listing 5.53 shows the use of the thread-local storage routines.

Listing 5.53 **Using POSIX Routines for Thread-Local Data**

```
#include <pthread.h>

pthread_key_t parameter;

void * threadFunc( void * param )
{
  pthread_setspecific( parameter, param );
  ...
  void * param2 = pthread_getspecific( parameter );
}

int main()
{
  pthread_t thread;
  pthread_key_create( &parameter, 0 );
```

```
pthread_create( &thread, 0, threadFunc, 0 );
pthread_join( thread );
pthread_key_delete( parameter );
}
```

The pthread_key_create() call takes an optional destructor function. This function is called when the thread terminates if the key still holds a value. This can be used to free any resources held by the thread. Listing 5.54 shows an example of this.

Listing 5.54 **Using a Destructor Function with thread-local Storage**

```
#include <pthread.h>
#include <stdlib.h>
#include <stdio.h>

pthread_key_t parameter;

void destructor( void * param )
{
  free( param );
  printf( "Memory freed\n" );
}

void * threadFunc( void * param )
{
  char * mem = malloc( 100 );
  pthread_setspecific( parameter, mem );
}

int main()
{
  pthread_t thread;
  pthread_key_create( &parameter, destructor );
  pthread_create( &thread, 0, threadFunc, 0 );
  pthread_join( thread, 0 );
  pthread_key_delete( parameter );
}
```

One disadvantage of thread-local variables is that the global thread is unable to see them. So, in some cases, it is useful to use arrays to hold values produced by the child thread.

Multiprocess Programming

An alternative to multithreaded applications is multiprocess applications, as suggested in Chapter 1, "Hardware, Processes, and Threads." The main advantage of multiprocess programming is that a failure of one process does not cause all the processes to die, and as a result, it might be possible to recover from such failures.

It is very easy to start multiple processes and have these processes load common initialization parameters from a file or from the command line to start communicating. However, it is often useful to do this programmatically.

The UNIX model of process creation is the Fork-Exec model. The `fork()` call makes a child process that receives an exact duplicate of the parent's memory. The `exec()` call replaces the current process with a new executable. The calls often go together so that one application calls `fork()` to create a new process; then the child process immediately calls `exec()` to replace itself with a new executable.

The `fork()` call is interesting because both the child and parent processes will return from this call. The only difference is the return value of the call. The child process will return with a value of zero, and the parent process will return with the process ID of the child process.

The code in Listing 5.55 uses `fork()` to create a new child process. The child process will execute a `sleep` command with a parameter of 10 so that it will sleep for ten seconds. The parent process will wait for the child to terminate and then report the exit status of the child process. The `execl()` call is used to execute the `sleep` command. The `execl()` call takes the path to the executable plus the arguments to be passed to that executable, and the first argument should be the name of the executable itself.

Listing 5.55 **Using Fork to Create a Child Process**

```
#include <unistd.h>
#include <stdio.h>
#include <sys/wait.h>

int main()
{
  int status;
  pid_t f = fork();
  if ( f == 0 )
  { /* Child process */
    execl( "/usr/bin/sleep", "/usr/bin/sleep", "10" );
  }
  else
  {
    waitpid( f, &status, 0 );
    printf( "Status = %i\n", status );
  }
}
```

If the `fork()` call is not followed by an `exec()` call, we have two copies of the same process. The process state, up to the point at which the fork call was made, is duplicated in both processes. We will see how this can be useful in the following sections on setting up communications between multiple processes.

Sharing Memory Between Processes

Usually different processes share nothing; however, it is possible to set up multiple processes to share the same memory. The `shm_open()` call creates a shared memory segment. This call takes a name for the segment, a size, and a set of flags for the created shared memory, together with the permission bits. The return value from the call is a file descriptor of the shared memory segment.

The name is a string with the first character as /, and no subsequent slashes. The flags used by the call are familiar from creating files. `O_RDONLY` will create a read-only segment. `O_RDWR` will create a segment that permits reading and writing. `O_CREAT` will create the segment if it does not exist or return a handle to it if it does exist. `O_EXCL` will return an error if the segment already exists. The final parameters are the file access permissions.

The memory segment will be created, if it does not already exist, with a size of 0 bytes. The size of the reserved segment can be set with a call to `ftruncate()`, passing the file descriptor of the segment together with the requested size.

Once the segment exists, the process can attach to it with a call to `mmap()`. Table 5.1 shows the parameters to `mmap`.

Table 5.1 **Parameters Passed to** `mmap()`

Parameter Type	Comment
`void *`	The preferred start address of the segment in memory.
`size_t`	The size of the segment in bytes.
`int`	The protection flags for the segment. These can be `PROT_EXEC` for pages that can be executed, `PROT_READ` for pages that can be read, and `PROT_WRITE` for pages that can be written. The permissions will usually match those set up in the call to `shm_open()`.
`int`	The sharing flags for the segment, either `MAP_SHARED` to share the segment with other processes or `MAP_PRIVATE` to keep the segment private to the current process.
`int`	The file descriptor of the shared memory.
`off_t`	An offset into the shared memory region.

The return value of the call to `mmap()` is a pointer to the shared memory segment.

Once the process has finished with the shared memory segment, it can unmap it from its address space using the `munmap()` call, which takes a pointer to the memory region together with its size as parameters.

The shared memory can be removed from the system with a call to `shm_unlink()`, which takes the name for the shared region originally given to `shm_open()`. This causes the shared memory to be deleted when the last process detaches from it.

Listing 5.56 shows an example of creating using and deleting shared memory. When compiling this code on Solaris, it is necessary to define at least `_POSIX_C_SOURCE=199309L` in order to get the header files to define `shm_open()` and `shm_unlink()`.

Listing 5.56 **Creating, Using, and Deleting Shared Memory**

```
#include <sys/mman.h>
#include <fcntl.h>
#include <unistd.h>

int main()
{
  int handle = shm_open( "/shm", O_CREAT|O_RDWR, 0777 );
  ftruncate( handle, 1024*1024*sizeof(int) );
  char * mem  = (char*) mmap( 0, 1024*1024*sizeof(int),
                      PROT_READ|PROT_WRITE, MAP_SHARED, handle, 0 );

  for( int i=0; i<1024*1024; i++ ) { mem[i] = 0; }

  munmap( mem, 1024*1024*sizeof(int) );
  shm_unlink( "/shm" );
}
```

One use for shared memory is as a location for placing mutexes shared between processes. Listing 5.57 illustrates how a process can form a child process and share a mutex with the child process.

Listing 5.57 **Sharing a Mutex Between Processes**

```
#include <sys/mman.h>
#include <sys/wait.h>
#include <fcntl.h>
#include <unistd.h>
#include <stdio.h>
#include <pthread.h>

int main()
{
  pthread_mutex_t * mutex;
  pthread_mutexattr_t attributes;
  pthread_mutexattr_init( &attributes );
  pthread_mutexattr_setpshared( &attributes, PTHREAD_PROCESS_SHARED );
```

```
int handle = shm_open( "/shm", O_CREAT|O_RD_WR, 0777 );
ftruncate( handle, 1024*sizeof(int) );
char * mem = mmap( 0, 1024*sizeof(int), PROT_READ|PROT_WRITE,
                   MAP_SHARED, handle,0 );

mutex = (pthread_mutex_t*)mem;
pthread_mutex_init( mutex, &attributes );

pthread_mutexattr_destroy( &attributes );

int ret = 0;
int * pcount = (int*)( mem + sizeof(pthread_mutex_t) );
*pcount = 0;

pid_t pid = fork();
if (pid == 0)
{   /* Child process */
  pthread_mutex_lock( mutex );
  (*pcount)++;
  pthread_mutex_unlock( mutex );
  ret = 57;
}
else
{
  int status;
  waitpid( pid, &status, 0 );
  printf( "Child returned %i\n", WEXITSTATUS(status) );
  pthread_mutex_lock( mutex );
  (*pcount)++;
  pthread_mutex_unlock( mutex );
  printf( "Count = %i\n", *pcount );
  pthread_mutex_destroy( mutex );
}
munmap( mem, 1024*sizeof(int) );
shm_unlink( "/shm" );
return ret;
}
```

The first thing the parent process does is to set up a mutex that is shared between the parent and child processes. Once this is complete, the parent process forks a child process. The parent process then waits for the child to complete.

When the child process is forked, it receives a copy of the memory of the parent process. This gives it access to the shared memory segment as well as the mutex and variables contained in the shared memory segment. The child process acquires the mutex, increments the shared variable, and releases the mutex before unmapping and unlinking the shared memory segment and exiting.

Once the child process has exited, the parent process continues to execute, obtaining the return value of the child process from the call to `waitpid()`. The macro `WEXITSTATUS` converts the exit status from `waitpid()` into the return value from the child process.

The parent process also acquires the mutex and increments the shared variable before releasing the mutex. It then prints the value of the shared variable, which has the value two, indicating that both the parent and the child process incremented it. The final actions of the parent process are to destroy the mutex and then unmap and unlink the shared memory segment.

One thing to pay attention to is the alignment of objects created in shared memory segments. Depending on the operating system, there may be constraints on the alignment. For example, Solaris requires that mutexes are aligned on 8-byte boundaries.

Sharing Semaphores Between Processes

As discussed in the section on semaphores, it is very easy to create a named semaphore that is shared between multiple processes. Listing 5.58 shows a parent process creating a child process. Both the parent and child process open the same semaphore, and this semaphore is used to ensure that the child process completes before the parent process.

Listing 5.58 **Sharing a Named Semaphore**

```c
#include <unistd.h>
#include <stdio.h>
#include <semaphore.h>

int main()
{
  int status;
  pid_t f = fork();
  sem_t * semaphore;
  semaphore = sem_open( "/my_semaphore", O_CREAT, 0777, 1 );
  if ( f == 0 )
  { /* Child process */
    printf( "Child process completed\n" );
    sem_post( semaphore );
    sem_close( semaphore );
  }
  else
  {
    sem_t * semaphore;
    sem_wait( semaphore );
    printf( "Parent process completed\n" );
    sem_close( semaphore );
    sem_unlink( "/my_semaphore" );
  }
}
```

Message Queues

Message queues are a method of passing messages between threads or processes. Messages can be placed into a queue, and they will be read out of the queue in a prioritized first-in, first-out order.

To attach to a message queue, the `mq_open()` function needs to be called, which will return a handle to the message queue. This takes a minimum of the name of the message queue and some flags. The name of the message queue should start with a / and then be up to 13 further characters with no additional / characters. The flags need to be one of `O_RDONLY`, `O_WRONLY`, or `O_RDWR` to produce a read-only message queue, a write-only message queue, or a read-write message queue.

The open specified in this way will open an existing message queue or fail if the message queue does not exist. If the additional flag `O_CREAT` is passed, then the call will create the message queue if it does not already exist. The additional flag `O_EXCL` can be passed if the call to open the queue should succeed *only* if the message queue does not exist. If the flag `O_CREAT` is passed, the call to `mq_open()` requires two more parameters, a mode setting that is used to set the access permissions for the message queue and a pointer to the attributes for the message queue; if this pointer is null, default values are used for the message queue attributes.

The attributes for a message queue are held in an `mq_attr` structure, which contains the fields `mq_maxmsg`, which is the maximum number of messages that can be held in the message queue, and `mq_msgsize`, which is the maximum size of the messages that can be stored in the message queue.

The other flag that can be passed to `mq_open()` is `O_NONBLOCK`. If this flag is set, any attempts to write to a full message queue or read from an empty one will fail and return immediately. The default is for the thread to block until the message queue has space for sending an additional message, or has a message in it.

The function `mq_close()`, which takes the handle to a message queue as a parameter, will close the connection to the message queue. The message queue will continue to exist. To remove the message queue from the system, it is necessary to call `mq_unlink()`, which takes the name of the message queue as a parameter. After a call to `mq_unlink()`, the message queue will be removed once all current references to the message queue have been closed.

The code in Listing 5.59 demonstrates creating and deleting a message queue.

Listing 5.59 **Opening and Closing a Message Queue**

```
#include <mqueue.h>

int main()
{
  mq_attr attr;
  mqd_t mqueue;
  attr.mq_maxmsg = 1000;
```

```
attr.mq_msgsize = 500;
mqueue = mq_open( "/messages", O_RDWR+O_CREAT, 0777, &attr );
...
mq_close( mqueue );
mq_unlink( "/messages" );
}
```

Message queues are prioritized first-in, first-out (FIFO) queues. Messages are added to the queue using the call `mq_send()` and received from the queue using the call `mq_receive()`. If the message queue has been created with the `O_NONBLOCK` attribute, then these functions will return immediately whether or not they were successful. There are versions of these functions available, which will return after a timeout if they are unsuccessful; these are `mq_timedsend()` and `mq_timedreceive()`, which take an absolute time, and `mq_reltimedsend_np()` and `mq_reltimedreceive_np()`, which take a relative time.

The parameters to `mq_send()` are the message queue, a pointer to a buffer containing the message, the size of the message, and a priority. Messages with a higher priority will be placed before messages with a lower priority and after messages with the same or higher priorities. The message is copied from the buffer into the queue. The call to `mq_send()` will fail if the message size is greater than the `mq_msgsize` attribute for the queue.

The call to `mq_receive()` takes the message queue, a pointer to a buffer where the message can be copied, the size of the buffer, and either a null pointer or a pointer to an `unsigned int` where the priority of the message will be written. If the size of the buffer is smaller than the size of the message, then the call will fail.

Note that sending messages requires at least two copy operations to be performed on the message—once to copy it into the queue and once to copy it out of the queue. Hence, it is advantageous to send short messages and perhaps use shared memory to pass longer items of information.

Listing 5.60 shows an example of sending messages between a parent and child process. On Solaris, the code will need to be linked with the real-time extensions library using the compiler flag `-lrt`.

Listing 5.60 **Passing Messages Between a Parent Process and a Child Process**

```
#include <unistd.h>
#include <stdio.h>
#include <mqueue.h>
#include <string.h>

int main()
{
  int status;
  pid_t f = fork();
```

```
if ( f == 0 )
{ /* Child process */
  mqd_t * queue;
  char message[20];
  queue = mq_open( "/messages", O_WRONLY+O_CREAT, 0777, 0 );
  strncpy( message, "Hello", 6 );
  printf( "Send message %s\n", message );
  mq_send( queue, message, strlen(message)+1, 0 );
  mq_close( queue );
  printf( "Child process completed\n" );
}
else
{
  mqd_t * queue;
  char message[2000];
  queue = mq_open( "/messages", O_RDONLY+O_CREAT, 0777, 0 );
  mq_receive( queue, message, 2000, 0 );
  printf( "Receive message %s\n", message );
  mq_close( queue );
  mq_unlink( "/messages" );
  printf( "Parent process completed\n" );
}
}
```

Both the child and the parent process open the message queue with the O_CREAT flag, meaning that the queue will be created if it does not already exist. The parent process then waits for a message from the child. The child sends a message and then closes its connection to the message queue. The parent receives the message and then closes the connection to the message queue and deletes the queue.

Pipes and Named Pipes

A *pipe* is a connection between two processes. It can be either an *anonymous pipe* between two processes or a *named pipe*, which uses an entity in the file system for communication between processes or threads. The pipe is a streamed first-in, first-out structure.

A named pipe is created by a call to `pipe()` typically before the child process forks. The pipe call creates two file descriptors, one for reading from the pipe and a second for writing into the pipe. After the fork, both the parent and child inherit both file descriptors. Typically one pipe would be used for unidirectional communication between the parent and the child.

Reading and writing to pipes can use the functions that take file descriptors as parameters, such as `read` and `write`.

Listing 5.61 shows an example of using an anonymous pipe to communicate between a child and parent process.

Listing 5.61 **Using an Anonymous Pipe to Communicate Between a Parent and Child Process**

```
#include <unistd.h>
#include <stdio.h>

int main()
{
  int status;
  int pipes[2];
  pipe( pipes );
  pid_t f = fork();
  if ( f == 0 )
  { /* Child process */
    close( pipes[0] );
    write( pipes[1], "a", 1 );
    printf( "Child sent 'a'\n" );
    close( pipes[1] );
  }
  else
  {
    char buffer[11];
    close( pipes[1] );
    int len = read( pipes[0], buffer, 10 );
    buffer[len] = 0;
    printf( "Parent received %s\n", buffer );
    close (pipes[0] );
  }
  return 0;
}
```

The code creates file descriptors for the two pipes before forking. The parent closes the descriptor indicted by pipes[1] and then waits to receive data from pipes[0]. The child process closes the descriptor pipes[0] and then sends a character to pipes[1] to be read by the parent process. The child process then closes their copy of the write file descriptor. The parent process prints the character sent by the child before closing the pipe and exiting.

Named pipes are created using a call to mknod(), which takes the path to the file that is to be used as the identifier for the pipe; the mode, which is S_IFIFO for a named pipe; and the access permissions for the file. The two processes can then call open() to open the file and treat the returned handles in the same way as before. Once the processes have finished with the named pipe, it can be removed by calling unlink(). The code in Listing 5.62 implements the same parent and child communication as Listing 5.61, this time using named pipes instead of anonymous pipes.

Listing 5.62 **Parent and Child Process Communicating Using Named Pipes**

```
#include <unistd.h>
#include <stdio.h>
#include <sys/stat.h>
#include <fcntl.h>

int main()
{
  int status;
  mknod( "/tmp/pipefile", S_IFIFO|S_IRUSR|S_IWUSR, 0 );
  pid_t f = fork();
  if ( f == 0 )
  { /* Child process */
    int mypipe = open( "/tmp/pipefile", O_WRONLY );
    write( mypipe, "a", 1 );
    printf( "Child sent 'a'\n" );
    close( mypipe );
  }
  else
  {
    int mypipe = open( "/tmp/pipefile", O_RDONLY );
    char buffer[11];
    int len = read( mypipe, buffer, 10 );
    buffer[len] = 0;
    printf( "Parent received %s\n", buffer );
    close( mypipe );
  }
  unlink( "/tmp/pipefile" );
  return 0;
}
```

The parent process calls `mknod()` to create the pipe and then forks. Both the child and parent processes open the pipe—the child for writing and the parent for reading. The child writes into the pipe, closes the file descriptor, unlinks the pipe, and then exits. The parent process reads from the pipe before it too closes it, unlinks it, and exits.

Using Signals to Communicate with a Process

Signals are used extensively in UNIX and UNIX-like operating systems. Pressing ^C on a terminal keyboard to stop an application actually results in the SIGKILL signal being sent to that process. It is relatively straightforward to set up a signal handler for the various signals that might be sent to a process. It is not possible to install a handler for SIGKILL, but many of the other signals can be intercepted and handled.

A signal handler is installed by calling `signal()` with the signal number and the routine that should handle the signal. A signal can be sent by calling `kill()` with the PID of the process that the signal should go to and the signal number. Listing 5.63 shows an example of this.

Listing 5.63 **Sending and Receiving a Signal**

```
#include <signal.h>
#include <stdio.h>
#include <unistd.h>

void hsignal( int signal )
{
}

int main()
{
  signal( SIGRTMIN+4, hsignal );
  kill( getpid(), SIGRTMIN+4 );
  return 0;
}
```

The example installs a handler for the signal SIGRTMIN+4. The values SIGRTMIN and SIGRTMAX are system-specific values that represent the range of values that are reserved for user-defined signals.

It is tempting to imagine that the code in Listing 5.64 would be appropriate for a signal handler. The problem with this code is that the function printf() is not guaranteed to be signal-safe. That is, if the application happened to be performing a printf() call when the signal arrived, it would not be safe to call the printf() in the signal handler.

Listing 5.64 **Unsafe Signal Handler Code**

```
void hsigseg( int signal )
{
  printf( "Got signal\n" );
}
```

The POSIX guarantees that a set of function calls are async-signal-safe, in particular that the write() call can be used in a signal handler, so the code in Listing 5.65 can be used.

Listing 5.65 **Printing Output in a Signal Handler**

```
#include <stdio.h>
#include <unistd.h>

void hsignal( int signal )
```

```
{
  write( 1, "Got signal\n", 11 );
}
```

Running this on an Ubuntu system produces the expected output shown in Listing 5.66.

Listing 5.66 **Output Printed by Signal Handler**

```
$ gcc signal.c
$ ./a.out
Got signal
```

Sometimes, the code already performs an operation on receiving a particular signal, but it is desired to add an additional handler. What should be done is to add a signal handler to the chain and then call the default one.

The function that allows us to create a chain of signal handlers is `sigaction()`. This takes a signal number and two `sigaction` structures. The first `sigaction` structure contains information about the new signal handler, while the second returns information about the existing signal handler.

The code in Listing 5.67 installs a new handler for the `SIGPROF` signal but stores the details of the old handler. Then, when a signal is received, the new handler does its processing and then installs the old handler to perform the default action. The handler structure has an `sa_sigaction` field, which indicates the routine to be called in the event of a signal arriving. It also has an `sa_mask` field, which sets the list of signals that are to be blocked while this signal is handled. The other field of interest is `sa_flags`, which allows tuning of the behavior of the signal handler.

Listing 5.67 **Chaining Signal Handlers**

```
#include <signal.h>
#include <unistd.h>

struct sigaction oldhandler;

void hsignal( int signal, siginfo_t* info, void* other )
{
  write( 1, "Got signal\n", 11 );
  if (oldhandler.sa_sigaction)
  {
    oldhandler.sa_sigaction( signal, info, other );
  }
}

int main()
```

```
{
  struct sigaction newhandler;
  newhandler.sa_sigaction = hsignal;
  newhandler.sa_flags = 0;
  sigemptyset( &newhandler.sa_mask );
  sigaction( SIGPROF, &newhandler, &oldhandler );
  kill( getpid(), SIGPROF );
}
```

Signals can also be used for communicating between processes. Listing 5.68 demonstrates a parent process sending a signal to a child process.

Listing 5.68 **Parent Process Signaling to a Child Process**

```
#include <unistd.h>
#include <stdio.h>
#include <signal.h>
#include <sys/wait.h>

volatile int go = 0;

void handler( int sig )
{
  go = 1;
  write( 1, "Signal arrived\n", 16 );
}

int main()
{
  signal( SIGRTMIN+4, handler );
  pid_t f = fork();
  if ( f == 0 )
  { /* Child process */
    while ( !go ){}
    printf( "Child completed\n" );
  }
  else
  {
    kill( f, SIGRTMIN+4 );
    waitpid( f, 0, 0 );
    printf( "Parent completed\n" );
  }
}
```

Compiling and running the code produces the output shown in Listing 5.69.

Listing 5.69 **Output from Parent Process Communicating with Child Process**

```
$ gcc sigchild.c
$ ./a.out
Signal arrived
Child completed
Parent completed
```

It might be sufficient to signal another process, but it is more useful to be able to pass data between the processes. It is possible to do this using sigaction(), as the code in Listing 5.70 demonstrates. The code also uses sigqueue() to send the signal containing the data; on Solaris, this is found in the real-time extensions library, and the application requires linking with –lrt.

Listing 5.70 **Using Signals to Transfer Information**

```
#include <unistd.h>
#include <stdio.h>
#include <signal.h>
#include <sys/wait.h>

volatile int go = 0;
struct sigaction oldhandler;

void handler( int sig, siginfo_t *info, void *context )
{
  go = (int)info->si_value.sival_int;
  write( 1, "Signal arrived\n", 16 );
}

int main()
{
  struct sigaction newhandler;
  newhandler.sa_sigaction = handler;
  newhandler.sa_flags = SA_SIGINFO;
  sigemptyset( &newhandler.sa_mask );
  sigaction( SIGRTMIN+4, &newhandler, &oldhandler );

  pid_t f = fork();
  if ( f == 0 )
  { /* Child process */
    while ( !go ){}
    printf( "Child completed go=%i\n", go );
  }
  else
  {
```

```
    union sigval value;
    value.sival_int = 7;
    sigqueue( f, SIGRTMIN+4, value );
    waitpid( f, 0, 0 );
    printf( "Parent completed\n" );
  }
}
```

The signal handler is set up with `sa_flags` including `SA_SIGINFO`. This flag causes the signal handler to receive the `siginfo_t` data. If the flag is not specified, the signal handler will not receive the data. The signal is sent by the parent process by calling `sigqueue()`. This takes a `sigval` union as a parameter, and the code sets the integer field of this union to the value seven. When the child process receives the signal, it can extract the value of this field from the `sigval` union passed into it.

Compiling and running the code produces the output shown in Listing 5.71.

Listing 5.71 **Parent Process Sending Information to the Child Process**

```
$ gcc sigchild2.c
$ ./a.out
Signal arrived
Child completed go=7
Parent completed
```

The parent process creates a child process and then sends a `SIGRTMIN+4` signal to the child. The child process loops until the variable `go` becomes nonzero. When the child process receives the signal, it sets the variable `go` to be nonzero, and this enables the process to print a message and exit. In the meantime, the parent process has been waiting for the child process to exit. When the child process does eventually exit, the parent process prints a message and also exits.

One significant problem with using signals is that they can disrupt a system call that the thread is making at the time the signal is received. If this happens, the system call will set `errno` to the value `EINTR` indicating that the call should be retried. However, the exact behavior is system dependent and should be carefully explored before relying on signals.

Sockets

A full treatment of *socket* programming is beyond the scope of this book. However, sockets remain an important way that processes or threads can communicate, so it is worth examining the use of sockets for communication within the same system. A particular advantage of using sockets for communication is that scaling beyond a single system becomes a relatively minor change to the code.

The use of sockets is different from other communication mechanisms because the client that opens the socket has different responsibilities than the server connected to the socket. So, it is appropriate to tackle the client and server as two entirely separate applications.

The first thing that any process that uses sockets has to do is request a socket. The socket is a potential connection to the network. The call to `socket()` takes three parameters: the family of socket being requested, the type of socket within that family, and the protocol. The protocol should usually be set to zero to indicate that the default protocol should be used. The protocol family should be `AF_INET` or `AF_INET6`, and the protocol type for these two families is either `SOCK_STREAM` for TCP/IP or `SOCK_DGRAM` for UDP/IP.

Once a socket has been established, it is necessary to connect it to an address. We can best illustrate this by initially working through the code necessary to write a server process that waits for a connection from a client, before discussing the code that would be found in such a client. This makes sense because the two scenarios have little code in common.

A server will call `bind()` with the address of the local host and the port on which it will listen for connections. The function `bind()` takes as parameters the previously established socket, a pointer to a structure containing the details of the address to bind to, the value `INADDR_ANY` is typically used for this, and the size of the structure. The particular structure that needs to be used will depend on the protocol, which is why it is passed by the pointer.

Once a server has been bound to an address, the server can then call `listen()` on the socket. The parameters to this call are the socket and the maximum number of queued connections as a parameter.

After a call to listen, the server can wait for a connection from a client by calling `accept()`. The parameters to the `accept()` call are the socket, an optional pointer to a socket address structure, and the size of the structure. If the pointer to the socket address structure is not zero, the call to `accept()` will write details of the client into the socket address structure. The call will return a new socket descriptor that is the connection to the client.

The server can read from or write to the new socket until the connection is terminated by either the client or the server calling `close()` on the new socket.

Data can be sent through the socket using either the `write()` call or the `send()` call. The `send()` call affords some additional flexibility in sending data. Similarly, data can be received from the socket using either the `read()` or `recv()` call. A socket that has been closed is indicated by a return of an error from the calls.

The code in Listing 5.72 shows the part of the server code that handles echoing data back. While there is still data in the socket, the thread will read that data, write it to `stdout`, and then echo it back to the socket where it came from. One complexity is that we do not want the server process to call `pthread_join()` for every thread that it creates to handle an incoming connection. To avoid the call to `pthread_join()`, each thread immediately calls `pthread_detach()` once it has been created. This detaches the thread and ensures that any resources that the thread uses are returned to the process when the thread terminates.

Listing 5.72 **Code for Echo Server Thread**

```
#include <pthread.h>
#include <stdio.h>
#include <unistd.h>

void * handleecho( void * param )
{
   char buffer[1024];
   int count;
   pthread_detach( pthread_self() );
   int s = (int)param;
   while ( count = read( s, buffer, 1023 ) > 0 )
   {
     buffer[count] = 0;
     printf( "Received %s \n", buffer );
     write( s, buffer, count );
   }
   close( s );
}
```

The more interesting part of the code is the code to set up the server, as shown in Listing 5.73. The server sets up a socket and binds this to port 7779. It also configures the socket to hold a queue of up to five connections. The server then listens on the socket for incoming connections. When a connection arrives, the server creates a new thread to handle this connection and passes the socket number as a parameter to the new thread. The resulting application needs to be linked with the socket library (−lsocket) and the network services library (−lnsl).

Listing 5.73 **Code to Set Up the Server**

```
#include <sys/types.h>
#include <sys/socket.h>
#include <strings.h>
#include <arpa/inet.h>

int main()
{
  int newsocket;
  int s = socket( AF_INET, SOCK_STREAM, 0 ); // TCP/IP socket
  struct sockaddr_in server;
  bzero( &server, sizeof(server) );          // Clear address structure
  server.sin_family = AF_INET;               // TCP/IP family
```

```
  server.sin_addr.s_addr = INADDR_ANY;      // Any address
  server.sin_port = 7779;                   // Port to bind to
  bind( s, (struct sockaddr*)&server, sizeof(server) );
  listen( s, 5 ); // Queue of five outstanding connections

  while ( newsocket = accept( s, 0, 0 ) )
  {
    pthread_t thread;
    pthread_create( &thread, 0, handleecho, (void*) newsocket );
  }
}
```

Listing 5.74 shows the client code. In a similar way to the server, the client sets up
a socket. However, the client calls `connect()` with the address and port of the system
that it wants to connect to. Once the call to `connect()` completes, the client can start
sending data to the server and receiving data back from the server using the socket. In
Listing 5.74, the client sends a string to the server and then prints out the data returned
by the server.

Listing 5.74 **Client Code That Sends Data to a Server and Prints Response**

```
#include <sys/types.h>
#include <sys/socket.h>
#include <strings.h>
#include <arpa/inet.h>
#include <unistd.h>
#include <stdio.h>

int main()
{
  int s = socket( AF_INET, SOCK_STREAM, 0 ); // TCP/IP socket
  struct sockaddr_in server;
  bzero( &server, sizeof(server) );          // Clear address structure
  server.sin_family = AF_INET;               // TCP/IP family
  server.sin_addr.s_addr = inet_addr( "127.0.0.1" );
                                             // Local machine
  server.sin_port = 7779;                    // Port to bind to
  if ( connect( s, (struct sockaddr*)&server, sizeof(server) ) == 0 )
  {
    printf( "Sending 'abcd' to server\n" );
    char buffer[1024];
    strncpy( buffer, "abcd", 4 );
    write( s, buffer, strlen(buffer) );
    int count = read( s, buffer, 1024 );
    buffer[count] = 0;
    printf( "Got %s from server\n", buffer );
```

```
    shutdown( s, SHUT_RDWR );
  }
}
```

Sockets represent a convenient way of communicating between a number of independent processes that are spread over one or more systems. They are a good approach if it is expected that the application will end up scaling beyond a single system.

Reentrant Code and Compiler Flags

Depending upon the platform and compiler, it may be necessary to compile with special flags to indicate that the application is multithreaded. On some platforms, gcc has the flag -pthread, which links in the POSIX threading library and defines _REENTRANT. The Solaris Studio compiler has the flag -mt, which performs the same task; only the flag defined is __REENTRANT.

Defining the preprocessor flag includes a set of "reentrant" functions to go with the usual set. The reentrant versions are denoted by the _r postfix. The reason these functions exist is that many of the C library functions are stateful, meaning that a call to the function sets up some state that is then used in later function calls. This statefulness means that multiple threads cannot call the function at the same time without the state becoming corrupted. The reentrant versions of the functions typically use a structure that the calling thread provides to hold the state for that calling thread. The code in Listing 5.75 uses the readdir() call to print out the contents of the current directory.

Listing 5.75 **Multithread Unsafe Code for Listing a Directory**

```
#include <dirent.h>
#include <stdio.h>

int main()
{
  DIR * directory = opendir( "." );
  while ( 1 )
  {
    struct dirent * entry = readdir( directory );
    if (entry!=0)
    {
      printf( "%s\n", entry->d_name );
    }
    else
    {
      closedir( directory );
      break;
    }
  }
}
```

The code works when compiled as a single-threaded application but could, on some operating systems, fail if multiple threads were to use the `readdir()` function simultaneously. The code can easily be modified to use the reentrant version of `readdir()`, `readdir_r()`. Listing 5.76 shows the modified code.

Listing 5.76 Using Multithread-Safe Code to Print Out a Directory Listing

```c
#include <dirent.h>
#include <stdio.h>
#include <stdlib.h>

int main()
{
  DIR * directory = opendir( "." );
  struct dirent * entry;
  struct dirent * result;
  entry = (struct dirent*)malloc( sizeof(struct dirent) +
                                  FILENAME_MAX + 1 );
  while ( ( readdir_r( directory, entry, &result ) ==0 ) && result )
  {
    printf( "%s\n", entry->d_name );
  }
  closedir( directory );
  free( entry );
}
```

The reentrant version of `readdir()` places the results into a `dirent` structure that is passed into the call. However, not all operating systems declare the `dirent` structure with storage for the filename by default. The code shown will compile on Solaris with `_POSIX_C_SOURCE` defined to be greater than or equal to `199506L`.

Summary

As a result of reading this chapter, you should have a good understanding of creating threads and processes using the POSIX standard library calls. You will also have knowledge of the various synchronization and communication constructs provided by the POSIX standard.

6

Windows Threading

Multithreading support under the Microsoft Windows operating system is broadly similar to the support provided by POSIX threads. The differences are largely in the names of the functions in the API rather than any significant differences in the actual functionality. This chapter compares the Windows threading support with that of POSIX threads. By the end of the chapter, the reader should be familiar with Windows threading and will be able to convert code between Windows and POSIX threading conventions.

Creating Native Windows Threads

A basic Windows application will start with a single thread. The function call to request that Windows create a child thread is `CreateThread()`. This call takes the parameters shown in Table 6.1.

Table 6.1 **Parameters Passed to** `CreateThread()`

Parameter Type	Comment
LPTHREADATTRIBUTES	The security attributes of the thread; a discussion of this is outside the scope of this text. However, passing zero will suffice for the purposes of creating child threads.
SIZE_T	The stack size for the thread. The default is for each thread to get 1MB of stack space. A thread created using a POSIX API would have its stack size provided by a separate attributes structure.
LPTHREAD_START_ROUTINE	The address of the function that the thread will execute.
LPVOID	The parameters that are to be passed to the thread.
DWORD	Whether the thread should be created in a suspended state. A suspended thread needs to be started by a call to the `ResumeThread()` function.
LPDWORD	A pointer to a variable where the thread ID can be written.

The return value from the function call is a handle for the created thread, which is a different construct than the thread ID. Handles will be discussed in more detail later. A return value of zero means that the call was unsuccessful.

All of the parameters, with the exception of the address of the function to execute, will take sensible defaults if they are provided the null value. Listing 6.1 shows code to create a child thread using the `CreateThread()` call. The call to `GetCurrentThreadId()` will return an integer ID for the calling thread.

Listing 6.1 **Creating a Thread Using a Call to** `CreateThread()`

```
#include <Windows.h>

DWORD WINAPI mythread(__in  LPVOID lpParameter)
{
  printf( "Thread %i \n", GetCurrentThreadId() );
  return 0;
}

int _tmain( int argc, _TCHAR* argv[] )
{
  HANDLE handle;
  handle = CreateThread( 0, 0, mythread, 0, 0, 0 );
  getchar();
  return 0;
}
```

If it is important to capture the ID of the created thread, the code shown in Listing 6.2 could be used. The thread ID is not very useful, because most functions take the thread handle as a parameter.

Listing 6.2 **Capturing the ID of the Created Thread**

```
int _tmain( int argc, _TCHAR* argv[] )
{
  HANDLE handle;
  DWORD threadid;
  handle = CreateThread( 0, 0, mythread, 0, 0, &threadid );
  printf( "Thread %i \n", threadid );
  getchar();
  return 0;
}
```

Calling `CreateThread()` tells the operating system to produce a new thread but does not set that thread up to work with the libraries provided by the developer environment. Windows essentially creates the thread and returns a handle to that thread.

However, the runtime libraries have not had the opportunity to set up the thread-local data structures that they need. In most instances, the libraries will create any structures that they need the first time that they are called, but not all library calls are able to do that. Therefore, it is recommended that instead of calling `CreateThread()`, the calls provided by the runtime libraries are used. The two recommended ways of creating a thread are the calls `_beginthread()` and `_beginthreadex()`. The two functions take different parameters. Table 6.2 provides the parameters for `_beginthread()`.

Table 6.2 **Parameters Passed to** `_beginthread()`

Parameter Type	Comment
`void(*)(void*)`	The address of the function that the thread will execute
`unsigned int`	The stack size for the thread
`void*`	The pointer to the parameters that are to be passed to the thread

Table 6.3 shows the parameters for `_beginthreadex()`. These are the same as the parameters taken by `CreateThread()`.

Table 6.3 **Parameters Passed to** `_beginthreadex()`

Parameter Type	Comment
`void*`	A pointer to the security attributes of the thread
`unsigned int`	The stack size for the thread
`unsigned int(*)(void*)`	The address of the function that the thread will execute
`void*`	A pointer to the arguments that should be passed to the thread
`unsigned int`	A flag indicating whether the thread should be created in a suspended state
`unsigned int *`	An optional pointer to a variable where the thread ID can be written

There is another difference between these two routines other than the parameters that they take. A thread created by a call to `_beginthread()` will close the handle to the thread when the thread exits. The handle returned by `_beginthreadex()` will have to be explicitly closed by the programmer by calling `CloseHandle()`. This requirement is similar to the concept of detached threads in POSIX.

The two functions also differ by the type of function that the thread will execute. `_beginthread()` is a **void** function and uses the default calling convention `__cdecl`, whereas `_beginthreadex()` returns an unsigned **int** and uses the `__stdcall` calling convention.

Both the `_beginthread()` and `_beginthreadex()` functions return handles to the newly created threads. However, the actual return type of the function call is `uintptr_t`, which has to be type cast to a HANDLE before it can be used in function calls that expect an object handle.

Listing 6.3 provides example code for creating threads using the three different approaches discussed. The call to WaitForSingleObject() waits for an object to signal its readiness; in this instance, the routine is passed the handle to a thread and waits for that thread to terminate.

Listing 6.3 **Three Different Ways of Creating Threads**

```
#include <windows.h>
#include <process.h>

DWORD WINAPI mywork1( __in  LPVOID lpParameter )
{
  printf( "CreateThread thread %i\n", GetCurrentThreadId() );
  return 0;
}

unsigned int __stdcall mywork2( void * data )
{
  printf( "_beginthreadex thread %i\n", GetCurrentThreadId() );
  return 0;
}

void mywork3( void * data )
{
  printf( "_beginthread thread %i\n", GetCurrentThreadId() );
}

int _tmain( int argc, _TCHAR* argv[] )
{
  HANDLE h1, h2, h3;
  h1 = CreateThread( 0, 0, mywork1, 0, 0, 0 );

  h2 = (HANDLE)_beginthreadex( 0, 0, &mywork2, 0, 0, 0 );
  WaitForSingleObject( h2, INFINITE );
  CloseHandle( h2 );

  h3 = (HANDLE)_beginthread( &mywork3, 0, 0 );
  getchar();
}
```

Although calling _beginthread() looks appealing because it takes fewer parameters and cleans up the handle after the thread exits, it is better to use _beginthreadex().

The call to _beginthreadex() avoids a difficulty with _beginthread(). If the thread terminates, the handle returned by the call to _beginthread() will be invalid or even reused, so it is impossible to query the status of the thread or even be confident that the handle to the thread is a handle to the same thread to which it originally pointed. Listing 6.4 shows an example of this problem.

Listing 6.4 **Code Where a Thread Handle Could Be Reused**

```
#include <windows.h>
#include <process.h>

void mywork1( void * data )
{
}

void mywork2( void * data )
{
  volatile int i;
  for (i=0; i<100000; i++)
  {}    // because i is volatile most compilers will not
       // eliminate the loop
}

int _tmain( int argc, _TCHAR* argv[] )
{
   HANDLE h1, h2;
   h1 = (HANDLE)_beginthread( &mywork1, 0, 0 );
   h2 = (HANDLE)_beginthread( &mywork2, 0, 0 );
   WaitForSingleObject( h1, INFINITE );
   WaitForSingleObject( h2, INFINITE );
}
```

The routine mywork1() in Listing 6.4 terminates quickly and may have already terminated by the time that the main thread reaches the call to create the second thread. If the first thread has terminated, the handle to the first thread may be reused as the handle to the second thread. Queries using the handle of the first thread might succeed, but they will work on the wrong thread. In the code shown in Listing 6.4, the calls to WaitForSingleObject() may not be using a correct or valid handle for either of the threads depending on the completion time of the threads.

Listing 6.5 shows an equivalent code that uses _beginthreadex(). Threads created with _beginthreadex() need to be cleaned up with a call to CloseHandle(). Consequently, the calls to WaitForSingleObject() are certain to get the correct handles.

Listing 6.5 **Creating Threads Using _beginthreadex() to Ensure That Handles Are Not Reused**

```
#include <windows.h>
#include <process.h>

unsigned int __stdcall mywork1( void * data )
{
  return 0;
}

unsigned int __stdcall mywork2( void * data )
{
  volatile int i;
  for (i=0; i<100000; i++)
  {}   // because i is volatile most compilers will not
       // eliminate the loop
  return 0;
}

int _tmain( int argc, _TCHAR* argv[] )
{
    HANDLE h1, h2;
    h1 = (HANDLE)_beginthreadex( 0, 0, &mywork1, 0, 0, 0);
    h2 = (HANDLE)_beginthreadex( 0, 0, &mywork2, 0, 0, 0);
    WaitForSingleObject( h1, INFINITE );
    WaitForSingleObject( h2, INFINITE );
    CloseHandle( h1 );
    CloseHandle( h2 );
}
```

Terminating Threads

Although there are multiple ways to cause a thread to terminate, the recommended approach is for the thread to exit the function that it was instructed to run. In Listing 6.6, the thread will print out its ID and then exit.

Listing 6.6 **Printing Thread ID and Exiting**

```
DWORD WINAPI mythread( __in  LPVOID lpParameter )
{
        printf( "Thread %i \n", GetCurrentThreadId() );
        return 0;
}
```

It is also possible to cause threads to terminate using the call `ExitThread()` or `TerminateThread()`. However, these are not recommended because they may leave the application in an unspecified state. The thread does not get the opportunity to release any held mutexes or free any other allocated resources. They also do not give the run-time libraries the opportunity to clean up any resources that they have allocated on behalf of the thread.

As long as care is taken to ensure that resources the thread has acquired are appropriately freed, a thread may terminate with a call to `_endthread()` or `_endthreadex()`. This call needs to match the call that was used to create the thread. If the thread exits with a call to `_endthreadex()`, the handle to the thread still needs to be closed by another thread calling `closeHandle()`.

In a fork-join type model, there will be a master thread that creates multiple worker threads and then waits for the worker threads to exit. There are two routines that the master thread can use to wait for the worker to complete: `WaitForSingleObject()` or `WaitForMultipleObjects()`. As indicated by their names, these two routines will wait either for the completion of a single thread or for the completion of an array of threads. The routines take the handle of the thread as a parameter together with a timeout value that indicates how long the master thread should wait for the worker thread to complete; usually the value `INFINITE` will be appropriate. Listing 6.7 shows the code necessary to wait for a single thread to complete.

Listing 6.7 **Using** `WaitForSingleObject()`

```
#include <windows.h>
#include <process.h>

unsigned int __stdcall mywork( void * data )
{
  printf( "Thread %i\n", GetCurrentThreadId() );
  return 0;
}



int _tmain( int argc, _TCHAR* argv[] )
{
   HANDLE h[2];
   for (int i=0; i<2; i++)
   {
     h[i] = (HANDLE)_beginthreadex( 0, 0, &mywork, 0, 0, 0 );
   }
   for (int i=0; i<2; i++)
   {
     WaitForSingleObject( h[i], INFINITE );
     CloseHandle( h[i] );
   }
```

```
    getchar();
}
```

Listing 6.8 shows the equivalent code using `WaitForMultipleObjects()`. The first parameter to the function call is the number of threads that are to be waited for. The second parameter is a pointer to the array of handles to these threads. The third parameter is a boolean that, if `true`, indicates that the function should return when all the threads are complete or, if `false`, indicates the function should return on the completion of the first worker thread. The final parameter is the length of time that the master thread should wait before returning anyway. Listing 6.8 shows an example of calling this.

Listing 6.8 **Using `WaitForMultipleObjects()`**

```
int _tmain( int argc, _TCHAR* argv[] )
{
    HANDLE h[2];
    for (int i=0; i<2; i++)
    {
      h[i] = (HANDLE)_beginthreadex( 0, 0, &mywork, 0, 0, 0 );
    }
    WaitForMultipleObjects( 2, h, true, INFINITE );
    for (int i=0; i<2; i++)
    {
      CloseHandle( h[i] );
    }
    getchar();
}
```

Even after a thread created by a call to `_beginthreadex()` has exited, it will continue to hold resources. These resources need to be freed by calling the `CloseHandle()` function on the handle to the thread. Listing 6.9 shows the complete sequence of creating a thread, waiting for it to complete, and then freeing its resources.

Listing 6.9 **Complete Thread Life Cycle**

```
int _tmain( int argc, TCHAR* argv[] )
{
    HANDLE handle;
    handle = (HANDLE)_beginthreadex( 0, 0, &routine, 0, 0, 0 );
    returnvalue = WaitForSingleObject( handle, INFINITE );
    CloseHandle( handle );
    return 0;
}
```

Creating and Resuming Suspended Threads

A *suspended* thread is one that is not currently running. Threads can be created in the suspended state and then started at a later time. If a thread is in the suspended state, then the call to start the thread executing is `ResumeThread()`, which takes the handle of the thread as a parameter. There is a `SuspendThread()` call that will cause a running thread to be suspended. This call is expected to be used only by tools such as debuggers; suspending a running thread may lead to problems if the thread currently holds resources such as mutexes. Listing 6.10 shows the creation of a suspended thread and then calling `ResumeThread()` on that thread. The code uses a call to `getchar()`, which waits for the enter key to be pressed, to separate the creation of the thread from the act of resuming the thread.

Listing 6.10 **Creating and Resuming a Suspended Thread**

```
#include <windows.h>
#include <process.h>

unsigned int __stdcall mywork( void * data )
{
  printf( "Thread %i\n", GetCurrentThreadId() );
  return 0;
}



int _tmain( int argc, _TCHAR* argv[] )
{
  HANDLE handle;
  handle = (HANDLE)_beginthreadex(0,0, &mywork, 0, CREATE_SUSPENDED, 0);
  getchar();
  ResumeThread( handle );
  getchar();
  WaitForSingleObject( handle, INFINITE );
  CloseHandle( handle );
  return 0;
}
```

The suspension state of the thread is handled as a counter, so multiple calls to `SuspendThread()` need to be matched with multiple calls to `ResumeThread()`.

Using Handles to Kernel Resources

Many of the Windows API functions return *handles*. As can be seen from the earlier discussion of type casting, these are really just unsigned integers. However, they have a particular purpose. Windows API calls that return handles have actually caused a resource to be created within the kernel space. The handle is just an index for that resource. When the application has finished with the resource, the call to `CloseHandle()` enables the kernel to free the associated kernel space resources.

Resources with handles can be shared between processes. Once a resource exists, other processes can open a handle to that resource or duplicate an existing handle to the resource. It is important to realize that the handle of a kernel resource makes sense only within the context of the process that has access to the resource. Passing the value of the handle to another process does not enable the other process to get access to the resource; the kernel needs to enable access to the resource and provide a new handle for the existing resource in the new process.

Some functions do not return a handle. For these functions, there is no associated kernel resource; hence, it is not necessary to call `CloseHandle()` once the resource is no longer needed.

Methods of Synchronization and Resource Sharing

The range of synchronization objects provided by Windows is very similar to those specified in POSIX:

- Mutex locks ensure that only one thread has access to a resource at a time. If the lock is held by another thread, the thread attempting to acquire the lock will sleep until the lock is released. A timeout can also be specified so that lock acquisition will fail if the lock does not become available within the specified interval. If multiple threads are waiting for the lock, the order in which the waiting threads will acquire the mutex is not guaranteed. Mutexes can be shared between processes.

- Critical sections are similar to mutex locks. The difference is that critical sections cannot be shared between processes; consequently, their performance overhead is lower. Critical sections also have a different interface from that provided by mutex locks. Critical sections do not take a timeout value but do have an interface that allows the calling thread to try to enter the critical section. If this fails, the call immediately returns, enabling the thread to continue execution. They also have the facility of spinning for a number of iterations before the thread goes to sleep in the situation where the thread is unable to enter the critical section.

- Slim reader/writer locks provide support for the situation where there are multiple threads that read shared data, but on rare occasions the shared data needs to be written. Data that is being read can be simultaneously accessed by multiple threads without concern for problems with corruption of the data being shared. However, only a single thread can have access to update the data at any one time, and other threads cannot access that data during the write operation. This is to prevent threads from reading incomplete or corrupted data that is in the process of being written. Slim reader/writer locks cannot be shared across processes.

- Semaphores provide a means of restricting access to a finite set of resources or of signaling that a resource is available. These are essentially the same as the semaphores provided by POSIX. As is the case with mutex locks, semaphores can be shared across processes.

- Condition variables enable a thread to be woken when a condition becomes true. Condition variables cannot be shared between processes.

- Events are a method of signaling within or between processes. They provide similar functionality to the signaling capability of semaphores.

An Example of Requiring Synchronization Between Threads

We'll start an example where two multiple threads are used to calculate all the prime numbers in a given range. Listing 6.11 shows one test to indicate whether a number is prime.

Listing 6.11 **Test for Whether a Number Is Prime**

```
#include <math.h>

int isprime( int number )
{
  int i;
  for ( i=2; i < (int)(sqrt((float)number)+1.0); i++ )
  {
    if ( number % i == 0 ) { return 0; }
  }
  return 1;
}
```

We will create two threads, both of which will keep testing numbers until all the numbers have been computed. Listing 6.12 shows the code to create the two threads.

Listing 6.12 **Code to Create Two Threads and Wait for Them to Complete Their Work**

```
int _tmain( int argc, _TCHAR* argv[] )
{
  HANDLE h1, h2;
  h1 = (HANDLE)_beginthreadex( 0, 0, &test, (void*)0, 0, 0 );
  h2 = (HANDLE)_beginthreadex( 0, 0, &test, (void*)1, 0, 0 );
  WaitForSingleObject( h1, INFINITE );
  WaitForSingleObject( h2, INFINITE );
  CloseHandle( h1 );
  CloseHandle( h2 );
  getchar();
  return 0;
}
```

The tricky part of the code is where we want each thread to test a different number. Listing 6.13 shows a serial version of the code to do this.

Listing 6.13 **Algorithmic Version of Code to Test Range of Numbers for Primality**

```
volatile int counter = 0;

unsigned int __stdcall test( void * )
{
  while ( counter<100 )
  {
    int number = counter++;
    printf( "ThreadID %i; value = %i, is prime = %i\n",
            GetCurrentThreadId(), number, isprime(number) );
  }
  return 0;
}
```

However, using two threads to perform this algorithm would cause a data race if both threads accessed the variable counter at the same time. If we did choose to select this particular algorithm, we would need to protect the increment of the variable counter to avoid data races. The following sections will demonstrate various approaches to solving this problem.

Protecting Access to Code with Critical Sections

Critical sections are one method of ensuring only a single thread executes a region of code. They are declared within a process and are not resources provided by the kernel (they have no handles). Since they are entirely within the process, access to them is quicker than it would be if access had to be brokered by the kernel.

The code in Listing 6.14 declares a critical section structure, initializes it with a call to InitializeCriticalSection(), and, once the program has finished with it, deletes it with a call to DeleteCriticalSection().

Listing 6.14 **Using Initialization and Deletion of Critical Sections**

```
CRITICAL_SECTION critical;

...
    InitializeCriticalSection(&critical);
...
    DeleteCriticalSection(&critical);
...
```

When a thread wants to enter the critical section, it calls `EnterCriticalSection()`. If no other thread is in the critical section, the calling thread acquires it and continues execution. If another thread is in the critical section, the calling thread will sleep until the thread executing the critical section leaves it with the call `LeaveCriticalSection()`. The thread that calls `EnterCriticalSection()` will not return until it has obtained access to the critical section; there is no concept of a timeout.

Listing 6.15 shows an example of using a critical section to protect access to the variable `counter`.

Listing 6.15 Using a Critical Section to Protect Access to a Variable

```
volatile int counter = 0;
CRITICAL_SECTION critical;

unsigned int __stdcall test( void * )
{
  while ( counter<100 )
  {
    EnterCriticalSection( &critical );
    int number = counter++;
    LeaveCriticalSection( &critical );
    printf( "ThreadID %i; value = %i, is prime = %i\n",
            GetCurrentThreadId(), number, isprime(number) );
  }
  return 0;
}

int _tmain( int argc, _TCHAR* argv[] )
{
    HANDLE h1, h2;
    InitializeCriticalSection( &critical );
    h1 = (HANDLE)_beginthreadex( 0, 0, &test, (void*)0, 0, 0);
    h2 = (HANDLE)_beginthreadex( 0, 0, &test, (void*)1, 0, 0);
    WaitForSingleObject( h1, INFINITE );
    WaitForSingleObject( h2, INFINITE );
    CloseHandle( h1 );
    CloseHandle( h2 );
    getchar();
    DeleteCriticalSection( &critical );
    return 0;
}
```

Putting threads to sleep and waking them up again is time-consuming, because it involves entering the kernel. All critical sections should be designed to be as short-lived as possible. With that in mind, it is likely that by the time the thread has been put to sleep, the thread that was in the critical section will already have left it. Therefore, making the waiting thread sleep and then waking it up again is just a waste of time.

There are two alternatives. The programmer can call `TryEnterCriticalSection()`, which will return immediately returning either true, meaning that the thread has acquired access to the critical section, or false, meaning that another thread is currently in the critical section. The code that protects access to the `counter` variable could be written using `TryEnterCriticalSection()`, as shown in Listing 6.16.

Listing 6.16 **Using `TryEnterCriticalSection()` to Avoid Putting Calling Threads to Sleep**

```
while (counter<100)
{
  while ( !TryEnterCriticalSection( &critical ) ) {}
  int number = counter++;
  LeaveCriticalSection( &critical );
  printf( "ThreadID %i; value = %i, is prime = %i\n",
          GetCurrentThreadId(), number, isprime(number) );
}
```

This would cause the process to spin continuously until it got the lock. One of the problems with having a thread spin is that it is potentially depriving other threads of processor time. Of particular concern would be the case where the spinning thread stops the other thread, which is currently in the critical section, from getting back onto the processor. Consequently, this style of programming is one that should only be undertaken with care.

The other approach is to have the thread wanting to enter the critical section spin briefly in the hope that the thread currently in the critical section will soon leave. If the other thread leaves the critical section, the spinning thread can immediately enter the critical section. Once the thread has spun for a predetermined count, the thread goes to sleep until the other thread eventually leaves the critical section. This approach represents a trade-off between the immediacy of spinning for access to the critical section and the poor utilization of resources that spinning causes.

Critical sections support this idea of spinning for a short time before sleeping. There are two ways of setting the number of times that a thread calling `EnterCriticalSection()` will spin before it goes to sleep. The critical section can be initialized with the value through the initialization call `InitializeCriticalSectionAndSpinCount()`, which takes the pointer to the critical section, and the spin count as parameters. Or, once the critical section has been created, the spin count can be set through a call to `SetCriticalSectionSpinCount()`. Listing 6.17 shows calls to these routines.

Listing 6.17 **Methods of Setting the Spin Count for a Critical Section**

```
InitializeCriticalSectionAndSpinCount( &critical, 1000 );
SetCriticalSectionSpinCount( &critical, 1000 );
```

Protecting Regions of Code with Mutexes

Mutexes are kernel objects, which enables them to be shared between processes. This also means that mutex-protected sections are heavier weight than critical sections.

Mutexes are created with a call to `CreateMutex()` or `CreateMutexEx()`, which was introduced in Windows Vista. The call will return the handle to the newly created mutex object.

The first parameter to the `CreateMutex()` call is a pointer to the security attributes, or zero if the default security attributes should be used. The second parameter is a boolean that indicates if the mutex should be created in the state of being already acquired by the calling thread. The final parameter is an optional name for the mutex.

The `CreateMutexEx` call takes the security attributes; an optional name for the mutex; a flag that has either the value 0 or the value `CREATE_MUTEX_INITIAL_OWNER`, which indicates that the mutex should be created as owned by the calling thread; and a mask that sets the access permissions for the mutex (this can be left as zero).

Once the application has finished with the mutex, the kernel resources need to be freed by a call to `CloseHandle()`. Listing 6.18 shows the process of creating and releasing a mutex.

Listing 6.18 **Creating and Disposing of Mutexes**

```
HANDLE mutex;
...
   mutex = CreateMutex( 0, 0, 0 );
...
   CloseHandle( mutex );
```

To acquire the mutex, the application makes a call to `WaitForSingleObject()`, which either returns with the mutex acquired or returns after the specified timeout. Once the thread has completed, the section of code protected by the mutex can be released with a call to `ReleaseMutex()`. The code in Listing 6.19 shows how to acquire and release the mutex.

Listing 6.19 **Acquiring and Releasing a Mutex**

```
volatile int counter = 0;
HANDLE mutex;
```

```
unsigned int __stdcall test( void * )
{
  while ( counter<100 )
  {
    WaitForSingleObject( mutex, INFINITE );
    int number = counter++;
    ReleaseMutex( mutex );
    printf( "ThreadID %i; value = %i, is prime = %i\n",
            GetCurrentThreadId(), number, isprime(number) );
  }
  return 0;
}

int _tmain(int argc, _TCHAR* argv[])
{
  HANDLE h1, h2;
  mutex = CreateMutex( 0, 0, 0 );
  h1 = (HANDLE)_beginthreadex( 0, 0, &test, (void*)0, 0, 0);
  h2 = (HANDLE)_beginthreadex( 0, 0, &test, (void*)1, 0, 0);
  WaitForSingleObject( h1, INFINITE );
  WaitForSingleObject( h2, INFINITE );
  CloseHandle( h1 );
  CloseHandle( h2 );
  getchar();
  CloseHandle(mutex);
  return 0;
}
```

Slim Reader/Writer Locks

Windows Vista introduced support for the *slim reader/writer lock,* which is useful in situations where data needs to be either read or updated. The lock allows multiple threads to have read access or a single thread to have write access to the data. The lock is initialized using a call to `InitializeSRWLock()`. Since the locks are essentially user variables and use no kernel resource, there is no equivalent function to delete a lock.

The call to acquire a lock as a reader is `AcquireSRWLockShared()`, and the call for a reader to release it is `ReleaseSRWLockShared()`. Multiple readers can share access to the lock; however, a writer must obtain exclusive access. The call to acquire the lock as a writer is `AcquireSRWLockExclusive()`, and the call for a writer to release the lock is `ReleaseSRWLockExclusive()`.

Listing 6.20 shows an example of using a slim reader/writer lock. The reader/writer lock is useful in this situation because both the update and the read require access to two elements. If there were not a lock around the update and read of the array, it would be likely that an update would cause a read to return inconsistent data from the array.

Listing 6.20 **Creating and Using a Slim Reader/Writer Lock**

```c
#include <process.h>
#include <windows.h>

int array[100][100];
SRWLOCK lock;

unsigned int __stdcall update( void *param )
{
  for (int y=0; y<100; y++)
    for (int x=0; x<100; x++)
    {
      AcquireSRWLockExclusive( &lock );
      array[x][y]++;
      array[y][x]--;
      ReleaseSRWLockExclusive( &lock );
    }
  return 0;
}

unsigned int __stdcall read( void * param )
{
  int value=0;
  for (int y=0; y<100; y++)
    for (int x=0; x<100; x++)
    {
      AcquireSRWLockShared( &lock );
      value = array[x][y] + array[y][x];
      ReleaseSRWLockShared( &lock );
    }
  printf( "Value = %i\n", value );
  return value;
}

int _tmain( int argc, _TCHAR* argv[] )
{
  HANDLE h1, h2;
  InitializeSRWLock( &lock );
  h1 = (HANDLE)_beginthreadex( 0, 0, &update, (void*)0, 0, 0);
  h2 = (HANDLE)_beginthreadex( 0, 0, &read,   (void*)0, 0, 0);
  WaitForSingleObject( h1, INFINITE );
  WaitForSingleObject( h2, INFINITE );
  CloseHandle( h1 );
  CloseHandle( h2 );
  getchar();
  return 0;
}
```

Windows 7 introduced two further function calls into the slim reader/writer API. In the Windows Vista API, function calls to acquire the reader/writer lock will return only once the lock has been acquired. In some situations, it is better to perform some other operation in the event that the lock is not available. The two functions that provide this are `TryAcquireSRWLockExclusive()` and `TryAcquireSRWLockShared()`. These two functions return immediately. If the lock is available, the function call will have acquired the lock for the thread, and the return value will be nonzero; if the lock is unavailable, the return value will be zero.

Semaphores

Semaphores are a way of keeping track of a count of numbers, as well as a way of communicating resource availability between threads. At the simplest level, they can be used as an alternative implementation of a mutex, while a more complex use would be to communicate readiness between multiple threads.

A semaphore can be created through a call to `CreateSemaphore()`, which takes four parameters. The first parameter is the security attributes, or it is null if the default is to be used. The second parameter is the initial value for the semaphore. The third parameter is the maximum value for the semaphore. The final parameter is an optional name for the semaphore. The name can be used when other threads or processes want to attach to the same semaphore. If a semaphore of the given name exists and it was created with the `SEMAPHORE_ALL_ACCESS` access right, then the function will return a handle to the existing semaphore.

The second way of creating a semaphore is through the `CreateSemaphoreEx()` call. This takes the same first four parameters but adds two more. The fifth parameter is a set of flags, but it must be passed the value zero. The sixth parameter is for access rights. Passing `SEMAPHORE_ALL_ACCESS` as this parameter will create a semaphore that can be shared between processes. The name of the shared semaphore also needs to be placed in the global namespace. Creating shared semaphores will be covered later in this chapter.

The final way of getting a handle to a semaphore is to call `OpenSemaphore()`, passing in three parameters. The first parameter gives the desired access rights. The second parameter is a boolean that indicates whether the handle to the semaphore should be inherited by child processes. This is one of the options available through the security attribute used by `SemaphoreCreate()` and `SemaphoreCreateEx()`. The third parameter is the name of the semaphore. This function call will not create the semaphore if it does not already exist.

Semaphores are kernel objects, so the create function will return a handle to the new semaphore. When the application has finished with the semaphore, it should release it with a call to `CloseHandle`. Once there are no outstanding handles to the semaphore, the kernel object is disposed of.

A semaphore can be decremented through a call to one of the wait functions. The one that is most likely to be useful is `WaitForSingleObject()`, which takes the handle of the semaphore and a timeout. The function will either return having decremented the semaphore or return when the timeout expires.

A semaphore can be incremented through a call to `ReleaseSemaphore()`. This call takes three parameters: the handle of the semaphore, the amount to increment the semaphore by, and an optional pointer to a LONG variable where the previous value will be written. Attempts to increment the semaphore beyond the maximum value that it can hold are ignored. It is important to notice that a semaphore has no concept of ownership, so it cannot tell whether a thread attempts to increment the semaphore by a greater amount than it was decremented.

Listing 6.21 shows an example of a semaphore being used as a replacement for a mutex. The semaphore is created to hold a maximum value of 1 and an initial value of 1. Two threads are created, and both threads execute the same code, which increments the variable `value` by 200. The end result of this is that the variable `value` should contain 400 when the application terminates.

Listing 6.21 **Using a Semaphore as a Mutex**

```
#include <windows.h>
#include <process.h>
#include <stdio.h>

HANDLE semaphore;
int value;

void addToValue( int increment )
{
  WaitForSingleObject( semaphore, INFINITE );
  value+=increment;
  ReleaseSemaphore( semaphore, 1, 0 );
}

unsigned int __stdcall test( void * )
{
  for ( int counter=0; counter<100; counter++ )
  {
    addToValue( 2 );
  }
  return 0;
}

int _tmain( int argc, _TCHAR* argv[])
{
  HANDLE h1, h2;
  value = 0;
  semaphore = CreateSemaphore( 0, 1, 1, 0 );
  h1 = (HANDLE)_beginthreadex( 0, 0, &test, (void*)0, 0, 0);
  h2 = (HANDLE)_beginthreadex( 0, 0, &test, (void*)0, 0, 0);
  WaitForSingleObject( h1, INFINITE );
```

```
    WaitForSingleObject( h2, INFINITE );
    CloseHandle( h1 );
    CloseHandle( h2 );
    CloseHandle( semaphore );
    printf( "Value = %i\n", value );
    getchar();
    return 0;
}
```

Condition Variables

Condition variables were introduced in Vista. They work with either a critical section or a slim reader/writer lock to allow threads to sleep until a condition becomes true. They are user constructs, so they cannot be shared across processes. The call `InitializeConditionVariable()` initializes the condition variable for use.

A thread uses a condition variable either by acquiring a slim reader/writer lock and then calling `SleepConditionVariableSRW()` or by entering a critical section and calling `SleepConditionVariableCS()`. When the threads are woken from the sleep call, they will again have acquired either the critical section lock or the reader/writer lock (depending on how the condition variable is being used). The first thing that the thread needs to do is test to determine whether the conditions it is waiting on are true, since it is possible for the thread to be woken when the conditions are not met. If the conditions have not been met, the thread should return to sleeping on the condition variable.

There are two calls to wake threads sleeping on a condition variable. `WakeConditionVariable()` wakes one of the threads waiting on a condition variable. `WakeAllConditionVariable()` wakes all the threads sleeping on a condition variable.

Listing 6.22 shows an example of using a condition variable to mediate a producer-consumer pairing of threads. The producer thread would add items onto a queue. To do this, the thread first needs to enter the critical section where it is safe to manipulate the queue data structure. Once the item has been added to the queue, it is safe to exit the critical section. The number of items originally in the queue is returned by the `addItemToQueue()` function. If there were no items in the queue, then it is possible that other threads are waiting on the condition variable and need to be woken up by the producer thread.

Listing 6.22 **Producer-Consumer Example Using a Condition Variable**

```
#include <windows.h>

CONDITION_VARIABLE CV;
CRITICAL_SECTION CS;

void addItem( int value )
{
```

```
  LONG oldQueueLength;
  EnterCriticalSection( &CS );
  oldQueueLength = queueLength;
  addItemToQueue( value );
  LeaveCriticalSection( &CS );
  if ( oldQueueLength==0 )          // If the queue was empty
  {
     WakeConditionVariable( &CV ); // Wake one sleeping thread
  }
}

int removeItem()
{
  int item;
  EnterCriticalSection( &CS );
  while ( QueueLength==0 )          // If the queue is empty
  {
     SleepConditionVariableCS( &CV, &CS, INFINITE );   // Sleep
  }
  item = removeItemFromQueue();
  LeaveCriticalSection( &CS );
  return item;
}

void _tmain()
{
  InitializeCriticalSection( &CS );
  InitializeConditionVariable( &CV );
  …
  DeleteCriticalSection( &CS );
}
```

The consumer thread enters the critical section to remove an item from the queue. If there are no items on the queue, it sleeps on the condition variable. When it is woken, either it is a spurious wake-up or there is an item in the queue. If the wake-up was spurious, the thread will return to sleep. Otherwise, it will remove an item from the queue, exit the critical section, and return the item from the queue to the calling function.

Signaling Event Completion to Other Threads or Processes

Events are used to signal the fact that an event has happened to one or more threads. It is possible to use semaphores, mutexes, or condition variables to perform the same task. The threads waiting for an event to occur will wait on that event object. The thread that completes the task will set the event into the signaled state and the waiting threads are then released. Events can be of two types, a *manually reset* event type, which requires the event to be reset before other threads will once again wait on it, or an *automatically reset* type, which will reset itself after a single thread has been allowed to pass.

Events are kernel objects, so the call to `CreateEvent()` will return a handle. The call requires four parameters. The first parameter is the security attribute that determines whether the handle will be inherited by child processes. The second parameter is a boolean that, when true, indicates that the event requires a manual reset or, when false, indicates that the event will automatically reset after a single thread has been released. The third parameter indicates whether the event should be created in a signaled state. The fourth parameter is an optional name for the event.

Existing events can be opened using a call to `OpenEvent()`. This call requires three parameters. The first parameter is the access permissions; if this is zero, default access permissions are requested. The second parameter is a boolean that indicates whether the handle should be inherited by child processes. The third parameter is the name of the event.

Since the event is a kernel object, it should be freed with a call to `CloseHandle()`.

A call to `SetEvent()` places the event into the signaled state. This allows threads waiting on the event using `WaitForSingleObject` to be released. If the event requires a manual reset to get out of the signaled state, then this can be achieved with a call to `ResetEvent()`, which also takes the handle to the event. If the event object resets automatically, then only a single thread will be released before the event is reset.

Listing 6.23 shows an example of using an event object to order two threads. An event object is created by the call to `CreateEvent()`. This object requires manual reset and is created in the unsignaled state. Two threads are then created. The first thread executes the routine `thread1()` and waits on the event. The second thread executes the routine `thread2()`, which prints a message and then signals the event object. The signal allows the first thread to continue execution, and it prints a second message.

Listing 6.23 **Using an Event Object to Enforce Execution Order**

```
#include <windows.h>
#include <process.h>
#include <stdio.h>

HANDLE hevent;

unsigned int __stdcall thread1(void *param)
{
  WaitForSingleObject(hevent,INFINITE);
  printf("Thread 1 done\n");
  return 0;
}

unsigned int __stdcall thread2(void *param)
{
  printf("Thread 2 done\n");
  SetEvent(hevent);
```

```
   return 0;
}


int _tmain(int argc, _TCHAR* argv[])
{
  HANDLE hthread1, hthread2;
  hevent=CreateEvent(0,0,0,0);
  hthread1=(HANDLE)_beginthreadex(0,0,&thread1,0,0,0);
  hthread2=(HANDLE)_beginthreadex(0,0,&thread2,0,0,0);
  WaitForSingleObject(hthread1,INFINITE);
  WaitForSingleObject(hthread2,INFINITE);
  CloseHandle(hthread2);
  CloseHandle(hthread1);
  CloseHandle(hevent);
  getchar();
  return 0;
}
```

Wide String Handling in Windows

Before we discuss the handling of multiple processes in Windows, it is necessary to have a short discussion of the handling of strings.

Since Windows NT 4, Windows has used Unicode as its default text encoding format. Unicode defines support for greater than 8-bit encoding of characters. Windows uses UTF-16 format, known as *wide character* encoding, which uses two bytes per character. Many Windows functions are defined with two entry points: a Unicode version that has a W appended, for wide character, or an ANSI character entry point that is appended with an A. For example, the `CreateMutex()` function call has a supporting `CreateMutexW()` and a `CreateMutexA()`. At compile time, the appropriate function call will be made depending on whether UNICODE is defined. Since Windows uses wide characters internally, the ANSI entry points are just wrappers around the wide versions of the function calls with appropriate string conversion.

The 16-bit character type is `wchar_t`. This can be used as a replacement for the `char` type. WCHAR is an equivalent method of specifying a wide string. However, strings of characters in source code are interpreted as being ANSI 8-bit characters, which is why they need to be specified as being wide characters. This can be performed using the L specifier or using the `TEXT()` macro, as demonstrated in Listing 6.24. We will need to use these macros in later examples when we specify string constants.

Listing 6.24 **Assigning a Compile-Time Value to a Wide Character String**

```
wchar_t mystring1[] = L"Some text";
WCHAR   mystring2[] = TEXT("More text");
```

The TEXT() macro is useful in that when UNICODE is defined, it translates a string to wide character format. When UNICODE is not defined, it leaves the string as ANSI 8-bit text. The TCHAR type behaves in a similar way, resolving to wchar_t when UNICODE is defined, or char otherwise.

Some functions are defined as macros that resolve differently depending on whether UNICODE is defined. For example, the main function _tmain() resolves either to wmain() when UNICODE is defined or to main() otherwise. Similarly, _tprintf() will either resolve to wprintf() or printf().

Creating Processes

To create a new process, the first process calls CreateProcess(), which takes a number of parameters. The three critical parameters are the name (and any parameters) of the process to be run, together with a pointer to a STARTUPINFO structure and a PROCESS_INFORMATION structure. Table 6.4 shows the full parameters to this function.

Table 6.4 **Parameters Passed to CreateProcess()**

Parameter Type	Comment
LPCWSTR	Name of the application.
LPWSTR	Command line.
LPSECURITY_ATTRIBUTES	Pointer to security attributes for the child process.
LPSECURITY_ATTRIBUTES	Pointer to security attributes for the first thread in the child process.
BOOL	A boolean that indicates whether the created process should inherit the handles from the calling process.
DWORD	An optional set of process creation flags and process priority flags. These flags control various characteristics of the created process such as whether the process has a window or whether the main thread is created in the suspended state. The flags also control the scheduling priority for the process, which in turn determines how much share of the CPU the process is given.
LPVOID	An optional pointer to a new set of runtime environment strings. If this is null, the new process will inherit the runtime environment of the calling process.
LPCWSTR	An optional pointer to a string containing the current directory for the process. If this parameter is null, the process inherits the runtime directory of the calling process.
LPSTARTUPINFOW	Pointer to the STARTUPINFO structure.
LPPROCESS_INFORMATION	Pointer to the PROCESS_INFORMATION structure.

The first parameter is the application name, and the second parameter is the command line. These two parameters work together. If either is null, the other is used as the entire command line. Otherwise, the application named by the first argument is executed but passed the command line given by the second argument. This means that the first parameter of the command line should be a repeat of the name of the application.

There are two further considerations: The Unicode version of this function, `CreateProcessW()`, is called, and the command line can be modified; hence, it should always be stored in a variable rather than a constant string. Second, if the application name is null, then the application executed will be the first whitespace-delimited text in the command line. If the path to the application contains a space, then the entire path and name should be enclosed in quotes.

The third and fourth parameters are optional pointers to `SECURITY_ATTRIBUTES`. The first gives the attributes for the created process, and the second of these is attributes for the first thread of the created process. These attributes principally determine whether child processes of the created process will inherit any handles owned by the created process. A null value for these pointers provides the created process with the default attributes.

Both the `STARTUPINFO` and `PROCESS_INFORMATION` structures should be zero-filled before the call. The `cb` member of the `STARTUPINFO` structure needs to be set to the size of the structure. The call to `CreateProcess()` will record information in these structures. The most important information will be the handle of the new process that is recorded in the `hProcess` member of the `PROCESS_INFORMATION` structure.

Listing 6.25 shows the steps necessary to create a new process. If the application is started with a command-line parameter, the process will print this out and then create a child process without any parameters. If the process is started without any parameters, it prints out a message indicating this and exits.

Listing 6.25 **Starting a New Process**

```
#include <Windows.h>

int _tmain( int argc, _TCHAR* argv[] )
{
  STARTUPINFO startup_info;
  PROCESS_INFORMATION process_info;

  if ( argc>1 )
  {
    wprintf( L"Argument %s\n", argv[1] );
    wprintf( L"Starting child process\n" );

    ZeroMemory( &process_info, sizeof(process_info) );
    ZeroMemory( &startup_info, sizeof(startup_info) );
    startup_info.cb = sizeof(startup_info);
```

```
       if (CreateProcess( argv[0], 0, 0, 0, 0, 0, 0, 0,
                          &startup_info, &process_info )==0 )
     {
        printf( "ERROR %i\n", GetLastError() );
     }
     WaitForSingleObject( process_info.hProcess, INFINITE );
   }
   else
   {
      printf( "No arguments\n" );
   }
   getchar();
}
```

The handle of the created process is returned in `process_info.hProcess`. This handle is used in the call to `WaitForSingleObject()`. This call returns when the child process exits.

The call to `getchar()` at the end of the code is there to wait for the Enter key to be pressed before the process exits.

To pass arguments to a child process, it is necessary to repeat the application name as the first command-line parameter. The entire command line gets passed to the child process. Listing 6.26 shows the situation where the child process is started with a single additional argument.

Listing 6.26 **Passing Arguments to a New Process**

```
#include <Windows.h>

int _tmain( int argc, _TCHAR* argv[] )
{
  STARTUPINFO startup_info;
  PROCESS_INFORMATION process_info;

  if ( argc==1 )
  {
    printf( "No arguments given starting child process\n" );
    wchar_t argument[256];
    wsprintf( argument, L"\"%s\" Hello", argv[0] );
    ZeroMemory( &process_info, sizeof(process_info) );
    ZeroMemory( &startup_info, sizeof(startup_info) );
    startup_info.cb = sizeof(startup_info);

    if (CreateProcess( argv[0], argument, 0, 0, 0, 0, 0, 0,
                       &startup_info, &process_info )==0 )
    {
      printf( "ERROR %i\n", GetLastError() );
    }
```

```
    WaitForSingleObject( process_info.hProcess, INFINITE );
  }
  else
  {
    wprintf( L"Argument %s\n", argv[1] );
  }
  getchar();
}
```

Sharing Memory Between Processes

It is possible to share memory between processes. Once one process has set up a region of memory with suitable sharing attributes, another process can open that region of memory and map it into its address space.

Shared memory uses the file mapping function `CreateFileMapping()` with parameter `INVALID_HANDLE_VALUE` to create a handle to a region of shared memory. This can then be mapped into the process with a call to `MapViewOfFile()`. The steps for attaching to an existing region of shared memory are similar, except that the function `OpenFileMapping()` is used to obtain the handle.

The call to `CreateFileMapping()` takes six parameters, as shown in Table 6.5.

Table 6.5 **Parameters Passed to** `CreateFileMapping()`

Parameter Type	Comment
HANDLE	INVALID_HANDLE_VALUE that indicates this call should create shared memory.
LPSECURITY_ATTRIBUTES	Optional pointer to security attributes that determine whether the handle can be inherited by child processes.
DWORD	Page protection attributes for the created memory. For shared memory, this will most likely be some combination of read or write access.
DWORD	High-order DWORD (an unsigned 4-byte integer) of the size of the region.
DWORD	Low-order DWORD of the size.
LPCTSTR	Optional name of the mapping object.

An object can be shared between processes either by sharing the object's handle, which will be discussed in the section "Inheriting Handles in Child Processes," or by using a common name. The name can contain any character except a backslash and must start with either the global namespace identifier `Global\` or the local namespace identifier `Local\`. The global namespace is shared by all users, whereas the local namespace is private to each user.

The `OpenFileMapping()` call that opens an existing file mapping object takes three parameters. The first parameter gives the security attributes for the mapping object, which usually will be `FILE_MAP_ALL_ACCESS` to allow both reading and writing to the shared memory. The second parameter is a boolean that determines whether the handle can be inherited by child processes. The third parameter is the name of the mapping object.

Although the `CreateFileMapping()` call creates the mapping object in the kernel, it does not actually map the object into user space. The call to `MapViewOfFile()` causes the shared object to be mapped into memory. The return value of this call is a pointer to the base address of the memory. This call takes five parameters, as shown in Table 6.6.

Table 6.6 **Parameters Passed to** `MapViewOfFile()`

Parameter Type	Comment
`HANDLE`	Handle from either `CreateFileMapping()` or `OpenFileMapping()`.
`DWORD`	Access permissions for the memory. This is likely to be `FILE_MAP_ALL_ACCESS` for processes that need to both read and write the shared memory.
`DWORD`	High-order DWORD of an offset into the shared memory.
`DWORD`	Low-order DWORD of an offset into the shared memory.
`SIZE_T`	Size of the shared memory region. Passing zero as this parameter makes the size the same as the size allocated in the mapping object.

The third and fourth parameters are the high-order and low-order DWORDs of an offset into the shared memory. This will be returned as the base address of the pointer. In general, the required offset into the shared memory will be zero, so both of these parameters will also be zero.

Once the process has finished with the shared memory, it needs to be unmapped with a call to `UnmapViewOfFile()`, which takes the base address of the shared memory as a parameter, and then the handle can be closed with a call to `CloseHandle()`.

The example in Listing 6.27 shows how a region of memory can be created and then shared between two processes. If the application is started without any parameters, it will create a child process. The parent process will also create a region of shared memory and store a string into the shared memory. The shared memory is given the name **shared-memory** and is created in the **Local** namespace. Hence, it is visible to all the processes owned by the user.

Listing 6.27 **Creating and Using Shared Memory**

```
#include <Windows.h>
#include <Windows.h>
```

```c
int _tmain(int argc, _TCHAR* argv[])
{
  STARTUPINFO startup_info;
  PROCESS_INFORMATION process_info;

  HANDLE filehandle;
  TCHAR ID[] = TEXT("Local\\sharedmemory");
  char* memory;

  if (argc==1)
  {
    filehandle = CreateFileMapping( INVALID_HANDLE_VALUE,
                               NULL, PAGE_READWRITE, 0, 1024, ID);
    memory = (char*)MapViewOfFile( filehandle, FILE_MAP_ALL_ACCESS,
                             0, 0, 0 );
    sprintf_s( memory, 1024, "%s", "Data from first process" );
    printf( "First process: %s\n", memory );

    ZeroMemory( &process_info, sizeof(process_info) );
    ZeroMemory( &startup_info, sizeof(startup_info) );
    startup_info.cb = sizeof(startup_info);

    wchar_t commandline[256];
    wsprintf( commandline, L"\"%s\" Child\n", argv[0] );

    CreateProcessW( argv[0], commandline, 0, 0, 0, 0, 0, 0,
                    &startup_info, &process_info );
    WaitForSingleObject(process_info.hProcess,INFINITE);

    UnmapViewOfFile( memory );
    CloseHandle( filehandle );
  }
  else
  {
    filehandle = OpenFileMapping( FILE_MAP_ALL_ACCESS, 0, ID );
    memory = (char*)MapViewOfFile( filehandle, FILE_MAP_ALL_ACCESS,
                              0, 0, 0 );

    printf( "Second process: %s\n", memory );

    UnmapViewOfFile( memory );
    CloseHandle( filehandle );
  }
  getchar();
  return 0;
}
```

The child process attaches to the shared memory and can print out the value of the string stored there by the parent process. One the child process has printed this string, it unmaps the memory and closes the file handle before exiting. Once the child process has exited, the parent process is free to unmap the memory, close the file handle, and exit.

Inheriting Handles in Child Processes

Child processes can inherit the handles to resources owned by the parent process. In this instance, the handles are identical values, but the parent process needs to pass these values to the child. The simplest way of achieving this is to pass the values through the command line.

The other constraint on this is that the handles must have been created with the property of being inherited by the child process, and the child process must be created with the parameter that enables it to inherit the handles from its parent.

Listing 6.28 shows an example of passing a handle to shared memory to the child process through the command line. The program is broadly the same as the one shown in Listing 6.27. However, there are a number of changes indicated in bold.

Listing 6.28 **Passing a Handle to Shared Memory to a Child Process**

```
#include <Windows.h>

int _tmain( int argc, _TCHAR* argv[] )
{
  STARTUPINFO startup_info;
  PROCESS_INFORMATION process_info;
  SECURITY_ATTRIBUTES secat;
  HANDLE filehandle;
  TCHAR ID[] = TEXT("Local\\foo");
  wchar_t* memory;

  if ( argc==1 )
  { // Parent process
    secat.nLength = sizeof(secat);   // Set up security attibutes
    secat.bInheritHandle = true;     // So handle can be inherited
    secat.lpSecurityDescriptor = NULL;

    filehandle = CreateFileMapping( INVALID_HANDLE_VALUE, &secat,
                         PAGE_READWRITE, 0, 1024, ID );
    memory = (wchar_t*)MapViewOfFile( filehandle,
                         FILE_MAP_ALL_ACCESS, 0, 0, 0);

    // Setup command line using shared memory
    swprintf( memory, 1024, L"\"%s\" %i", argv[0], filehandle);
    printf( "First process memory: %S handle:%i\n", memory, filehandle);
```

```
    ZeroMemory( &process_info, sizeof(process_info) );
    ZeroMemory( &startup_info, sizeof(startup_info) );
    startup_info.cb = sizeof(startup_info);

    // Start child process
    CreateProcess( NULL, memory, 0, 0, true, 0, 0, 0,
                   &startup_info, &process_info);
    WaitForSingleObject( process_info.hProcess, INFINITE );

    UnmapViewOfFile( memory );
    CloseHandle( filehandle );
  }
  else
  {
    filehandle=(HANDLE)_wtoi( argv[1] );   // Get handle from argv[1]
    memory = (wchar_t*)MapViewOfFile( filehandle,
                                  FILE_MAP_ALL_ACCESS, 0, 0, 0 );

    printf( "Second process memory: %S handle: %i\n",
            memory, filehandle );

    UnmapViewOfFile( memory );
    CloseHandle( filehandle );
  }
  getchar();
  return 0;
}
```

The first important change is the use of SECURITY_ATTRIBUTES when the mapping object is created. These security attributes have the bInheritHandle property set to true, which will allow the handle to the mapping object to be inherited by any child processes.

The command line to the child process is built up out of the process name, which is argv[0] and the handle of the mapping object.

The final change in creating the child process is that now the call to CreateProcess() passes true for the parameter, which determines whether the child process should inherit the handles of the parent process.

The code for the child process is similar to the previous code with the exception that the handle to the mapping object is extracted from the command-line parameter argv[1].

Naming Mutexes and Sharing Them Between Processes

The easiest way to share a mutex between processes is for the mutex to be created with a name. Then other processes can use the OpenMutex() or CreateMutex() function to obtain a handle to the mutex. There are several complexities involved in this:

- Only one of the processes can create the mutex. The others can only open the existing mutex.
- The name of the mutex needs to be unique. If any object of the same name already exists, then the mutex will fail to be created.
- The name of the mutex needs to be passed to the other processes.

All of these issues are surmountable, but they add some complexity.

The code in Listing 6.29 creates two copies of the same processes and enables them to share a mutex.

Listing 6.29 **Sharing Mutexes Between Processes**

```
#include <Windows.h>

int _tmain( int argc, _TCHAR* argv[] )
{
  HANDLE sharedmutex;
  STARTUPINFO startup_info;
  PROCESS_INFORMATION process_info;


  ZeroMemory( &process_info, sizeof(process_info) );
  ZeroMemory( &startup_info, sizeof(startup_info) );
  startup_info.cb = sizeof(startup_info);

  sharedmutex=CreateMutex( 0, 0, L"mymutex12234" );
  if ( GetLastError() != ERROR_ALREADY_EXISTS )
  {
    if ( CreateProcess( argv[0], 0, 0, 0, 0, 0, 0, 0,
                        &startup_info, &process_info )==0 )
    {
      printf( "ERROR %i\n", GetLastError() );
    }

    WaitForInputIdle( process_info.hProcess, INFINITE );
  }

  WaitForSingleObject( sharedmutex, INFINITE );

  for (int i=0; i<1000; i++)
  {
    printf( "Process %i Count %i\n", GetCurrentProcessId(), i );
  }
  ReleaseMutex( sharedmutex );
  CloseHandle( sharedmutex );
```

```
    getchar();
    return 0;
}
```

The mutex is created through a call to `CreateMutex()`. If the mutex already exists, then a handle to the existing mutex is returned, and the error condition is set to `ERROR_ALREADY_EXISTS`. If this is not the error condition, then it is assumed by the code that this means that the mutex was created by the calling process and therefore that the calling process needs to start a second copy of itself.

The call to `CreateMutex()` takes the name of the mutex. In this case, the name is `mymutex12234`. The string is specified with an uppercase `L`, which tells the compiler to make it a wide-character string. The same effect could have been achieved by wrapping the string in `TEXT(...)`.

In this example, the shared mutex is used to ensure that only one of the two processes counts up to 1,000 at a time. If there was no mutex, then both processes could be active simultaneously, and the console output would be a mix of the output from both processes. Using the mutex, the output is from just one of the processes at a time.

Communicating with Pipes

Pipes are a method of streamed communication where data written to a pipe by one thread can be read from the pipe by a different thread. Pipes on Windows enable communication between threads within a process, between threads in different processes, or even between threads on different systems.

Pipes are available in two flavors. A *named pipe* can be used to uniquely identify a connection by name. An *anonymous pipe* does not have an explicit name, so processes wanting to communicate need to obtain its handle. On Windows, anonymous pipes are implemented using a unique name, but this name is not specified by the application when the pipe is created.

To create an anonymous pipe, the application should call `CreatePipe()`. This takes four parameters. The first and second parameters are pointers to the variables to hold the read and write handles for the pipe. The third parameter is the security attributes for the pipe, which, if null, gives the default attributes that do not allow child processes to inherit the handle of the pipe. Passing a pointer to a security attributes object is necessary if inheritance of the handle is desired. The fourth parameter is a hint as to the appropriate size of buffer to use for the pipe. A value of zero indicates that the default value should be used.

To create a named pipe, an application needs to call `CreateNamedPipe()`. This creates a pipe and returns a handle to the pipe. The same handle can be used for read or write operations on the pipe, assuming the pipe was set up to allow the operation. This function takes eight parameters; these are listed in Table 6.7.

Table 6.7 Parameters Passed to `CreateNamedPipe()`

Parameter Type	Comment
LPCWSTR	The name of the pipe. This needs to be of the format '\\.\pipe\name' where name is replaced by the desired name of the pipe. Pipes on the local machine are specified using '\\.'. The next part of the name is the 'pipe\' declaration, followed by the actual name of the desired pipe.
DWORD	The access mode for the pipe. The typical values of this flag will be PIPE_ACCESS_DUPLEX, which creates a pipe that can be read or written to; PIPE_ACCESS_INBOUND, which creates a pipe that can only be read from; or PIPE_ACCESS_OUTBOUND, which creates a pipe that can only be written to. PIPE_ACCESS_OUTBOUND and PIPE_ACCESS_INBOUND need to be used as a pair in order to make a successful connection.
DWORD	The mode that the pipe operates. They can enable the pipe to carry a stream of data or a stream of messages.
DWORD	The number of instances allowed for the pipe. The value PIPE_UNLIMITED_INSTANCES indicates that the maximum number of instances is limited only by system resources.
DWORD	The size in bytes of the output buffer.
DWORD	The size in bytes of the input buffer.
DWORD	The timeout value for reads or writes. A value of zero uses the default time out of 50ms.
LPSECURITY_ ATTRIBUTES	An optional pointer to security attributes that can be set if the handle to the pipe should be inherited by child processes.

Once a pipe has been created, data can be sent through the pipe using the `WriteFile()` call and read from the pipe using the `ReadFile()` call. The parameters used in both calls are similar and are shown in Table 6.8.

Table 6.8 Parameters Passed to `ReadFile()` and `WriteFile()`

Parameter Type	Comment
HANDLE	The handle of the pipe
LPVOID	The address of the buffer where data is to be stored if the call is to ReadFile() or sent if the call is to WriteFile().
DWORD	The size of the buffer for ReadFile() or the amount of data to be sent for WriteFile().
LPDWORD	Pointer to a variable where the amount of data is read or the amount of data written will be recorded.
LPOVERLAPPED	A pointer to an OVERLAPPED structure, the use of which would enable the function call to return immediately and allow the processing of the read or write to complete later.

The pipe must be closed with a call to `CloseHandle()` once the application has finished using it.

Listing 6.30 shows an example of two threads using an anonymous pipe to communicate. The pipe is created through a call to `CreatePipe()` that returns both a read and a write handle for the pipe.

Listing 6.30 **Using an Anonymous Pipe to Communicate Between Two Threads**

```
#include <windows.h>
#include <process.h>

HANDLE readpipe,writepipe;

unsigned int __stdcall stage1( void * param )
{
  char buffer[200];
  DWORD length;
  for ( int i=0; i<10; i++ )
  {
    sprintf( buffer, "Text %i", i );
    WriteFile( writepipe, buffer, strlen(buffer)+1, &length, 0 );
  }
  CloseHandle( writepipe );
  return 0;
}

unsigned int __stdcall stage2( void * param )
{
  char buffer[200];
  DWORD length;
  while ( ReadFile( readpipe, buffer, 200, &length, 0 ) )
  {
    DWORD offset=0;
    while ( offset<length )
    {
      printf( "%s\n", &buffer[offset] );
      offset += strlen( &buffer[offset] )+1;
    }
  }
  CloseHandle( readpipe );
  return 0;
}


int _tmain( int argc, _TCHAR* argv[] )
{
  HANDLE thread1,thread2;
```

```
CreatePipe( &readpipe, &writepipe, 0, 0 );
thread1 = (HANDLE)_beginthreadex( 0, 0, &stage1, 0, 0, 0 );
thread2 = (HANDLE)_beginthreadex( 0, 0, &stage2, 0, 0, 0 );
WaitForSingleObject( thread1, INFINITE );
WaitForSingleObject( thread2, INFINITE );
getchar();
return 0;
}
```

The application in Listing 6.30 models a pipeline where one thread does the initial processing before passing the data onto a second thread for more processing. In the code, the first thread places text messages into the pipe using a call to `WriteFile()`. The second thread receives and prints out these messages.

There is a slight complication in the processing necessary to handle messages placed in a pipe. The pipe is a stream of bytes, so multiple messages become concatenated. The thread that handles the incoming messages must have some additional processing to ensure that all the messages in the buffer are processed before attempting to read the next set of messages. Notice that in this simplified example, the buffer is large enough to hold all the messages sent. In a more realistic example, the receiving thread would have to handle the situation where one message was split between two reads from the pipe.

Communicating Using Sockets

The Windows Sockets API is based on the BSD Sockets API, so many of the calls are very similar. There are some minor differences in setup. The most obvious differences are the requirements for header files. Listing 6.31 shows the steps necessary to include the networking sockets functions. The Windows header automatically includes the 1.1 version of the Windows socket library. The `#define WIN32_LEAN_AND_MEAN` avoids the inclusion of this header and allows the application to include the 2.0 version of the Windows socket library.

The Microsoft compiler also allows the source to contain a directive indicating which libraries are to be linked into the executable. In this case, the library is `ws2_32.lib`; this is more convenient than having to specify it on the command line. We also allocate a global variable that will be used to store the handle of an event object. The event object will be used to ensure that the server thread is ready before the client thread sends any data.

Listing 6.31 **Including the Header Files for Windows Sockets**

```
#ifndef WIN32_LEAN_AND_MEAN
#define WIN32_LEAN_AND_MEAN
#endif
#include <windows.h>
#include <process.h>
```

```
#include <winsock2.h>
#include <stdio.h>

#pragma comment( lib, "ws2_32.lib" )

  HANDLE hEvent;
```

Listing 6.32 shows the code for the main thread. The first action that the main thread needs to take is to start the Windows sockets library with a call into `WSAStartup()`; this takes two parameters. The first parameter is the version number of the library that the application requires; version 2.2 is current. The second parameter is the address of a `WSADATA` structure where the description of the sockets implementation will be stored.

Listing 6.32 **The Main Thread Is Responsible for Starting Both the Client and Server Threads**

```
int _tmain( int argc, _TCHAR* argv[] )
{
  HANDLE serverthread, clientthread;
  WSADATA wsaData;

  WSAStartup( MAKEWORD(2,2), &wsaData );
  hEvent = CreateEvent( 0, true, 0, 0 );

  serverthread = (HANDLE)_beginthreadex( 0, 0, &server, 0, 0, 0 );

  clientthread = (HANDLE)_beginthreadex( 0, 0, &client, 0, 0, 0 );
  WaitForSingleObject( clientthread, INFINITE );
  CloseHandle( clientthread );

  CloseHandle( hEvent );
  getchar();
  WSACleanup();
  return 0;
}
```

As previously mentioned, the code uses an event object to ensure that the server thread starts up before the client thread sends a request. The event is created through a call to `CreateEvent()`. The event is created unsignaled so that it can be signaled by the server thread, and this signaling will enable the client thread to progress. The event is set up to require a manual reset so that once it has been signaled, it remains in that state. This ensures that any later client threads will not block on the event.

The main thread then starts the server thread and the client thread using calls to `_beginthreadex()`. It waits until the client thread completes before exiting. The final action of the main thread is to call `WSACleanup()` to close down the sockets library.

Listing 6.33 shows the code for the client thread. The client thread is going to send data to the server and then print the response from the server. The client thread first opens up a socket and then waits for the event object to become signaled, indicating that the server is ready, before continuing.

Listing 6.33 **Code for the Client Thread**

```
unsigned int __stdcall client( void * data )
{
  SOCKET ConnectSocket = socket( AF_INET, SOCK_STREAM, 0 );

  WaitForSingleObject( hEvent, INFINITE );

  struct sockaddr_in server;
  ZeroMemory( &server, sizeof(server) );
  server.sin_family = AF_INET;
  server.sin_addr.s_addr = inet_addr( "127.0.0.1" );
  server.sin_port = 7780;

  connect( ConnectSocket, (struct sockaddr*)&server, sizeof(server) );

  printf( "Sending 'abcd' to server\n" );
  char buffer[1024];
  ZeroMemory( buffer, sizeof(buffer) );
  strncpy_s( buffer, 1024, "abcd", 5 );
  send( ConnectSocket, buffer, strlen(buffer)+1, 0 );

  ZeroMemory( buffer, sizeof(buffer) );
  recv( ConnectSocket, buffer, 1024, 0 );
  printf( "Got '%s' from server\n", buffer );

  printf( "Close client\n" );
  shutdown( ConnectSocket, SD_BOTH );
  closesocket( ConnectSocket );
  return 0;
}
```

The code uses the socket to connect to port 7780 on the localhost (localhost is defined as the IP address 127.0.0.1). Once connected, it sends the string "abcd" to the server and then waits to receive a string back from the server. Once it receives the returned string, it shuts down the connection and then closes the socket.

Listing 6.34 shows the code for the server thread. The server thread does not actually handle the response to any client thread. It exists only to accept incoming connections and to pass the details of this connection onto a newly created thread that will handle the response.

Listing 6.34 **Code for the Server Thread**

```
unsigned int __stdcall server( void * data )
{
  SOCKET newsocket;
  SOCKET ServerSocket =  socket( AF_INET, SOCK_STREAM, 0 );

  struct sockaddr_in server;
  ZeroMemory( &server, sizeof(server) );
  server.sin_family = AF_INET;
  server.sin_addr.s_addr = INADDR_ANY;
  server.sin_port = 7780;

  bind( ServerSocket,(struct sockaddr*)&server, sizeof(server) );
  listen( ServerSocket, SOMAXCONN );

  SetEvent(hEvent);

  while ( (newsocket = accept( ServerSocket, 0, 0) )!=INVALID_SOCKET )
  {
    HANDLE newthread;
    newthread=(HANDLE)_beginthread( &handleecho, 0, (void*)newsocket);
  }

  printf( "Close server\n" );
  shutdown( ServerSocket, SD_BOTH );
  closesocket( ServerSocket );
  return 0;
}
```

Listing 6.35 shows the code for the thread that will actually respond to the client. This thread will loop around, receiving data from the client thread and sending the same data back to the client thread until it receives a return value that indicates the socket has closed or some other error condition. At that point, the thread will shut down and close the socket.

Listing 6.35 **Code for the Echo Thread**

```
void handleecho( void * data )
{
   char buffer[1024];
   int count;
   ZeroMemory( buffer, sizeof(buffer) );
   int socket=(int)data;
   while ( (count = recv( socket, buffer, 1023, 0) ) >0 )
   {
```

```
    printf( "Received %s from client\n", buffer );
    int ret = send( socket, buffer, count, 0 );
  }
  printf( "Close echo thread\n" );
  shutdown( socket, SD_BOTH );
  closesocket( socket );
}
```

The first activity of the server thread is to open a socket. It then binds this socket to accept any connections to port 7780. The socket also needs to be placed into the listen state; the value SOMAXCONN contains the maximum number of connections that will be queued for acceptance. Once these steps have been completed, the server thread signals the event, which then enables the client thread to attempt to connect.

The main thread then waits in a loop accepting connections until it receives a connection identified as INVALID_SOCKET. This will happen when the Windows socket library is shut down and is how the server thread will exit cleanly when the other thread exits.

Every time the server thread accepts a connection, a new thread is created, and the identification of this new connection is passed into the newly created thread. It is important to notice that the call to create the thread that will actually handle the work is _beginthread(). The _beginthread() call will create a new thread that does not leave resources that need to be cleaned up with a call to CloseHandle() when it exits. In contrast, the client and server threads were created by the master thread with a call to _beginthreadex(), which means that they will have resources assigned to them until a call to CloseHandle() is made.

When the loop finally receives an INVALID_SOCKET, the server thread shuts down and then closes the socket.

The code for Windows is sufficiently similar to that for Unix-like operating systems that it is possible to convert between the two. Although the example program is relatively simple, it illustrates the key steps necessary for communication between two threads, two processes, or two systems.

Atomic Updates of Variables

The Windows API provides a large number of atomic operations, which are referred to in Windows terminology as *interlocked functions*. For the full list of functions, refer to the Windows documentation. An example of one such function is InterlockedExchangeAdd(), which atomically adds a value to a variable of type LONG (in Windows a long variable is 32 bits in size, and a LONGLONG is 64 bits in size; the size does not change depending on whether the application is 32-bit or 64-bit). Listing 6.36 shows an example of using InterlockedExchangeAdd() to atomically increment a variable by ten.

Listing 6.36 **Example of Using** `InterlockedAdd()`

```
#include <windows.h>

void update( LONG* value )
{
  InterlockedExchangeAdd( value, 10 );
}
```

The range of atomic operations available encompasses *and*, *or*, *xor*, *add*, *increment*, and *decrement*. All the functions are available for `long` and `longlong` data types; some of them are also available for smaller data types like `char`.

There are also some functions that modify the variable and return the old value. `InterlockedCompareExchange()` performs a compare and swap operation where if the value of the variable matches the expected value, the value of the variable is exchanged with a new value. `InterlockedBitTestAndSet()` returns the value of a specified bit in the variable and sets its new value to one. Similarly, `InterlockedBitTestAndReset()` provides the same return value but sets the new value to zero.

The code in Listing 6.37 creates two threads and uses `InterlockedIncrement()` to increment the variable `counter` shared between the two threads. This approach is lower latency than using a mutex or some other synchronization mechanism.

Listing 6.37 **Using Atomic Operations to Protect a Shared Variable**

```
#include <math.h>
#include <stdio.h>
#include <windows.h>
#include <process.h>

int isprime( int number )
{
  int i;
  for (i = 2; i < (int)( sqrt( (float)number )+1.0 ); i++ )
  {
    if ( number%i == 0) { return 0; }
  }
  return 1;
}
volatile long counter = 0;

unsigned int __stdcall test( void * )
{
  while ( counter<100 )
  {
```

```
    int number = InterlockedIncrement( &counter );
    printf( "ThreadID %i; value = %i, is prime = %i\n",
            GetCurrentThreadId(), number, isprime(number) );
  }
  return 0;
}

int _tmain( int argc, _TCHAR* argv[] )
{
    HANDLE h1, h2;
    h1 = (HANDLE)_beginthreadex( 0, 0, &test, (void*)0, 0, 0);
    h2 = (HANDLE)_beginthreadex( 0, 0, &test, (void*)0, 0, 0);
    WaitForSingleObject( h1, INFINITE );
    WaitForSingleObject( h2, INFINITE );
    CloseHandle( h1 );
    CloseHandle( h2 );
    getchar();
    return 0;
}
```

Most of these functions enforce full memory ordering, so all memory operations prior to the call become visible to other processors before the atomic operation completes and any operations performed after the atomic operation becomes visible to other processors as happening after the atomic operation.

Allocating Thread-Local Storage

Thread-local storage enables each thread in an application to store private copies of data. Each thread accesses the data in the same way but cannot see the values held by other threads. In essence, it is "global" data that has scope limited to the executing thread.

There are two approaches to thread-local storage. The easiest approach is to use the __declspec(thread) specifier to allocate a thread-local variable. Listing 6.38 shows an example of this. In this code, each thread holds the value passed into it in a thread-local variable.

Listing 6.38 **Using** __declspec(thread) **to Allocate a Thread-Local Variable**

```
#include <windows.h>
#include <process.h>

__declspec(thread) int number=0;

unsigned int __stdcall work( void *param )
{
  number = (int)param;
```

```
  printf( "Number = %i\n", number );
  return 0;
}

int _tmain( int argc, _TCHAR* argv[] )
{
  HANDLE hthreads[8];
  for (int i=0; i<8; i++)
  {
    hthreads[i]=(HANDLE) _beginthreadex(0, 0, &work, (void*)i, 0, 0 );
  }

  WaitForMultipleObjects( 8, hthreads, 1, INFINITE );

  for (int i=0; i<8; i++) { CloseHandle( hthreads[i] ); }
  getchar();
  return 0;
}
```

An alternative approach is to use the thread-local storage API. A global index needs to be allocated by a call to `TlsAlloc()`. This index is shared between all threads, but the data that each thread stores in the index will be private to the calling thread. The call `TlsFree()` can be used to release a global index when the thread-local storage that it provides is no longer needed.

Each thread can store data at the index with a call to `TlsSetValue()` and can read the thread-local data with a call to `TlsGetValue()`.

In Listing 6.39, thread-local storage is used to hold the value passed into each thread. When each thread is created, it gets passed a unique value. This value is stored in thread-local storage by the routine `setdata()`. The routine `getdata()` retrieves the thread-local value. Each thread calls `setdata()` and then sleeps for a second to allow the other threads to run before retrieving the data with a call to `getdata()`.

Listing 6.39 **Using Thread-Local Storage**

```
#include <windows.h>
#include <process.h>
#include <stdio.h>

DWORD TLSIndex;

void setdata( int value )
{
  printf( "Thread %i: Set value = %i\n", GetCurrentThreadId(), value );
  TlsSetValue( TLSIndex, (void*)value );
}
```

```
void getdata()
{
  int value;
  value = (int)TlsGetValue( TLSIndex );
  printf( "Thread %i: Has value = %i\n", GetCurrentThreadId(), value );
}

unsigned int __stdcall workerthread( void * data )
{
  int value = (int)data;
  printf( "Thread %i: Got value = %i\n", GetCurrentThreadId(), value );
  setdata( value );
  Sleep( 1000 );
  getdata();
  return 0;
}

int _tmain( int argc, _TCHAR* argv[] )
{
  HANDLE handles[8];
  TLSIndex = TlsAlloc();
  for (int i=0; i<8; i++)
  {
    handles[i] = (HANDLE)_beginthreadex( 0, 0, &workerthread,
                                         (void*)i, 0, 0 );
  }
  for (int i=0; i<8; i++)
  {
    WaitForSingleObject( handles[i], INFINITE );
  }
  TlsFree( TLSIndex );
  getchar();
  return 0;
}
```

Setting Thread Priority

Windows uses a priority system to determine which thread gets the next slice of CPU
resources. The higher the priority of a thread, the more CPU time it will get, and con-
versely a thread with a low priority will get fewer CPU resource than other higher-
priority threads. In some instances, it can be useful to adjust the priority of different
threads in an application. The obvious example is when the application is performing a
long-running background task. A background task is best run at a low priority in order
to keep the machine responsive, while a high-priority background task could consume

all the CPU resources over a long period of time and stop the machine from performing other short-lived compute-intensive tasks.

Consider burning a CD or DVD. Here the system needs to keep feeding data to the burner, and any interruption to the data stream could cause an error resulting in an unusable disk being written. To avoid this, it might be appropriate to run the burning application at a higher than usual priority level.

The function that sets the priority of the thread is `SetThreadPriority()`, which takes a handle to the thread plus the desired priority level. There is a corresponding function `GetThreadPriority()` that takes a handle to a thread and returns the priority level of that thread.

Listing 6.40 shows code that manipulates the priority levels of two threads to ensure that one of the threads gets more CPU resources than the other. All threads are created with a priority level of `THREAD_PRIORITY_NORMAL`. The slow thread is created first and sets its own priority to be below normal. Then the fast thread is created, and it sets its own priority level to be above normal. The slow thread is created first in order to give it the chance to complete first. On a system with one core, the slow thread will get less CPU resources than the fast thread and will therefore complete later. On an idle multicore system, both threads will be scheduled simultaneously so they will complete at the same time.

Listing 6.40 **Setting Thread Priority**

```
#include <windows.h>
#include <process.h>

unsigned int __stdcall fastthread( void * data )
{
  double d=0.0;
  printf( "Fast thread started\n" );
  SetThreadPriority( GetCurrentThread(), THREAD_PRIORITY_ABOVE_NORMAL );
  for (int i=0; i<100000000; i++)
  {
    d += d;
  }
  printf( "Fast thread finished\n" );
  return 0;
}

unsigned int __stdcall slowthread( void * data )
{
  double d=0.0;
  printf( "Slow thread started\n" );
  SetThreadPriority( GetCurrentThread(), THREAD_PRIORITY_BELOW_NORMAL );
  for (int i=0; i<100000000; i++)
  {
    d += d;
  }
```

```
  printf( "Slow thread finished\n" );
  return 0;
}

int _tmain( int argc, _TCHAR* argv[] )
{
  HANDLE hfast,hslow;
  hslow = (HANDLE)_beginthreadex( 0, 0, &slowthread, 0, 0, 0 );
  hfast = (HANDLE)_beginthreadex( 0, 0, &fastthread, 0, 0, 0 );
  WaitForSingleObject( hfast, INFINITE );
  WaitForSingleObject( hslow, INFINITE );
  getchar();
  return 0;
}
```

One of the issues caused by adjusting the priority of threads (or processes) is *priority inversion*, which occurs when a higher-priority thread ends up waiting for a lower-priority thread to complete some task. The classic example of this is when a lower-priority thread enters a critical region but because of its priority ends up taking a long time to exit the critical region. While this is happening, a higher-priority thread can be waiting to enter the critical region.

Summary

The Windows threading API provides support for threads, shared memory, and synchronization primitives. At the end of this chapter, you should feel comfortable with the various methods of creating threads and have an appreciation of where they might be appropriately used. You should also understand the various synchronization methods supported and be able to see the commonality with the objects provided as part of the POSIX standard.

7

Using Automatic Parallelization and OpenMP

Previous chapters have covered low-level approaches to creating processes or threads and sharing data between them. Fortunately, many approaches enable the developer to focus on higher levels of application design and leave the mechanics of managing threads and sharing data to runtime libraries and the compiler. In an ideal case, the compiler manages everything, from identifying parts of the code to run in parallel through providing the mechanisms to support that parallelism. However, without some help from the developer, current compiler technology will rarely be able to exploit all the parallelism in an application. The most commonly used and commonly available language extension for parallelism is the OpenMP API.[1]

The OpenMP specification defines an API that enables a developer to add directives to their serial code that will cause the compiler to produce a parallel version of the application. This chapter describes both automatic parallelism provided by many compilers and how the OpenMP API can produce parallel applications from serial codes.

Using Automatic Parallelization to Produce a Parallel Application

Most compilers are able to perform some degree of automatic parallelization. In an ideal world, automatic parallelization would be just another compiler optimization, but currently there are significant limitations on what can be achieved. This is undoubtedly an area that will improve in time. However, in many instances, it is possible to assist the compiler in making the code parallel.

In this section, we will explore the ability of both the Oracle Solaris Studio and Intel compilers to perform automatic parallelization. As well as the ability to perform automatic parallelization, it is also important for the compilers to be able to provide feedback

1. www.openmp.org

on which parts of the code were parallelized and what inhibited parallelization of other regions of code.

Current compilers can only automatically parallelize loops. Loops are a very good target for parallelization because they are often iterated, so the block of code will therefore accumulate significant time. As previously discussed, any parallel region must perform significant work to overcome any costs that the parallelization incurs.

Listing 7.1 shows a simple example of a loop that might be automatically parallelized.

Listing 7.1 **Code to Set Up a Vector of Double-Precision Values**

```
#include <stdlib.h>

void setup( double *vector, int length )
{
  int i;
  for ( i=0; i<length; i++ )         // Line 6
  {
     vector[i] += 1.0;
  }
}

int main()
{
  double *vector;
  vector = (double*)malloc( sizeof(double)*1024*1024 );
  for ( int i=0; i<1000; i++ )      // Line 16
  {
    setup( vector, 1024*1024 );
  }
}
```

The Solaris Studio C compiler uses the flag −xautopar to enable automatic parallelization and the flag −xloopinfo to report information on the degree of parallelization obtained. Listing 7.2 shows the results of compiling this code snippet.

Listing 7.2 **Compiling Code with Autopar**

```
$ cc -g -xautopar -xloopinfo -O -c omp_vector.c
"setvector.c", line 6: PARALLELIZED, and serial version generated
"setvector.c", line 16: not parallelized, call may be unsafe
```

There are two loops in the code, and although the compiler has managed to parallelize the first loop, it has not been able to parallelize the second loop. The compiler reports that the function call in the second loop stopped the parallelization of the loop. We will discuss avoiding this problem later in the section.

The Intel compiler uses the option -parallel to enable parallelization and the option -par-report to report its success. The compiler also has the option -par-threshold{n}, which controls the threshold at which the compiler will parallelize a loop. The option -par-threshold0 will make the compiler parallelize all candidate loops; the default of -par-threshold100 indicates that the compiler should parallelize only those loops that are certain to benefit. Listing 7.3 shows the output from the Intel compiler on the same source file. The flag -fno-inline-functions disables function inlining in the compiler and ensures that the generated code is the same for the two compilers.

Listing 7.3 **Automatic Parallelization Using the Intel Compiler**

```
$ icc -std=c99 -O -parallel -par-report1 -par-threshold0 \
  -fno-inline-functions omp_vector.c
omp_vector.c(6): (col. 3) remark: LOOP WAS AUTO-PARALLELIZED.
```

The number of parallel threads used in the loop is controlled by the environment variable OMP_NUM_THREADS. Listing 7.4 shows the performance of the code when run with one and two threads. It is useful to examine the time reported for the serial and parallel codes. The user time is the same in both instances, which indicates that the two codes did the same amount of work. However, the real, or wall, time is less for the parallel version. This is to be expected. Spreading a constant amount of work over two threads would ideally lead to each thread completing half the work.

Listing 7.4 **Performance of the Parallel Code with One and Two Threads**

```
$ export OMP_NUM_THREADS=1
$ timex a.out
real           3.55
user           3.55
sys            0.02
$ export OMP_NUM_THREADS=2
$ timex a.out
real           2.10
user           3.55
sys            0.04
```

As a more complex example of automatic parallelization, consider the loop in Listing 7.5, which multiplies a matrix by a vector and places the result in a second vector.

Listing 7.5 **Code to Multiply a Matrix by a Vector**

```
void matVec( double **mat, double *vec, double *out,
             int *row, int *col )
{
  int i, j;
  for ( i=0; i<*row; i++ )          // Line 5
```

```
  {
    out[i]=0;
    for ( j=0; j<*col; j++ )          // Line 8
    {
      out[i] += mat[i][j] * vec[j];
    }
  }
}
}
```

Listing 7.6 shows the results of compiling this code with the Solaris Studio compiler.

Listing 7.6 **Compiling Code with Autopar**

```
$ cc -g -xautopar -xloopinfo -O -c fploop.c
"fploop.c", line 5: not parallelized, not a recognized for loop
"fploop.c", line 8: not parallelized, not a recognized for loop
```

The compiler does not recognize either of the `for` loops as loops that can be parallelized. The reason for this is the possibility of aliasing between the store to `out[i]` and the values used to determine the loop bound, `*row` and `*col`. A requirement for the compiler to automatically parallelize the loop is that the loop bounds must remain constant. A store to either of the loop boundaries would violate that restriction. Therefore, it is not a form of loop that can be automatically parallelized. As a programmer, it would be unusual to write code that relies on stores to elements in the array changing the loop boundaries, but for the compiler, the only safe assumption is that these might alias.

The most general-purpose way of correcting this is to place the loop limits into local temporary variables. This removes the possibility that the loop limit might alias with one of the stores in the loop. For the code shown in Listing 7.5, it is easy to perform the equivalent change and pass the loop bounds by value rather than passing them as pointers to the values. Listing 7.7 shows the modified loop.

Listing 7.7 **Code Modified to Avoid Aliasing with Loop Counter**

```
void matVec( double **mat, double *vec, double *out,
             int row, int col )
{
  int i, j;
  for ( i=0; i<row; i++ )          // Line 5
  {
    out[i]=0;
    for ( j=0; j<col; j++ )        // Line 8
    {
      out[i] += mat[i][j] * vec[j];
    }
  }
}
```

Listing 7.8 shows the output from the compiler when this new variant of the code is compiled.

Listing 7.8 **Compiling Modified Code with Automatic Parallelization**

```
$ cc -g -xautopar -xloopinfo -O -c fploop.c
"fploop.c", line 5: not parallelized, unsafe dependence
"fploop.c", line 8: not parallelized, unsafe dependence
```

The code modification has enabled the compiler to recognize the loops as candidates for parallelization, but the compiler has hit a problem because the elements pointed to by out might alias with the elements pointed to either by the matrix, mat, or by the vector, vec. One way to resolve this is to use a restrict-qualified pointer to hold the location of the output array. Listing 7.9 shows the modified code for this.

Listing 7.9 **Using Restrict-Qualified Pointer for Address of Output Array**

```
void matVec(double **mat, double *vec, double * restrict out,
            int row, int col)
{
  int i,j;
  for (i=0; i<row; i++)          // Line 5
  {
    out[i]=0;
    for (j=0; j<col; j++)        // Line 8
    {
      out[i]+=mat[i][j]*vec[j];
    }
  }
}
```

After this adjustment to the source code, the compiler is able to produce a parallel version of the loop, as shown in Listing 7.10.

Listing 7.10 **Compiling Code Containing Restrict-Qualified Pointer**

```
$ cc -g -xautopar -xloopinfo -O -c fploop.c
"fploop.c", line 5: PARALLELIZED, and serial version generated
"fploop.c", line 8: not parallelized, unsafe dependence
```

The Solaris Studio compiler generates two versions of the loop, a parallel version and a serial version. At runtime, the compiler will determine whether the trip count of the loop is high enough for the parallel version to run faster than the serial version.

The compiler reports that the loop at line 8 in Listing 7.9 has an unsafe dependence; the reason for this decision will be discussed in the next section, "Identifying and Parallelizing Reductions."

Of the two loops in the code, the compiler parallelizes the outer loop but not the inner loop. This is the best decision to make for performance. The threads performing the work in parallel need to synchronize once the parallel work has completed. If the outer loop is parallelized, then the threads need to synchronize only once the outer loop has completed. If the inner loop were to be made parallel, then the threads would have to synchronize every time an iteration of the outer loop completed. The number of synchronization events would equal the number of times that the outer loop was iterated. Hence, it is much more efficient to make the outer loop parallel.

Identifying and Parallelizing Reductions

When a loop reduces a large amount of data down to a smaller set of values, the operation is called a *reduction*. The classic example of a reduction is computing the sum of an array of numbers, as shown in Listing 7.11.

Listing 7.11 Calculating the Sum of an Array of Numbers

```
double sum( double* array, int length )
{
  double total=0;
  int i;
  for ( i=0; i<length; i++ )
  {
    total += array[i];
  }
  return total;
}
```

To create a reduction in parallel, the reduction operator needs to be commutative—performing the operations in a different order must not cause an incorrect result. The possible reduction operations are addition, subtraction, multiplication, and the logical operations, such as AND or OR, as well as the operations MIN and MAX when applied to an array of numbers.

However, some operations on floating-point numbers cannot be reordered without causing some potential numeric differences to the output. The addition of floating-point values is a good example of this. There are situations where adding A and B and then C will give a different numeric value than adding C and A and then B. The order of the operations is important. This is not a problem unique to parallel codes; serial codes have the same ordering constraints. However, for parallel codes, this constraint may stop a compiler from producing a parallel version of a code construct.

To consider a contrived example, assume you have an array of floating point numbers sorted from the largest element to the smallest element. When you sum the elements in this array, the value may reach a point where the sum has become so large that adding the small elements onto this sum causes no impact, because the increase is less than can be registered as an increase in the variable holding the total.

Suppose you take this same array and use two threads to compute the result. Each thread computes a partial total over half of the range of numbers. The first thread calculates the sum of the first half of the array, which contains the list of the large numbers. The second thread calculates the sum of the second half of the array, which contains the list of the small numbers. Now the second thread will compute a much smaller value for its partial total. When two small positive values are added together, it is more likely that the result is greater than the largest of the two values. In contrast, if a small value is added to a much larger value, it is likely that the result will be identical to the larger value. The consequence of this is that the small values will accumulate and be recorded in the summation computed by the second thread.

At the end of the parallel region, the values from both threads are added to produce the final result. The value that the second thread computes is potentially large enough to cause a small change in value when added to the large result from the first thread. The result in the computation by using two threads is likely to be different from the result computed using only one thread. The difference might only be in the smallest significant figure, or it might even be a rounding difference. But, the result could potentially be different.

Some compilers place the decision of whether to perform reductions under the control of the user. The Solaris Studio compiler requires that the user specify the flag -xreduction to parallelize reduction operations. The Intel compiler does not require an additional flag to recognize reductions. We can see the results of using this flag on the code from Listing 7.5 in the output shown in Listing 7.12.

Listing 7.12 **Parallelization of Reduction Operations**

```
$ cc -g -xautopar -xloopinfo -xreduction -O -c fploop.c
"fploop.c", line 5: PARALLELIZED, and serial version generated
"fploop.c", line 8: not parallelized, not profitable
```

The compiler output shows that it recognized the inner loop at line 8 and did not declare it an unsafe dependency. Instead, the loop is reported as not being profitable to parallelize. This is the expected behavior; as we have previously discussed, it is much more effective to parallelize the outer loop and leave the inner loop as serial code.

Reductions are present in many codes, and it is usually appropriate to parallelize them as long as the developer is aware that this may cause a difference in the generated results.

Automatic Parallelization of Codes Containing Calls

We discussed the impact made on performance by calls to other routines in Chapter 2, "Coding for Performance." The basic problem with calling another function is that the compiler has no idea what that routine might do—it could change global data or perhaps never return. For this reason, a loop that contains function calls cannot, in general, be automatically parallelized.

Obviously, this restriction would preclude a large number of loops that could otherwise be safely parallelized. The most obvious place where this would be a problem
would be in calling mathematical functions. This limitation can be demonstrated using
the modified version of the matrix-vector code from Listing 7.9. Listing 7.13 shows this
modified code.

Listing 7.13 **Modified Matrix-Vector Code That Makes a Function Call**

```
#include <math.h>

void matVec( double **mat, double *vec, double * restrict out,
             int row, int col )
{
  int i,j;
  for ( i=0; i<row; i++ )      // Line 7
  {
    out[i]=0;
    for ( j=0; j<col; j++ )  // Line 10
    {
      out[i] += sin( mat[i][j] * vec[j] );
    }
  }
}
```

When compiled, the call to `sin()` causes automatic parallelization to fail, as shown in
Listing 7.14.

Listing 7.14 **Automatic Parallelization Failing in the Presence of a Function Call**

```
$ cc -g -xautopar -xloopinfo -O -c fploops.c
"fploops.c", line  7: not parallelized, call may be unsafe
"fploops.c", line 10: not parallelized, call may be unsafe
```

The Solaris Studio compiler considers `sin()` to be a "built-in" function, but because
a developer might provide an alternative implementation or perhaps interpose on the
function calls, it does not recognize these calls unless specifically told to do so. The flag
to enable recognition of built-in functions is `-xbuiltin`. When this flag is provided, the
output from the compiler is shown in Listing 7.15.

Listing 7.15 **Automatic Parallelization Recognizing Call to `sin()` as Safe**

```
$ cc -g -xbuiltin -xautopar -xloopinfo -O -c fploops.c
"fploops.c", line  7: PARALLELIZED, and serial version generated
"fploops.c", line 10: not parallelized, unsafe dependence
```

However, calls to mathematical functions represent a small proportion of the calls that might be encountered in loops. There is no standard way to denote that a call to a particular function can be safely made in parallel, although individual compilers might implement mechanisms that could be used. The best way to enable a loop containing a function call to be parallelized automatically is by inlining the function. Inlining replaces a call to a function with the actual code for the called function. Function inlining can be enabled with a general compiler flag or a flag enabling a specific routine to be inlined. Listing 7.16 shows a variant of the code where part of the calculation is performed by a routine.

Listing 7.16 **Code Where Part of the Calculation Is Performed by Another Function**

```
#include <math.h>

double calc( double a, double b )
{
  return a * b;
}

void matVec( double **mat, double *vec, double * restrict out,
             int row, int col )
{
  int i,j;
  for ( i=0; i<row; i++ )         // Line 12
  {
    out[i]=0;
    for ( j=0; j<col; j++ )       // Line 15
    {
      out[i] += calc( mat[i][j], vec[j] );
    }
  }
}
```

When this code is compiled, the compiler fails to automatically parallelize the loops because they contain a call that may be unsafe. However, when the code is compiled at an optimization level of –xO4 or higher, the compiler automatically performs inlining optimizations, which eliminates the call and allows the loop to be parallelized. This is shown in Listing 7.17.

Listing 7.17 **Inlining Enables the Compiler to Automatically Parallelize Loop**

```
$ cc -g -xautopar -xloopinfo -xO4 -c fploops.c
"fploop.c", line 12: PARALLELIZED, and serial version generated
"fploop.c", line 15: not parallelized, unsafe dependence
```

Assisting Compiler in Automatically Parallelizing Code

The code shown in Listing 7.18 has a potential aliasing issue. Changes to the elements in the array `myarray` might also change the value pointed to by `length` if it happens to be a member of `myarray`.

Listing 7.18 **Incrementing All the Values Held in an Array of Numbers**

```
void sum( double* myarray, int *length )
{
  int i;
  for ( i=0; i<*length; i++ )
  {
    myarray[i] += 1;
  }
}
```

It is possible to modify the code so that a compiler can automatically parallelize it. One way to resolve this would be to specify that `length` was a `restrict`-qualified pointer so that the compiler would know that stores to `array` would not alter the value pointed to by `length`. Another approach would be to place the value pointed to by `length` into a temporary variable. This second approach has an advantage in that it does not rely on support for the `restrict` keyword.

In many situations, the compiler will be able to parallelize loops if some of the potential aliasing issues are resolved using temporary variables or type casting using `restrict`-qualified pointers. The code shown in Listing 7.19 exhibits a number of potential aliasing issues.

Listing 7.19 **Code That Passes Data Using Structures**

```
typedef struct s
{
  int length;
  double *array1, *array2;
} S;

void calc( S *data )
{
  int i;
  for ( i=0; i < data->length; i++ )        // Line 10
  {
    data->array1[i] += data->array2[i];     // Line 12
  }
}
```

The first issue that the compiler finds is that it fails to recognize the loop at line 10 as one that can be parallelized. This is because changes to `data->array1` might change the value of the variable `data->length`. The problem is that the compiler cannot know how many iterations of the loop will be performed, so it cannot divide those iterations between multiple threads. This issue can be resolved by taking a local copy of the variable `data->length` and using that as the loop iteration limit.

This converts the loop into one that can be recognized by the compiler, but the compiler is still unable to parallelize it because there is potential aliasing between reads from `data->array2` and writes to `data->array1`. This issue can be resolving by making local `restrict`-qualified pointers that point to the two arrays. Listing 7.20 shows the modified source.

Listing 7.20 **Modified Code That Passes Data Using Structures**

```
typedef struct s
{
  int length;
  double * array1, *array2;
} S;

void calc( S *data )
{
  int i;
  int length = data->length;
  double * restrict array1 = data->array1;
  double * restrict array2 = data->array2;
  for (i=0; i < length; i++)
  {
    array1[i] += array2[i];
  }
}
```

In some instances, the compiler may be able to use *versioning* of the loop to automatically parallelize code similar to that in Listing 7.19. The compiler produces multiple versions of the loop, and the appropriate version is selected at runtime. A serial version of the loop is used when there is aliasing between stores to memory in the loop and variables used by the loop. In the code in Listing 7.19, the stores to `data->array1` might alias with `data->array2`, `data->length`, or the structure pointed to by `data`. A parallel version is generated for use when there is no such aliasing.

The techniques to improve the chance that a compiler can automatically parallelize an application can be summarized as follows:

- By default, most compilers will assume that all pointers may alias. This can be resolved by making local copies of invariant data, by specifying a stronger aliasing assumption, or by declaring pointers with the `restrict` keyword.

- The compiler may require additional flags for it to produce parallel versions of all loops. This may be a flag to give it permission to perform parallelization of reductions, such as the `-xreduction` flag needed by the Solaris Studio compiler. Alternatively, it may be a flag that alters the threshold at which the compiler will consider a loop profitable to parallelize. For example, the Intel compiler has the `-par-threshold0` flag. Finally, there may be additional flags for the compiler to recognize loops containing calls to intrinsic functions as being safe to parallelize; the Solaris Studio compiler requires the `-xbuiltin` flag for this purpose.

- Compilers cannot parallelize loops containing calls to functions unless they are certain that the function calls are without side effects. In some cases, there may be compiler directives that can be placed into the source code of the application to provide this assertion. In other cases, it may be possible to force the compiler to inline the function, which would then enable it to parallelize the resulting loop.

From this section, it should be apparent that compilers are able to automatically extract some parallelism from a subset of applications. The size of the subset can be increased using the feedback provided by the compiler and some of the techniques described here. However, the ability of current compilers to perform automatic parallelization is limited, and some of the source code changes proposed here may reduce the clarity of the source code.

Alternatively, the OpenMP API provides a way to expose the parallelism in a code by making minimal changes to the source code. With most compilers, it can be used in addition to automatic parallelization so that more of the application can be parallelized.

Using OpenMP to Produce a Parallel Application

With OpenMP, directives in the source code are used to express parallel constructs. These directives start with the phrase `#pragma omp`. Under appropriate compilation flags, they are read by the compiler and used to generate a parallel version of the application. If the required compiler flags are not provided, the directives are ignored. The OpenMP API specification details these directives as well as library calls to determine or modify runtime parameters such as the current number of threads. As we saw in Chapter 3, "Identifying Opportunities for Parallelization," a benefit of using OpenMP directives is that it separates the parallelism from the algorithm. The code can be read without having to worry about how the parallelization is implemented. Some other advantages to using OpenMP are as follows:

- The directives are recognized only when compiled with a particular compiler flag, so the same source base can be used to generate the serial and parallel versions of the code. This simplifies debugging since it is relatively easy to determine whether, for a given problem, the parallel version produces a different answer to the serial version and therefore whether a bug is because of the parallelization or the original algorithm.

- Each directive is limited in scope to the region of code to which it applies. Consequently, the developer can focus on making the critical section of the code parallel without having to be concerned about changing the rest of the code to support this parallelization. This is often referred to as the ability to perform *incremental parallelization*.

- Possibly the biggest advantage is that the compiler and supporting library are responsible for all the parallelization work and the runtime management of threads.

It is probably easiest to demonstrate the use of OpenMP directives through the simple example shown in Listing 7.21. The OpenMP directive is indicated in bold.

Listing 7.21 **Loop Parallelized Using OpenMP**

```
void calc( double* array1, double * array2, int length )
{
  #pragma omp parallel for
  for ( int i=0; i<length; i++ )
  {
    array1[i] += array2[i];
  }
}
```

The code in Listing 7.21 shows how the OpenMP directive can be placed above the loop to which it applies. The OpenMP directive places the burden of ensuring the code is safe to execute in parallel on the developer, not on the compiler. Although the compiler will produce a parallel version of the loop, it is up to the developer to ensure that this is a safe optimization to make. An instance of where this might be unsafe is if the two arrays had some degree of overlap, then the parallel version might not produce the same result as the serial version.

The OpenMP directive has three parts:

- `#pragma omp` indicates to the compiler that what follows is an OpenMP directive.

- `parallel` tells the compiler to start a new parallel region. Unless otherwise specified, all the threads will execute the code in the parallel region.

- `for` tells the compiler that the next `for` loop should be executed in parallel.

Multiple threads will work on independent parts of the range of iterations. At the end of the loop, the threads will wait until all the iterations have completed before the next part of the code is executed.

The statement given in this code snippet is the simplest possible example, but it illustrates exactly what the OpenMP specification aims to achieve.

Using OpenMP to Parallelize Loops

OpenMP places some restrictions on the types of loops that can be parallelized. The runtime library needs to be able to determine the start points and end points for the work assigned to each thread. Consequently, the following constraints are needed:

- The loop has to be a `for` loop of this form:

  ```
  for (init expression; test expression; increment expression)
  ```

- The loop variable needs to be of one of the following types: a signed or unsigned integer, a C pointer, or a C++ random access iterator.
- The loop variable needs to be initialized to one end of the range.
- The variable needs to be incremented (or decremented) by a loop invariant increment.
- The test expression needs to be one of >, >=, <, or <=. The comparison needs to be with a loop invariant value.

Under these conditions, it is possible for the runtime to take the loop and partition the iteration ranges to the threads completing the work. Loops that do not adhere to these specifications will need to be restructured before they can be parallelized using an OpenMP `parallel for` construct.

Runtime Behavior of an OpenMP Application

OpenMP works using a combination of compiler support plus a runtime library. The compiler uses the directives in the source code to produce appropriate blocks of code together with the necessary calls into the runtime library.

For example, when the compiler encounters a directive defining a parallel region, the compiler will produce a new block of code that will be executed by the threads in parallel. The runtime library is responsible for assigning the work to the various threads.

OpenMP follows a fork-join type model. The runtime library will create a team of threads. When a parallel region is encountered, the work will be divided between members of this team of threads. At the end of the region, the original thread, called the *master thread*, will continue executing the code after the region. The other threads, called the *worker threads*, will wait until the master thread reaches the next parallel region and new work is assigned to them. The number of threads that will be used is set by the environment variable `OMP_NUM_THREADS`, but this can be adjusted by the application at runtime by calls into the runtime support library. For example, consider the code in Listing 7.22.

Listing 7.22 **OpenMP Parallel Region**

```c
#include <stdio.h>

void main()
{
```

```
#pragma omp parallel
{
  printf( "Thread\n" );
}
}
```

When compiled and run, each thread of the number of threads specified by OMP_NUM_THREADS will execute the parallel region. For the Solaris Studio compiler to recognize the OpenMP directives, it needs the flag -xopenmp. The flag -xloopinfo tells the compiler to provide information about the parallelization it has undertaken. Listing 7.23 shows the output of compiling and running this program. Each of the two threads executes the parallel region and prints the output Thread.

Listing 7.23 **OpenMP Parallel Region**

```
$ cc -O -xopenmp -xloopinfo omptest.c
$ export OMP_NUM_THREADS=2
$ ./a.out
Thread
Thread
```

Variable Scoping Inside OpenMP Parallel Regions

One of the trickier aspects of parallelization is the scoping of variables used in the parallel region. In Listing 7.24, there are four variables used in the parallel region: i, length, array1, and array2. The variables can be scoped either as *shared*, so each thread shares the same variable, or as *private*, where each thread gets its own copy of the variable.

The loop counter i needs to be private to each thread so that each thread gets its own copy of the variable. The variables array1 and array2 are shared. Each thread works on a separate range of values, so there is no actual sharing of data. The variable length is also shared between the threads, but since it is not modified, it does not matter whether it is scoped as shared or private. It is possible to see how the Solaris Studio compiler has scoped these variables using the code analysis tool er_src on the generated object file, as shown in Listing 7.24.

Listing 7.24 **Using er_src to Examine Variable Scoping for Parallel Region**

```
% cc -c -g -O -xopenmp -xloopinfo omploop.c
"omploop.c", line 4: PARALLELIZED, user pragma used
% er_src omploop.o
...
    1. void calc( double * array1, double * array2, int length )
    2. {
       <Function: calc>
```

```
Source OpenMP region below has tag R1
Private variables in R1: i
Shared variables in R1: array2, length, array1
  3.   #pragma omp parallel for

Source loop below has tag L1
L1 parallelized by explicit user directive
...
  4.   for( int i=0; i<length; i++ )
  5.   {
  6.     array1[i] += array2[i];
  7.   }
  8. }
```

The rules governing the default variable scoping in OpenMP are quite complex. The simplified summary of the rules is that they define the loop induction variable as being private, variables defined in the parallel code as being private, and variables defined outside the parallel region as being shared. This should be appropriate in simple situations but may not be appropriate in more complex ones. In these situations, it is better to manually define the variable scoping. The default scoping rules can be disabled using the clause `default(none)`, which will cause the compiler to issue an error for any variables whose scoping is not specified. Variables can be scoped as private or shared using the clause `private(variables)` or `shared(variables)`, respectively. Listing 7.25 shows the original source modified to manually specify variable scoping.

Listing 7.25 Loop Parallelized Using OpenMP with Explicitly Stated Variable Scoping

```
void calc( double* array1, double * array2, int length )
{
  int i;
  #pragma omp parallel for private(i) shared(length, array1, array2)
  for ( i=0; i<length; i++ )
  {
    array1[i] += array2[i];
  }
}
```

Parallelizing Reductions Using OpenMP

Not all variables can be scoped as either shared or private. The most obvious example of a more complex situation is a reduction. Listing 7.26 shows an example of a reduction. The variable `total` is computed by adding all the elements in an array.

Listing 7.26 **Loop Containing a Reduction Operation**

```
double calc( double* array, int length )
{
  double total = 0.0;
  for ( int i=0; i<length; i++ )
  {
    total += array[i];
  }
  return total;
}
```

The result returned by the variable `total` will need contributions from every thread. One way of making this happen would be to serialize access to the variable using a mutex or an atomic operation, but this would render any parallelization of the loop pointless.

The OpenMP specification allows for a reduction operation to be applied over a parallel region. The reduction gives each thread a private copy of the reduction variable, which it uses for computation in the parallel region. At the end of the parallel region, the private copies of the reduction variable are combined to produce the final result. The syntax for the reduction clause is `reduction(`*`operator`*`:`*`variable`*`)`. Listing 7.27 shows the loop parallelized using a reduction clause.

Listing 7.27 **Loop Containing a Reduction Operation**

```
double calc( double* array, int length )
{
  double total = 0.0;
  #pragma omp parallel for reduction( +: total )
  for ( int i=0; i<length; i++ )
  {
    total += array[i];
  }
  return total;
}
```

The operator to which the reduction applies is not limited to additions. It includes a number of other operations such as subtraction; multiplication; the bitwise operations AND, OR, and XOR; and the logical operations AND and OR.

Accessing Private Data Outside the Parallel Region

When a variable is declared as private, each thread gets a private copy of the variable. However, the variable does not get initialized at the start of the parallel region, and its value does not get propagated beyond the end of the region. Listing 7.28 shows an example of code where the value of the variable before the parallel region is important.

Listing 7.28 Parallel Region That Accesses the Value of a Private Variable

```
#include <stdio.h>

int main()
{
  int data=1;
  #pragma omp parallel for private(data)
  for ( int i=0; i<100; i++ )
  {
    printf( "data=%i\n", data );
  }
  return 0;
}
```

Although the variable `data` is initialized to the value one outside the parallel region, this value is not passed into the private copy that each thread obtains inside the parallel region. Hence, the value that is printed is undefined. To initialize the value of the variable in the parallel region to the value it held before the region, the variable needs to be declared using the clause `firstprivate(variables)`. This tells the compiler to include code that copies the existing value into the private copy held by each thread in the parallel region. Listing 7.29 shows the modified code.

Listing 7.29 Declaring a Variable as `firstprivate` to Pass Its Value into the
**   Parallel Region**

```
#include <stdio.h>

int main()
{
  int data=1;
  #pragma omp parallel for firstprivate(data)
  for ( int i=0; i<100; i++ )
  {
    printf( "data=%i\n", data );
  }
  return 0;
}
```

Another situation is where the value of a variable is used after a parallel region. In this case, it is important to retain the value that was written into this variable by the thread that executed the last iterations of the loop. This preserves the semantics of the serial program. The clause that enables this to happen is `lastprivate(variables)`. This clause is also supported on `parallel sections`, which will be introduced later. Listing 7.30 shows an example of using `lastprivate` to retain the last value written into the variable.

Listing 7.30 **Passing the Value of a Variable Out of a Parallel Region Using**
                `lastprivate`

```
#include <stdio.h>

int main()
{
  int data=1;
  #pragma omp parallel for lastprivate(data)
  for ( int i=0; i<100; i++ )
  {
    data = i*i;
    printf( "data=%i\n", data );
  }
  printf( "Final value=%i\n", data );
  return 0;
}
```

Improving Work Distribution Using Scheduling

The default scheduling for a parallel for loop is called *static scheduling*. The iterations are divided evenly, in chunks of consecutive iterations, between the threads. If there are two threads working to complete 100 iterations, the first thread will complete the first 50 iterations, and the second thread will complete the second 50 iterations. This scheme works well in situations where each iteration takes the same amount of time. However, in some cases, a different amount of work will be performed in each iteration. Consequently, both threads may complete the same number of iterations, but one may have more work to do in those iterations. Listing 7.31 shows an example of this. The number of iterations performed in the routine `calc()` depends on the value passed into it. The value passed into the routine largely depends on the value of the loop induction variable i. With static scheduling, threads that get assigned the higher values of i will take longer to complete their work.

Listing 7.31 **Code Where Each Iteration Has Different Computational Costs**

```
double calc( int count )
{
  double d = 1.0;
  for( int i=0; i < count*count; i++ )
  {
    d += d;
  }
  return d;
}
```

```
int main()
{
  double data[200][100];
  int i,j;
  #pragma omp parallel for private(i,j) shared(data)
  for ( int i=0; i<200; i++ )
  {
    for ( int j=0; j<200; j++ )
    {
      data[i][j] = calc( i+j );
    }
  }
  return 0;
}
```

Listing 7.32 shows the results of compiling and running this code using one and two threads.

Listing 7.32 Compiling and Running Code with One and Two Threads

```
$ cc -O -xopenmp -xloopinfo schedule.c
"schedule.c", line 4: not parallelized, unsafe dependence
"schedule.c", line 16: PARALLELIZED, user pragma used
"schedule.c", line 18: not parallelized, loop inside OpenMP region
$ export OMP_NUM_THREADS=1
$ timex a.out
real           4.96
user           4.94
sys            0.01
$ export OMP_NUM_THREADS=2
$ timex a.out
real           3.55
user           4.94
sys            0.01
```

In this case, going from one to two threads decreases the runtime from about 5 seconds to about 3.5 seconds. This is less than linear scaling. Ideally, doubling the thread count should halve the runtime. The reason for this poor scaling is that the work is unevenly distributed between the two threads. The thread that computes the results for the lower values of i will have fewer iterations to complete in the innermost loop than the thread that computes the higher values of i.

We can resolve this by changing the scheduling of the loop. Instead of having a static schedule, we can use a *dynamic schedule*. A dynamic schedule means that the work is divided into multiple chunks of work. As each thread completes a chunk of work, it takes the next chunk of work. This ensures that a thread that completes its work faster ends up doing more chunks, whereas a thread that takes a lot of time to complete each chunk of work will end up completing fewer of them. Dynamic scheduling is selected using the `schedule(dynamic)` clause. Listing 7.33 shows the modified code.

Listing 7.33 **Code Where Each Iteration Has Different Computational Costs**

```
double calc( int count )
{
  double d = 1.0;
  for( int i=0; i < count*count; i++ )
  {
    d += d;
  }
  return d;
}

int main()
{
  double data[200][100];
  int i, j;
  #pragma omp parallel for private(i,j) shared(data) schedule(dynamic)
  for ( int i=0; i<200; i++ )
  {
    for ( int j=0; j<200; j++ )
    {
      data[i][j] = calc(i+j);
    }
  }
  return 0;
}
```

Running this modified code on the same platform results in a runtime of 2.5 seconds—half the original single-threaded runtime.

Dynamic scheduling avoids the issue of distributing work evenly across the threads. However, it also incurs greater runtime overheads. This is not so apparent in this small example. Rather than use another code sequence to demonstrate it, it is relatively simple to explain the reason for this increase in overhead.

With static scheduling, the threads get their iteration limits when they start, and once completed, they can wait at a barrier until all other threads have completed. There is no synchronization between threads in the parallel region.

In contrast, dynamic scheduling requires that each thread complete a unit of work that is much shorter than their share of the total iteration count. Every time a thread completes this short chunk of work, it has to fetch the next chunk. Every fetch of a chunk of work is a potential serialization point, because all the threads have to cooperate to determine who gets the next chunk. So, the increase in overhead comes from two potential factors: the number of places where a new chunk of work is fetched and the interthread communication costs when each new chunk of work is fetched.

The default size of the chunks for a dynamic schedule is one. Each thread performs a single iteration before returning for more work. This can be too low a value, resulting in significant synchronization overhead. An additional parameter can be given to the schedule clause to govern the chunk size used. This parameter can be a static value or can be calculated at runtime. Listing 7.34 shows an example of using dynamic scheduling with a chunk size value calculated at runtime.

Listing 7.34 **Dynamic Scheduling with Chunk Size Calculated at Runtime**

```
double sum( double *a, int n )
{
  double total = 0.0;
  #pragma omp parallel for reduction( +: total) schedule( dynamic, n/50)
  for ( int i=0; i<n; i++ )
  {
    total += a[i];
  }
  return total;
}
```

Another scheduling mode is *guided*. With guided scheduling, the size of the chunk of work assigned is proportional to the amount of work remaining. So, initially the threads will get assigned large chunks of work, but then they will get smaller chunks until all the work is completed. Guided scheduling can also take an optional parameter that determines the smallest chunk size to be used. The default minimum chunk size is a single iteration. Listing 7.35 shows an example of guided scheduling.

Listing 7.35 **Guided Scheduling with Chunk Size Calculated at Runtime**

```
double sum( double *a, int n )
{
  double total = 0.0;
  #pragma omp parallel for reduction( +: total) schedule( guided, n/50)
  for ( int i=0; i<n; i++ )
  {
    total += a[i];
  }
  return total;
}
```

There are two more scheduling modes: *automatic* and *runtime*. The `schedule(auto)` clause will leave the scheduling decisions for the runtime system to determine automatically. The `schedule(runtime)` clause enables the environment variable `OMP_SCHEDULE` to determine the type of schedule used.

Static scheduling can also take an optional chunk size parameter. If a chunk size is specified for static scheduling, the work is split into equal units of the specified chunk size. These are distributed round-robin to the worker threads. This may mean that some worker threads have no work assigned to them or that some threads end up with more chunks of work than others. In the absence of a specified chunk size, the work is divided evenly over all the threads.

Using Parallel Sections to Perform Independent Work

OpenMP *parallel sections* provide another way to parallelize a code into multiple independent units of work that can be assigned to different threads. Parallel sections allow the developer to assign different sections of code to different threads. Consider a situation where in the process of being initialized an application needs to set up two linked lists. Listing 7.36 shows an example.

Listing 7.36 **Using Parallel Sections to Perform Independent Work in Parallel**

```
#include <stdlib.h>

typedef struct s
{
  struct s* next;
} S;

void setuplist( S *current )
{
  for(int i=0; i<10000; i++)
  {
    current->next = (S*)malloc( sizeof(S) );
    current = current->next;
  }
  current->next = NULL;
}

int main()
{
  S var1, var2;
  #pragma omp parallel sections
  {
    #pragma omp section
    {
      setuplist( &var1 );    // Set up first linked list
    }
    #pragma omp section
```

```
  {
    setuplist( &var2 );    // Set up second linked list
  }
  }
}
```

The parallel region is introduced using the `#pragma omp parallel` directive. In this example, it is combined with the `sections` directive to produce a single statement. This identifies the region of code as containing one or more sections of code that can be executed in parallel. Each individual section is identified using the directive `#pragma omp section`. It is important to notice the open and close braces that denote the range of code included in the parallel sections and also denote the code in each parallel section. In the absence of the braces, the parallel section would apply only to the following line of code.

All the threads wait at the end of the `parallel sections` region until all the work has been completed, before any of the subsequent code is executed.

Although parallel sections increase the range of applications that can be parallelized using OpenMP, it has the constraint that the parallelism is statically defined in the source code. This static definition of parallelism limits the degree of scaling that can be expected from the application. Parallel sections are really effective only in situations where there is a limited, static opportunity for parallelism. In most other cases, parallel tasks, which we will discuss later, may be a better solution.

Nested Parallelism

The OpenMP API also supports *nested* parallelism. Here, a parallel region is encountered inside another parallel region. This can be a useful way of attaining increased parallelism by having `tasks` or `parallel sections` that provide course-grained parallelism and then using a `parallel for` to gain further parallelism within the task or region. Nested parallelism is also useful in situations where the algorithm is recursive in nature.

Listing 7.37 shows an example of nested parallelism where two parallel sections contain `parallel for` directives that initialize two arrays of values. Support for nested parallelism can be enabled through the environment variable `OMP_NESTED` or through a call to the routine `omp_set_nested()` with a value other than zero. However, support of `omp_set_nested()` is optional. It can be determined whether nested parallelism is enabled or not through a call to `omp_get_nested()`.

Listing 7.37 **Using Nested Parallelism to Perform Array Set Up in Parallel**

```
#include <stdlib.h>
#include <omp.h>

int main()
{
  double * array1, *array2;
```

```
omp_set_nested( 1 );
#pragma omp parallel sections shared( array1, array2 )
{
  #pragma omp section
  {
    array1 = (double*)malloc( sizeof(double)*1024*1024 );
    #pragma omp parallel for shared(array1)
    for ( int i=0; i<1024*1024; i++ )
    {
      array1[i] = i;
    }
  }
  #pragma omp section
  {
    array2 = (double*)malloc( sizeof(double)*1024*512 );
    #pragma omp parallel for shared(array2)
    for ( int i=0; i<1024*512; i++ )
    {
      array2[i] = i;
    }
  }
}
}
```

However, nested parallelism is complex, so detailed discussion is left to specialist texts on the topic of OpenMP.

Using OpenMP for Dynamically Defined Parallel Tasks

The OpenMP 3.0 specification introduced *tasks*. A task is a block of code that will be executed at some point in the future by one of the team of threads. Every time the `task` directive is encountered at runtime, a new task is created and added to the list of tasks to be completed. This facility enables OpenMP to tackle many of the problems that previously could only be elegantly addressed using threads. As an example, it is possible to write a version of the echo server from Chapter 5, "Using POSIX Threads," using OpenMP tasks. This example combines parallelization across loops, parallel sections, and nested parallelization, together with parallel tasks.

The application uses `parallel sections` to start both a client and a driver thread. Listing 7.38 shows the source code to do this. The code uses nested parallelism, so this needs to be explicitly enabled by calling `omp_set_nested()` with a nonzero value. The parallel section explicitly requests two threads using the `num_threads(2)` clause. Note that for correct execution, the code relies on having at least two virtual CPUs. If the code is run on a system with only a single virtual CPU, the code will not function correctly because it will stall while executing the `echothread()` code and will never get to execute the `driverthread()`.

Listing 7.38 Using OpenMP Parallel Sections to Start Two Threads

```
#include <stdio.h>
#include <unistd.h>
#include <stdlib.h>
#include <sys/types.h>
#include <sys/socket.h>
#include <netinet/in.h>
#include <netdb.h>
#include <arpa/inet.h>
#include <strings.h>
#include <pthread.h>
#include <errno.h>
#include <omp.h>

...

int main()
{
  omp_set_nested( 1 );
  #pragma omp parallel sections num_threads( 2 )
  {
    #pragma omp section
    {
      echothread();
    }
    #pragma omp section
    {
      driverthread();
    }
  }
}
```

Listing 7.39 shows the code for the driver or client part of the application. This code uses a `parallel for` loop in the driver code to launch multiple requests to the server in parallel. The driver code shares a single `sockaddr_in` structure between all the threads. Each thread gets a private copy of the variable `s`, which holds the ID of the socket that the thread has opened to the server. Each iteration of the loop will send a string to the server and then wait for its response.

Listing 7.39 Driver Thread That Generates Multiple Connections to the Server

```
void driverthread()
{
  int s;
  struct sockaddr_in addr;
  bzero( &addr, sizeof(addr) );
```

```
    addr.sin_family = AF_INET;
    addr.sin_addr.s_addr = inet_addr( "127.0.0.1" );
    addr.sin_port = htons( 5000 );

    #pragma omp parallel for shared( addr ) private( s )
    for( int count=0; count<10000; count++ )
    {
      s = socket( PF_INET, SOCK_STREAM, 0 );
      printf( "Driver thread %i ready\n", omp_get_thread_num() );

      if ( connect( s, (struct sockaddr*)&addr, sizeof(addr) )==0 )
      {
        char buffer[1024];

        for ( int i=0; i<10; i++ )
        {
          sprintf( buffer, "Sent %i\n", i );
          if ( send( s, buffer, strlen(buffer)+1 ,0 )!= strlen(buffer)+1 )
          {
             printf( "send size mismatch\n" );
          }
          bzero( buffer, sizeof(buffer) );
          read(s, buffer, sizeof(buffer) );
        }

      }
      else
      {
        perror( "Connection refused" );
        exit( 0 );
      }

    shutdown( s, SHUT_RDWR );
    close( s );
  }
}
```

Listing 7.40 shows the server code. This takes an incoming connection and launches a new task to handle that incoming connection.

Listing 7.40 **Server Code to Handle Incoming Connections**

```
void echothread()
{
  int s;
  int true = 1;
  struct sockaddr_in addr;
```

```c
s = socket( PF_INET, SOCK_STREAM, 0 );
if ( s == -1 ) { printf( "Socket error %i\n", errno ); }

if ( setsockopt(s, SOL_SOCKET, SO_REUSEADDR, &true, sizeof(int))==-1 )
   { printf( "setsockopt error %i\n", errno ); }

bzero( &addr, sizeof(addr) );
addr.sin_family = AF_INET;
addr.sin_addr.s_addr = htonl( INADDR_ANY );
addr.sin_port = htons( 5000 );

if ( bind( s, (struct sockaddr*)&addr, sizeof(addr) ) != 0 )
   { printf( "Bind error %i\n", errno ); }

listen( s, 4 );
#pragma omp parallel
{
  #pragma omp single
  while( 1 )
  {
    struct sockaddr client;

    int size = sizeof(client);
    int stream = accept( s, &client, &size );
    #pragma omp task
    {
      char buffer[1024];

      if ( stream >= 0 )
       { printf("Accepted by thread ID %i\n", omp_get_thread_num()); }
      else
       { printf("Accept error %i\n", errno); }

      while ( recv( stream, buffer, sizeof(buffer), 0 ) )
      {
        send( stream, buffer, strlen(buffer)+1, 0 );
      }

      close( stream );
      printf( "Stream closed\n" );
    }
  }
}
```

The code uses three OpenMP directives. We have already met the `omp parallel` directive, which denotes the start of a parallel region, but not the `omp single` directive, which tells the compiler that only one thread is to execute the enclosed code. As discussed earlier, all the threads will execute the code in the parallel region by default. This single thread is responsible for accepting incoming connections and then producing the new tasks that handle the details of the connection.

Finally, the `omp task` directive encloses the region of code that is to be executed as the task. The variable `stream` is scoped as `firstprivate` by default, so each task gets a private copy of the variable. Within the task, this variable is assigned the value that it holds at the time that the task was created. The new task then handles the echoing back of data that is sent on that particular socket.

Listing 7.41 shows the results of compiling and running this code on a four-way machine. The resulting applications needs to be linked with the socket library (`-lsocket`) and the network services library (`-lnsl`). The key thing to observe is that the threads sending and receiving the sockets change, indicating that the work is being distributed across all the available threads.

Listing 7.41 **Output from Client-Server Code Parallelized Using Nested OpenMP Directives**

```
% cc -O -xopenmp -xloopinfo omp_sockets.c -lsocket -lnsl
"omp_sockets.c", line 24: PARALLELIZED, user pragma used
"omp_sockets.c", line 33: not parallelized, loop inside OpenMP region
"omp_sockets.c", line 76: not parallelized, loop has multiple exits
"omp_sockets.c", line 95: not parallelized, not a recognized for loop
% ./a.out
Echo socket setup
Driver thread 0 ready
Driver thread 1 ready
Driver thread 3 ready
Driver thread 2 ready
Accepted by thread ID 1
Accepted by thread ID 3
Accepted by thread ID 2
Driver thread 3 ready
Stream closed
Accepted by thread ID 3
Driver thread 1 ready
Driver thread 0 ready
Stream closed
Accepted by thread ID 2
...
```

Keeping Data Private to Threads

It is possible to set up thread-local data using the OpenMP directive `threadprivate`. This directive works in a similar way to the `__thread` declaration, described in Chapter 5, in making each thread hold a private copy of some variable. Listing 7.42 shows an example of declaring a `threadprivate` variable.

Listing 7.42 **Declaring a `threadprivate` Variable**

```
int i;
#pragma omp threadprivate( i )

int main()
{
  ...
}
```

The value of the `threadprivate` variable can persist between parallel regions. The rules governing when this will happen are slightly complex but can be summarized as the requirement that the active thread count is the same for the two parallel regions.

There are other constraints on `threadprivate` variables. If the code is parallelized using tasks and the value of the variable depends on the order that the tasks are completed, then its value will be unpredictable.

During serial portions of the application's execution, the variable will return the value held by the master thread. This can be demonstrated using the code shown in Listing 7.43. The variable `i` is thread private. In the master thread, it is set to hold the value –1, but in the parallel region, it is set to hold the thread ID. Each thread will set the value of `i` to its thread ID. The ID of the master thread is zero. Outside the parallel region, the reference to the variable `i` resolves to the value held by the master thread. So, the final version of the variable `i` will be zero.

Listing 7.43 **Printing the Value of a `threadprivate` Variable**

```
#include<stdio.h>
#include<omp.h>

int i;
#pragma omp threadprivate( i )

int main()
{
  i = -1;
  #pragma omp parallel
  {
    i = omp_get_thread_num();
```

```
    printf( "Parallel value %i\n", i );
  }
  printf( "Serial value %i\n", i );
}
```

The main reason for using `threadprivate` variables is to hold a value within a parallel region, not necessarily across parallel regions. Consequently, there may be requirements to copy a value into a region. The `copyin` clause copies the value from the master thread into the `threadprivate` values held by the worker threads. This clause can be placed on parallel regions. Listing 7.44 shows an example of using the `copyin` clause. The value of the variable `i` within the parallel region will be –1 for all threads.

Listing 7.44 **Using `copyin` to Copy Data from the Master Thread**

```
#include<stdio.h>
#include<omp.h>

int i;
#pragma omp threadprivate( i )

void main()
{
  i = -1;
  #pragma omp parallel copyin( i )
  {
    printf( "Parallel value %i\n", i );
  }
}
```

The `copyprivate` directive can be used to propagate the value of a `threadprivate` variable calculated in a `single` region to all threads. Although this applies to the `single` directive, the impact of the clause is at the end of the `single` region where the value is copied from the single thread to all the other threads. This can be used for the initialization of the `threadprivate` variables or dissemination of a new value to all threads. Listing 7.45 shows an example of using `copyprivate`. In this example, all threads will receive the value 2 for their private copy of the variable `i`.

Listing 7.45 **Using `copyprivate` to Copy Data a Single Thread to All Other Threads**

```
#include<stdio.h>
#include<omp.h>

int i;
#pragma omp threadprivate( i )
```

```
int main()
{
  i = -1;
  #pragma omp parallel
  {
    #pragma omp single copyprivate( i )
    {
      i = 2;
    }
    printf( "Parallel value %i\n", i );
  }
}
```

Controlling the OpenMP Runtime Environment

The OpenMP runtime environment can be controlled in up to three different ways. We have already encountered the environment variable OMP_NUM_THREADS to set the number of threads that the program uses. However, it is also possible to set this through programmatic calls to the runtime library or even as clauses placed onto the directives in the source code. Clauses will override the settings from calls to API functions, and these will override any environment settings. This section discusses the various settings that can be configured and the options available for configuring them.

Setting the Number of Threads

As previously seen, the number of threads used by an OpenMP application can be set through the environment variable OMP_NUM_THREADS. It is also possible to set the number of threads using the function call omp_set_num_threads(), as shown in Listing 7.46. Calls to omp_set_num_threads() change the default value for all subsequent parallel regions. It is possible to determine the number of threads using the function call omp_get_max_threads(). The function call omp_get_thread_num() will return a unique ID for each thread.

Listing 7.46 **Setting the Number of Threads**

```
#include <omp.h>
#include <stdio.h>

int main()
{
  double total = 0.0;
  double array[1000];
  omp_set_num_threads( 2 );
  #pragma omp parallel for reduction( +: total )
  for ( int i=0; i<1000; i++ )
```

```
  {
    total += array[i];
  }
  printf( "Total=%f\n", total );
  printf( "Threads=%i\n", omp_get_max_threads() );
}
```

The number of threads for a parallel region can be specified in the source code using the num_threads(*threads*) clause. The value for the number of threads can be fixed, or it can be an integer calculated based on some other factors. Listing 7.47 shows an example of using a fixed value for this.

Listing 7.47 **Setting the Number of Threads**

```
#include <omp.h>
#include <stdio.h>

int main()
{
  double total = 0.0;
  double array[1000];
  #pragma omp parallel for reduction( +: total ) num_threads( 2 )
  for ( int i=0; i<1000; i++ )
  {
    total += array[i];
  }
  printf( "Total=%f\n", total);
  printf( "Threads=%i\n", omp_get_max_threads() );
}
```

The num_threads clause will override the default value just for this single parallel region. The next parallel region will again take the default value for the number of threads, unless this too has a num_threads clause.

There is one other environment variable that can set the number of threads. OMP_THREAD_LIMIT sets the maximum number of threads that are allowed. It is an implementation defined as to whether this limit will be imposed on all attempts to use more threads than this limit. The value for this limit can be obtained through the function call omp_get_thread_limit().

An OpenMP implementation can honor the environment variable OMP_DYNAMIC. This environment variable can be set to either true or false. If it is set to true, then the OpenMP implementation can react to runtime conditions and use fewer threads than requested for any parallel region. This variable can be set at runtime with a call to omp_set_dynamic(), and its value can be read by a call to omp_get_dynamic().

Setting Runtime Loop Scheduling

The scheduling for loops with the runtime scheduling clause is controlled with the environment variable OMP_SCHEDULE. The schedule can also be set at runtime through a call to omp_set_schedule(), and the current schedule can be obtained through a call to omp_get_schedule(). The function calls to get and set the schedule take two parameters. The first is an integer that indicates the scheduling requested. The second is the chunk size (the second parameter will be ignored for schedules that do not require a chunk size). The available schedules are omp_sched_static, omp_sched_dynamic, omp_sched_guided, and omp_sched_auto. Listing 7.48 demonstrates using the calls to get and set the schedule.

Listing 7.48 **Getting and Setting the Schedule**

```
#include <omp.h>
#include <stdio.h>

int main()
{
  omp_sched_t schedule;
  int chunksize;
  omp_get_schedule( &schedule, &chunksize );
  printf( "Schedule = %i, chunksize = %i\n", schedule, chunksize );
  omp_set_schedule( omp_sched_guided, 10 );
}
```

Specifying the Stack Size for Worker Threads

The stack size of the master thread is set through the normal operating system environment. This can be changed using the ulimit command on UNIX-like platforms. On Windows, the default stack size is set at link time.

The default stack size for each worker thread created by the OpenMP runtime library is implementation specific. Depending on the requirements for stack space, this default may not be sufficient. The environment variable OMP_STACKSIZE determines the stack space for the worker threads. There is no call into the runtime library that sets this size.

The environment variable takes a number with an optional suffix. A number with no suffix is interpreted as kilobytes, the suffix B indicates that the number is in bytes, the suffix K indicates that it is in kilobytes, the suffix M is interpreted as megabytes, and the suffix G indicates gigabytes.

Waiting for Work to Complete

For most parallel constructs, there is an implicit barrier at the end to ensure that all threads complete their work before the next block of code is started. This section describes the options in OpenMP for changing the default barrier behavior.

Allowing Threads to Continue Execution Beyond a Parallel Region

The `nowait` clause applies to `parallel for`, `parallel sections`, and `single` directives. All of these directives have an implied wait at the end of the parallel region. Use of the directive means that the threads in the parallel region will continue into the next code region once they have completed the current one without waiting for the other worker threads to complete their work. Listing 7.49 contains an example of two `for` loops that iterate over two different ranges on two different sets of variables. Once the threads have completed the first loop, there is no reason why they should not start work on the second loop. This preference can be denoted by labeling the first loop with the `nowait` clause. The second loop keeps the implicit wait clause, so execution will not continue until all the threads complete their work on the second loop.

Listing 7.49 **Using the** `nowait` **Clause**

```
double calc( double *a, int lena, double *b, int lenb )
{
  double totala = 0.0, totalb = 0.0;
  #pragma omp parallel
  {
    #pragma omp for nowait reduction( +: totala )
    for ( int i=0; i<lena; i++ )
    {
      totala += a[i];
    }
    #pragma omp for reduction( +:totalb )
    for ( int i=0; i<lenb; i++ )
    {
      totalb += b[i];
    }
  }
  return totala + totalb;
}
```

Causing Threads to Wait Until All the Threads Have Completed Their Work

The `barrier` directive places an explicit barrier in a parallel region. In Listing 7.50, the `barrier` directive is used with the `master` directive to ensure that all threads wait while the master thread completes its task. The `master` directive does not have an implicit wait clause, so without the barrier directive, the single thread may print its output before the master thread. With this barrier in place, the code will always print out the string `"Master thread"` before it prints the string `"Single thread"`.

Listing 7.50 **Using the** `barrier` **Directive to Cause Other Threads to Wait for Master Thread**

```c
#include <stdio.h>

int main()
{
  #pragma omp parallel
  {
    #pragma omp master
    {
      printf( "Master thread\n" );
    }
    #pragma omp barrier
    #pragma omp single
    {
      printf( "Single thread\n" );
    }
  }
}
```

Waiting for All Child Tasks to Complete

When an application has been parallelized using tasks, it can be useful to wait for all the current child tasks from a parallel region to complete before continuing execution. The `taskwait` directive ensures that this condition is met. Consider the code shown in Listing 7.51.

Listing 7.51 **Using the** `taskwait` **Directive Wait for Child Tasks to Complete**

```c
#include <stdio.h>

int work( int i )
{
  if ( i > 0 )
  {
    #pragma omp parallel
    {
      #pragma omp task
      {
        work( i-1 );
      }
      #pragma omp task
      {
        work( i-1 );
      }
      #pragma omp taskwait
```

```
        printf( "Completed %i\n", i );
      }
    }
  }
}

void main()
{
  work( 3 );
}
```

In this example, the `taskwait` directive is used to ensure that the child tasks complete before the parent task performs its work, which is printing the value of the variable i. In the absence of the `taskwait` directive, it would be possible for the parent task to print its output before the child tasks printed theirs. Listing 7.52 shows the output from this application.

Listing 7.52 **Output Showing Effect of Task Wait on Ordering of Task Execution**

```
% cc -O -xopenmp -xloopinfo taskwait.c
% ./a.out
Completed 1
Completed 1
Completed 2
Completed 1
Completed 1
Completed 2
...
```

Restricting the Threads That Execute a Region of Code

There are situations where it is necessary to restrict the number of threads that can execute a block of code. For example, there might be algorithmic reasons where only a single thread should execute a region of code. Alternatively, for correctness, it may be necessary to ensure that only a single thread at a time executes a region of code. It may also be necessary to restrict the number of threads executing a parallel region if there is insufficient work for more threads to complete. This section describes multiple ways that the number of threads can be restricted.

Executing a Region of Code Using a Single Thread

We met the `single` directive in the section "Using OpenMP for Dynamically Defined Parallel Tasks." The `single` directive specifies that only one thread will execute the code in the region. All the other threads will wait for this code to be executed before continuing. The `nowait` clause can be used if the other threads should continue execution before the single thread completes execution. For an example of the `single` directive, see Listing 7.40.

Allowing Only the Master Thread to Execute a Region of Code

The `master` directive is similar to the `single` directive in that it specifies only one thread should execute the enclosed region. There are two differences between the directives. The first is that it identifies that the master thread is the one that will do the work; the `single` directive does not specify which thread will perform the work. The second difference is that the `master` directive does not cause the other threads to wait for the work in the region to be completed before they continue.

The `master` directive is useful in situations where only one thread needs to complete the work. It ensures that the same thread always executes the region of code, so any thread-local variables will carry over from previous executions. This can be useful for broadcasting and sharing the value of variables between threads. An example of the `master` directive can be seen in Listing 7.50.

Restricting Execution of a Region of Code to a Single Thread

For correctness, it is sometimes necessary to restrict a region of code so that it is executed only by a single thread at a time. This can be achieved using the `critical` directive. Listing 7.53 shows a very inefficient way of performing a reduction using a `critical` directive to ensure that only one thread changes the reduction variable at any time.

Listing 7.53 **Reduction Operation Implemented Using a `critical` Directive**

```
double calc( double* array, int length )
{
  double total = 0.0;
  #pragma omp parallel for
  for ( int i=0; i<length; i++ )
  {
    #pragma omp critical
    {
      total += array[i];
    }
  }
  return total;
}
```

The `critical` directive takes an optional name. This enables the same critical section to protect multiple regions of code. For example, all accesses to the variable `total` could be protected by a `critical` section of the name `total_critical_section`, as shown in Listing 7.54.

Listing 7.54 **Named Critical Section**

```
#pragma omp critical( total_critical_section )
{
  total += array[i];
}
```

Performing Operations Atomically

Sometimes, all that is necessary is the atomic modification of a variable. OpenMP supports this through the `atomic` directive that applies only to the following modification of a variable. Listing 7.55 shows how the reduction could be coded using an `atomic` directive. The `atomic` directive ensures correct behavior but may not be any faster than using a critical section.

Listing 7.55 **Reduction Implemented Using an Atomic Directive**

```
double calc( double* array, int length )
{
  double total = 0.0;
  #pragma omp parallel for
  for ( int i=0; i<length; i++ )
  {
    #pragma omp atomic
    total += array[i];
  }
  return total;
}
```

Using Mutex Locks

OpenMP also supports the flexibility offered by mutex locks, which are supported through OpenMP locks. A *lock* is declared to be of the type `omp_lock_t` and initialized through a call to `omp_init_lock()`. The lock is destroyed with a call to `omp_destroy_lock()`.

To acquire the lock, the code calls `omp_set_lock()`, and to release the lock, the code calls `omp_unset_lock()`. The code can test whether the lock is available by calling `omp_test_lock()`. It is possible to rewrite the reduction code to use OpenMP locks, as shown in Listing 7.56.

Listing 7.56 **Reduction Implemented Using an OpenMP Lock**

```
#include <omp.h>

omp_lock_t lock;

double calc( double* array, int length )
{
  double total = 0.0;
  #pragma omp parallel for
  for ( int i=0; i<length; i++ )
  {
    omp_set_lock( &lock );
    total += array[i];
    omp_unset_lock( &lock );
  }
```

```
    return total;
}

int main()
{
  double array[1024];
  omp_init_lock( &lock );
  calc( array, 1024 );
  omp_destroy_lock( &lock );
}
```

Conditional Serial Execution of Parallel Regions

In some instances, it can be useful to identify conditions when a parallel region should be executed by a single thread. This saves having to place both a serial version and a parallel version of the block of code in the source of the application.

The most obvious occasion for doing this would be when there is insufficient work to justify using more than one thread. The `if()` clause can be applied to a `parallel` directive to determine the conditions when the region should be executed in parallel. Listing 7.57 shows an example of using this directive. The code will execute the region using multiple threads only if the variable `length` has a value greater than 1,000.

Listing 7.57 **Conditional Parallel Execution Using the `if` Clause**

```
double calc( double * array, int length )
{
  double total = 0.0;
  #pragma omp parallel for reduction( +: total ) if( length > 1000 )
  for ( int i=0; i<length; i++ )
  {
    total += array[i];
  }
  return total;
}
```

Another use for the `if()` clause would be in situations where using multiple threads to execute a region of code would cause correctness issues. For example, if a loop calculates some function of two vectors, the code is sometimes called with vectors that alias. The `if()` clause can be used to check whether the vectors alias and execute the code in parallel only if no aliasing is present.

Ensuring That Code in a Parallel Region Is Executed in Order

In some cases, it may be necessary to ensure that a section of code is executed in the same order as the serial code would execute it. Unfortunately, such an ordering is unlikely to allow the code to get the full benefit of using multiple threads, but it should enable some gains to be attained from parallelization.

OpenMP supports the `ordered` directive, which ensures that the order of parallel execution is the same as the serial ordering. The directive needs to be applied to the parallel region, and the loop also needs to be identified as an ordered loop using the `ordered` clause on the `parallel for` directive.

Listing 7.58 shows how the ordered directive can be used to ensure that the loop iterations are printed in the correct order.

Listing 7.58 **Using the Ordered Directive to Ensure Code Executes in the Serial Order**

```
#include <stdio.h>
#include <omp.h>

int main()
{
  #pragma omp parallel for ordered
  for ( int i=0; i<100; i++ )
  {
    #pragma omp ordered
    {
      printf(" Iteration %i, thread ID %i\n", i, omp_get_thread_num() );
    }
  }
}
```

The `ordered` directive is most useful when applied to loops that do not use static scheduling. With the default static scheduling used in the example, the first thread will execute the first portion of the iterations, the second thread the second portion, and so on. Since the `ordered` region needs to be executed in the serial order, the second thread ends up waiting at the `ordered` code block until the first thread has completed all of its assigned work. This means that the work is serialized, but each serial chunk of work has been performed by a different thread.

The `ordered` directive is a useful way of exploring the impact of the scheduling on the order in which iterations are assigned to threads. Listing 7.59 shows the code modified to use dynamic scheduling.

Listing 7.59 **Using the Ordered Directive to Explore the Scheduling Directive**

```c
#include <stdio.h>
#include <omp.h>

int main()
{
  #pragma omp parallel for ordered schedule( dynamic )
  for ( int i=0; i<100; i++ )
  {
    #pragma omp ordered
    {
      printf( "Iteration %i, thread ID %i\n", i, omp_get_thread_num() );
    }
  }
}
```

Listing 7.60 shows the effect of this change in scheduling. Dynamic scheduling causes the two threads to work with the default chunk size of a single iteration, so the two threads alternate performing iterations.

Listing 7.60 **Exploring the Impact of Dynamic Scheduling**

```
$ cc -O -xopenmp ordered.c
$ export OMP_NUM_THREADS=2
$ ./a.out
Iteration 0 Thread 0
Iteration 1 Thread 1
Iteration 2 Thread 0
Iteration 3 Thread 1
...
```

Collapsing Loops to Improve Workload Balance

The `parallel for` directive applies only to the next loop. As always, it is best to apply parallelization at the outermost loop, because this reduces the number of synchronizations necessary. However, a low trip count for the outer loop will limit the maximum number of threads that can be used in parallel. In these cases, it might be appropriate to parallelize the inner loop, since this could have a higher iteration count. Without knowing the trip counts for the two loops, it is not possible to decide which strategy is more appropriate.

However, OpenMP provides a way of avoiding issues with the outermost loop having a low trip count, which is to collapse the inner and outer loops into a single loop. The clause to do this is `collapse`, which takes the number of loops to collapse as a parameter. Listing 7.61 shows an example of a code where the outer loop has a low trip count, and using the `collapse` clause enables scaling to higher numbers of threads.

Listing 7.61 **Using the `collapse` Clause to Improve Scaling**

```
#include <math.h>

void main()
{
  double array[2][10000];
  #pragma omp parallel for collapse( 2 )
  for( int i=0; i<2; i++ )
    for( int j=0; j<10000; j++ )
      array[i][j] = sin( i+j );
}
```

Without the `collapse` clause, the outermost loop will only ever scale to two threads. With the `collapse` clause, the combined loop can be up to a theoretical 20,000 threads (although the synchronization overheads would cause the code to run slowly far before that count was reached). Using the `collapse` clause may introduce additional overhead into the parallel region, so it is worth evaluating whether the clause will improve performance or cause a performance loss.

Enforcing Memory Consistency

Memory consistency is when the values held in registers by a thread match those held in memory. If another thread modifies a variable held in a register by this thread, the value has become inconsistent and needs to be refetched from memory. OpenMP directives already enforce appropriate memory consistency, so it is rare for it to be a concern for codes parallelized using OpenMP. However, there could be situations where it is necessary to manually enforce consistency.

OpenMP allows the developer to explicitly specify the places in the code where variables need to be saved to memory or loaded from memory using the `flush` directive. Unless the directive specifies a list of variables, it applies to all the thread visible state. If a list of variables is specified, these variables will either be stored to memory or be reloaded from memory depending on which action is necessary.

The example shown in Listing 7.62 uses the `flush` directive to produce a synchronization barrier between a pair of threads.

Listing 7.62 **Using the `flush` Directive to Produce a Barrier**

```
#include <stdio.h>
#include <omp.h>
#include <stdlib.h>
```

```
void main()
{
  int *ready = calloc( sizeof(int), 2 );

  #pragma omp parallel num_threads( 2 )
  {
     printf( "Thread %i is ready\n", omp_get_thread_num() );
     ready[ omp_get_thread_num() ] = 1;
     int neighbour = ( omp_get_thread_num()+1 ) % omp_get_num_threads();

     while( ready[neighbour] == 0 )
     {
       #pragma omp flush
     }

     printf( "Thread %i is done\n", omp_get_thread_num() );
  }
  free( ready );
}
```

The master thread allocates an array with a single element per thread. In the parallel region, each thread sets their index in the array to be one and then waits for their neighboring thread to set their index to be nonzero. Each thread is released from the barrier when its neighboring thread arrives. The flush directive is used to ensure that the current thread stores its value into the array and that the current thread constantly reloads its neighbor's value until the neighboring thread sets it to one.

An Example of Parallelization

As an example of automatic parallelization and parallelization using OpenMP, we will consider a short code that determines whether each point in a matrix is in or out of the Mandelbrot set. Listing 7.63 shows the code.

Listing 7.63 **Code to Determine Whether a Point Is in the Mandelbrot Set**

```
int inSet( double ix, double iy )
{
  int    iterations = 0;
  double x = ix, y = iy;
  double x2 = x*x, y2 = y*y;
  while ( (x2 + y2 < 4) && (iterations < 1000) )  /* Line 9 */
  {
    y = 2*x*y + iy;
    x = x2 − y2 + ix;
    x2= x*x;
    y2= y*y;
```

```
    iterations++;
  }
  return iterations;
}
```

The code in Listing 7.63 contains a single loop. This loop is not suitable for automatic parallelization for two reasons:

- Each iteration of the loop depends on the previous iteration. It is not possible for the calculation of the next iteration to start until the previous iteration has completed. This fact means that the loop can be calculated only in serial.

- The loop iterates until the point either escapes a circle of radius 2 centered around the origin or the maximum iteration count is exceeded. Since the trip count is unknown until the loop is executed, it is not possible to assign the work to multiple threads because it is not known how much work there is to perform.

Listing 7.64 shows the main code, including OpenMP parallelization directives. This allocates a large matrix to hold the results of the calculations and then computes for every point in the matrix whether it is in or out of the Mandelbrot set. The final loop in the code is purely there to ensure that the compiler does not eliminate the main loops because the values are not used.

Listing 7.64 **Main Loop for Mandelbrot Code**

```
#define SIZE 4000

int main()
{
  int *matrix[SIZE];
  for ( int i=0; i<SIZE; i++ )    /* Line 24 */
  {
    matrix[i] = (int*)malloc( SIZE*sizeof(int) );
  }

  #pragma omp parallel for
  for ( int x=0; x<SIZE; x++ )    /* Line 30 */
   for ( int y=0; y<SIZE; y++ )   /* Line 31 */
   {
     double xv = ( (double)x - (SIZE/2) ) / (SIZE/4);
     double yv = ( (double)y - (SIZE/2) ) / (SIZE/4);
     matrix[x][y] = inSet(xv,yv);
   }

  for ( int x=0; x<SIZE; x++ )    /* Line 38 */
   for ( int y=0; y<SIZE; y++ )   /* Line 39 */
     if ( matrix[x][y] == -7 ) { printf(""); }
}
```

To get automatic parallelization to work, the routine inSet must be inlined so that the compiler can determine that parallelization is safe. Solaris Studio compilers require an optimization level of at least -xO4. Listing 7.65 shows the result of compiling the code. The compiler has parallelized the inlined call to inSet, but it has only been able to parallelize the innermost loop. The outermost loop iterates over an array of pointers, and multiples of those pointers could point to the same memory address; hence, the compiler cannot parallelize the outer loop because of aliasing issues.

Listing 7.65 **Results of Using Automatic Parallelization on the Mandelbrot Example**

```
$ cc -xO4 -xautopar -xloopinfo mandle.c
"mandle.c", line 9: not parallelized, loop has multiple exits
"mandle.c", line 9: not parallelized, loop has multiple exits (inlined loop)
"mandle.c", line 24: not parallelized, call may be unsafe
"mandle.c", line 30: not parallelized, unsafe dependence
"mandle.c", line 31: PARALLELIZED
"mandle.c", line 38: not parallelized, call may be unsafe
"mandle.c", line 39: not parallelized, call may be unsafe
```

The source code in Listing 7.64 already includes an OpenMP directive to make the outermost loop parallel. Listing 7.66 shows the result of compiling and running the OpenMP code with various numbers of threads.

Listing 7.66 **Performance of Code Parallelized with OpenMP**

```
% export OMP_NUM_THREADS=1
% timex ./a.out
real          28.83
user          28.69
sys            0.07
% export OMP_NUM_THREADS=2
% timex ./a.out
real          20.92
user          28.69
sys            0.07
% export OMP_NUM_THREADS=3
% timex ./a.out
real          23.35
user          28.69
sys            0.06
```

The code takes about 29 seconds of wall time to run with a single thread, roughly 21 seconds with two threads and just over 23 seconds with three threads. This is far from ideal scaling, which would be that the runtime decreased in proportion to the number of running threads. Notice that the user time for the code remains constant. This means that the same amount of work is performed, regardless of the number of threads used. This indicates that the poor scaling is not the result of the threads having to perform an increasing amount of work. If the amount of work is not increasing, it suggests that the scaling problems are the result of that work being poorly distributed between the threads.

Figure 7.1 shows the timeline view from the Solaris Studio Performance Analyzer running the code with two threads. This view shows the activity of the two threads over the entire duration of the run. There are three lines shown. The top line shows the activity of all the threads in the application. This shows that initially both threads were running entirely in user mode, and around 8 seconds into the run, only one of the two threads was in user mode while the other thread was idle.

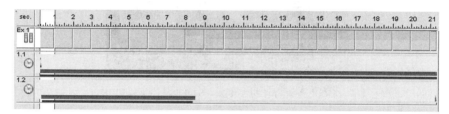

Figure 7.1 Timeline view of Mandelbrot code run with two threads

The other two lines indicate the activity of the two threads. The top one shows that the master thread was active over the entire duration of the run, as is to be expected by the OpenMP execution model. The second thread was active only during the first 8.5 seconds of the run. This confirms that the poor scaling is because of an unequal distribution of work between the two threads.

It is easy to understand where this workload imbalance comes from when the actual image being computed is viewed. Figure 7.2 shows the image that is being computed. One thread is computing the left half, the other the right half. For a large number of the points, colored black in the image, it takes only a few iterations to determine that the point is not in the set. However, it takes the maximum limit on the iteration count to determine that a point is, or might be, in the set; these points are colored white.

The areas that are shaded black in the figure take relatively few iterations and are computed quickly. The areas that are shaded white take many iterations and therefore take some time to compute. Comparing the left and right halves of the image, it is apparent that the right half contains more black pixels than the left half. This means that the thread computing the right half will take less time than the thread computing the left half. This is the source of the workload imbalance between the two threads.

Fixing the workload imbalance is relatively easy since it is just a matter of changing the scheduling clause for the parallel code. Either dynamic or guided scheduling could be used. Listing 7.67 shows the code modified to use dynamic scheduling.

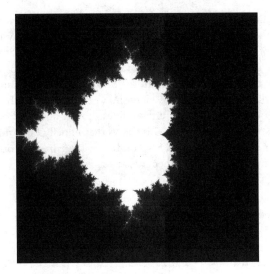

Figure 7.2 Mandelbrot image calculated by two threads

Listing 7.67 **Mandelbrot Code Modified to Use Dynamic Scheduling**

```
#define SIZE 4000

int main()
{
  int *matrix[SIZE];
  for (int i=0; i<SIZE; i++)
  {
    matrix[i]=(int*)malloc(SIZE*sizeof(int));
  }

  #pragma omp parallel for schedule( dynamic )
  for (int x=0; x<SIZE; x++)
   for (int y=0; y<SIZE; y++)
   {
     double xv = ((double)x-(SIZE/2))/(SIZE/4);
     double yv = ((double)y-(SIZE/2))/(SIZE/4);
     matrix[x][y]=inSet(xv,yv);
   }

  for (int x=0; x<SIZE; x++)
   for (int y=0; y<SIZE; y++)
     if (matrix[x][y]==-7){printf("");}
}
```

Listing 7.68 shows the resulting scaling from this code. With dynamic scheduling, the work is evenly distributed across the threads, leading to nearly linear performance gains as the number of threads increases.

Listing 7.68 **Scaling of Dynamically Scheduled Code**

```
% setenv OMP_NUM_THREADS 1
% timex ./a.out
real         28.84
user         28.69
sys           0.07
% setenv OMP_NUM_THREADS 2
% timex ./a.out
real         15.42
user         28.69
sys           0.07
% setenv OMP_NUM_THREADS 3
% timex ./a.out
real         10.49
user         28.70
sys           0.08
```

Summary

This chapter has discussed how the compiler can enable parallelization either automatically or by adding OpenMP directives to the source code. You should now be familiar with the limitations of automatic parallelization and the typical issues in the source code that reduce the ability of the compiler to automatically parallelize code. You should also be able to identify and fix these issues, leading to code with improved scaling.

You should also understand how OpenMP directives can be used to produce parallel applications. You will know the various synchronization directives and objects that are provided by the OpenMP specification. You will also know how to apply or modify OpenMP directives to improve the scaling of an application.

8

Hand-Coded Synchronization and Sharing

The synchronization mechanisms provided by the operating system are typically designed to be fully featured, fast, and correct. In most cases, these will be the appropriate mechanism to use. However, there will be situations where it is desirable to have a different mechanism for synchronization and sharing, and often the motivation for this is one of improved efficiency.

Many pitfalls are associated with coding synchronization primitives. The objective of this chapter is to describe the issues that need to be faced when writing synchronization and communication primitives, both to provide information when doing this and to explain why the operating system–provided mechanisms are coded the way that they are.

This chapter starts with a discussion of atomic operations and the atomic operations that are provided by the operating system. This is a useful warm-up for a discussion of how atomic operations can be hand-coded. The final section of the chapter discusses the issues around writing synchronization primitives.

Atomic Operations

Atomic memory operations appear to the rest of the system as operations that either succeed or fail; there's no partial state or state where the operation completes but the result is incorrect. Loads and stores, in most instances, are atomic. A load instruction will not fetch half the data from the most recent store to that cache line and half from what was previously held in the cache line. Similarly, a store will not perform a partial update of a memory address.

More complex operations are not atomic. For example, incrementing a value held in memory is usually implemented as a load of the value, the increment, and then a store of the new value back to memory. Unfortunately, in a multithreaded environment, another thread could interrupt this sequence and replace the original value held in memory with a new value. The final store would store the calculated value back to memory, but the entire operation would not reflect an increment of the new value held in memory. This is an example of a data race, as we have previously discussed.

In this situation, it would be useful to have an atomic increment instruction. This would take the value in memory, increment it, and replace it back to memory as a single operation without the possibility of other threads updating the value between the load and store parts of the operation. On x86 processors, the xadd instruction can be combined with the lock prefix to produce an atomic add, or the inc instruction can be combined with the lock prefix to produce an atomic increment. Listing 8.1 shows the code snippets to do this.

Listing 8.1 x86 Assembly Language Atomic Addition Variants

```
int atomic_add_int( volatile int *address, int value )
{
  asm volatile( "lock xadd %0,%1":
                "+r"(value):
                "+m"(*address):
                "memory" );
  return value;
}

int atomic_inc_int( int *address )
{
  asm volatile ( "lock inc %0": :
                "+m"(*address):
                "memory" );
  return (*address);
}
```

The routines are coded using gcc inline assembly language. Although it is not the intention of this book to dwell at this low level, it is appropriate to describe how the statements are put together. The keyword asm identifies the following text as an assembly language statement that will be inlined directly into the code. The keyword volatile tells the compiler not to move the statement from where it has been placed, because such movement could cause a difference to the statement's semantics.

The assembly language code is enclosed in the parentheses. There are multiple parts to the code. The first item in the parentheses, surrounded by quotes, is the instruction. The instruction uses virtual registers %0 and %1 as parameters. The compiler will allocate real registers later and will be responsible for populating these registers with the appropriate values.

After the assembly language instruction, there are up to three colon-delimited lists. These are optional extended syntax. The first list is of output variables and whether these are accesses to registers or memory. In the example, the expression "+r"(value) means that the output parameter is a register that should be used to update the variable value. The plus sign means that the register will be both read and written by the instruction.

The second list contains the input values and where these are located. Both routines take the pointer address as an input value, and the expression "+m"(*address) indicates that this pointer is used as a memory access. The plus sign indicates that the instruction will both read and write the location in memory.

The third list is the "clobber" list indicating what the instruction will modify. In both instances, the instruction will modify memory.

The virtual registers are numbered from the input registers, so register %0 is assigned the value of the variable `address`. The output registers are the next set of virtual registers, so the variable `value` gets assigned to register %1.

It is also useful to look at the actual assembly language instructions. The `xadd` instruction is an exchange add, so it adds the variable `value` to the value held at the memory address, but it also returns the value held at the address before the add operation was performed; this is the exchange operation. The `inc` instruction just adds one to the value held in memory but does not return a value in any register. Both instructions are prefixed with the `lock` operation. The `lock` operation locks the system bus so that no other processors can touch the memory location that is being updated; hence, it is the `lock` prefix that actually makes these instructions atomic. Without it, the result of the operations would be undefined if there were multiple threads acting on the same memory location.

The routine `atomic_add_int()` adds the specified amount to the value held at the memory location and returns the value held in memory before the atomic operation.

The routine `atomic_inc_int()` increments the value held at the memory location and returns the value currently held in memory. Since the `inc` instruction does not return the new value, the return value is a load of the value held in memory. This need not be the true result of the operation; the value could have been modified between the atomic operation and the final load.

Using Compare and Swap Instructions to Form More Complex Atomic Operations

Not all processors implement atomic add or increment instructions. However, most processors do implement a variant of the compare and swap instruction. This instruction can form the basis of most atomic operations.

An atomic compare and swap (CAS) operation compares the value held at a memory location with the value held in a register. If the value at that location matches the desired value passed to the instruction, then the value held in memory will be atomically updated with a second value passed into the instruction. The return value from CAS is the original value that was held in memory. If the operation was successful, the return value will be the same as the desired value. If the operation did not succeed, the return value will be some other value. This enables the code to determine whether the operation succeeded.

This operation can be useful in a number of situations. For example, assume a mutex lock is implemented using a variable that holds one when the lock is held or zero when the lock is available. The CAS operation can be used to transition the lock from free to taken. To acquire the lock, the variable `lock` must hold the value zero, and the instruction needs to atomically replace the zero with a one. Listing 8.2 shows the code for a simple spinlock. The `volatile` keyword ensures that the compiler repeats the CAS operation on every iteration.

Listing 8.2 **A Simple Spinlock Implemented Using CAS**

```
#ifdef __sparc
int CAS( volatile int* addr, int ov, int nv )
{
  asm volatile( "cas %1, %2, %0":
                "=r"(nv):
                "m"(*addr), "r"(ov), "0"(nv):
                "memory" );
  return nv;
}
#else
int CAS( volatile int* addr, int ov, int nv )
{
  asm volatile( "lock; cmpxchg %2, %1":
                "=a"(ov):
                "m"(*addr), "r"(nv), "a"(ov):
                "memory" );
  return ov;
}
#endif

void lock_spinlock( volatile int * lock )
{
  while ( CAS(lock, 0, 1) != 0 ) {} // Spin until lock acquired
}

void free_spinlock( volatile int * lock )
{
  *lock = 0;
}
```

It is tempting to imagine that a spinlock could be implemented without using atomic operations, as shown in Listing 8.3. The problem with the code is that it does not guarantee that only a single thread will acquire the lock. If a thread observes that the lock is free, it will then assume that it has acquired it. The atomic operation used in Listing 8.2 ensures that the only way the thread can exit is if it actually has acquired the lock.

Listing 8.3 **An Incorrect Implementation of a Spinlock**

```
void lock_spinlock( volatile int * lock )
{
  while ( *lock == 1 ) {}  // Spin while lock busy
```

```
    *lock = 1 ;
}

void free_spinlock( volatile int * lock )
{
    *lock = 0;
}
```

The CAS instruction can also be used in situations where atomic modification of an unusual variable type is required. Consider the situation where atomic increment of a floating-point value is required. Listing 8.4 shows code to perform this.

Listing 8.4 **Code to Atomically Increment a Floating-Point Value**

```
void atomic_add_float( volatile float * variable, float increment )
{
    union
    {
        int asint;
        float asfp;
    } oldvalue, newvalue;

    do
    {
        oldvalue.asfp = *variable;                      // Line 11
        newvalue.asfp = oldvalue.asfp + increment;  // Line 12
    }
    while ( CAS( variable, oldvalue.asint, newvalue.asint )
            != oldvalue.asint );
}
```

The code to perform the atomic update of a floating-point variable appears rather complex. A fair amount of the complexity is because the CAS operation takes integer parameters; hence, the floating-point values need to be converted into integers. This is the function of the union in the code.

The code reads the value of the variable to be modified and then prepares the modified version of this variable. In the code, the variable is read only once, at line 11, and then held in the local variable oldvalue. This is to avoid a data race where the value changes between the first read of the variable and its use as one operand in the addition, at line 12. The race is subtle. Suppose that the first time the variable is read, at line 11, it has the value 20; this is recorded as the original value of the variable. At this point, another thread changes the value of the variable, so the second time it is read, at line 12, it has the value 21. The value 21 is incremented to 22, and this will become the new value of the variable if the operation is successful. Suppose now that the other thread has returned the value of the variable to 20 by the time the CAS operation is tried. Since the variable contains 20 and this is the expected value, the CAS operation will store the value 22 into the variable, rather than the correct value of 21.

We can explore this problem of reloading values with another example. Listing 8.5 shows code that adds an element to the top of a list. The code creates a new element and stores the appropriate value in this. The loop keeps attempting to add this new element to the front of the list until it succeeds. Each iteration of the loop sets the next field of the new element to be the next element in the list and then attempts to atomically compare and swap the head of the list with a pointer to the new element. If the compare and swap succeeded, the return value will be the pointer to the element that used to be the top of the list. If this happens, the code has succeeded, and the loop can exit.

Listing 8.5 **Code to Add an Element to the Top of a List**

```
void addelement( element_t ** head, int value )
{
  element_t * element = (element_t*)malloc(sizeof(element_t));
  element->value = value;
  while (element!=0)
  {
    element->next = *head;
    if ( CAS( head, element->next, element ) == element->next)
    {
      element = 0;
    }
  }
}
```

The problem with this code is that the CAS() function call causes the compiler to reload the value of element->next. There is a short window of opportunity for another thread to take the top element from the list between the CAS() function call and the load of element->next. If this other thread takes the element off the list and modifies the value of element->next, then the compare and swap will not match with the new value of element->next, and the loop will assume that it failed to add the element to the queue, even though it actually succeeded. So, the code will attempt to add the element a second time, causing an error. The solution is to hold the original value of *head in a local variable and use this in the comparison to determine whether the compare and swap was successful.

The opportunity for this data corruption to occur is only a few cycles in duration. However, for a sufficiently long-running program, this will eventually occur. In common with all data-race type errors, the result of this data corruption will be detected arbitrarily far from when the corruption occurred.

Returning to the atomic add operation, notice that the operation is actually a loop. Although the observable effect is that the value in the variable is incremented atomically, this operation can take an arbitrary number of iterations around the loop to complete. This is actually a *lock-free* algorithm for updating the variable. This is really to contrast with the obvious implementation using mutex locks shown in Listing 8.6.

Listing 8.6 **Addition of Values Using Mutex Locks**

```
void atomic_add_float( pthread_mutex_t * lock, float * var, float inc )
{
  pthread_mutex_lock( lock );
  *var += inc;
  pthread_mutex_unlock( lock );
}
```

As mutex locks can be implemented using CAS operations, the resulting code for the two situations is structurally not too dissimilar—both codes have a single loop. The difference is that the mutex lock loops on the CAS of the *lock*, whereas the lock-free variant loops on the CAS of the *variable*.

Enforcing Memory Ordering to Ensure Correct Operation

In the previous section, we looked at the implementation of a simple spinlock. Unfortunately, there is the potential for more implementation complexity. When writing any multithreaded code, it is important to consider the memory-ordering characteristics of the system. When a thread running on a multithread system performs a memory operation, that operation may or may not become visible to the rest of the system in the order in which it occurred.

For example, an application might perform two store operations. On some processors, the second store operation could become visible to other processors before the first store operation becomes visible. This is called *weak* memory ordering.

Consider this in the context of a mutex lock. The application updates a variable and stores it back to memory. It then frees the lock by writing a zero into the lock. If the system implements a weak memory ordering, the store to free the lock might become visible to other processors in the system before the store to update the data. Another processor that was waiting on the lock might see that the lock is free and read the value of the variable protected by the lock before the update of that variable is visible.

To stop this kind of error, it may be necessary to include instructions that enforce the desired memory ordering. Determining whether a particular processor requires these instructions typically requires a careful read of the documentation. However, code that assumes that these instructions are necessary will run correctly on hardware that does not need the instructions, whereas the converse is not true.

First, we'll consider the release of a mutex lock in more detail. The release operation is performed by storing a zero to the lock variable. The code executed while the mutex lock is held will update memory. It must be ensured that all the memory updates performed while the mutex is held are completed before the mutex is released. In the context of this discussion, the memory updates performed while the mutex was held must become visible to the rest of the system before the freeing of the mutex lock becomes visible.

To ensure that the correct order of operations is observed, it is sometimes necessary to use a *memory barrier* or *memory fence*. These stop the processor from executing further memory operations until the previous memory operations have completed. These instructions usually have different variants to enforce an order on different types of memory operations. In the case of the mutex lock release after a store operation, the memory barrier needs to enforce store ordering—no future store operations should become visible to the system until all proceeding stores have completed. Store ordering is the default for SPARC and x86 processors, so neither processor requires a memory barrier between two adjacent stores to enforce the order of the store operations.

It is less immediately obvious why loads have a similar constraint. Imagine that we have a reader-writer lock where a reader thread will only read data protected by the mutex and a writer thread can update those values. If a reader thread acquires the mutex, it wants to read those values while it still holds the mutex. The act of acquiring the mutex must complete before the load of the data protected by the mutex can start. A similar ordering constraint occurs when the mutex is freed. It is critical that the value of the variable protected by the mutex is read before the release of the mutex becomes visible to the system.

Loads and stores that occur after the mutex has been released can be speculated so that they occur before the barrier. This is safe because access to these variables is not protected by the mutex and can be completed by either holding or not holding the mutex. This kind of barrier is called a *release barrier*.

A similar process must take place when a mutex is acquired. Memory operations that occur after the mutex has been acquired must not be visible to the system until after the mutex has been safely acquired. Again, memory operations that occur before the mutex is acquired can still be ongoing after the mutex has been acquired. This is referred to as an *acquire barrier*.

Returning to the spinlock that we implemented in Listing 8.2, we can now update this in Listing 8.7 to include the appropriate barrier calls.

Listing 8.7 **Spinlock with Appropriate Memory Barriers**

```
void lock_spinlock( volatile int* lock )
{
  while ( CAS(lock, 0, 1) != 0 ) {}
  acquire_memory_barrier();  // Ensure that the CAS operation
                             // has become visible to the system
                             // before memory operations in the
                             // critical region start
}

void free_spinlock( volatile int * lock )
{
  release_memory_barrier();  // Ensure that all past memory operations
                             // have become visible to the system
                             // before the following store starts
  *lock = 0;
}
```

The kinds of memory barriers available are defined by the architecture. The x86 architecture defines the following:

- `mfence`. Ensures that all previous loads and stores are visible to the system before any future loads and stores become visible

- `sfence`. Ensures that all previous stores are visible to the system before any future stores become visible

- `lfence`. Ensures that all previous loads are visible to the system before any future loads become visible

The SPARC architecture defines a slightly finer set of memory barrier semantics. The instruction `membar` takes a combination of options to indicate the particular type of barrier required. The following types of memory barrier can be combined:

- `membar #StoreStore`. Ensures that all stores complete before the following stores

- `membar #StoreLoad`. Ensures that all stores complete before the following loads

- `membar #LoadStore`. Ensures that all loads complete before the following stores

- `membar #LoadLoad`. Ensures that all loads complete before the following loads

Modern SPARC and x86 processors implement a strong memory-ordering model. This means that memory-ordering operations are rarely needed. However, writing software that is safe for future processors where the memory-ordering constraints may have changed and older processors that implemented a weaker memory ordering requires that these instructions are included in the code. Processors that do not need the operations will typically ignore them and therefore get only minimal performance penalty.

On x86, the `mfence` instruction provides sufficient constraints on memory ordering for it to be used as both an acquire and a release barrier. On SPARC, it is sufficient to use `membar #LoadLoad|#LoadStore` to provide acquire barrier semantics to ensure that all previous loads have completed before any following memory operations. Release semantics are provided by `membar #LoadStore|#StoreStore` to ensure that all previous memory operations have completed before the following store instruction.

On both SPARC and x86 processors, atomic operations enforce total memory ordering; the atomic operation enforces an ordering between loads and older stores and loads and stores that are to be issued. Hence, in general, no memory barrier is required before or after an atomic operation.

Compiler Support of Memory-Ordering Directives

Windows provides the `MemoryBarrier()` macro, which causes the compiler to emit memory-ordering instructions. OS X provides `OSMemoryBarrier()`, which provides the same functionality.

gcc and Solaris Studio support using inline assembly to generate memory-ordering instructions. For example, `asm volatile ("mfence":::"memory")` would insert an `mfence` instruction at the desired location in the code.

Reordering of Operations by the Compiler

Although the hardware can reorder operations, it is also possible for the compiler to do the same. Although the compiler will try to do the "right thing," there will be situations where it needs hints in order to produce code that runs correctly.

It is often thought that the `volatile` keyword provides a safety net that stops the compiler from optimizing code. Unfortunately, this is not true. The `volatile` keyword determines that the compiler needs to reload data from memory when it needs to use it and should store it back to memory as soon as it is modified. It does not stop the compiler from performing optimizations around the data nor does it form any kind of protection against data races.

However, the `volatile` keyword is necessary to avoid the compiler optimizing away accesses to a variable. Consider the code in Listing 8.8. The variable `start` is declared as `volatile`. If this were not the case, then the compiler would determine that the loop was either not entered or entered and infinite.

Listing 8.8 **Code Where `volatile` Keyword Is Necessary to Ensure Reloading of Variable `start`**

```
volatile int start;

void waitforstart()
{
   while( start == 0 ) {}
}
```

A very similar situation exists with the code in Listing 8.9. In this case, the code contains a function call. Function calls, generally, cause the compiler to reload global data. However, if the variable `count` is not declared to be volatile, it is still possible for the compiler to generate an infinite loop. The reason for this is that if `count` does equal zero and it is not a volatile variable, then the call to `getElementFromList()` will not be made, and the variable will remain zero. An optimizing compiler may identify this situation and replace the `else` branch of the `if` statement with an infinite loop.

Listing 8.9 **Function Calls Do Not Always Enforce Reloading of All Variables**

```
volatile int count;

int* getnextelement()
{
   int element = 0;
   while( element == 0 )
   {
     if (count>0)
     {
       element = getElementFromList();
```

```
      }
    }
    return element;
}
```

The code shown in Listing 8.10 demonstrates a situation where the compiler can merge two loops, resulting in a change of behavior. The code creates four threads. Each thread runs the same routine that prints out a statement that the thread is ready and then waits on the `volatile` variable `start`. When the thread is started, it prints out a message before completing a short amount of work, printing a message indicating that it has completed its work and exiting.

The main code creates the threads and, once all the threads are created, signals to the threads that they can start working. Once this has been done, it waits for all the threads to complete their work, before calling `pthread_join()` on each of the threads.

Listing 8.10 **Code Where the Compiler May Reorder Operations**

```
#include <stdio.h>
#include <pthread.h>

volatile int start[4];
volatile int done[4];

void * work( void* param )
{
  int id = (int)param;
  while ( start[id] == 0 ) {}
  printf( "Thread %i started\n", id );
  double total=0;
  for ( int i=0; i<100000000; i++ ) { total += i; }
  printf( "Thread %i done\n", id );
  done[id] = 1;
}

int main()
{
  pthread_t thread[4];
  for ( int i=0; i<4; i++ )
  {
    pthread_create( &thread[i], 0, work, (void*)i );
    done[i]=0;
  }
  for ( int i=0; i<4; i++ )
  {
    start[i] = 1;
  }
```

```
for ( int i=0; i<4; i++ )
{
  while( done[i] == 0 ){}
}
for ( int i=0; i<4; i++ )
{
  pthread_join( thread[i], 0 );
}
}
```

Listing 8.11 shows the output from the code with and without optimization. There is a pronounced difference between the codes. When compiled without optimization, all the threads proceed at the same time, so the output from the application shows all the threads starting and then all the threads completing. When compiled with optimization, the threads are serialized, so each thread prints the message that it has started followed by the message that it has completed.

Listing 8.11 **Output Without and with Optimization**

```
$ cc loop_merge.c
$ ./a.out
Thread 1 started
Thread 2 started
Thread 0 started
Thread 3 started
Thread 1 done
Thread 0 done
Thread 2 done
Thread 3 done
$ cc -O loop_merge.c
$ ./a.out
Thread 0 started
Thread 0 done
Thread 1 started
Thread 1 done
Thread 2 started
Thread 2 done
Thread 3 started
Thread 3 done
```

With optimization, the compiler has merged the code in the two loops that set the start variable and read the end variable. This produces code similar to that shown in Listing 8.12. The two loops contain no function calls, and the compiler considers the accesses to the volatile variables to be without side effects. Hence, the compiler considers it safe to merge the two loops.

Listing 8.12 **Compiler-Optimized Code**

```
int main()
{
  pthread_t thread[4];
  for( int i=0; i<4; i++ )
  {
    pthread_create( &thread[i], 0, work, (void*)i );
    done[i] = 0;
  }
  for ( int i=0; i<4; i++ )
  {
    start[i] = 1;
    while( done[i] == 0 ){}
  }
  for ( int i=0; i<4;i++ )
  {
    pthread_join( thread[i], 0 );
  }
}
```

To correct this situation, we need to modify the code so that the compiler is unable to merge the two loops. The easiest way to do this is to place a function call either in one of the loops or between the two loops. An alternative approach would be to separate the two loops with serial code that is unable to be moved because of some dependency or potential aliasing issue. However, both of these approaches will add some unnecessary instructions into the code, and both approaches run the risk that a "smart" compiler might identify the instructions as unnecessary and remove them.

There is a gcc `asm(""::: "memory")` construct, supported by multiple compilers, that can be used to cause the compiler to correctly order the loops. Listing 8.13 shows the code modified to use this statement. This statement stops the loops from merging and adds no additional instructions into the code.

Listing 8.13 **Using gcc `asm( )` Statement to Cause Correct Operation Ordering**

```
int main()
{
  pthread_t thread[4];
  for ( int i=0; i<4; i++ )
  {
    pthread_create( &thread[i], 0, work, (void*)i );
    done[i] = 0;
  }
  for ( int i=0; i<4; i++ )
  {
    start[i] = 1;
  }
```

```
asm volatile( "": : : "memory" );
for ( int i=0; i<4; i++ )
{
  while( done[i] == 0 ){}
}
for ( int i=0; i<4;i++ )
{
  pthread_join( thread[i], 0 );
}
}
```

Windows provides intrinsics for this purpose. The functions `_ReadBarrier()`,
`_WriteBarrier()`, and `_ReadWriteBarrier()` are defined in `<intrin.h>`. These
intrinsics tell the compiler not to reorder the operations. A `_ReadBarrier()` call
ensures that all reads will have completed at that point, while a `_WriteBarrier()` call
ensures that all writes have completed. These instructions only enforce the compiler
ordering and do not generate any instructions.

Volatile Variables

It should be apparent from the previous discussions that the `volatile` keyword is useful
in the context of multithreaded code but does not stop the compiler from reordering
operations. The `volatile` keyword just tells the compiler to reload variables from memory before using them and store them back to memory after they have been modified.
This behavior imposes an overhead on the access of any volatile variables. They must be
held in memory and cannot be cached in a variable.

Using the `volatile` keyword is necessary to avoid undesirable caching, in registers,
of the values held in memory locations. However, the keyword also stops desirable
caching of the variable, so any use of the variable can be expensive.

It may be possible to reduce this cost by typecasting the variable to be `volatile` or
using function calls that would cause the compiler to believe that the variable might
have been modified.

However, it should be observed that judicious use of compiler memory barriers can
be low cost and a more accurate way of ensuring that variables are stored back to memory and reloaded from memory at the desired point in the code. Listing 8.14 modifies
the code shown in Listing 8.6 to avoid having to declare the variable start as volatile and
instead uses a compiler barrier to ensure that the value is reloaded from memory.

Listing 8.14 **Code Where Compiler Barrier Ensures Reloading of Variable start**

```
extern int start;

void waitforstart()
{
    while(start==0) { asm volatile( "": : : "memory" ); }
}
```

Operating System–Provided Atomics

Using the information in this chapter, it should be possible for you to write some fundamental atomic operations such as an atomic add. However, these operations may already be provided by the operating system. The key advantage of using the operating system–provided code is that it should be correct, although the cost is typically a slight increase in call overhead. Hence, it is recommended that this code be taken advantage of whenever possible.

gcc provides the operations such as `__sync_fetch_and_add()`, which fetches a value from memory and adds an increment to it. The return value is the value of the variable before the increment. Windows defines `InterlockedExchangeAdd()`, which provides the same operation, and Solaris has a number of `atomic_add()` functions to handle different variable types. Table 8.1 on page 311 provides a mapping between the atomic operations provided by gcc, Windows, OS X, and Solaris. An asterisk in the function name indicates that it is available for multiple different types.

The code in Listing 8.15 uses the gcc atomic operations to enable multiple threads to increment a counter. The program creates ten threads, each of which completes the function `work()`. The original program thread also executes the same code. Each thread increments the variable `counter` 10 million times so that at the end of the program, the variable holds the value 110 million. If the atomic add operation is replaced with a normal unprotected increment operation, the output of the program is unpredictable because of the data race that this introduces.

Listing 8.15 **Using Atomic Operations to Increment a Counter**

```
#include <stdio.h>
#include <pthread.h>

volatile int counter=0;

void *work( void* param )
{
  int i;
  for( i=0; i<1000000; i++ )
  {
    __sync_fetch_and_add( &counter, 1 );
  }
}

int main()
{
  int i;
  pthread_t threads[10];
  for( i=0; i<10; i++ )
  {
```

```
    pthread_create( &threads[i], 0, work, 0 );
}
work( 0 );
for( i=0; i<10; i++ )
{
    pthread_join( threads[i], 0 );
}
printf( "Counter=%i\n", counter );
}
```

The main advantage of using these atomic operations is that they avoid the overhead of using a mutex lock to protect the variable. Although the mutex locks usually also have a compare and swap operation included in their implementation, they also have overhead around that core operation. The other difference is that the mutex lock operates at a different location in memory from the variable that needs to be updated. If both the lock and variable are shared between threads, there would typically be cache misses incurred for obtaining the lock and performing an operation on the variable. These two factors combine to make the atomic operation more efficient.

Atomic operations are very effective for situations where a single variable needs to be updated. They will not work in situations where a coordinated update of variables is required. Suppose an application needs to transfer money from one bank account to another. Each account could be modified using an atomic operation, but there would be a point during the entire transaction where the money had been removed from one account and had not yet been added to the other. At this point, the total value of all accounts would be reduced by the amount of money in transition. Depending on the rules, this might be acceptable, but it would result in the total amount of money held in the bank being impossible to know exactly while transactions were occurring.

The alternative approach would be to lock both accounts using mutex locks and then perform the transaction. The act of locking the accounts would stop anyone else from reading the value of the money in those accounts until the transaction had resolved.

Notice that there is the potential for a deadlock situation when multiple transactions of this kind exist. Suppose an application needs to move x pounds from account A to account B and at the same time another thread in the application needs to move y pounds from account B to account A. If the first thread acquires the lock account A and the second thread acquires the lock on account B, then neither thread will be able to make progress. The simplest way around this is to enforce an ordering (perhaps order of memory addresses, low to high) on the acquisition of locks. In this instance, if all threads had to acquire lock A before they would attempt to get the lock on B, only one of the two threads would have succeeded in getting the lock on A, and consequently the deadlock would be avoided.

Table 8.1 Atomic Operations Provided by gcc, Windows, OS X, and Solaris

gcc	Windows	Solaris	Mac OS X
__sync_fetch_and_add()	InterlockedExchangeAdd()	atomic_add*()	OSAtomicAdd*()
__sync_fetch_and_or()	InterlockedOr()	atomic_or*()	OSAtomicOr32()
__sync_fetch_and_and()	InterlockedAnd()	atomic_and*()	OSAtomicAnd32()
__sync_fetch_and_xor()	InterlockedXor()	-	OSAtomicXor32()
__sync_val_compare_and_swap()	InterlockedCompareExchange()	atomic_cas*()	OSAtomicCompareAndSwap*()
No equivalent	InterlockedExchange()	atomic_swap*()	-
	InterlockedIncrement()	atomic_inc*()	OSAtomicIncrement*()
	InterlockedDecrement()	atomic_dec*()	OSAtomicDecrement*()
	InterlockedBitTestAndSet()	atomic_set_long_excl()	OSAtomicTestAndSet()
	InterlockedBitTestAndReset()	atomic_clear_long_excl()	OSAtomicTestAndClear()
__sync_lock_test_and_set()	No equivalent		
__sync_lock_release()			
__sync_fetch_and_sub()			
__sync_fetch_and_nand()			
__sync_add_and_fetch()			
__sync_sub_and_fetch()			
__sync_or_and_fetch()			
__sync_and_and_fetch()			
__sync_xor_and_fetch()			
__sync_nand_and_fetch()			

Lockless Algorithms

The other approach to lockless algorithms is to code the algorithms so that they do not require locks. This can be complicated to achieve because it requires consideration of the state of the data and the transitions between data states to ensure that the system remains in legal states all the time.

Dekker's Algorithm

One of the first lockless algorithms was Dekker's algorithm for mutual exclusion. Without using any atomic operations, the algorithm ensures that only one thread at a time out of a pair of threads can enter a critical region. Listing 8.16 shows an implementation of Dekker's algorithm. To increment the counter a thread would call the function `increment()` with its thread ID.

Listing 8.16 Implementation of Dekker's Algorithm for Mutual Exclusion

```
volatile int priority = 0;
volatile int counter = 0;
volatile int waiting[2];

void increment( int id )
{
  waiting[id] = 1;

  while( waiting[1-id] == 1 )
  {
    if ( priority != id )
    {
      waiting[id] = 0;
      while ( priority != id ){}
      waiting[id] = 1;
    }
  }
  /* Critical section */
  counter++;
  /* Exit critical section */
  priority = 1-id;
  waiting[id] = 0;
}
```

The algorithm works because each thread signals that it is waiting to get into the critical section. If the other thread has not signaled that it is waiting for or has already entered the critical section, then the current thread can enter it. If both threads are waiting, then one of the threads gets priority, and the other thread waits until it gets priority.

The variables `priority` and `counter`, together with the array `waiting`, are shared between the two threads and as such need to be declared as being `volatile`. This ensures that the compiler stores these variables immediately after modification and loads them immediately before use. To test the correctness of this implementation, we can place the code in a harness. Listing 8.17 shows the harness. This harness creates the two threads. Each thread increments the variable counter 1 million times, so at the end of the program, the variable should contain the value 2 million. The program reports the difference between this value and what the counter actually contains.

Listing 8.17 **Test Harness for Dekker's Algorithm**

```
#include <stdio.h>
#include <pthread.h>

void * worker( void * param )
{
  for ( int i=0; i<1000000; i++ )
  {
    increment( (int)param );
  }
}

int main()
{
  pthread_t threads[2];
  pthread_create( &threads[0], 0, worker, (void*)0 );
  pthread_create( &threads[1], 0, worker, (void*)1 );
  pthread_join( threads[1], 0 );
  pthread_join( threads[0], 0 );
  printf( "Errors = %i\n", 2*1000000 - counter );
}
```

Listing 8.18 shows the results of compiling and running the program. Unfortunately, the program reports that the variable did not get incremented the correct number of times, and this means that there were some situations when the two threads managed to enter the critical region at the same time.

Listing 8.18 **Results of Compiling and Running Test Harness**

```
$ cc -O -mt dekker.c
$ ./a.out
Errors = 14
```

The problem with the code is one of memory ordering. The two threads can simultaneously indicate that they are waiting to enter the critical section by storing to their index in the `waiting` array. In the very next cycle, they load the other thread's waiting status. Since the other thread has only just issued the store, the store has not yet made its way through the pipeline to be visible to the rest of the system. So, the load instruction picks up a zero, indicating that the other thread is not waiting for the critical section. Both threads fail to see the other thread waiting, and both threads enter the critical region.

The way to fix this is to put memory barriers into the code. The memory barriers ensure that previous memory operations have completed before the next memory operation issues. In this case, we want to ensure that the store to indicate a thread is waiting is completed before the load to check whether the other thread is also waiting. Now consider the sequence of operations. Both threads hit the store at the same time; both threads now wait until the stores are visible to the other processor before issuing their load. So, both threads will get the data that was stored by the other thread.

On SPARC processors, the appropriate memory barrier to use is `membar #StoreLoad`, which ensures that all previous stores have completed before the following load is issued. On x86 processors, it is necessary to use an `mfence` operation that ensures that all previous memory operations complete before the next memory operation is issued.

Listing 8.19 shows the modified code for Dekker's algorithm. The code requires two memory barriers, once before the loop is entered and a second barrier inside the loop. With this modification, the code produces the correct result when run in the test harness.

Listing 8.19 **Dekker's Algorithm with Memory Barriers**

```
#include <stdio.h>
#include <pthread.h>

volatile int priority = 0;
volatile int counter = 0;
volatile int waiting[2];

void increment( int i )
{
  waiting[i] = 1;

#ifdef __sparc
  asm( "membar #StoreLoad": : : "memory" );
#else
  asm( "mfence": : : "memory" );
#endif
  while( waiting[1-i] == 1 )
  {
    if ( priority != i )
    {
      waiting[i] = 0;
      while ( priority != i ){}
      waiting[i] = 1;
```

```
#ifdef __sparc
  asm( "membar #StoreLoad": : : "memory" );
#else
  asm( "mfence": : :"memory" );
#endif
    }
  }
  counter++;
  priority = 1-i;
  waiting[i] = 0;
}
```

Producer-Consumer with a Circular Buffer

Consider the case where there is a producer-consumer pair of threads that communicate through a circular buffer. It is possible to write code that does not require locks or atomic operations to handle this situation. The code shown in Listing 8.20 defines two functions: one to add an item to a circular buffer and one to remove an item.

Listing 8.20 **Adding and Removing Elements from a Circular List**

```
#include <stdio.h>
#include <pthread.h>
#include <stdlib.h>

volatile int volatile buffer[16];
volatile int addhere;
volatile int removehere;

void clearbuffer()
{
  addhere = 0;
  removehere = 0;
  for( int i=0; i<16; i++ ) { buffer[i] = 0; }
}

int next( int current )
{
  return ( current+1 ) & 15;
}

void addtobuffer( int value )
{
  while( next(addhere) == removehere ) {} // Spin waiting for room
  if ( buffer[addhere] != 0 )
     { printf( "Circular buffer error\n" ); exit(1); }
```

```
    buffer[addhere] = value;              // Add item to buffer
    addhere = next(addhere);              // Move to next entry
}

int removefrombuffer()
{
  int value;
  while( ( value = buffer[removehere] ) == 0 ){}  // Spin until
                                                   // something in buffer
  buffer[removehere] = 0;                 // Zero out element
  removehere = next(removehere);          // Move to next entry
  return value;
}
```

The code works without memory barriers because one thread is responsible for adding elements to the array and the other thread is responsible for removing elements for the array.

There are actually two implicit constraints that ensure that the code works. One constraint is that stores and loads are themselves atomic. The other constraint is that stores do not become reordered.

Hardware ensures that a correctly aligned load cannot get half of its data from the old value at the address and half from the new value stored at that address. If this were to happen, there would be a problem when returning the value stored in the array. Imagine that either the store or the load was nonatomic. If an element was transitioning from holding the value zero to holding a nonzero value, then a nonatomic load might get the old upper half of the value (which would be zero) and the new lower half of the value (which would be nonzero). The resulting value would be incorrect.

The requirement for ordering stores comes from the code that removes elements from the array. The location containing the element to be removed is zeroed out, then the pointer to the end element to be removed is advanced to the next location in the array. If these actions became visible to the producer thread in the wrong order, the producer thread would see that the end pointer had been advanced. This would allow it to enter the code that adds a new element. However, the first test this code performs is to check that the new location is really empty. If the store of zero to the released array position was delayed, this location would still contain the old value, and the code would exit with an error. The check is "logically" unnecessary but validates that the code is behaving correctly.

Several characteristics of the algorithm enable it to work correctly. There are two pointers that point to locations in the array. Only one thread is responsible for updating each of these variables. The other thread only reads the variable. As long as the reading thread sees the updates to memory in the correct order and each variable is updated atomically, the thread will continue to wait until the data is ready and only then read that data.

A subtle characteristic of the code is that the updates of the pointers into the array are carried out by a function call. The function call acts as a compiler memory barrier and forces the compiler to store variables back to memory. Otherwise, there would be the risk that the compiler might reorder the store operations.

The handling of the array that forms the basis for communication between the two threads is also of concern. There is only one thread responsible for reading from the array and one thread responsible for writing to it. In fact, the code could be simplified so that the act of reading and writing the array was the synchronization mechanism. Listing 8.21 shows this modification. In the modified code, the application adds an entry into the buffer only if there is a space. The two pointers are entirely independent.

Listing 8.21 **Using Reads and Writes to Coordinate Thread Activity**

```c
#include <stdio.h>
#include <pthread.h>
#include <stdlib.h>

volatile int volatile buffer[16];
volatile int addhere;
volatile int removehere;

void clearbuffer()
{
  addhere = 0;
  removehere = 0;
  for ( int i=0; i<16;i++ ) { buffer[i] = 0; }
}

int next( int current )
{
  return ( current + 1 ) & 15;
}

void addtobuffer( int value )
{
  while( buffer[ next(addhere) ] != 0 ) {}
  buffer[addhere] = value;
  addhere = next(addhere);
}

int removefrombuffer()
{
  int value;
  while( ( value = buffer[removehere] ) == 0 ) {}
  buffer[removehere] = 0;
  removehere = next(removehere);
  return value;
}
```

The code in Listing 8.22 provides the remainder of the test program. It creates two threads and sets one up as the producer and the other as the consumer. Both threads run until 10 million elements have been passed from the producer to the consumer.

Listing 8.22 **Code to Set Up Producer and Consumer Thread**

```
void * producer( void *param )
{
  for( int i=1; i<10000000; i++ )
  {
    addtobuffer( i );
  }
}

void * consumer ( void *param )
{
  while ( removefrombuffer() != 9999999 ) {}
}

int main()
{
  clearbuffer();
  pthread_t threads[2];
  pthread_create( &threads[0], 0, producer, 0 );
  pthread_create( &threads[1], 0, consumer, 0 );
  pthread_join( threads[1], 0 );
  pthread_join( threads[0], 0 );
}
```

Scaling to Multiple Consumers or Producers

The code in Listing 8.21 works for a single producer and consumer without synchronization because one thread is responsible for adding items to the circular buffer and one thread is responsible for removing items. If the code were to be scaled to multiple consumers or producers, this would no longer be true, and in general, the code would require some kind of locking.

There are some cases where the use of synchronization could be avoided. If the code scales to either multiple consumers or multiple producers, but not both, then the number of circular buffers could also be scaled. This would maintain the one-to-one relationship between producers and circular buffers and between circular buffers and consumers. If there were multiple producers and multiple consumers, then synchronization could be avoided if each of these were paired. So, one producer can feed only a single consumer, and that consumer can take work from only a single producer. Finally, if there was a single circular buffer for every producer-consumer pair, then synchronization could again be avoided.

All of the previous scenarios reflect different trade-offs, memory footprints, and run-time behaviors. Assuming that the amount of work does indeed need to scale, it is most likely that some kind of "many producer to many consumer" mapping will be necessary. It would be possible to code an NxM system of queues that would provide a circular buffer for every producer-consumer pair, but this approach would likely be less efficient than using some amount of either atomic operations or mutex locks.

Scaling the Producer-Consumer to Multiple Threads

The simplest way to share the circular buffer between threads would be to use some kind of mutual exclusion that would ensure that only a single thread at a time could modify the structure. We previously encountered spinlocks in Listing 8.7, and these would be appropriate to ensure that only a single thread manipulates the circular list at a single time. Listing 8.23 shows the code modified so that access to the circular buffer is protected with a spinlock.

Listing 8.23 **Using Mutual Exclusion to Ensure Exclusive Access to the Circular Buffer**

```
#include <stdio.h>
#include <pthread.h>

volatile int volatile buffer[16];
volatile int addhere;
volatile int removehere;
volatile int lock = 0;

void lock_spinlock( volatile int* lock )
{
  while ( CAS( lock, 0, 1 ) != 0 ) {}
  acquire_memory_barrier();
}

void free_spinlock( volatile int *lock )
{
  release_memory_barrier();
  *lock = 0;
}

void clearbuffer()
{
  addhere = 0;
  removehere = 0;
  for( int i=0; i<16; i++ ) { buffer[i] = 0; }
}

int next( int current )
```

```
{
  return ( current + 1 ) & 15;
}

void addtobuffer( int value )
{
  lock_spinlock( &lock );
  while( buffer[ next(addhere) ] != 0 ) {}
  buffer[addhere] = value;
  addhere = next(addhere);
  free_spinlock( &lock );
}

int removefrombuffer()
{
  int value;
  lock_spinlock( &lock );
  while( ( value = buffer[removehere] ) == 0 ){}
  buffer[removehere] = 0;
  removehere = next(removehere);
  free_spinlock( &lock );
  return value;
}
```

There are several points to make about the code as it stands. The first is that the circular buffer has 16 entries, and although this might be adequate for a single producer-consumer pair, it is unlikely to remain so as the number of threads increases.

The second, more important, point is that the code now contains a deadlock. Imagine that the circular buffer is empty and a consumer thread acquires the lock and starts waiting for something to appear in the buffer. A producer thread eventually arrives but now has to acquire the lock before it can add anything into the buffer. Both threads end up spinning, waiting for an event that can never happen.

There are two solutions to this particular instance of the problem. The first solution is perhaps the most trivial, and that is to provide two locks—one for threads waiting to add elements to the buffer and the second for threads waiting to remove an item from the list. This solution works in this situation because it reduces the problem down to the one described earlier where there are only two threads present in the system. One lock ensures that only one producer thread can access the circular buffer at a time. The other lock ensures that only one consumer thread can access the circular buffer at a time. The other producer and consumer threads cannot interfere and cause correctness problems.

This solution relies on the original semantics of the code to provide a thread-safe version in the presence of two threads. For illustrative purposes, consider how we could modify the code so that only a single lock was necessary.

One way of doing this is to place the critical section inside another loop, which repeats the loop until the critical section is successfully executed. This requires modification to the `addtobuffer()` and `removefrombuffer()` routines so that they no longer loop inside the critical section and instead quickly return success or failure. Listing 8.24 shows code modified to remove the loops inside the critical section.

Listing 8.24 Using Mutual Exclusion to Ensure Exclusive Access to the Circular Buffer

```
void addtobuffer( int value )
{
  int success = 0;
  while( !success )
  {
    lock_spinlock( &lock );
    if( buffer[ next(addhere) ] == 0 )
    {
      buffer[addhere] = value;
      addhere = next(addhere);
      success = 1;
    }
    free_spinlock( &lock );
  }
}

int removefrombuffer()
{
  int value;
  int success = 0;
  while ( !success )
  {
    lock_spinlock( &lock );
    if ( ( value = buffer[removehere] ) != 0 )
    {
      buffer[removehere] = 0;
      removehere = next(removehere);
      success = 1;
    }
    free_spinlock( &lock );
  }
  return value;
}
```

The code uses a variable `success` to determine whether the critical region was successful. Although this change results in the desired behavior for the code, it is not the best code to run on the system. The problem with the code is that while threads are unable to add or remove items from the queue, the spinlock is constantly being acquired and released. This results in significant traffic between the cores invalidating and fetching the cache line containing the `lock` variable. Both the acquisition and release of the variable `lock` result in a store operation, which causes all the other caches to invalidate the cache line containing the lock. When the next thread acquires the spinlock, it has to fetch it from the cache of the processor that last updated the lock. This activity causes the cache line containing the variable lock to be constantly being passed between the caches of different virtual CPUs and may have an impact on the performance of the system.

For this code, a thread can easily determine whether it is likely to be successful in accessing the buffer. This test for success is to load the next element in the `buffer` array and see whether it is zero. The advantage of using load instructions is that the cache line fetched by a load remains resident in cache until it is invalidated by a store operation. In practical terms, each thread will spin on the appropriate variable waiting for it to be modified. This causes no invalidation of the values held in other caches until the variable is actually updated. Consequently, there is little risk of there being a performance impact from this scheme.

When the next element in the buffer array becomes zero, it indicates that the thread may be successful if it enters the critical region. Only at that point will the thread attempt to enter the critical region, and only at that point will there be any invalidation of data in cache lines. Listing 8.25 shows a modified version of the source code.

Listing 8.25 **Avoiding Unnecessary Invalidations of Cache Lines**

```
void addtobuffer( int value )
{
  int success = 0;
  while ( !success )
  {
    if ( buffer[ next(addhere) ] == 0 ) // Wait for an empty space
    {
      lock_spinlock( &lock );
      if( buffer[ next(addhere) ] == 0 )
      {
        buffer[addhere] = value;
        addhere = next(addhere);
        success = 1;
      }
      free_spinlock( &lock );
    }
  }
}

int removefrombuffer()
{
  int value;
  int success = 0;
  while ( !success )
```

```
  {
    if ( buffer[removehere] != 0 ) // Wait for an item to be added
    {
      lock_spinlock( &lock );
      if ( ( value = buffer[removehere] ) != 0 )
      {
        buffer[removehere] = 0;
        removehere = next(removehere);
        success = 1;
      }
      free_spinlock( &lock );
    }
  }
  return value;
}
```

The modified code contains the same mechanism that keeps the thread spinning until it is successful. Within that loop, the thread tests to see whether it might be successful before actually obtaining the lock. Although this reduces the number of invalidations of the shared data and reduces the memory traffic, it is still not an optimal solution.

The problem with this code is that every time a new item is added to the circular buffer or every time a space becomes free, all the waiting threads recognize this and attempt to acquire the lock, even though only one thread can actually succeed. This is an example of the *thundering herd problem* where a number of threads are waiting for a condition to become true and only one thread can successfully proceed, so all the other threads end up using unnecessary resources. This problem can be resolved by ordering the list of threads such that only one thread is allowed to proceed.

However, the problem is worse than this. All the threads that identify the opportunity to access the circular buffer will enter the `if` statement and can exit only after they have acquired and released the spinlock. So, these threads will end up spinning on the spinlock, which was not the intention of the code.

To remove this problem, we should change the code so that instead of spinning on the spinlock, the threads try to acquire it, and if they do not, then they should return to the outer loop and wait for the next opportunity to access the circular buffer. Listing 8.26 shows the modified code. It introduces a function called `try_spinlock()` that will either acquire the spinlock and return true or fail to acquire the lock and return false. With this modification, the threads spin on the variable, indicating the state of the circular buffer. This variable is shared so it does not produce much memory traffic. If the state changes, the threads attempt to get the spinlock. Only one thread will succeed, and this thread gets to access the buffer while the other threads go back to spinning on the shared variable. With this change, the spinlock has ceased to be used as a spinlock since the threads spin before attempting to acquire the lock.

Listing 8.26 Avoiding Unnecessary Invalidations of Cache Lines Using `try_spinlock()`

```
int try_spinlock( volatile int* lock )
{
  if ( CAS( lock, 0, 1 ) == 1 ) { return 0; }
  else
  {
    acquire_memory_barrier();
    return 1;
  }
}

void addtobuffer( int value )
{
  int success = 0;
  while ( !success )
  {
    if ( buffer[ next(addhere) ] == 0 )
    {
      if (try_spinlock( &lock ) )
      {
        if ( buffer[ next(addhere) ] == 0 )
        {
          buffer[addhere] = value;
          addhere = next(addhere);
          success = 1;
        }
        free_spinlock( &lock );
      }
    }
  }
}

int removefrombuffer()
{
  int value;
  int success = 0;
  while ( !success )
  {
    if ( buffer[removehere] != 0 )
    {
      if ( try_spinlock( &lock ) )
      {
        if ( ( value = buffer[removehere] ) !=0 )
        {
          buffer[removehere] = 0;
          removehere = next(removehere);
```

```
        success = 1;
      }
      free_spinlock( &lock );
    }
  }
}
return value;
}
```

A further improvement to the code would be to rewrite the spinlock so that it has these semantics. Listing 8.27 shows this improvement to the spinlock code. This code spins until the lock has been acquired by the calling thread. Every iteration, the loop tests whether the lock is available. If the lock is available, the code attempts to acquire the lock atomically. If successful, the code exits the loop having acquired the spinlock. If unsuccessful, the loop continues to spin.

Listing 8.27   **Reducing Number of CAS Operations When Spinning**

```
void lock_spinlock( volatile int* lock )
{
  int acquired = 0;
  while ( !acquired )
  {
    if ( ( *lock == 0 ) && ( CAS( lock, 0, 1 ) == 0) )
    {
      acquired = 1;
    }
  }
  acquire_memory_barrier();
}

void addtobuffer( int value )
{
  int success = 0;
  while ( !success )
  {
    if ( buffer[ next(addhere) ] == 0 )
    {
      lock_spinlock( &lock );
      if ( buffer[ next(addhere) ] == 0 )
      {
        buffer[addhere] = value;
        addhere = next(addhere);
        success = 1;
      }
      free_spinlock( &lock );
```

```
      }
    }
  }

int removefrombuffer()
{
  int value;
  int success = 0;
  while ( !success )
  {
    if ( buffer[removehere] != 0 )
    {
      lock_spinlock( &lock );
      if ( ( value = buffer[removehere] ) !=0 )
      {
        buffer[removehere] = 0;
        removehere = next(removehere);
        success = 1;
      }
      free_spinlock( &lock );
    }
  }
  return value;
}
```

Modifying the Producer-Consumer Code to Use Atomics

Since adding an item into the circular list and removing an item from the list look like
single operations, it is tempting to imagine that they could be implemented using atomic
operations. We will explore this scenario using the modified code shown in Listing 8.28.
In this code, each producer thread waits until the next entry in the buffer is free and
then attempts to atomically add an item into that buffer location. If successful, it increments the pointer to the next entry in the list. Similarly, all the consumer threads wait
until an item is placed into the list and then try to atomically remove the new item. The
thread that succeeds increments the pointer to the next entry in the list.

Listing 8.28 **Using Atomic Operations to Handle a Circular List**

```
void addtobuffer( int value )
{
  int success = 0;
  while ( !success )
  {
    if ( buffer[ next(addhere) ] == 0 )
    {
```

```
      if ( CAS( &buffer[ next(addhere) ], 0, value ) == 0 )
      {
        addhere = next(addhere);
        success = 1;
      }
    }
  }
}

int removefrombuffer()
{
  int value;
  int success = 0;
  while ( !success )
  {
    if ( ( value = buffer[removehere] ) != 0 )
    {
      if ( CAS( &buffer[removehere], value, 0 ) == value )
      {
        removehere = next(removehere);
        success = 1;
      }
    }
  }
  return value;
}
```

At first, it appears that this should work. Only one thread at a time can successfully add or remove an element. Only that thread will alter the pointer so that it points to the next entry.

However, this is not the case. It is critical to realize that although instructions will execute in the expected order, the gaps between the execution of adjacent instructions are random. A pair of instructions could be executed on the same cycle or with a separation of only a few cycles. However, a thread may be context switched off the virtual CPU between the two instructions, and this would cause a gap of thousands of cycles to occur between the two operations.

Consider the situation shown in Figure 8.1 where multiple producer and consumer threads exist. At step A, two producer threads are attempting to add an item into the circular buffer. They both reach the CAS instruction at nearly the same time, but one of the threads gets context switched off the CPU at that very moment. At step B, the other thread successfully enters its value into the circular list and is just about to move the addhere pointer onto the next element when it too is context switched off the virtual CPU.

While the first thread is off-processor, one of the consumer threads come along and removes the recently inserted element, as shown in step C. At that point, the first thread

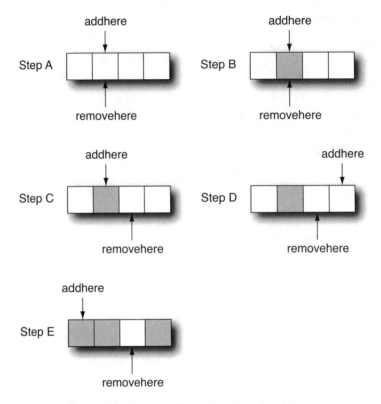

Figure 8.1 Example of stepping through a data race

is switched back onto the CPU, and it sees that the slot it was planning to use is now empty. It atomically inserts its item of data into the circular buffer and then increments the pointer to the next place to insert an element.

This is rapidly followed by the second producer thread being brought back onto a virtual CPU. It completes the operation it was performing when it was context switched off the virtual CPU, and it too increments the **addhere** pointer to the next place to insert an element. This causes the **addhere** pointer to skip a location, but the **removehere** pointer, which indicates where to remove elements from, is now pointing at the skipped location, as shown in step D. The skipped location is empty, so the consumer threads are left waiting for an element to be inserted there. This cannot happen until the producer threads have filled up the entire circular buffer. However, before the producer threads can fill the entire buffer, they hit a filled element in the buffer and cannot make progress until this element has been removed, which will never happen because of the stalled consumer threads.

Consequently, the application deadlocks with both the producer and consumer threads unable to make forward progress.

The ABA Problem

This example is an instance of a general problem called the *ABA problem*. The ABA problem is the situation where a thread is context switched off the virtual CPU when the program is in state A. While it is off-CPU, the system changes into a second state, B, before returning to state A. This state is different from the original state but looks identical to the thread that is now switched back onto a virtual CPU. When the first thread returns to the CPU, it continues to act as if the program state had not changed, and this causes an error.

In the circular buffer problem described in the previous section, the first thread is taken off the virtual CPU while believing it has a pointer to a free slot. When it returns to CPU, it has a pointer to what it believes is the free slot, but it has no indication that the state of the rest of the system has changed.

A general solution to the ABA problem is to encode a version number with any stored data. In this example of the circular buffer, the data would be accompanied by this version number, and the version number would be incremented every time the circular buffer was traversed.

With this version number, the thread that was taken off-CPU would have to match both the version number and the data for it to successfully add or remove an element from the buffer.

Adding the version number has reduced but not eliminated the possibility that a thread might return to the CPU to find a match of both version number and data. However, the probability can be made so small as to be practically impossible.

For example, if the version number is held as a 4-byte integer, then there are more than 4 billion possible values. If the code traverses the circular buffer 1,000 times a second, then it would take about one and a half months before the version number was repeated. The race condition can occur only if the version number when a thread is context switched off the virtual CPU matches the version number when the thread is switched back onto the CPU. No thread would be context switched off the CPU for a month and a half, so the race condition will not occur.

The code in Listing 8.29 is a modified version of the circular buffer code that includes a version number for each element of the buffer. The version is incremented in the routine `nextupdate()` every time the counter wraps around the buffer.

This code uses a structure of two integers to hold the value to be stored and the version number. It is necessary to use an atomic operation to perform the store. Most hardware supports an 8-byte atomic operation, but a 16-byte atomic is rarely supported, so the code will work only for 32-bit values.

Listing 8.29 **Using Version Numbers to Avoid the ABA Problem**

```
union ABAvalue
{
   long long llvalue;
   struct element
```

```
    {
      int version;
      int value;
    } nested;
};

union ABAvalue buffer[16];

int counter = 0;

void clearbuffer()
{
  addhere = 0;
  removehere = 0;
  for ( int i=0; i<16;i++ )
  {
    buffer[i].llvalue = 0;
  }
}



int next( int current )
{
  return ( current + 1 ) & 15;
}

int nextupdate( int current )
{
  if ( current == 15 ) { counter++; }
  return ( current + 1 ) & 15 ;
}
```

The code shown in Listing 8.30 is the modified version of the routines to add and remove elements from the circular buffer. The compare and swap operation needs to work on 8-byte values; hence, the assembly for the compare and swap needs to be modified, and the x86 code will work only when compiled to use 64-bit instruction set extensions.

Listing 8.30 **Adding and Removing Elements from Buffer**

```
#ifdef __sparc
long long CAS( volatile long long* addr, long long ov, long long nv)
{
  asm volatile( "casx %1, %2, %0":
                "=r"(nv):
                "m"(*addr),"r"(ov),"0"(nv):
                "memory" );
```

```
    return nv;
}
#else
long long CAS( volatile long long * addr, long long ov, long long nv )
{
    asm volatile( "lock; cmpxchg %2, %1":
                  "=a"(ov):
                  "m"(*addr),"r"(nv),"a"(ov):
                  "memory" );
    return ov;
}
#endif

void addtobuffer( int value )
{
    int success = 0;
    union ABAvalue current;
    while ( !success )
    {
        current = buffer[ next(addhere) ];
        if ( current.nested.value == 0 )
        {
            union ABAvalue nextvalue;
            nextvalue.nested.version = counter;
            nextvalue.nested.value = value;
            if ( CAS( &buffer[ next(addhere) ].llvalue,
                      current.llvalue,
                      nextvalue.llvalue )
                 == current.llvalue )
            {
                addhere = nextupdate(addhere);
                success = 1;
            }
        }
    }
}

int removefrombuffer()
{
    union ABAvalue current;
    int success = 0;
    int value;
    while ( !success )
    {
        current = buffer[ next(removehere) ];
        if ( current.nested.value != 0 )
        {
```

```
      value = current.nested.value;
      union ABAvalue nextvalue;
      nextvalue.nested.version = counter;
      nextvalue.nested.value = 0;
      if ( CAS( &buffer[ next(removehere)].llvalue,
                  current.llvalue,
                  nextvalue.llvalue )
          == current.llvalue )
        {
          removehere = next(removehere);
          success = 1;
        }
      }
    }
  }
  return value;
}
```

It should be apparent from the previous discussion that it is not trivial to use atomic operations to manage the addition and removal of elements from a circular buffer. The basic problem is that the atomic operation allows the atomic modification of the circular list but is a separate operation to update the shared pointer to the next element. These two operations would need to be somehow combined into a single atomic operation for the code to work correctly.

Summary

Having completed this chapter, you should have an appreciation of some of the issues that need to be considered when writing synchronization code. It is important to consider both the memory ordering observed by other threads and the possibility that a thread might be descheduled at any point.

Correct memory ordering needs to be enforced to ensure that memory operations become visible to other threads in the appropriate order. Failure to do this will result in other threads picking up stale or invalid values.

When threads become descheduled, they give other threads the opportunity to modify program state. However, rescheduled threads may not be able to observe the fact that it has missed some changes in program state. The risk with this is that a rescheduled thread may overwrite program state on the assumption that the state has not changed.

It is clearly possible to write safe synchronization mechanisms. However, it is usually best to look for primitives provided by the compiler or operating system because these will have been validated for correct operation. It is only when these prove to be high cost and the alternatives have been exhausted that it is worth investigating custom coding synchronization primitives.

9

Scaling with Multicore Processors

The key advantage of a multicore processor is that it is able to allocate more cores to solving a compute problem. Hence, to get the best out of a multicore processor, each thread of an application needs to be efficient, and the application needs to be able to effectively utilize multiple threads. An ideal application will double in performance when run with two hardware threads and will quadruple in performance with four.

This chapter discusses the issues surrounding application scaling. By the end of the chapter, you will have an understanding of the common ways that hardware and software limit the scaling of applications. You will also know how to recognize these issues and potentially solve them. You will also appreciate the difference between using multiple threads on a multicore processor and using multiple single-core processors.

Constraints to Application Scaling

Most applications, when run in parallel over multiple cores, will get less than linear speedup. We discussed this in Chapter 3, "Identifying Opportunities for Parallelism." Amdahl's law indicates that a section of serial code will limit the scalability of the application over multiple cores. If the application spends half of its runtime in a section of code that has been made parallel and half in a section of code that has not, then the best that can be achieved with two threads is that the application will run in three-quarters of the original time. The best that could ever be achieved would be for the code to run in about half the original time, given enough threads.

However, there will be other limitations that stop an application from scaling perfectly. These limitations could be hardware bottlenecks where some part of the system has reached a maximum capacity. Adding more threads divides this total amount of resources between more consumers but does not increase the amount available. Scaling can also be limited by hardware interactions where the presence of multiple threads causes the hardware to become less effective. Software limitations can also constrain scaling where synchronization overheads become a significant part of the runtime.

Performance Limited by Serial Code

As previously discussed, the serial sections of code will limit how fast an application can execute given unlimited numbers of threads. Consider the code shown in Listing 9.1. This application has two sections of code; one section is serial code, and the other section is parallel code.

Listing 9.1 **Application with Serial and Parallel Sections**

```
#include <math.h>
#include <stdlib.h>

void func1( double*array, int n )
{
  for( int i=1; i<n; i++ )
  {
    array[i] += array[i-1];
  }
}

void func2( double *array,int n )
{
  #pragma omp parallel for
  for( int i=0; i<n; i++ )
  {
    array[i] = sin(array[i]);
  }
}

int main()
{
  double * array = calloc( sizeof(double), 1024*1024 );
  for ( int i=0; i<100; i++ )
  {
    func1( array, 1024*1024 );
    func2( array, 1024*1024 );
  }
  return 0;
}
```

Listing 9.2 shows the profile from the application when it is parallelized using OpenMP and run with a single thread. The application runs for nearly 16 seconds; this is the wall time. The user time is the time spent by all threads executing user code. More than half of the wall time is spent in the `sin()` function, about five seconds is spent in `func2()`, and about two seconds is spent in `func1()`. So, 14 of the 16 seconds of runtime are spent in code that can be executed in parallel.

Listing 9.2 **Profile of Code Run with a Single Thread**

Excl. User CPU sec.	Excl. Wall sec.	Name
15.431	15.701	`<Total>`
8.616	8.756	`sin`
4.963	5.034	`func2`
1.821	1.831	`func1`
0.020	0.030	`memset`
0.010	0.010	`<OMP-overhead>`

If two threads were to run this application, we would expect each thread to take about seven seconds to complete the parallel code and one thread to spend about two seconds completing the serial code. The total wall time for the application should be about nine seconds. The actual profile, when run with two threads, can be seen in Listing 9.3.

Listing 9.3 **Profile of Code Run with Two Threads**

Excl. User CPU sec.	Excl. Wall sec.	Name
15.421	8.956	`<Total>`
8.526	4.413	`sin`
4.973	2.432	`func2`
1.831	1.851	`func1`
0.030	0.030	`memset`
0.030	0.140	`<OMP-implicit_barrier>`
0.030	0.040	`<OMP-overhead>`

The first thing that is important to notice is that the total amount of user time remained the same. This is the anticipated result; the same amount of work is being performed, so the time taken to complete it should remain the same.

The second observation is that the wall time reduces to about nine seconds. This is the amount of time that we calculated it would take.

The third observation is that the synthetic routines `<OMP-implicit_barrier>` and `<OMP-overhead>` accumulate a small amount of time. These represent the costs of the OpenMP implementation. The time attributed to the routines is very small, so they are not a cause for concern.

For a sufficiently large number of threads, we would hope that the runtime for the code could get reduced down to the time it takes for the serial region to complete, plus a small amount of time for the parallel code and any necessary synchronization. Listing 9.4 shows the same code run with 32 threads.

Listing 9.4 **Profile of Code Run with 32 Threads**

```
Excl.     Excl.   Name
User CPU  Wall
  sec.      sec.
17.162    3.192   <Total>
 9.527    0.410   sin
 5.594    0.190   func2
 1.911    1.991   func1
 0.090    0.520   <OMP-implicit_barrier>
 0.030    0.040   memset
 0.010    0.      <OMP-idle>
```

With perfect scaling, we would expect the runtime of the application with 32 threads to be 2 seconds of serial time plus 14 seconds divided by 32 threads, making a total of just under 3 seconds. The actual wall time is not that far from this ideal number. However, notice that the total user time has increased.

This code is actually running on a single multicore processor, so the increase in user time probably indicates that the processor is hitting some scaling limits at this degree of utilization. The rest of the chapter will discuss what those limits could be.

The other thing to observe is that although the user time has increased by two seconds, this increase does not have a significant impact on the total wall time. This should not be a surprising result. A 2-second increase in user time spread over 32 threads represents a 1/16th of a second increase in per thread, which is unlikely to be noticeable in the elapsed time, or wall time, of the application's run.

This code has scaled very well. There remains two seconds of serial time and no amount of threads will reduce that, but the time for the parallel region has scaled very well as the number of threads has increased.

Superlinear Scaling

Imagine that you hurt your hand and were no long able to use both hands to type but you still had a report to finish. For most people, it would take more than twice as long to produce the report using one hand as using two. When your hand recovers, the rate at which you can type will more than double. This is an example of *superlinear* speedup. You double the resources yet get more than double the performance as a result. It's easy to explain for this particular situation. With two hands, all the keys on the keyboard are within easy reach, but with only one hand, it is not possible to reach all the keys without having to move your hand.

In most instances, going from one thread to two will result in, at most, a doubling of performance. However, there will be applications that do see superlinear scaling—the application ends up running more than twice as fast. This is typically because the data that the application uses becomes cache resident at some point. Imagine an application that uses 4MB of data. On a processor with a 2MB cache, only half the data will be resident in the cache. Adding a second processor adds an additional 2MB of cache; then all the data becomes cache resident, and the time spent waiting on memory becomes substantially lower.

Listing 9.5 shows a modification of the program in Listing 9.1 that uses 64MB of memory.

Listing 9.5 **Program with 64MB Memory Footprint**

```
#include <stdlib.h>

double func1( double*array, int n )
{
  double total = 0.0;
  #pragma omp parallel for reduction(+:total)
  for( int i=1; i<n; i++ )
  {
    total += array[i^29450];
  }
  return total;
}

int main()
{
  double * array = calloc( sizeof(double), 8192*1024 );
  for( int i=0; i<100; i++ )
  {
    func1( array, 8192*1024 );
  }
}
```

When the program is run on a single processor with 32MB of second-level cache, the program takes about 25 seconds to complete. When run using two threads on the same processor, the code completes in about 12 seconds and takes 25 seconds of user time. This is the anticipated performance gain from using multiple threads. The code takes half the time but does the same amount of work. However, when run using two threads, with each thread bound to a separate processor, the program runs in just over four seconds of wall time, taking only eight seconds of user time.

Adding the second processor has increased the amount of cache available to the program, causing it to become cache resident. The data in cache has a lower access latency, so the program runs significantly faster.

It is a different situation on a multicore processor. Adding an additional thread, particularly if it resides on the same core, does not substantially increase the amount of cache available to the program. So, a multicore processor is unlikely to see superlinear speedup.

Workload Imbalance

Another common software issue is *workload imbalance*, when the work is not evenly distributed over the threads. We have already seen an example of this in the *Mandelbrot example* in Chapter 7. The code in Listing 9.6 has a very deliberate workload imbalance. The number of iterations in the `compute()` function is proportional to the square of the value passed into it; the larger the number passed into the function, the more time it will take to complete.

A parallel loop iterates over a range from small values up to large values, passing each value into the function. If the work is statically distributed, the threads that get the initial iterations will spend less time computing the result than the threads that get the later iterations.

Listing 9.6 **Code Exhibiting Workload Imbalance**

```c
#include <stdlib.h>

int compute( int value )
{
  value = value*value;
  while ( value > 0 )
  {
    value = value - 12.0;
  }
  return value;
}

int main()
{
  #pragma omp parallel for
  for( int i=0; i<3000; i++ )
  {
    compute( i );
  }
}
```

Figure 9.1 shows the timeline view of running the code with eight threads. Each horizontal bar represents a thread actively running user code. The duration of the run is governed by the time taken by the longest thread. The longest threads completed in just over nine seconds. In those 9 seconds, the eight threads accumulated 27 seconds of user time. The user time represents the amount of work that the threads actually completed. If those 27 seconds of user time had been spread evenly across the eight threads, then the application would have completed in about 3.5 seconds.

Changing the scheduling of the parallel loop to guided scheduling results in the timeline shown in Figure 9.2. After this change, the work is evenly distributed across the threads, and the application runs in just over 3.5 seconds.

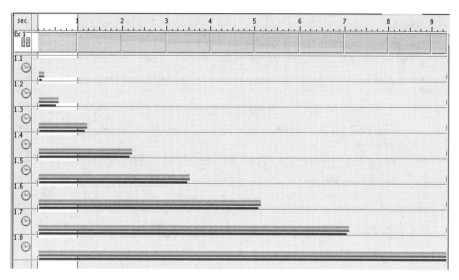

Figure 9.1 Timeline of code with eight threads

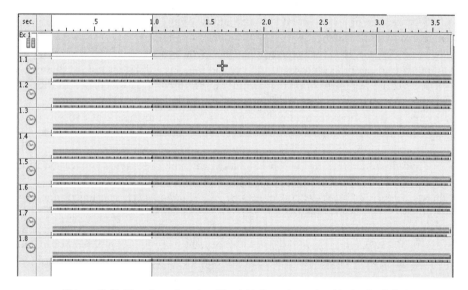

Figure 9.2 Timeline of code with eight threads and guided scheduling

Hot Locks

Contended (or hot) mutex locks are one of the common causes of poor application scaling. This comes about when there are too many threads contending for a single resource protected by a mutex. There are two attributes of the program conspiring to produce the hot lock.

- The first attribute is the number of threads needed to lock a single mutex. This is the usual reason for poor scaling; there are just too many threads trying to access this one resource.

- The second, more subtle, issue is that the interval between a single thread's accesses of the resource is too short. For example, imagine that each thread in an application needs to access a resource for one second and then does not access that resource again for nine seconds. In those nine seconds, another nine threads could access the resource without a conflict. The application would be able to scale very well to ten threads, but if an eleventh thread was added, the application would not scale as well, since this additional thread would delay the other threads from access to the resource.

These two factors result in the more complex behavior of an application with multiple threads. The application may scale to a particular number of threads but start scaling poorly because there is a contended lock that limits scaling. There are a number of potential fixes for this issue.

The most obvious fix is to "break up" the mutex or find some way of converting the single mutex into multiple mutexes. If each thread requires a different mutex, these mutex accesses are less likely to contend until the thread count has increased further.

Another approach is to increase the amount of time between each access to the critical resource. If the resource is required less frequently, then the chance of two threads requiring the resource simultaneously is reduced. An equivalent change is to reduce the time spent holding the lock. This change alters the ratio between the time spent holding the lock and the time spent not holding the lock, with the consequence that it becomes less likely that multiple threads will require the lock at the same time.

There are other approaches that can improve the situation, such as using atomic operations to reduce the cost of the critical section of code.

The code in Listing 9.7 simulates a bank that has many branch offices. Each branch holds a number of accounts and customers can move money between different accounts at the same branch. To ensure that the amounts held in each account are kept consistent, there is a single mutex lock that allows a single transfer to occur at any one time.

Listing 9.7 **Code Simulating a Bank with Multiple Branches**

```
#include <stdlib.h>
#include <strings.h>
#include <pthread.h>
```

```
#define ACCOUNTS 256
#define BRANCHES 128
int account[BRANCHES][ACCOUNTS];
pthread_mutex_t mutex;

void move( int branch, int from, int to, int value )
{
  pthread_mutex_lock( &mutex );
  account[branch][from] -= value;
  account[branch][to] += value;
  pthread_mutex_unlock( &mutex );
}

void *customers( void *param )
{
  unsigned int seed = 0;
  int count = 10000000 / (int)param;
  for( int i=0; i<count; i++ )
  {
      int  row = rand_r(&seed) & (BRANCHES-1);
      int from = rand_r(&seed) & (ACCOUNTS-1);
      int   to = rand_r(&seed) & (ACCOUNTS-1);
      move( row, from, to, 1 );
  }
}

int main( int argc, char* argv[] )
{
  pthread_t threads[64];
  memset( account, 0, sizeof(account) );
  int nthreads = 8;
  if ( argc > 1 ) { nthreads = atoi( argv[1] ); }

  pthread_mutex_init( &mutex, 0 );
  for( int i=0; i<nthreads; i++ )
  {
    pthread_create( &threads[i], 0, customers, (void*)nthreads );
  }
  for( int i=0; i<nthreads; i++ )
  {
    pthread_join( threads[i], 0 );
  }

  pthread_mutex_destroy( &mutex );
  return 0;
}
```

When run with a single thread, the program completes in about nine seconds. When run with eight threads on the same platform, it takes about five seconds to complete. The timeline view of the run of the application, shown in Figure 9.3, indicates the problem. The figure shows two seconds from the five-second run. Although all the threads are active some of the time, they are inactive for significant portions of the time. The inactivity is represented in the timeline view as gaps.

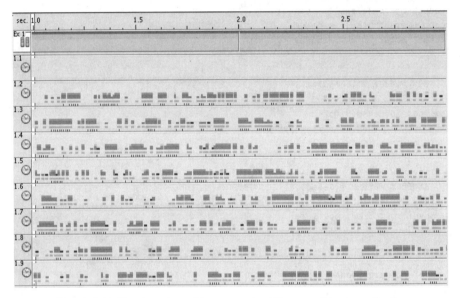

Figure 9.3 Timeline view of two seconds of the run of bank application

Looking at the profile, from the run of the application with eight threads, the user time is not significantly different from when it is run with a single thread. This indicates that the amount of work performed is roughly the same. The one place where the profiles differ is in the amount of time spent in user locks. Listing 9.8 shows the profile from the eight-way run. This shows that the eight threads accumulate about 10 seconds of time spent, in __lwp_park( ), parked waiting for user locks.

Listing 9.8 Profile of Bank Application Run with Eight Threads

Excl.	Excl.	Name
User CPU	User Lock	
sec.	sec.	
8.136	10.187	\<Total>
1.811	0.	rand_mt
1.041	0.	atomic_cas_32

```
0.991    0.         mutex_lock_impl
0.951    0.         move
0.881    0.         mutex_unlock
0.841    0.         experiment
0.520    0.         mutex_trylock_adaptive
0.490    0.         rand_r
0.350    0.         sigon
0.160    0.         mutex_unlock_queue
0.070    0.         mutex_lock
0.020    10.187     __lwp_park
```

On Solaris, the tool `plockstat` can be used to identify which locks are hot. Listing 9.9 shows the output from `plockstat`. This output indicates the contended locks. In this case, it is the lock named `mutex` in the routine `move()`.

Listing 9.9 **Output from `plockstat` Indicating Hot Lock**

```
% plockstat ./a.out 8
plockstat: pid 13970 has exited

Mutex block

Count   nsec Lock                    Caller
-------------------------------------------------------------------
  428 781859525 a.out`mutex               a.out`move+0x14
```

Alternatively, the call stack can be examined to identify the routine contributing to this time. Using either method, it is relatively quick to identify that particular contended lock.

In this banking example, there are multiple branches, and all account activity is restricted to occurring within a single branch. An obvious solution is to provide a single mutex lock per branch. This will enable one thread to lock up a transaction on a single branch, while other threads continue to process transactions at other branches. Listing 9.10 shows the modified code.

Listing 9.10 **Bank Example Modified So That Each Branch Has a Private Mutex Lock**

```
#include <stdlib.h>
#include <strings.h>
#include <pthread.h>

#define ACCOUNTS 256
#define BRANCHES 128
int account[BRANCHES][ACCOUNTS];
pthread_mutex_t mutex[BRANCHES];
```

```
void move( int branch, int from, int to, int value )
{
  pthread_mutex_lock( &mutex[branch] );
  account[branch][from] -= value;
  account[branch][to] += value;
  pthread_mutex_unlock( &mutex[branch] );
}

void *experiment( void *param )
{
  unsigned int seed = 0;
  int count = 10000000 / (int)param;
  for( int i=0; i<count; i++ )
  {
    int   row = rand_r(&seed) & (BRANCHES-1);
    int from = rand_r(&seed) & (ACCOUNTS-1);
    int   to = rand_r(&seed) & (ACCOUNTS-1);
    move( row, from, to, 1 );
  }
}

int main( int argc, char* argv[] )
{
  pthread_t threads[64];
  memset( account, 0, sizeof(account) );
  int nthreads = 8;
  if ( argc > 1 ) { nthreads = atoi( argv[1] ); }
  for( int i=0; i<BRANCHES; i++ )
    pthread_mutex_init( &mutex[i], 0 );
  for( int i=0; i<nthreads; i++ )
  {
    pthread_create( &threads[i], 0, experiment, (void*)nthreads );
  }
  for( int i=0; i<nthreads; i++ )
  {
    pthread_join( threads[i], 0 );
  }
  for( int i=0; i<BRANCHES; i++ )
    pthread_mutex_destroy( &mutex[i] );
  return 0;
}
```

With this change in the application, the original runtime remains at about nine seconds, but the runtime with eight threads drops to just over one second. This is the expected degree of scaling.

It is interesting to compare the scaling of three different configurations of the bank example. Figure 9.4 shows the scaling of the original code, with 128 branches and a single mutex, from one to eight threads; the scaling of the code with 128 branches, each with its own mutex; and the code that shows the scaling if there were only four branches, each with a single mutex.

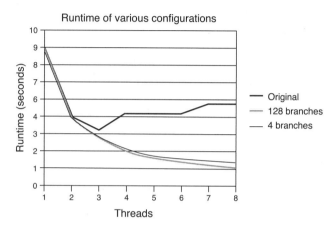

Figure 9.4 Scaling of three different configurations of the bank example

One point worth noting is that even the original code shows some limited degree of scaling going from one to three threads. This indicates that it is relatively easy to get some amount of scaling from most applications. However, the scaling rapidly degrades when run with more than three threads. Perhaps surprisingly, there is little difference in scaling between provided 128 mutex locks or providing four. This is perhaps not as surprising when considered in the context of the original mutex lock that provides the ability to scale to three times the original thread count. It might, therefore, be expected that four mutex locks might be sufficient to scale the code to eight to twelve threads, which is in fact what is revealed if the data collection is extended beyond eight threads.

Scaling of Library Code

Issues with scaling are not restricted to just the application. It is not surprising to find scaling issues in code provided in libraries. One of the most fundamental library routines is the memory allocation provided by `malloc()` and `free()`. The code shown in Listing 9.11 represents a very simple benchmark of `malloc()` performance as the number of threads increases. The benchmark creates a number of threads, and each thread repeatedly allocates and frees a chunk of 1KB memory. The application completes after a fixed number of `malloc()` and `free()` calls have been completed by the team of threads.

Listing 9.11 **Code to Testing Scaling of** `malloc()` **and** `free()`

```c
#include <stdlib.h>
#include <pthread.h>

int nthreads;

void *work( void * param )
{
  int count = 1000000 / nthreads;
  for( int i=0; i<count; i++ )
  {
    void *mem = malloc(1024);
    free( mem );
  }
}

int main( int argc, char*argv[] )
{
  pthread_t thread[50];
  nthreads = 8;
  if ( argc > 1 ) { nthreads = atoi( argv[1] ); }
  for( int i=0; i<nthreads; i++ )
  {
    pthread_create( &thread[i], 0, work, 0 );
  }
  for( int i=0; i<nthreads; i++ )
  {
    pthread_join( thread[i], 0 );
  }
  return 0;
}
```

Suppose a default implementation of `malloc()` and `free()` uses a single mutex lock to ensure that only a single thread can ever allocate or deallocate memory at any one time. This implementation will limit the scaling of the test code. The code is serialized, so performance will not improve with multiple threads. Consider an alternative `malloc()` that uses a different algorithm. Each thread has its own heap of memory, so it does not require a mutex lock. This alternative `malloc()` scales as the number of threads increases. Figure 9.5 shows the runtime of the application in seconds using the two `malloc()` implementations as a function of the number of threads.

As expected, the default implementation does not scale, so the runtime does not improve. The increase in runtime is because of more threads contending for the single mutex lock. The alternative implementation shows very good scaling. As the number of threads increases, the runtime of the application decreases.

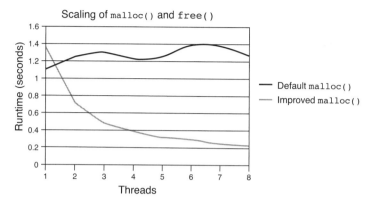

Figure 9.5 Scaling of two different implementations of `malloc()`
and `free()`

There is an interesting, though perhaps not surprising, observation to be made from the performance of the two implementations of `malloc()` and `free()`. For the single-threaded case, the default `malloc()` provides better performance than the alternative implementation. The algorithm that provides improved scaling also adds a cost to the single-threaded situation; it can be hard to produce an algorithm that is fast for the single-threaded case and scales well with multiple threads.

Insufficient Work

If we return to the Mandelbrot example used in Chapter 7, "Using Automatic Parallelization and OpenMP," we made the work run in parallel by having each thread compute a different range of iterations. A grid of 4,000 by 4,000 pixels was used, so there was plenty of work to be performed by each thread. On the other hand, if we were computing a grid of 64 by 64 pixels, then using the same scheme we would not get scaling beyond 64 threads; each thread would be able to compute a single row of the image.

Of course, the parallelization scheme could be modified so that there was a single outer loop that iterated over the range 0 to 64 * 64 = 4096. Listing 9.12 shows the modified outer loop nest. With this modification, the maximum theoretical thread count reaches 4,096. It is likely that, for this example on standard hardware, the synchronization costs would dwarf the cost of the computation long before 4,096 threads were reached.

Listing 9.12 **Merging Two Outer Loops to Provide More Parallelism**

```
#pragma omp parallel for
for( int i=0; i<64*64; i++ )
{
  y = i % SIZE;
  x = i / SIZE;
```

```
    double xv = ( (double)x - (SIZE/2) ) / (SIZE/4);
    double yv = ( (double)y - (SIZE/2) ) / (SIZE/4);
    matrix[x][y] = inSet( xv, yv );
  }
```

Of course, it is not uncommon to find that scalability is limited by the number of iterations performed by the outer loop. We have already met the OpenMP `collapse` clause, which tells the compiler to perform this loop merge, as shown in Listing 9.13.

Listing 9.13 **Using the OpenMP** `collapse` **Directive**

```
#pragma omp parallel for collapse(2)
for( int x=0; x<64; x++ )
 for( int y=0; y<64; y++ )
 {
   double xv = ( (double)x - (SIZE/2) ) / (SIZE/4);
   double yv = ( (double)y - (SIZE/2) ) / (SIZE/4);
   matrix[x][y] = inSet( xv, yv );
 }
```

However, if this code were to run with perfect scaling on 4,096 processors, then there would be no further opportunities for parallelization. If you recall, the routine `inSet()` has an iteration-carried dependence, so it cannot be parallelized, and we have exhausted all the parallelism available at the call site.

The only options to extract further parallelism in this particular instance would be to search for opportunities outside of this part of the problem. The easiest thing to do would be to increase the size of the problem; if there are spare threads, this might complete in the same amount of time and end up being more useful.

The problem size can also be considered as equivalent to the precision of the calculation. It may be possible to use a larger number of processors to provide a result with more precision. Consider the example of numerical integration using the trapezium rule shown in Listing 9.14.

Listing 9.14 **Numerical Integration Using the Trapezium Rule**

```
#include <math.h>
#include <stdio.h>

double function( double value )
{
  return sqrt( value );
}

double integrate( double start, double end, int intervals )
{
```

```
      double area = 0;
      double range = ( end - start ) / intervals;
      for( int i=1; i<intervals; i++ )
      {
         double pos = i*range + start;
         area += function( pos );
      }
      area += ( function(start) + function(end) ) / 2;
      return range * area;
}

int main()
{
   for( int i=1; i<500; i++ )
   {
      printf( "%i intervals %8.5f value\n", i, integrate( 0, 1, i ) );
   }
   return 0;
}
```

The code calculates the integral of `sqrt(x)` over the range 0 to 1. The result of this calculation is the value two-thirds. The time that the calculation takes depends on the number of steps used; the smaller the step, the more accurate the result.

The example illustrates this very nicely when it is run. When one step is used, the function calculates a value of 0.5 for the integral. Once a few more steps are being used, it calculates a value of 0.66665. The more steps used, the greater the precision. As the number of steps increases, there becomes more opportunity to spread the work over multiple threads.

The actual computation time is minimal, so from that perspective, the operation is not one that naturally needs to be sped up. However, the calculation of the interval is clearly a good candidate for parallelization. The only complication is the reduction implicit in calculating the value of the variable **area**. It is straightforward to parallelize the integration code using OpenMP, as shown in Listing 9.15.

Listing 9.15 Numerical Integration Code Parallelized Using OpenMP

```
double integrate( double start, double end, int intervals )
{
  double area = 0;
  double range = ( end - start ) / intervals;
  #pragma omp parallel for reduction( +: area )
  for( int i=1; i<intervals; i++ )
  {
     double pos = i*range + start;
     area += function( pos );
  }
```

```
  area += ( function(start) + function(end) ) / 2;
  return range * area ;
}
```

The other way of uncovering further opportunities for parallelization, in the event of insufficient work, is to look at how the results of the parallel computation are being used. Returning to the Mandelbrot example, it may be the case that the computation is providing a single frame in an animation. If this were the case, then the code could be parallelized at the frame level, which may provide much more concurrent work.

Algorithmic Limit

Algorithms have different abilities to scale to multiple processors. If we return to discussing sorting algorithms, bubble sort is an inherently serial process. Each iteration through the list of elements that require sorting essentially picks a single element and bubbles that element to the top.

It is possible to generalize this algorithm to a parallel version called the *odd-even sort*. This sort uses two alternate phases of sorting. In the first phase, all the even elements are compared with the adjacent odd element. If they are in the wrong order, then the two elements are swapped. In the second phase, this is repeated with each odd element compared to the adjacent even element. This can be considered as in the first phase comparing the pair of elements (0,1), (2,3), and so on, and performing a swap between the elements as necessary. In the second phase, the pairs are the elements (1,2), (3,4), and so on. In both phases, each element is part of a single pair, so all the pairs can be computed in parallel, using multiple threads, and the two elements in each pair can be reordered without requiring any locks.

Obviously, better sorting algorithms are available. The most obvious next step is the quicksort. The usual implementation of this algorithm is serial, but it actually lends itself to a parallel implementation because it recursively sorts shorter independent lists of values. When parallelized using tasks, each task performs computation on a distinct range of elements, so there is no requirement for synchronization between the tasks. The code shown in Listing 9.16 demonstrates how a parallel version of quicksort could be implemented using OpenMP. The code is called through the `quick_sort()` routine. This code starts off the parallel region that contains the entire algorithm but uses only a single thread to perform the initial pass. The initial thread is responsible for creating additional tasks that will be undertaken by other available threads.

Listing 9.16 **Quicksort Parallelized Using OpenMP**

```
#include <stdio.h>
#include <stdlib.h>

void setup( int * array,int len )
{
  for ( int i=0; i<len; i++ )
```

```
    {
      array[i] = (i*7 - 3224) ^ 20435;
    }
}

void quick_sort_range( int * array, int lower, int upper )
{
  int tmp;
  int mid = ( upper + lower ) / 2;
  int pivot = array[mid];
  int tlower = lower, tupper = upper;
  while ( tlower <= tupper )
  {
    while ( array[tlower] < pivot ) { tlower++; }
    while ( array[tupper] > pivot ) { tupper--; }
    if ( tlower <= tupper )
    {
      tmp            = array[tlower];
      array[tlower] = array[tupper];
      array[tupper] = tmp;
      tupper--;
      tlower++;
    }
  }
  #pragma omp task shared(array) firstprivate(lower,tupper)
  if ( lower < tupper ) { quick_sort_range( array, lower, tupper ); }
  #pragma omp task shared(array) firstprivate(tlower,upper)
  if ( tlower < upper ) { quick_sort_range( array, tlower, upper ); }
}

void quick_sort( int *array, int elements )
{
  #pragma omp parallel
  {
    #pragma omp single nowait
    quick_sort_range( array, 0, elements );
  }
}

void main()
{
  int size = 10*1024*1024;
  int * array = (int*)malloc( sizeof(int) * size );
  setup( array, size);
  quick_sort( array, size-1 );
}
```

To summarize this discussion, some algorithms are serial in nature, so to parallelize an application, the algorithm may need to change. Not all parallel algorithms will be equally effective. Critical characteristics are the number of threads an algorithm scales to and the amount of overhead that the algorithm introduces.

In the context of the previous discussion, bubble sort is serial but can be generalized to an odd-even sort. This makes better use of multiple threads but is still not a very efficient algorithm. Changing the algorithm to a quick sort provides a more efficient algorithm that still manages to scale to many threads.

In this particular instance, we have been fortunate in that our parallel algorithm also happened to be more efficient than the serial version. This need not always be the case. It will sometimes be the case that the parallel algorithm scales well, but at the cost of lower serial performance. In these instances, it is worth considering whether both algorithms need to be implemented and a runtime selection made as to which is the more efficient.

There is another approach to algorithms that is not uncommon in some application domains, particularly those where the computation is performed across clusters with significant internode communication costs. This is to use an algorithm that iteratively converges. The number of iterations required depends on the accuracy requirements for the calculation. This provides an interesting tuning mechanism for parallelizing the algorithm.

It is probably easiest to describe this with an example. Suppose the problem is to model the flow of a fluid along an obstructed pipe. It is easy to split the pipe into multiple sections and allocate a set of threads to perform the computation for each section. However, the results for one section will depend on the results for the adjacent sections. So, the true calculation requires a large volume of data to be exchanged at the intersections.

This exchange of data would serialize the application and limit the amount of scaling that could be achieved. One way around this is to approximate the values from the adjacent sections and refine those approximations as the adjacent sections refine their results. In this way, it is possible to make the computations nearly independent of each other. The cost of this approximation is that it will take more iterations of the solver for it to converge on the correct answer.

This kind of approach is often taken with programs run on clusters where there is significant cost associated with exchanging data between two nodes. The approximations enable each node to continue processing in parallel. Despite the increased number of iterations, this approach can lead to faster solution times.

Hardware Constraints to Scaling

The design and implementation of the hardware will have a substantial impact on the scaling of applications run on it. There are three critical areas that can make a large difference to scaling. The amount of bandwidth to cache and the memory will be divided among the active threads on the system. The design of the caches will determine how much time is lost because of capacity and conflict-induced cache misses. The way that the processor core pipelines are shared between active software threads will determine how instruction issue rates change as the number of active threads increases.

Bandwidth Sharing Between Cores

Bandwidth is another resource shared between threads. The bandwidth capacity of a system depends on the design of the processor and the memory system as well as the memory chips and their location in the system. A consequence of this is that two systems can contain the same processor and same motherboard yet have two different measurements for bandwidth. Typically, a system configuring a system for best possible performance requires expensive memory chips.

The bandwidth a processor can consume is a function of the number of outstanding memory requests and the rate at which these can be returned. These memory requests can come from either hardware or software prefetches, as well as from load or store operations. Since each thread can issue memory requests, the more threads that a processor can run, the more bandwidth the processor can consume.

Many of the string-handling library routines such as `strlen()` or `memset()` can be large consumers of memory bandwidth. Since these routines are provided as part of the operating system, they are often optimized to give the best performance for a given system. The code in Listing 9.17 uses multiple threads calling `memset()` on disjoint regions of memory in order to estimate the available memory bandwidth on a system. Bandwidth can be measured by dividing the amount of memory accessed by the time taken to complete the accesses.

Listing 9.17 **Using `memset` to Measure Memory Bandwidth**

```
#include <stdio.h>
#include <stdlib.h>
#include <strings.h>
#include <pthread.h>
#include <sys/time.h>

#define BLOCKSIZE 1024*1025
int nthreads = 8;
char * memory;

double now()
{
  struct timeval time;
  gettimeofday( &time, 0 );
  return (double)time.tv_sec + (double)time.tv_usec / 1000000.0;
}
```

```
void *experiment( void *id )
{
  unsigned int seed = 0;
  int count = 20000;
  for( int i=0; i<count; i++ )
  {
    memset( &memory[BLOCKSIZE * (int)id], 0, BLOCKSIZE );
  }
  if ( seed == 1 ){ printf( "" ); }
}

int main( int argc, char* argv[] )
{
  pthread_t threads[64];
  memory = (char*)malloc( 64*BLOCKSIZE );
  if ( argc > 1 ) { nthreads = atoi( argv[1] ); }
  double start = now();
  for( int i=0; i<nthreads; i++ )
  {
    pthread_create( &threads[i], 0, experiment, (void*)i );
  }
  for ( int i=0; i<nthreads; i++ )
  {
    pthread_join( threads[i], 0 );
  }
  double end = now();
  printf( "%i Threads Time %f s Bandwidth %f GB/s\n", nthreads,
          (end - start) ,
          ( (double)nthreads * BLOCKSIZE * 20000.0 ) /
          ( end - start) / 1000000000.0 );
  return 0;
}
```

The results in Listing 9.18 show the bandwidth measured by the test code for one to eight virtual CPUs on a system with 64 virtual CPUs. For this particular system, the bandwidth scales nearly linearly with the number of threads until about six threads. After six threads, the bandwidth reduces. This might seem like a surprising result, but there are several effects that can cause this.

Listing 9.18 **Memory Bandwidth Measured on a System with 64 Virtual CPUs**

```
1 Threads Time  7.082376 s Bandwidth  2.76 GB/s
2 Threads Time  7.082576 s Bandwidth  5.52 GB/s
3 Threads Time  7.059594 s Bandwidth  8.31 GB/s
4 Threads Time  7.181156 s Bandwidth 10.89 GB/s
5 Threads Time  7.640440 s Bandwidth 12.79 GB/s
```

```
6 Threads Time 11.252412 s Bandwidth 10.42 GB/s
7 Threads Time 14.723671 s Bandwidth  9.29 GB/s
8 Threads Time 17.267288 s Bandwidth  9.06 GB/s
```

One possibility is that the threads are interfering on the processor. If multiple threads are sharing a core, the combined set of threads might be fully utilizing the instruction issue capacity of the core. We will discuss the sharing of cores between multiple threads in the section "Pipeline Resource Starvation." A second interaction effect is if the threads start interfering in the caches, such as multiple threads attempting to load data to the same set of cache lines.

One other effect is the behavior of memory chips when they become saturated. At this point, the chips start experiencing queuing latencies where the response time for each request increases. Memory chips are arranged in banks. Accessing a particular address will lead to a request to a particular bank of memory. Each bank needs a gap between returning two responses. If multiple threads happen to hit the same bank, then the response time becomes governed by the rate at which the bank can return memory.

The consequence of all this interaction is that a saturated memory subsystem may end up returning data at less than the peak memory bandwidth. This is clearly seen in the example where the bandwidth peaks at five threads.

Listing 9.19 shows memory bandwidth measured on system with four virtual CPUs. This is a very different scenario. In this case, adding a second thread does not increase the memory bandwidth consumed. The system is already running at peak bandwidth consumption. Adding additional threads causes the system memory subsystem to show reduced bandwidth consumption for the reasons previously discussed.

Listing 9.19 **Memory Bandwidth Measured on a System with Four Virtual CPUs**

```
1 Threads Time  7.437563 s Bandwidth  2.63 GB/s
2 Threads Time 15.238317 s Bandwidth  2.57 GB/s
3 Threads Time 24.580981 s Bandwidth  2.39 GB/s
4 Threads Time 37.457352 s Bandwidth  2.09 GB/s
```

False Sharing

False sharing is the situation where multiple threads are accessing items of data held on a single cache line. Although the threads are all using separate items of data, the cache line itself is shared between them so only a single thread can write to it at any one time. This is purely a performance issue because there is no correctness issue. It would be a correctness issue if it were a single variable on the cache line being shared between the threads.

The performance impact comes from the fact that each thread requires the cache line to be present and writable in the cache of the processor where the thread is executing. If another thread recently wrote to the cache line, then the modified data needs to be written back to memory and then sent to the next processor that wants to write to it.

This can cause accesses to the cache line to take a similar length of time as a miss to memory. In the case of false sharing, the line is constantly being bounced between processors, so most accesses to it end up requiring another processor to write the line back to memory—so the line does not ever get the benefit of being cache resident.

It is easy to demonstrate the cost of false sharing using the code in Listing 9.20. The code assigns each thread a volatile variable to use as a counter. The fact that the variable is volatile ensures that the code must store and reload it with every iteration. It also ensures that the compiler cannot eliminate the loop, even though the work it performs is redundant. The code creates multiple threads and then times how long it takes the first thread to complete the same amount of work as the other threads.

Listing 9.20 **Example of False Sharing**

```
#include <stdio.h>
#include <stdlib.h>
#include <pthread.h>
#include <sys/time.h>

double now()
{
  struct timeval time;
  gettimeofday( &time, 0 );
  return (double)time.tv_sec + (double)time.tv_usec / 1000000.0;
}

#define COUNT 100000000
volatile int go = 0;
volatile int counters[20];

void *spin( void *id )
{
  int myid = (int)id + 1;
  while( !go ) {}
  counters[myid] = 0;
  while ( counters[myid]++ < COUNT ) {}
}

int main( int argc, char* argv[] )
{
  pthread_t threads[256];
  int nthreads = 1;
  if ( argc > 1 ) { nthreads = atoi( argv[1] ); }
  for( int i=1; i<nthreads; i++ )
  {
    pthread_create( &threads[i], 0, spin, (void*)i );
  }
```

```
  double start = now();
  go = 1;
  spin( 0 );
  double end = now();
  printf("Time %f ns\n", ( end - start ) );

  for( int i=0; i<nthreads; i++ )
  {
    pthread_join( threads[i], 0 );
  }
  return 0;
}
```

If we take the code from Listing 9.20 and run a single thread, the thread completes its work in about nine seconds on a system with two dual-core processors. Using four threads on the same system results in a runtime for the code of about 100 seconds—a slowdown of about 10 times.

It is very easy to solve false sharing by padding the accessed structures so that the variable used by each thread resides on a separate cache line. The cache line can then reside in the cache of the processor where the thread is running, and consequently, all accesses to that cache line are low cost, and the code runs much faster.

Listing 9.21 shows a modified version of the code where accesses to the counter structure have been padded so that each counter is located at 64-byte intervals. This will ensure that the variables are located on separate cache lines on machines with cache line sizes of 64 bytes or less.

Listing 9.21 **Data Padded to Avoid False Sharing**

```
#include <stdio.h>
#include <stdlib.h>
#include <pthread.h>
#include <sys/time.h>

double now()
{
  struct timeval time;
  gettimeofday( &time, 0 );
  return (double)time.tv_sec + (double)time.tv_usec / 1000000.0;
}

#define COUNT 100000000
volatile int go = 0;
volatile int counters[320];

void *spin( void *id )
{
```

```
  int myid = ( (int)id + 1) * 16;
  while( !go ) {}
  counters[myid] = 0;
  while ( counters[myid]++ < COUNT ) {}
}

int main( int argc, char* argv[] )
{
  pthread_t threads[256];
  int nthreads = 1;
  if ( argc > 1 ) { nthreads = atoi( argv[1] ); }
  nthreads--;
  for( int i=1; i<nthreads+1; i++ )
  {
    pthread_create( &threads[i], 0, spin, (void*)i );
  }

  double start = now();
  go=1;
  spin( 0 );
  double end = now();
  printf( "Time %f s\n", ( end - start ) );

  for( int i=0; i<nthreads; i++ )
  {
    pthread_join( threads[i], 0 );
  }
  return 0;
}
```

The modified code takes about nine seconds to run with four threads on the same machine.

Although fixing false sharing is easy to do in most cases, detecting performance loss from it is much harder. In general, false sharing will turn up as an elevated number of cache misses on a particular memory operation, and it is hard to distinguish this from the normal cache misses that occur in all applications. However, the important thing to realize from the previous description is that when significant time is lost to false sharing, there will be significant numbers of cache misses, indicating the points at which the false sharing occurs. Hence, tracking down false sharing can be as simple as locating the places in the code where there are unexpectedly high numbers of cache misses on variables that should be local to one thread.

One important thing to note is that false sharing is a significant issue for multiprocessor systems but is not nearly as critical for multicore systems. For example, if we take the code from Listing 9.20 that has the false sharing issue and run it on a CMT system, it

takes 24 seconds with one thread and 26 seconds with four; the runtime is not significantly changed by the presence of false sharing. The data is shared through the on-chip
caches, and this sharing has little impact on performance. This is a useful feature of multicore processors.

Cache Conflict and Capacity

One of the notable features of multicore processors is that threads will share a single
cache at some level. There are two issues that can occur with shared caches: capacity
misses and conflict misses.

A conflict cache miss is where one thread has caused data needed by another thread
to be evicted from the cache. The worst example of this is thrashing where multiple
threads each require an item of data and that item of data maps to the same cache line
for all the threads. Shared caches usually have sufficient associativity to avoid this being a
significant issue. However, there are certain attributes of computer systems that tend to
make this likely to occur.

Data structures such as stacks tend to be aligned on cache line boundaries, which
increases the likelihood that structures from different processes will map onto the same
address. Consider the code shown in Listing 9.22. This code creates a number of threads.
Each thread prints the address of the first item on its stack and then waits at a barrier for
all the threads to complete before exiting.

Listing 9.22 **Code to Print the Stack Address for Different Threads**

```
#include <pthread.h>
#include <stdio.h>
#include <stdlib.h>

pthread_barrier_t barrier;

void* threadcode( void* param )
{
  int stack;
  printf("Stack base address = %x for thread %i\n", &stack, (int)param);
  pthread_barrier_wait( &barrier );
}


int main( int argc, char*argv[] )
{
  pthread_t threads[20];
  int nthreads = 8;
  if ( argc > 1 ) { nthreads = atoi( argv[1] ); }
  pthread_barrier_init( &barrier, 0, nthreads );
  for( int i=0; i<nthreads; i++ )
```

```
  {
    pthread_create( &threads[i], 0, threadcode, (void*)i );
  }
  for( int i=0; i<nthreads; i++ )
  {
    pthread_join( threads[i], 0 );
  }
  pthread_barrier_destroy( &barrier );
  return 0;
}
```

The expected output when this code is run on 32-bit Solaris indicates that threads are created with a 1MB offset between the start of each stack. For a processor with a cache size that is a power of two and smaller than 1MB, a stride of 1MB would ensure the base of the stack for all threads is in the same set of cache lines. The associativity of the cache will reduce the chance that this would be a problem. A cache with an associativity greater than the number of threads sharing is less likely to have a problem with conflict misses.

It is tempting to imagine that this is a theoretical problem, rather than one that can actually be encountered. However, suppose an application has multiple threads, and they all execute common code, spending the majority of the time performing calculations in the same routine. If that routine performs a lot of stack accesses, there is a good chance that the threads will conflict, causing thrashing and poor application performance. This is because all stacks start at some multiple of the stack size. The same variable, under the same call stack, will appear at the same offset from the base of the stack for all threads. It is quite possible that the cache line will be mapped onto the same cache line set for all threads. If all threads make heavy use of this stack location, it will cause thrashing within the set of cache lines.

It is for this reason that processors usually implement some kind of hashing in hardware, which will cause addresses with a strided access pattern to map onto different sets of cache lines. If this is done, the variables will map onto different cache lines, and the threads should not cause thrashing in the cache. Even under this kind of hardware feature, it is still possible to cause thrashing, but it is much less likely to happen because the obvious causes of thrashing have been eliminated.

The other issue with shared caches is capacity misses. This is the situation where the data set that a single thread uses fits into the cache, but adding a second thread causes the total data footprint to exceed the capacity of the cache.

Consider the code shown in Listing 9.23. In this code, each thread allocates an 8KB array of integers. When the code is run with a single thread on a core with at least 8KB of cache, the data the thread uses becomes cache resident, and the code runs quickly. If a second thread is started on the same core, the two threads would require a total 16KB of cache for the data required by both threads to remain resident in cache.

Listing 9.23 **Code Where Each Thread Uses an 8KB Chunk of Data**

```
#include <pthread.h>
#include <stdio.h>
#include <sys/time.h>
#include <stdlib.h>
#include <sys/types.h>
#include <sys/processor.h>
#include <sys/procset.h>

void * threadcode( void*id )
{
  int *stack = calloc( sizeof(int), 2048 );
  processor_bind( P_LWPID, P_MYID, ((int)id*4) & 63, 0 );
  for( int i=0; i<1000; i++ )
  {
    hrtime_t start = gethrtime();
    double total = 0.0;
    for( int h=0; h<100; h++ )
     for( int k=0; k<256*1024; k++ )
      total += stack[ ( (h*k) ^ 20393 ) & 2047 ]
              *stack[ ( (h*k) ^ 12834 ) & 2047 ];
    hrtime_t end = gethrtime();
    if ( total == 0 ){ printf( "" ); }
    printf( "Time %f ns %i\n", (double)end - (double)start, (int)id );
  }
}



int main( int argc, char*argv[] )
{
  pthread_t threads[20];
  int nthreads = 8;
  if ( argc > 1 ) { nthreads = atoi( argv[1] ); }
  for( int i=0; i<nthreads; i++ )
  {
    pthread_create( &threads[i], 0, threadcode, (void*)i );
  }
  for( int i=0; i<nthreads; i++) { pthread_join( threads[i], 0 ); }
  return 0;
}
```

Running this code on an UltraSPARC T2 processor with one thread reports a time of about 0.7 seconds per iteration of the outermost loop. The 8KB data structure fits into the 8KB cache. When run with two threads, this time nearly doubles to 1.2 seconds per iteration, as might be expected, because the required data exceeds the size of the first-level cache and needs to be fetched from the shared second-level cache.

Note that this code contains a call to the Solaris function `processor_bind()`, which binds a thread to a particular CPU. This is used in the code to ensure that two threads are placed on the same core. Binding will be discussed in the section "Using Processor Binding to Improve Memory Locality."

Obviously, when multiple threads are bound to the same processor core, there are other reasons why the performance might not scale. To prove that the problem we are observing is a cache capacity issue, we need to eliminate the other options.

In this particular instance, the only other applicable reason is that of instruction issue capacity. This would be the situation where the processor was unable to issue the instructions from both streams as fast as it could issue the instructions from a single stream.

There are two ways to determine whether this was the problem. The first way is to perform the experiment where the size of the data used by each thread is reduced so that the combined footprint is much less than the size of the cache. If this is done and there is no impact performance from adding a second thread, it indicates that the problem is a cache capacity issue and not because of the two threads sharing instruction issue width.

However, modifying the data structures of an application is practical only on test codes. It is much harder to perform the same experiments on real programs. An alternative way to identify the same issue is to look at cache miss rates using the hardware performance counters available on most processors.

One tool to access the hardware performance counters on Solaris is `cputrack`. This tool reports the number of hardware performance counter events triggered by a single process. Listing 9.24 shows the results of using `cputrack` to count the cache misses from a single-threaded version of the example code. The tool reports that for the active thread there are about 450,000 L1 data cache misses per second and a few hundred L2 cache miss events per second.

Listing 9.24 Cache Misses Reported Hardware Performance Counters from a Single-Threaded Run

```
% cputrack -c  DC_miss,L2_dmiss_ld ./a.out 1
   time lwp      event      pic0        pic1
   0.034    2 lwp_create       0           0
Time 698595172.000000 ns 0
   1.017    1      tick     4984         362
   1.127    2      tick   445576         138
Time 712353418.000000 ns 0
   2.017    1      tick        0           0
   2.127    2      tick   390764         107
Time 705177694.000000 ns 0
Time 700679442.000000 ns 0
   3.017    1      tick        0           0
   3.127    2      tick   402203          97
```

This can be compared to the cache misses encountered when two threads are run on the same core, as shown in Listing 9.25. In this instance, the L1 data cache miss rate increases to 26 million per second for each of the two active threads. The L2 cache miss rate remains near to zero.

Listing 9.25 **Cache Misses Reported When Two Threads Run on the Same Core**

```
% cputrack -c  DC_miss,L2_dmiss_ld ./a.out 2
   time lwp       event      pic0      pic1
  0.032   2 lwp_create         0         0
  0.046   3 lwp_create         0         0
  1.021   1       tick      5022       580
  1.181   2       tick  26332010        18
  1.211   3       tick  27171551         0
Time 1228276726.000000 ns 1
Time 1261119600.000000 ns 0
  2.021   1       tick         0         0
  2.181   2       tick  18846208         9
  2.031   3       tick  19188273        54
```

This indicates that when a single thread is running on the core, it is cache resident and has few L1 cache misses. When a second thread joins this one on the same core, the combined memory footprint of the two threads exceeds the size of the L1 cache and causes both threads to have L1 cache misses. However, the combined memory footprint is still smaller than the size of the L2 cache, so there is no increase in L2 cache misses.

Therefore, it is important to minimize the memory footprint of the codes running on the system. Most memory footprint optimizations will tend to appear to be common good programming practice and are often automatically implemented by the compiler. For example, if there are unused local variables within a function, then the compiler will not allocate stack space to hold them.

Other issues might be less apparent. Consider an application that manages its own memory. It would be better for this application to return recently deallocated memory to the thread that deallocated it rather than return memory that had not been used in a while. The reason is that the recently deallocated memory might still be cache resident. Reusing the same memory avoids the cache misses that would occur if the memory manager returned an address that had not been recently used and the thread had to fetch the cache line from memory.

Pipeline Resource Starvation

If a single thread is running on a core, its performance is limited by the rate at which the core can issue instructions and the number of stalls that the thread encounters. For example, a core might be able to sustain only a single load every cycle, so a code that contained only load instructions could at most issue a single instruction per cycle. Similarly, a code that consisted of a stream of dependent load instructions would only be able to issue the next instruction once the previous load had completed, and the time the load would take would represent the latency of the memory system.

When multiple threads share a core, the rate at which the threads can issue instructions is limited by two constraints. The first constraint is the maximum rate at which the hardware can issue instructions. For example, if there is only one load pipeline, then only one load instruction can be issued per cycle. The second constraint is that all the threads have to share the available hardware resources. If there is one load pipeline and two threads, then only one thread can issue a load instruction at a time.

It is instructive to think of this in terms of cache misses. When one thread is stalled waiting for data to be returned from memory, then all the other threads on that core can take instruction issue slots from the stalled thread. If all threads are stalled waiting for data from memory, then the issue width of the processor is not the dominating constraint on performance. This is the ideal situation for a CMT processor. If the threads are stalled waiting for memory, then it is more effective to have a large number of these threads all making forward process. Although individual threads might run slowly, the aggregate throughput of the system is impressive because of the number of threads.

When threads are not stalled on memory, such as when the data is cache resident or the code is compute intensive, the threads can become limited on instruction issue width. A single core supporting multiple threads relies on gaps where each thread is stalled to find cycles where an instruction from a different thread can be executed. If there are too many compute-intensive threads running on the core, then instruction issue width becomes a limiting factor in performance.

Consider the code shown in Listing 9.26, which runs a number of threads, and each thread is performing a simple set of integer operations on an item of data. Integer operations are typically single-cycle instructions, so one thread will desire to execute a single instruction every cycle. This is achievable when there is a single thread running on the core, but it can be limited on some processors when multiple threads are assigned to the same core.

Listing 9.26 **Worker Threads That Perform Sequences of Single-Cycle Integer Operations**

```
#include <stdio.h>
#include <stdlib.h>
#include <strings.h>
#include <pthread.h>

#include <sys/types.h>
#include <sys/processor.h>
#include <sys/procset.h>

int nthreads = 8;

void *experiment( void *id )
{
  unsigned int seed = 0;
```

```
    processor_bind( P_LWPID, P_MYID, ((int)id*2), 0 );
    int count = 100000000;
    for( int i=0; i<count; i++ )
    {
        seed += (seed<<2) ^ (seed|33556);
        seed += (seed<<2) ^ (seed|33556);
        seed += (seed<<2) ^ (seed|33556);
        seed += (seed<<2) ^ (seed|33556);
        seed += (seed<<2) ^ (seed|33556);
        seed += (seed<<2) ^ (seed|33556);
        seed += (seed<<2) ^ (seed|33556);
        seed += (seed<<2) ^ (seed|33556);
        seed += (seed<<2) ^ (seed|33556);
        seed += (seed<<2) ^ (seed|33556);
    }
    if ( seed == 1 ) { printf( "" ); }
}

int main( int argc, char* argv[] )
{
  pthread_t threads[64];
  if ( argc > 1 ) { nthreads = atoi( argv[1] ); }
  for( int i=0; i<nthreads; i++ )
  {
    pthread_create( &threads[i], 0, experiment, (void*)i );
  }
  for( int i=0; i<nthreads; i++ )
  {
    pthread_join( threads[i], 0 );
  }
  return 0;
}
```

The code shown in Listing 9.26 uses the Solaris `processor_bind` call to bind threads to particular virtual CPUs. This is necessary because the operating system will typically try to locate threads so that each thread gets the maximal resources. In this instance, we do not want that to happen because we want to investigate what happens when threads are scheduled on the same core. Doing this correctly requires knowledge of how the virtual CPU number maps to cores. This mapping often falls into one of two types.

The one common mapping is that virtual CPU numbers are assigned to cores in groups. If a core supports four threads, then virtual CPUs 0 to 3 would correspond to the four threads on the the first core.

The other common mapping scheme is to interleave cores. In this case, if there were two cores, then all the odd-numbered virtual CPUs would map to one core and all the even-numbered virtual CPUs would map to the other core.

The code as shown is for a machine where the virtual CPUs are interleaved. The particular Intel machine this was run on had two hyperthreading-enabled cores, making a total of four virtual CPUs. Virtual CPUs 0 and 2 are located on core 0, and virtual CPUs 1 and 3 are located on core 1.

When the bit manipulation code is run with one thread, it takes about two seconds. When run with two threads on the same core, it runs in two and a half seconds. If the runtime had remained the same, then twice as much work would have been achieved in the same time. However, this was not the case—twice as much work was achieved in 25% more time. To put it another way, this represents a 60% gain in throughput.

The same code was also run on an UltraSPARC T2 machine, with the binding suitably modified. The topology of this machine is interesting because each core can support eight threads, and these threads are arranged into two groups of four. Each group of four can issue one integer operation per cycle, but the two groups share a single load/store pipeline and a single floating-point pipeline. When run on this machine, using a single thread, the code took four seconds. When two threads were assigned to the same group on the same core, the threads completed in seven seconds, achieving only slightly more work per unit time than a single thread. When the two threads are assigned to different groups on the same core, the threads complete their work in four seconds. With this distribution of threads, the amount of work achieved per unit time is doubled.

As more threads become active, the scaling of a processor depends on the architecture of the core. The more available capacity, the more the throughput of the core will increase as the number of threads increases. An alternative view is that cores that work very hard to extract every bit of performance from a single-threaded code will end up with fewer spare cycles for a second thread to use. Once a core becomes fully utilized, additional threads will steal cycles from those that are already running and will cause all the active threads to run slightly slower.

If all the threads are busy performing useful work, then to a large extent it does not matter how well the processor scales—as long as it is completing more work than it was when running with a single thread.

Where performance is potentially lost is when one of the threads is spinning, waiting for some signal. The spinning thread will be taking instruction issue opportunities from the other threads running on the core. The code in Listing 9.27 demonstrates how a spinning thread can detract from the performance of the worker thread. This code creates multiple spinning threads and then attempts to complete a predefined amount of work.

Listing 9.27 **Spinning Threads That Take Instruction Issue Width from the Thread Performing the Work**

```
#include <stdio.h>
#include <stdlib.h>
#include <strings.h>
#include <pthread.h>
```

```c
#include <sys/types.h>
#include <sys/processor.h>
#include <sys/procset.h>

int nthreads = 8;
volatile int busy = 1;

void * spin( void *id )
{
  processor_bind( P_LWPID, P_MYID, (int)id, 0 );
  while ( busy ) {}
}

void experiment( int id )
{
  unsigned int seed = 0;
  processor_bind( P_LWPID, P_MYID, id, 0 );
  int count = 100000000;
  for( int i=0; i<count; i++ )
  {
      seed += (seed<<2) ^ (seed|33556);
      seed += (seed<<2) ^ (seed|33556);
      seed += (seed<<2) ^ (seed|33556);
      seed += (seed<<2) ^ (seed|33556);
      seed += (seed<<2) ^ (seed|33556);
      seed += (seed<<2) ^ (seed|33556);
      seed += (seed<<2) ^ (seed|33556);
      seed += (seed<<2) ^ (seed|33556);
      seed += (seed<<2) ^ (seed|33556);
      seed += (seed<<2) ^ (seed|33556);
  }
  if ( seed == 1 ) { printf( "" ); }
}

int main( int argc, char* argv[] )
{
  pthread_t threads[64];
  if ( argc > 1 ) { nthreads = atoi( argv[1] ); }
  for( int i=0; i<nthreads; i++ )
  {
    pthread_create( &threads[i], 0, spin, (void*)(i+1) );
  }
  experiment( 0 );
  busy = 0;
  for( int i=0; i<nthreads; i++ )
  {
    pthread_join( threads[i], 0 );
```

```
    }
    return 0;
}
```

On a test machine, the code takes four seconds to complete when there are no other threads scheduled to the same core. With one spinning thread scheduled to the same core, the code takes five and a half seconds to complete. With two threads it takes 8 seconds, and with three spinning threads it takes 12 seconds.

The progression of runtimes is interesting. The first spinning thread slows the original thread by only about 25% because the spinning thread mainly performs load and branch instructions, both of which have a latency of a few cycles before the thread is again ready to execute a new instruction. The net result is that the first spinning thread wants to issue an instruction every four cycles, which leaves three cycles for the original thread to execute instructions. The second spinning thread follows the same pattern, so now there are two threads that want to issue an instruction every four cycles. This leaves the original thread able to issue an instruction every other cycle, so it runs twice as slowly. When the third spinning thread is added, the core is already fully occupied by running the original thread and the two spinning threads, so adding an additional thread takes the situation from one where the three threads are getting to issue about one instruction every three cycles to a situation where they get to issue an instruction every four cycles. This is a 33% slowdown, which takes the runtime from 8 to 12 seconds.

One way of reducing the impact of spinning threads is to cause the thread to pause and consume no instruction issue resources. Most processors have a long latency instruction that can be used for this purpose even if they do not have an explicit instruction for delaying.

For example, on SPARC processors the operation to read the tick register takes a few cycles. The modified spin function shown in Listing 9.28 uses this to insert pauses into the spin cycle.

Listing 9.28 **Reading the Tick Register to Insert Delays into the Spin Code**

```
void * spin( void *id )
{
  processor_bind( P_LWPID, P_MYID, (int)id, 0 );
  while( busy )
  {
    asm( "rd %tick,%o0": : :"" );
  }
}
```

Inserting this delay takes the runtime of the code from 12 seconds with three spinning threads down to 7 seconds. Repeating the same instruction a couple of times or identifying a longer latency operation could be used to further reduce the impact of spinning threads.

Recent x86 processors have implemented a `pause` instruction, which causes the thread to pause for a number of cycles before issuing the next instruction. On older processors, the `pause` instruction maps onto a `no-op` instruction; therefore, the use of the instruction is fine on older hardware, but the old hardware will not actually pause. Windows implements a `yieldprocessor()` macro for pause/delay to provide an easy way of accessing this operation.

Operating System Constraints to Scaling

Most limitations to scaling are caused by either limitations of the hardware or inefficiencies in the implementation of the actual application. However, as the number of cores increases, it is not uncommon to uncover problems in the operating system or the libraries provided with it.

Oversubscription

Oversubscription is when there are too many active threads on a system. This is not a constraint on the absolute number of threads on the system, only on the number of active threads. If there are continuously more threads requesting CPU time than there are virtual CPUs, then the system may be considered to be oversubscribed.

Although quiescent threads take resources such as memory, they do not tend to consume much processor time, so a system can sustain a high count of idle threads. A system can sustain more active threads than there are virtual CPUs, but each active thread will only get a share of the available CPU resources. On a system where there are twice as many active software threads as there are hardware threads to sustain them, each active software thread will end up with 50% of the time of one of the virtual CPUs.

Having multiple threads share the same virtual CPU will typically lead to a greater than linear reduction in performance because of a number of factors such as overheads due to the cost of switching context between the active threads, the eviction of useful data from the cache, and the costs associated with the migration of threads between virtual CPUs. It is also worth considering that each thread requires some memory footprint, and a proliferation of threads is one way of causing a shortage of memory.

A key point to observe is that having more active threads than there are virtual CPUs can only decrease the rate at which each thread completes work. There is one situation where there is likely to be a benefit from having more threads than virtual CPUs. Threads that are sleeping or blocked waiting for a resource do not consume CPU and should not impact the performance of the active threads. An example of this is where there are many threads waiting for disk or network activity to complete.

It may be useful to have many threads waiting for the results of network requests or to have threads waiting for disk I/O to complete. In fact, this is a critical way of improving the performance of applications that have significant I/O—the main thread can continue computation, while a child thread waits for the completion of an I/O request.

The code in Listing 9.29 can be used to demonstrate how the performance of a single thread can suffer in the presence of other active threads. The code measures how long it takes the main thread to complete its work. However, before the main thread starts the timed section, it spawns multiple child threads that spin on a lock until the main thread completes its work.

Listing 9.29 Code to Demonstrate the Costs Associated with Oversubscription

```c
#include <stdio.h>
#include <stdlib.h>
#include <pthread.h>
#include <sys/time.h>

double now()
{
  struct timeval time;
  gettimeofday( &time, 0 );
  return (double)time.tv_sec + (double)time.tv_usec / 1000000.0;
}

#define COUNT 100000000
volatile int stop = 0;

void *spin( void *id )
{
  while( !stop ) {}
}

int main( int argc, char* argv[] )
{
  pthread_t threads[256];
  int nthreads = 1;
  if ( argc > 1 ) { nthreads = atoi( argv[1] ); }
  nthreads--;
  for( int i=0; i<nthreads; i++ )
  {
    pthread_create( &threads[i], 0, spin, (void*)0 );
  }

  double start=now();
  int total = 0;
  for( int h=0; h<COUNT; h++ )
    total += ( total << 2 ) ^ ( total | 33556 );
  if ( total == 0 ) { printf( "total==0\n" ); }
  double end=now();
  printf( "Time %f s\n", ( end - start ) );
  stop = 1;
  for( int i=0; i<nthreads; i++ )
```

```
{
    pthread_join( threads[i], 0 );
}
return 0;
}
```

The chart in Figure 9.6 shows the runtime of the code on a system with four virtual CPUs. The runtime of this code will depend on the number of software threads per virtual CPU. If there are eight or more software threads, then the runtime will be at least twice what it was for four or fewer threads. There are two lines in the chart: a line indicating how long the code would have taken to run if the runtime scaled linearly with the number of threads and a line that shows the actual runtime of the code. After about 64 threads, it is apparent that the oversubscription causes the runtime to be greater than might be expected from linear scaling. In other words, after about 64 threads, the performance of the system suffers because of oversubscription.

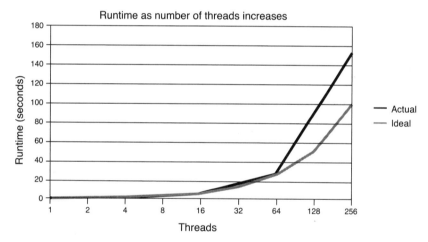

Figure 9.6 Scaling of oversubscribed system

Using Processor Binding to Improve Memory Locality

Thread migration is the situation where a thread starts running on one virtual processor but ends up migrated to a different virtual processor. If the new virtual processor shares the same core or if it shares cache with the original virtual processor, then the cost of this migration is low. For a multicore processor, the effect of thread migration tends to be minor since the new location of the thread shares a close level of cache with the old location of the thread. However, if the migration is from one physical chip to another, the cost can be quite high.

One cost of thread migration is related to the fact that the data the thread was using now resides in the cache of the old virtual processor. The data will need to be fetched into the cache of the new process. It is important to notice that this is likely to be a cache to cache transfer, rather like the situation with false sharing. For some systems, fetching data from another processor's cache may be lower cost than fetching that data from memory. However, on some systems the cost of fetching data from another cache may be higher than fetching the data from memory. The typical reason for this is that the data needs to be stored to memory before the new processor can fetch it.

However, there is an additional potential cost to thread migration in a multiprocessor system. Modern operating systems typically have some idea of the topology of the memory subsystem. Hence, the operating system can provide a thread with memory that has the lowest access latency. Unfortunately, if a thread is migrated, it can be located on a different processor with a much higher memory latency. This issue causes operating systems to attempt to keep threads, if not exactly where they were originally running, at least within the group of virtual CPUs that share the same memory access latencies.

This gives rise to the idea of locality groups, groups of threads that share the same memory access latencies. If a thread is moved within a locality group, there will be no change in memory latency costs; the only migration cost is a small cost due to the thread moving to a potentially cold cache.

Linux provides the tool `numactl` both to query the topology of the hardware and to allow the user to specify the virtual processor where the application will be run. Listing 9.30 shows the output from `numactl` that indicates that the system has two nodes, physical processors, and the amount of memory associated with each node.

Listing 9.30 **NUMA Characteristics from Linux**

```
$ numactl --hardware
available: 2 nodes (0-1)
node 0 size: 2047 MB
node 0 free: 88 MB
node 1 size: 1983 MB
node 1 free: 136 MB
```

Solaris provides the tool `lgrpinfo`, which reports on the locality groups on the system. The output shown in Listing 9.31 is from a system with two locality groups. Solaris provides the separate tool `pbind` to specify the binding of a process to virtual CPUs.

Listing 9.31 **Locality Group Information from Solaris**

```
$ lgrpinfo
lgroup 0 (root):
        Children: 1 2
        CPUs: 0-3
        Memory: installed 18G, allocated 2.7G, free 15G
```

```
       Lgroup resources: 1 2 (CPU); 1 2 (memory)
       Latency: 20
lgroup 1 (leaf):
       Children: none, Parent: 0
       CPUs: 0-1
       Memory: installed 9.0G, allocated 1.0G, free 8.0G
       Lgroup resources: 1 (CPU); 1 (memory)
       Load: 0.139
       Latency: 10
lgroup 2 (leaf):
       Children: none, Parent: 0
       CPUs: 2-3
       Memory: installed 9.0G, allocated 1.7G, free 7.3G
       Lgroup resources: 2 (CPU); 2 (memory)
       Load: 0.0575
       Latency: 10
```

In most instances, the developer should be able to trust that the operating system performs the optimal placement of the threads of the application. There are instances where this may not be optimal.

Memory is typically allocated with some policy that attempts to place the memory used by the thread close to the processor where the thread will be run. In many instances, this will be first-touch placement, which locates memory close to the thread that first accesses the memory.

There is a subtle point to be made. The act of allocating memory is often considered as the call that the application makes to `malloc()`. Although this is the call that causes an address range of memory to be reserved for the use of the process, physical memory is often only mapped into the process when a thread touches the memory. First touch works well in situations where the memory is used only by the thread that first touches it. If the memory is initialized by one thread and then utilized by another, this is less optimal, because the memory will be located close to the thread that initialized it and not close to the thread that is using it.

To demonstrate the effect of memory placement on performance, consider the code shown in Listing 9.32. This example estimates memory latency by pointer chasing through memory. This setup allows us to measure the impact of memory placement by allocating memory close to one chip and then using it with a thread on a different chip. The routine `setup()` sets up a circular linked list of pointers that will be used in timing memory latency. The code includes a call to the routine `threadbind()`, which will be defined shortly. This routine binds the particular thread to virtual CPU 0.

The routine `use()` is executed multiple times by the main thread. Each execution calls `threadbind()` to bind the thread to the desired virtual CPU. This enables the code to measure the memory latency from the virtual CPU where the code is running to the memory where the data is held. This routine uses two calls to the routine `now()` to calculate the elapsed time for the critical pointer chasing loop. The routine `now( )` will be defined shortly. The end result of this activity is an estimate of the latency of every memory access for the timed pointer chasing loop.

Listing 9.32 **Code to Measure Memory Latency**

```c
#include <pthread.h>
#include <stdlib.h>
#include <stdio.h>
#include <sys/types.h>
#include <sys/time.h>
#include <unistd.h>

#define SIZE 128*1024*1024
int** memory;

void setup()
{
  int i, j;
  threadbind( 0 );
  memory = (int**)calloc( sizeof(int*), SIZE+1 );
  for( j=0; j<16; j++ )
  {
    for( i=16+j; i<=SIZE; i++)
    {
      memory[i] = (int*)&memory[ i-16 ];
    }
    memory[j] = (int*)&memory[ SIZE-16+j+1 ];
  }
}

void *use( void* param )
{
  if ( threadbind( (int)param ) == 0 )
  {
    int* next;
    int i;
    double start = now();
    next = memory[0];
    for( i=0; i<SIZE; i++ )
    {
      next = (int*)*next;
    }
    if ( (int)next == 1 ) { printf( "a" ); }
    double end = now();
```

```
    printf( "Time %14.2f ns Binding %i/s\n",
            (end - start) * 1000000000.0 / ((double)SIZE), (int)param );
  } else { perror( "Error" ); }
}

int main( int argc, char* argv[] )
{
  pthread_t thread;
  int nthreads = 1;
  int i;
  if ( argc > 1 ) { nthreads = atoi( argv[1] ); }
  setup();
  for( i=0; i<nthreads; i++ )
  {
    pthread_create( &thread, 0, use, (void*)i );
    pthread_join( thread, 0 );
  }
  return 0;
}
```

Before the code can be run, two critical routines need to be provided. The easiest one to provide is the timing routine now(), which returns the current time in seconds as a double. The system function call gettimeofday() provides a very portable way on *NIX systems of getting seconds and microseconds since the system was booted. Listing 9.33 shows the code for wrapping this as returning a double.

Listing 9.33 **Code for Returning Current Time in Seconds**

```
double now()
{
  struct timeval time;
  gettimeofday( &time, 0 );
  return (double)time.tv_sec + (double)time.tv_usec / 1000000.0;
}
```

Controlling the location where the thread is run is not portable. The code in Listing 9.34 shows how the Solaris call processor_bind() can be used to control the binding of a thread to a virtual processor. The variables P_LWPID and P_MYID bind the calling thread to the particular virtual processor.

Listing 9.34 **Controlling Processor Binding on Solaris**

```
#ifdef __sun
#include <sys/processor.h>
#include <sys/procset.h>
```

```
int threadbind( int proc )
{
  return processor_bind( P_LWPID, P_MYID, proc, 0 );
}
#endif
```

Linux provides the same functionality through the `sched_setaffinity()` call. This call sets the affinity of a thread so that it will run on any of a group of virtual CPUs. The call requires a CPU set that indicates which virtual CPUs the thread can run on. The macro `CPU_ZERO()` clears a CPU set, and the macro `CPU_SET()` adds a virtual CPU to a CPU set. However, there are a couple of complexities. First, the macros `CPU_ZERO()` and `CPU_SET()` are defined only if the `#define _GNU_SOURCE` is set. To ensure the macros are available, this should be set as the first thing in the source file or on the compile line. The second issue is that `gettid()`, which returns the ID of the calling thread, may not be defined in the system header files. To rectify this, `gettid()` needs to be explicitly coded. Listing 9.35 shows the complete code to bind a thread to a particular virtual CPU.

Listing 9.35 **Binding a Thread to a Virtual CPU on Linux**

```
#ifdef linux
#include <sched.h>
#include <sys/syscall.h>

pid_t gettid()
{
  return syscall( __NR_gettid );
}

int threadbind( int proc )
{
  cpu_set_t cpuset;
  CPU_ZERO( &cpuset );
  CPU_SET( proc, &cpuset );
  return sched_setaffinity( gettid(), sizeof(cpu_set_t), &cpuset );
}
#endif
```

Listing 9.36 shows the equivalent Windows code for these two routines. The call to `GetTickCount()` returns a value in milliseconds rather than the microseconds returned by `gettimeofday()`. However, the code runs for sufficiently long enough that this reduction in accuracy does not cause a problem. The call to bind a thread to a virtual CPU is `SetThreadAffinityMask()`, and this call takes a mask where a bit is set for every virtual CPU where the thread is allowed to run.

Listing 9.36 Windows Code for Getting Current Time and Binding to a Virtual CPU

```
#include <stdio.h>
#include <windows.h>
#include <process.h>

double now()
{
  return GetTickCount() / 1000.0;
}

int threadbind( int proc )
{
  DWORD_PTR mask;
  mask = 1<<proc ;
  return SetThreadAffinityMask( GetCurrentThread(), mask );
}
```

Listing 9.37 shows the remainder of the code modified to compile and run on Windows.

Listing 9.37 Latency Code for Windows

```
#include <stdio.h>
#include <windows.h>
#include <process.h>

#define SIZE 128*1024*1024
int** memory;

void setup()
{
  int i, j;
  threadbind( 0 );
  memory = (int**)calloc( sizeof(int*), SIZE+1 );
  for( j=0; j<16; j++ )
  {
    for( i=16+j; i<=SIZE; i++ )
    {
      memory[i] = (int*)&memory[ i-16 ];
    }
    memory[j] = (int*)&memory[ SIZE-16+j+1 ];
  }
}

unsigned int __stdcall use( void* param )
{
  if ( threadbind( (int)param ) != 0 )
```

```
  {
    int* next;
    int i;
    double start = now();
    next = memory[0];
    for( i=0; i<SIZE;i++ )
    {
      next = (int*)*next;
    }
    if ( (int)next == 1 ) { printf( "a" ); }
    double end = now();
    printf( "Time %14.2f ns Binding %i/s\n",
            (end-start)*1000000000.0 / ((double)SIZE), (int)param );
  } else { printf( "Error" ); }
  return 0;
}


int _tmain( int argc, _TCHAR* argv[] )
{
  HANDLE thread;
  int nthreads = 8;
  int i;
  if ( argc > 1 ) { nthreads = _wtoi( argv[1] ); }
  setup();
  for( i=0; i<nthreads; i++ )
  {
    thread = (HANDLE)_beginthreadex( 0, 0, &use, (void*)i, 0, 0 );
    WaitForSingleObject( thread, INFINITE );
    CloseHandle( thread );
  }
  getchar();
  return 0;
}
```

Listing 9.38 shows the results of running the latency test code on a Solaris system where there are two chips each with associated local memory. In this instance, the remote memory latency is 50% greater than the local memory latency.

Listing 9.38 Latency on Solaris System with Two Memory Locality Groups

```
$ ./a.out 4
Time         98.24 ns Binding 0/s
Time        145.69 ns Binding 1/s
```

Although it is tempting to use processor binding to get the best possible performance from an application, it is not a general-purpose solution. On a shared system, it is relatively easy to end up with multiple applications bound to the same group of virtual CPUs. This would result in reduced performance for all the threads bound to shared virtual CPUs and an inefficient use of the system's resources. This is why it is usually best to let the operating system manage resources. For situations where some kind of static allocation of threads to virtual CPUs is desirable, it may be worth investigating some of the virtualization or resource allocation facilities provided by the operating system. There may be a way to divide the resources between applications without running the risk that some of the resources might be oversubscribed and some undersubscribed.

There is a potentially interesting situation when binding threads to virtual CPUs on a processor. If threads work on the memory regions with close proximity, then best performance will be obtained when these threads are bound to cores with close proximity. This binding would ensure that data that is shared between the threads ends up in caches that are also shared. As an example, thread 0 and thread 1 might access a set of overlapping array elements. If thread 0 happens to fetch all the elements into cache, then thread 1 may be able to access them from there, rather than also having to fetch them from memory.

However, consider the situation where work is unevenly distributed between the threads. Suppose the amount of work done by each thread diminishes such that thread 0 does the most work and thread 15 does the least work. If threads 0 and 1 are bound to virtual CPUs on the same core, then both threads will be competing for pipeline resources and will consequently run slowly. On the other hand, if thread 0 were paired with thread 15, then thread 15 would rapidly complete its work leaving all the resources of the core available for use by thread 0.

Processor binding is not something that should be undertaken without some careful consideration of the situation. Although it has the potential to improve performance, it also restricts the freedom of the operating system to dynamically schedule for best performance, and this can lead to the bound application taking many times longer than its unbound runtime.

Priority Inversion

All processes and threads can have some associated priority. The operating system uses this to determine how much CPU time to assign to the thread. So, a thread with a higher priority will get more CPU time than a thread with a lower priority. This enables the developer to determine how time is distributed between the threads that comprise an application.

For example, the threads that handle the user interface of an application are often assigned a high priority. It is important for these threads to accept user input and refresh the screen. These activities make the application feel responsive to the user. However, the application might also need to be doing some background processing. This background processing could be quite compute intensive. Run at a low priority, the background task gets scheduled into the gaps where the interface does not need attention. If it were scheduled with a high priority, then it would be competing with the user interface threads for compute resources, and there would be a noticeable lag between the user performing an action and the application responding.

One problem with priority is that of priority inversion, where one thread is waiting for the resources held by another thread. If the thread holding the resources is of lower priority, then the priority is said to be inverted.

A potential issue in this situation is when a low-priority thread holds a mutex. A thread with a higher priority wakes up and causes the low-priority thread to be descheduled from the CPU. The thread waiting for the mutex could be of an even higher priority, but it will now have to wait for both the lower-priority threads to complete before it can acquire the mutex.

A common solution for this problem is for the thread holding the resources to temporarily acquire the max priority of the waiting threads, ideally reducing the time that it holds the resources. Once the thread releases the resources, it resumes its original lower priority, and the higher-priority thread continues execution with its original higher priority.

An alternative solution is to boost the priority of any thread that acquires a particular resource so that the thread is unlikely to be preempted while it is holding the resource.

Multicore Processors and Scaling

The two big advantages of multicore processors are their ability to run multiple threads and the low synchronization costs between those threads. Synchronization costs govern scaling in two important ways. Low synchronization costs mean that the code will scale more effectively to higher thread counts. A similar reasoning leads to the enticing possibility that low synchronization costs enable developers to produce parallel versions of routines that were previously too small to parallelize. Consequently, there is a fortuitous convergence that processors with low synchronization costs that enable scaling to high thread counts also provide the threads that will perform that scaling.

The low synchronization costs lead to one further advantage for multicore processors. This section has discussed a number of reasons that scaling could be limited, and a number of these are implicitly functions of the communication costs between cores. The most obvious example of this is false sharing.

The cost of false sharing is that updates to a cache line depend on the cache to cache communication latency between the cores where the threads are running. This cost is typically of the order of memory latency. On a multicore processor, the communication cost between two threads is the latency of the closest shared level of cache between the two processors. Since this cache is usually on chip, the latency is often an order of magnitude less than memory latency. If we take the code demonstrating false sharing from Listing 9.20 and run it on a multicore system, the increase in runtime due to false sharing is minimal.

However, these benefits from multicore processors are likely to disappear if the system is a multiprocessor system. If the system has multiple processors, then it becomes more important to consider the memory locality of the data that a thread is using. The migration of a thread between processors will cause local data to become remote. If data is shared between threads, some of those threads might see local, and some might see remote access costs. For optimal performance, it may be appropriate to consider binding threads to virtual CPUs.

With a multicore, multiprocessor system, there is the question of whether it is better to spread the work across all the chips or whether it is better to constrain it to within a single chip. Using multiple chips may provide more instruction issue bandwidth, and it may also provide more memory bandwidth, but the cost will be increased communication latency between threads. Constraining all the threads to reside on a single chip will provide the best communication latency but may not provide optimal instruction issue width and memory bandwidth.

Although multicore processors present great opportunities for running parallel workloads, they also have constraints. Most critical is the sharing of resources between the virtual CPUs. These resources might be processor bandwidth, instruction pipeline, or cache. These constraints will have an impact on the scaling of a single process as the number of threads increases. Scaling to low numbers of threads will often be close to linear, but scaling to higher numbers of threads may demonstrate limitations of both the hardware and software.

Even within a single multicore chip, it may be worth considering binding threads to virtual processors. The optimal assignment for work will probably be achieved by placing as few threads as possible on each core. This is a task that operating systems should perform automatically, but there may be situations where this does not happen. One example might be when there are multiple processes active on the machine, making it hard for the OS. The OS may make the decision to place the threads where there is spare compute resource rather than placing threads optimally for the process.

Summary

This chapter described the common reasons why an application may not reach ideal scaling. The discussions should provide you with the ability to identify the particular hardware- or software-related reasons for restricted scaling and understand the limiting factors. You should be able to determine ways of solving those problems that have solutions.

An important discussion in this chapter has been the comparison between multicore processors and multiprocessors systems. Multicore processors avoid or reduce some of the scaling limitations of multiprocessors systems. Understanding the differences will enable you to write code that works well on both kinds of systems. This is an important consideration because applications need to perform well regardless of the underlying hardware.

Other Parallelization Technologies

Previous chapters have dealt with some of the mainstream approaches to developing parallel applications. There are many alternative ways of producing applications that take advantage of multicore processors. This chapter introduces a number of alternative approaches ranging from the use of GPU hardware by OpenCL and CUDA to the C++ library provided by Intel's Threading Building Blocks.

This chapter also covers some cluster technologies such as MPI. Although running a cluster of machines is outside the scope of this text, it is interesting to realize that a single machine can now offer an equivalent number of processors as might have been found in a cluster a few years ago. Although most users may not experience using an actual cluster, some of the technologies that are appropriate for clusters are now also appropriate for single systems.

By the end of the chapter, you should have a good appreciation for some other approaches to parallelization. You will also have some understanding of what the strengths and weaknesses are for the various approaches and also have some knowledge of how to write code to exploit the different methods.

GPU-Based Computing

An approach to parallelism that has recently evolved is the use of graphics co-processors as accelerators for computation. This came about because as the requirements for fast and detailed graphical representations evolved, the hardware to implement them began to increasingly resemble hardware that could perform fast parallel floating-point or integer computation. Recently, there have been multiple efforts to export the ability to perform computation on graphics processing units (GPUs) to common programming languages. The most well-known of these are Compute Unified Device Architecture (CUDA) and Open Computing Language (OpenCL). CUDA is specific to Nvidia, whereas OpenCL is supported on GPUs from both Nvidia and ATI.

Although this approach utilizes many cores to perform computations in parallel, the details of the approach are quite different from all the other approaches discussed in this book. The most important consideration is that GPUs represent compute co-processors, and there are several constraints with co-processors.

The first is that they need not, and in the case of GPUs do not, share the instruction set of the host processor. This means that producing code that runs on the GPU requires a more complex tool chain. This has to produce code for the host processor, together with code for the GPU, and then bind the two different sets of code together into a single executable.

The second problem is that GPUs do not share the same address space as the host processor. Data needs to be copied across to the GPU. The act of copying is time-consuming and forces the problem being tackled to have to be large enough to justify the cost of the copy operation.

These problems can be, if not hidden, at least reduced by the language used to program the GPU. Listing 10.1 shows a simple program written using CUDA. The program written in OpenCL would look broadly similar.

Listing 10.1 **Simple CUDA Program**

```
#include "cuda.h"

#define LEN 100000

// GPU code
__global__ void square( float *data, int length )
{
  int index = blockIdx.x * blockDim.x + threadIdx.x;
  if ( index < length )
  {
    data[index] = data[index] * data[index];
  }
}

//Host code
int main()
{
  float *host_data, *gpu_data;
  int ThreadsPerBlock, Blocks;

  // Allocate memory
  host_data = (float*)malloc( LEN * sizeof(float) );
  cudaMalloc( &gpu_data, LEN*sizeof(float) );

  // Initialize data on host
  for( int i=0; i<LEN; i++ )
```

```
  {
    host_data[i] = 2*i;
  }

  // Copy host data to GPU
  cudaMemcpy( gpu_data, host_data, LEN*sizeof(int),
              cudaMemcpyHostToDevice );

  // Perform computation on GPU
  ThreadsPerBlock = 128;
  Blocks = (int)( (LEN-1) / ThreadsPerBlock ) + 1;
  square <<<Blocks, ThreadsPerBlock>>>( gpu_data, LEN );

  // Copy GPU data back to host
  cudaMemcpy( gpu_data, host_data, LEN*sizeof(int),
              cudaMemcpyDeviceToHost);

  // Free allocated memory
  cudaFree( gpu_data );
  free( host_data );
}
```

The code is in two routines. The routine `square()` contains the code that is actually executed by the GPU. The routine `main()` is executed by the host processor.

It is best to describe the routine `main()` first because this code performs the preparation for the parallel work. This routine needs to allocate memory both on the host system, using `malloc()`, and on the GPU, using the call `cudaMalloc()`. The method of passing data between the host system and the GPU is to copy the data from the host system to the GPU. Hence, it is necessary to reserve space for the data in both places.

The `host_data` array is initialized and then copied over to the GPU by calling `cudaMemcpy()`. The `cudaMemcpy()` call is used for transferring data in both directions, and the direction of the copy is determined by the last parameter passed into the function.

Copying data to and from the GPU requires the data to be sent across the bus that connects the processor to the GPU. This bus provides relatively low bandwidth, perhaps 8GB/s to 16GB/s. Once the data is transferred, the GPU is able to sustain much higher aggregate bandwidths on the order of 100GB/s. Therefore, transferring data to and from the GPU is to be avoided as much as possible.

Each GPU supports a large number of software threads. These threads are arranged in groups called *blocks*. The main program assigns work to a block of threads, and each thread in the block executes the same routine. The number of threads in a block can be set by the code. It should be a multiple of 32 and can be as large as 512 threads.

The code takes the number of threads per block and uses this to calculate how many blocks are needed to complete the work. The function call syntax has been extended so that the call to `square()` takes both the normal parameters and the details of the number of blocks and the number of threads per block. This function call causes the GPU to execute the code using the specified number of blocks and threads per block.

Once the call to `square()` completes, the host copies the resulting data back from the device into host memory using a second `cudaMemcpy()` call. The last actions allow the host machine to free up the memory allocated on the host and on the GPU.

The function `square()` is declared with the `__global__` keyword to indicate that it is a function that executes on the GPU but can be called by the host code. Each hardware thread on the GPU will execute the routine. The first thing the hardware thread needs to do is determine the index of the element that it needs to compute. Information about the topology of the block of threads is passed into the thread in the structures `blockIdx`, `blockDim`, and `threadIdx`. These three structures allow the CUDA framework the flexibility to specify that the thread performs computation in some three-dimensional space. However, in this example we are working on only a single, `x`, dimension. The index that a particular thread should compute can be derived by multiplying the index of the block that is currently being computed by the size of each block and then adding the index of the current thread. The thread will then work on the element at that index.

In the Listing 10.1, the computation performed is trivial, but much more complex work can be performed on the GPU. The theoretical performance can reach teraflops of floating-point computations per second. This can make for a compelling solution for codes that require large amounts of computation.

There is another important point to make. The current trend is to see increasing numbers of general-purpose CPUs on the same chip. It is quite likely that in the future we will see processors that resemble today's GPUs. Consequently, understanding how codes can be scaled to this level of threading is likely to be a useful skill in the future.

Language Extensions

Perhaps the most obvious place to add support for parallelism is through extensions to existing languages. The language C++ because of its expressive power is a good vehicle for extensions such as Intel's Threading Building Blocks. Cilk++, again from Intel, provides a set of language extensions that can be preprocessed to generate the appropriate code. This section explores a number of ways that language extensions can be used to enable the development of parallel applications.

Threading Building Blocks

Intel's Threading Building Blocks (TBB) is a C++ library that uses templates to provide common parallelization functionality and supporting objects. For example, the library provides fundamental objects such as containers and synchronization objects. It also provides supporting functionality such as access to timers and memory management routines. The TBB library is open source and ported to multiple platforms.

Some of the functionality provided by the library could be used as objects in conventional code. The code in Listing 10.2 uses the concurrent queue template to manage communication between a producer and consumer thread.

Listing 10.2 **Using a Concurrent Queue in a Pthread Producer-Consumer Model**

```
#include "tbb/concurrent_queue.h"
#include <stdio.h>
#include <pthread.h>

using namespace tbb;
using namespace std;

concurrent_queue<int> queue;

extern "C"
{
  void * producer( void* )
  {
    for( int i=0; i<100; i++ ) { queue.push( i ); }
    return 0;
  }

  void * consumer( void* )
  {
    int value = 0;
    while ( value != 99 )
    {
      queue.pop( value );
      printf( "Value=%i\n", value );
    }
    return 0;
  }
}

int main()
{
  pthread_t threads[2];
  pthread_create( &threads[0], 0, producer, 0 );
  pthread_create( &threads[1], 0, consumer, 0 );
  pthread_join( threads[1], 0 );
  pthread_join( threads[0], 0 );
  return 0;
}
```

The two POSIX threads in the Listing 10.2 use the concurrent queue to pass integer values from the producer to the consumer. Although providing a large set of building block functionality is very useful, the more important features are those that manage performing parallel work. The use of TBB allows the developer to abstract away from POSIX threads and concentrate on the algorithm.

The code in Listing 10.3 uses TBB to parallelize the code to compute points in the Mandelbrot set. The code declares a `Mandle` object that contains all the methods that compute whether a given point is in the set. The `operator()` is overloaded to perform the computations over a 2D range. The computation is executed by a call to the `parallel_for` function, which takes the range over which the computation is to be performed as parameters and the object receiving that range.

Listing 10.3 **Using TBB to Parallelize Mandelbrot Set Generation**

```cpp
#include "tbb/parallel_for.h"
#include "tbb/blocked_range2d.h"

using namespace tbb;

const int SIZE = 500;

int data[SIZE][SIZE];

class Mandle
{
  int inset( double ix, double iy ) const
  {
    int iterations = 0;
    double x = ix, y = iy, x2 = x*x, y2 = y*y;
    double x3 = 0,y3 = 0;
    while (( x3 + y3 < 4 ) && ( x2 + y2 < 4 ) && ( iterations < 1000 ) )
    {
      y  = 2 * x * y + iy;
      x  = x2 - y2 + ix;
      x2 = x * x; x3 = x2;
      y2 = y * y; y3 = y2;
      iterations++;
    }
    return iterations;
  }

public:
  void operator()( const blocked_range2d<int,int>&range ) const
  {
    for( int y = range.rows().begin(); y != range.rows().end(); y++ )
    {
      for( int x = range.cols().begin(); x != range.cols().end(); x++ )
      {
        double xv = 0.75 * ( (double)(x - SIZE/2) ) / (double)(SIZE/4);
        double yv = 0.75 * ( (double)(y - SIZE/2) ) / (double)(SIZE/4);
        data[x][y] = inset(xv,yv);
      }
```

```
    }
  }
  Mandle(){}
};

int main()
{
  parallel_for( blocked_range2d<int,int>(0,500,10,0,500,10), Mandle() );
  return 0;
}
```

The code does not know what range it will be assigned until runtime. This enables the runtime library to decide how many threads are available and divide the work among the threads appropriately. The runtime will take the original range object and break it down into an appropriate number of smaller ranges. It will be these range objects that are actually passed into the `Mandle` object.

Cilk++

The Cilk++ language extensions from Intel provide parallel functionality for applications using a relatively small set of new keywords. Support is currently limited to x86 processors running either Windows or Linux. The language is very close to OpenMP in terms of what it provides. Listing 10.4 shows a Cilk++ version of the Mandelbrot example. To convert the C language code to Cilk++ code, it was necessary to replace the `main()` function with `cilk_main()`. This change ensures that the Cilk runtime environment is initialized. The other necessary change was to convert the outermost for loop into a `cilk_for` loop.

The program is built using the Cilk++ preprocessor `cilkpp`, which then invokes the C++ compiler on the resulting code.

Listing 10.4 **Mandelbrot Example Using** `cilk_for`

```
#define SIZE 300

int inset( double ix, double iy )
{
  int iterations = 0;
  double x = ix, y = iy, x2 = x*x, y2 = y*y;
  double x3 = 0,y3 = 0;
  while ( ( x3 + y3 < 4) && ( x2 + y2 < 4 ) && ( iterations < 1000 ) )
  {
    y  = 2 * x * y + iy;
    x  = x2 - y2 + ix;
    x2 = x * x; x3 = x2;
    y2 = y * y; y3 = y2;
    iterations++;
```

```
    }
    return iterations;
}

int cilk_main(int argc, _TCHAR* argv[])
{
  int data[SIZE][SIZE];
  cilk_for( int y=0; y<SIZE; y++ )
  {
    for( int x=0; x<SIZE; x++ )
    {
      double xv = 0.75 * ( (double)(x - SIZE/2) ) / (double)(SIZE/4);
      double yv = 0.75 * ( (double)(y - SIZE/2) ) / (double)(SIZE/4);
      data[x][y] = inset(xv,yv);
    }
  }
  getchar();
  return 0;
}
```

Cilk++ offers more than just a parallel for construct. A more important feature is `cilk_spawn/cilk_sync`. This allows the application to spawn worker threads and then wait for them to complete. This is close to the concept of OpenMP tasks.

We can take the OpenMP quicksort example from Listing 9.15 from the previous chapter and convert it into equivalent Cilk++ code shown in Listing 10.5. The `cilk_spawn` statement causes the following code to be, potentially, executed by another thread. Every function ends with an implicit `clik_sync` statement, so the function can spawn multiple threads but will not complete until those threads have also completed.

Listing 10.5 **Quicksort Written in Cilk++**

```
#include <stdio.h>
#include <stdlib.h>

void setup( int * array, int len )
{
  for( int i=0; i<len; i++ ) { array[i] = ( i*7 - 3224 ) ^ 20435; }
}

void output( int * array, int len )
{
  for( int i=0; i<len; i++ ) { printf( "%8i", array[i] ); }
}

void quick_sort_range( int * array, int lower, int upper )
{
```

```
  int tmp;
  int mid = ( upper + lower ) / 2;
  int pivot = array[mid];
  int tlower = lower, tupper = upper;
  while ( tlower <= tupper )
  {
    while ( array[tlower] < pivot ) { tlower++; }
    while ( array[tupper] > pivot ) { tupper--; }
    if ( tlower <= tupper )
    {
      tmp = array[tlower];
      array[tlower] = array[tupper];
      array[tupper] = tmp;
      tupper--;
      tlower++;
    }
  }
  if ( lower < tupper )
  {
    cilk_spawn quick_sort_range( array, lower, tupper );
  }
  if ( tlower < upper )
  {
    cilk_spawn quick_sort_range( array, tlower, upper );
  }
}

void quick_sort( int *array, int elements )
{
    quick_sort_range( array, 0, elements );
}


int cilk_main()
{
  int size = 10*1024*1024;
  int * array = (int*)malloc( sizeof(int)*size );
  setup( array, size );
  quick_sort( array, size-1 );
  output( array, size );
  return 0;
}
```

The Cilk++ environment also provides two tools that are useful for developers of parallel applications: a data race detection tool called `cilkscreen` and a performance prediction tool called `cilkview`. The data race tool `cilkscreen` provides functionality that is common to most similar tools. The performance tool `cilkview` provides something different—a high-level report on the scalability of the application. This is of less use than a line-by-line profile but does provide an interesting insight into how the application may scale as the number of threads increases. The output in Listing 10.6 shows `cilkview` run on the quicksort code (modified so as not to print out the list of the sorted values).

Listing 10.6 **Scalability Estimates from** `cilkview`

```
$ cilkview cilkquicksort
cilkview: generating scalability data
Whole Program Statistics:

Cilkview Scalability Analyzer V1.1.0, Build 8504
1) Parallelism Profile
   Work :                                5,216,903,917 instructions
   Span :                                  338,025,076 instructions
   Burdened span :                         339,522,925 instructions
   Parallelism :                                 15.43
   Burdened parallelism :                        15.37
   Number of spawns/syncs:                   9,106,354
   Average instructions / strand :                 190
   Strands along span :                            119
   Average instructions / strand on span :   2,840,546
   Total number of atomic instructions :     9,106,371
   Frame count :                            18,212,713

2) Speedup Estimate
   2 processors:        1.80 - 2.00
   4 processors:        3.00 - 4.00
   8 processors:        4.51 - 8.00
   16 processors:       6.02 - 15.43
   32 processors:       7.22 - 15.43
```

The tool reports a number of statistics about the run of the program. The more interesting result is in the section showing estimates of speedup for various numbers of threads. The tool reports that the best-case estimate for scaling is just over 15 times faster at 16 threads. A lower bound for scaling is that the code will never get much more than eight times faster regardless of the number of threads used.

Grand Central Dispatch

Grand Central Dispatch (GCD) from Apple is an approach to task-based parallelism. It is very similar to the concept of an OpenMP task or a `cilk_spawn` call. The core functionality of GCD is that a block of work can be placed onto a dispatch queue. When hardware resource is available, the work is removed from the queue and completed. There are various ways that work can be dispatched to a queue. For example, the dispatch_async() function dispatches work to a queue and immediately returns to the calling code, having placed the work on the queue for later completion. In contrast, the dispatch_apply() function places work on a queue but does not return until all the work is completed. Listing 10.7 shows an example of using the dispatch_apply() function to parallelize the calculation of the Mandelbrot set.

Listing 10.7 **Mandelbrot Example Using** dispatch_apply

```
#define SIZE 300

int inset( double ix, double iy )
{
  int iterations = 0;
  double x = ix, y = iy, x2 = x*x, y2 = y*y;
  double x3 = 0,y3 = 0;
  while ( ( x3 + y3 < 4 ) && ( x2 + y2 < 4 ) && ( iterations < 1000 ) )
  {
    y  = 2 * x * y + iy;
    x  = x2 - y2 + ix;
    x2 = x * x; x3 = x2;
    y2 = y * y; y3 = y2;
    iterations++;
  }
  return iterations;
}

int main( int argc, _TCHAR* argv[] )
{
  int data[SIZE][SIZE];
  dispatch_apply( SIZE, dispatch_get_global_queue( 0, 0 ),
  ^( size_t y )
  {
      for( int x=0; x<SIZE; x++ )
      {
        double xv = 0.75 * ( (double)(x - SIZE/2) ) / (double)(SIZE/4);
        double yv = 0.75 * ( (double)(y - SIZE/2) ) / (double)(SIZE/4);
        data[x][y] = inset( xv, yv );
      }
    }
  );
  getchar();
  return 0;
}
```

The `dispatch_apply()` call takes three parameters. The first parameter is the number of iterations. The second parameter is the queue to which the work is to be dispatched. An application may create and manage multiple queues; the global queue used in the example is the queue representing all available processors. The final parameter is a block variable. This contains a *block literal* containing the code that each iteration of the loop needs to execute. The block literal is denoted with a caret (^). This block of code is actually passed as a parameter into the routine; hence, the closing bracket of the function call is after the closing bracket for the block of code.

Features Proposed for the Next C and C++ Standards

The next revisions of both the C and C++ standards contain some features that will help in the development of multithreaded codes. In previous chapters, we looked at the differences between POSIX threads and Windows threads. The functionality provided by the two implementations is very similar, but there are many differences in how that functionality is exported to the developer. Incorporating some of this support into the language standards will be a huge improvement in the ability to write portable parallel code.

At the time of writing, it is not certain whether these features will be accepted or modified in the final version. Consequently, it is not possible to write compilable code that demonstrates these new features, both because the features may change in the final version and because there are no compilers that implement these features. However, there seems to be three areas that the languages are standardizing.

The first area is that of creating and managing threads. In C, there are likely to be a set of function calls, reminiscent of the POSIX function calls for creating and managing threads. The example in Listing 10.8 shows the current approach for creating and running a new thread. The resulting code looks very similar to both the Windows and POSIX code.

Listing 10.8 Creating a New Thread in the Proposed Next C Standard

```
#include <threads.h>
#include <stdio.h>

int * work( void * )
{
  printf( "Child thread\n" );
  return 0;
}

int main()
{
  thrd_t thread;
  thrd_create( &thread, work, 0 );
  thrd_join( &thread, 0 );
}
```

In C++ it is natural for threads to be objects. The code in Listing 10.9 is an equivalent code that creates and manages a child thread. The work that is to be performed is passed in as a function to the created thread object.

Listing 10.9 **Creating a New Thread in the Proposed Next C++ Standard**

```
#include <thread>
#include <iostream>

work()
{
  std::cout << "Child thread\n";
}

int main()
{
  std::thread mythread( work );
  mythread.join();
}
```

Both standards also propose support for atomic operations and memory ordering. In C, atomic operations are supported through providing atomic types and operations that can be performed on those types. The code in Listing 10.10 demonstrates how an atomic variable can be incremented.

Listing 10.10 **Atomic Increment in C Proposal**

```
#include <stdatomic.h>

int count()
{
  static struct atomic_int value = 0;
  atomic_fetch_add( &value, 1 );
  printf( "Counter=%i\n", value );
}
```

C++ defines the atomic types as structs and provides methods for accessing them. Listing 10.11 shows equivalent C++ code.

Listing 10.11 **Atomic Increment in C++ Proposal**

```
#include <atomic>
#include <iostream>

int count()
{
```

```
static atomic_int value = 0;
value += 1;
printf( "Counter=%i\n", value );
}
```

The final area of standardization treats mutexes and condition variables. The code in Listing 10.12 demonstrates how, with the proposed C standard, a mutex could be created and used to provide atomic access to a shared variable. The call to `mtx_init()` takes a parameter to describe the type of mutex that is required, which provides the facility for the mutex to have different runtime behaviors, such as having a timeout.

Listing 10.12 **Protecting a Shared Variable with a Mutex in C**

```c
#include <threads.h>
#include <stdio.h>

int counter = 0;
mtx_t mutex;

int * work( void * )
{
  mtx_lock( &mutex );
  counter++;
  printf( "Counter = %i\n", counter );
  mtx_unlock( &mutex );
  return 0;
}

int main()
{
  thrd_t thread;
  mtx_init( &mutex, mtx_plain );
  thrd_create( &thread, work, 0 );
  thrd_join( &thread, 0 );
  mtx_destroy( &mutex );
}
```

The C++ proposed standard implements a class hierarchy of different kinds of mutex. Listing 10.13 shows the equivalent code to protect a shared variable.

Listing 10.13 **Protecting a Shared Variable with a Mutex Object in C++**

```cpp
#include <thread>
#include <iostream>

int counter = 0;
```

```cpp
std::mutex mymutex;

struct work operator()
{
  mymutex.lock();
  std::cout<< "Counter " << counter << "\n";
  mymutex.unlock();
}

int main()
{
  std::thread mythread{ work() };
  mthread.join();
}
```

Microsoft's C++/CLI

Visual Studio supports a C++/Common Language Infrastructure (CLI), which is a C++-derived language that runs on the .NET Common Language Runtime (CLR). As with all managed languages, it compiles to bytecode, which is then run on a virtual machine. The language provides a set of objects for synchronization and threads.

The code in Listing 10.14 illustrates how a main thread can create a child thread. The main thread prints one set of output, and the child thread prints another. The main thread waits for a key press before exiting.

Listing 10.14 **Creating a Child Thread in C++/CLI**

```cpp
using namespace System;
using namespace System::Threading;


void work()
{
  Console::WriteLine( L"Work Thread" );
}

int main( array< System::String ^> ^args )
{
    Thread^ mythread = gcnew Thread( gcnew ThreadStart( &work ) );
    mythread->Start();
    Console::WriteLine( L"Main Thread" );
    Console::ReadKey();
    return 0;
}
```

The `Thread` object is the abstraction for a thread. To produce a running thread, an object needs to be created and then started by calling its `Start()` method. The `gcnew()` function creates a managed object on the garbage-collected heap and returns a handle to it. A variable that holds a handle to a particular type is indicated with a carat (^) character. The thread requires the address of a routine to execute. This is provided through a `ThreadStart` object, and this object is created with the address of the desired routine.

As previously mentioned, the language provides the familiar synchronization primitives. For example, we can use a mutex to ensure that the main thread prints its output before the child thread.

The code then becomes more complex because it is not possible to use managed global variables. One way around this is to convert the code that the child thread executes into a method in an object. Listing 10.15 defines a `ThreadWork` object that contains the handle of a `Mutex` object; this is set when the object is created.

Listing 10.15 **Using a Mutex to Enforce Ordering**

```
using namespace System;
using namespace System::Threading;

public ref class ThreadWork
{
private:
  Mutex^ mymutex;
public:
  ThreadWork( Mutex^ m )
  {
     mymutex = m;
  }

  void work()
  {
    mymutex->WaitOne();
    Console::WriteLine( L"Child thread" );
    mymutex->ReleaseMutex();
  }
};

int main( array<System::String ^> ^args )
{
    Mutex^ mymutex = gcnew Mutex();
    ThreadWork^ T = gcnew ThreadWork( mymutex );
    mymutex->WaitOne();
    Thread^ mythread = gcnew Thread( gcnew
                    ThreadStart( T, &ThreadWork::work ) );
    mythread->Start();
    Console::WriteLine( L"Main Thread" );
```

```
    mymutex->ReleaseMutex();
    mythread->Join();
    Console::ReadKey();
    return 0;
}
```

The `Mutex` object is acquired through a call to the method `WaitOne()` and released through a call to the method `ReleaseMutex()`.

The first thing the code does is to create the `Mutex` object, and the handle of this is passed into the `ThreadWork` object. The main thread acquires the mutex by calling `WaitOne()`. This will stop the child thread from executing until after the main thread has printed its output.

The `ThreadStart` object now needs to be initialized with two parameters. The first parameter is the instantiation, `T`, of a `ThreadWork` object, and the second parameter is the method to be run by the thread.

Once the main thread has printed its output to the console, it releases the mutex and then calls the `Join()` method of the `Thread` object to wait for the child thread to complete.

Alternative Languages

The languages described so far in this chapter have been extensions to what might be called standard C/C++. In some ways, C and C++ are not ideal languages for parallelization. One particular issue is the extensive use of pointers, which makes it hard to prove that memory accesses do not alias.

As a consequence of this, other programming languages have been devised that either target developing parallel applications or do not suffer from some of the issues that hit C/C++. For example, Fortress, initially developed by Sun Microsystems, has a model where loops are parallel by default unless otherwise specified. The Go language from Google includes the concept of go routines that, rather like OpenMP tasks, can be executed in parallel with the main thread.

One area of interest is functional programming. With pure functional programming, the evaluation of an expression depends only on the parameters passed into that expression. Hence, functions can be evaluated in parallel, or in any order, and will produce the same result. We will consider Haskell as one example of a functional language.

The code in Listing 10.16 evaluates the Nth Fibonacci number in Haskell. The language allows the return values for functions to be defined for particular input values. So, in this instance, we are setting the return values for 0 and 1 as well as the general return value for any other numbers.

Listing 10.16 **Evaluating the Nth Fibonacci Number in Haskell**

```
fib 0 = 0
fib 1 = 1
fib n = fib (n-1) + fib (n-2)
```

Listing 10.17 shows the result of using this function interactively. The command `:load` requests that the module `fib.hs` be loaded, and then the command `fib` is invoked with the parameter 10, and the runtime returns the value 55.

Listing 10.17 Asking Haskell to Provide the Tenth Fibonacci Number

```
GHCi, version 6.10.4: http://www.haskell.org/ghc/  :? for help
Loading package ghc-prim ... linking ... done.
Loading package integer ... linking ... done.
Loading package base ... linking ... done.
Prelude> :load fib.hs
[1 of 1] Compiling Main             ( fib.hs, interpreted )
Ok, modules loaded: Main.
*Main> fib 10
55
```

Listing 10.18 defines a second function, `bif`, a variant of the Fibonacci function. Suppose that we want to return the sum of the two functions. The code defines a serial version of this function and provides a `main` routine that prints the result of calling this function.

Listing 10.18 Stand-Alone Serial Program

```
main = print ( serial 10 10)

fib 0 = 0
fib 1 = 1
fib n = fib (n-1) + fib (n-2)

bif 0 = -1
bif 1 = 0
bif n = bif (n-1) + bif (n-2)

serial a b = fib a + bif b
```

Rather than interpreting this program, we can compile and run it as shown in Listing 10.19.

Listing 10.19 Compiling and Running Serial Code

```
C:\> ghc -O --make test.hs
[1 of 1] Compiling Main             ( test.hs, test.o )
Linking test.exe ...
C:\> test
21
```

The two functions should take about the same amount of time to execute, so it would make sense to execute them in parallel. Listing 10.20 shows the code to do this.

Listing 10.20 **Stand-Alone Parallel Program**

```
import Control.Parallel

main = print ( parallel 20 20)

fib 0 = 0
fib 1 = 1
fib n = fib (n-1) + fib (n-2)

bif 0 = -1
bif 1 = 0
bif n = bif (n-1) + bif (n-2)

parallel a b
  = let x = fib a
        y = bif b
        in x `par` (y `pseq` (x+y))
```

In the code, the `let` expressions are not assignments of values but declarations of local variables. The local variables will be evaluated only if they are needed; this is lazy evaluation. These local variables are used in the `in` expression, which performs the computation. The `import` statement at the start of the code imports the `Control.Parallel` module. This module defines the `par` and `pseq` operators. These two operators are used so that the computation of x=fib a and y=bif b is performed in parallel, and this ensures that the result (x+y) is computed after the calculation of y has completed. Without these elaborate preparations, it is possible that both parallel threads might choose to compute the value of the function x first.

The example given here exposes parallelism using low-level primitives. The preferred way of coding parallelism in Haskell is to use strategies. This approach separates the computation from the parallelization.

Haskell highlights the key advantage of pure functional programming languages that is helpful for writing parallel code. This is that the result of a function call depends only on the parameters passed into it. From this point, the compiler knows that a function call can be scheduled in any arbitrary order, and the results of the function call do not depend on the time at which the call is made. The advantage that this provides is that adding the `par` operator to produce a parallel version of an application is guaranteed not to change the result of the application. Hence, parallelization is a solution for improving performance and not a source of bugs.

Clustering Technologies

Historically, one of the ways of gathering large numbers of processors together was to use a cluster of machines. An advantage of doing this was that it increased the available disk space, memory, and memory bandwidth as well as the number of CPUs. The capacity of a single multicore processor has increased such that work that previously required a small cluster will now fit onto a single system. It is therefore interesting to consider technologies that might be used in this domain.

MPI

Message Passing Interface (MPI) is a parallelization model that allows a single application to span over multiple *nodes*. Each node is one or more software threads on a system, so it is quite permissible to host multiple nodes on the same system. Hence, a multicore system can host multiple MPI nodes.

Communication between the nodes is, as the name suggests, accomplished by passing messages between the nodes. The messages can be broadcast to all nodes or directed to a particular node. Since there is no addressable shared memory between the nodes, the communication costs depend on the size and frequency of the messages. Hence, the best scaling will be achieved if the application does minimal communication. A consequence of this is that MPI codes have to scale well by design. This means that they can often run well on a multicore or multiprocessor system so long as no other system resources, such as bandwidth or memory capacity, are exhausted.

Each node executes the same application. The first action the application needs to take is to initialize the MPI library with a call to `MPI_Init()`; the final action it needs to take is to shut down the library with a call to `MPI_Finalize()`. Each individual MPI process will need to know both the total number of processes in the application and its own rank in that group of processes. The call to `MPI_Comm_size()` returns the total number of processes, and the call to `MPI_Comm_rank()` provides each process with its identifier. Listing 10.21 shows the basic framework for a typical MPI program.

Listing 10.21 **A Bare-Bones MPI Program**

```
#include "mpi.h"

int main( int argc, char *argv[] )
{
  int numproc, myid;
  MPI_Init( &argc, &argv );
  MPI_Comm_size( MPI_COMM_WORLD, &numproc );
  MPI_Comm_rank( MPI_COMM_WORLD, &myid );
  ...
  MPI_Finalize();
  return 0;
}
```

MPI provides a very rich API for communicating between processes. The simplest level of this is the ability to pass an array of data to another MPI process using a call to `MPI_Send()` and for that process to receive the data using a call to `MPI_Recv()`. Other calls exist to provide more intrinsic functionality such as reductions.

Since the communication overhead is often quite large, it makes most sense to use MPI to solve problems that are too large for a single system. With multicore processors, the size of the problem that can be tackled has become less dependent on the number of threads and more dependent on considerations such as the memory footprint of the data set or the amount of bandwidth of the system. This highlights an important motivator for MPI programs—system characteristics such as amount of bandwidth or amount of available memory scale with the number of systems. For a problem that is limited by the time it takes to stream through a large amount of data, two systems will provide twice as much bandwidth, potentially solving the problem twice as fast. Using two threads on a single system does not necessarily provide the same doubling of bandwidth and certainly does not double the memory capacity of the system.

High communication costs also cause a change in the approach taken to using MPI to solve problems. As we have previously discussed, the best scalability will result from codes that have the fewest and smallest amounts of communication. Tuning algorithms to remove or reduce the need for communication will result in better performance. It may be more efficient for an algorithm to use approximations to estimate the return values from other processes rather than waiting for those processes to return the exact answers, even if this approximation causes the algorithm to iterate longer before terminating.

To illustrate the use of MPI, we'll use it to produce a larger image of the Mandelbrot set. The algorithm that we are going to use is a single master process and a number of worker processes. The worker processes compute a line of the Mandelbrot set at a time and pass this to the master process. Listing 10.22 shows the code necessary to compute a line of the Mandelbrot set.

Listing 10.22 Computing a Row of the Mandelbrot Set

```
#include "mpi.h"
#include <stdlib.h>

#define COLS 1000
#define ROWS 1000

int inset( double ix, double iy )
{
   int iterations = 0;
   double x = ix, y = iy, x2 = x*x, y2 = y*y;
   while ( ( x2 + y2 < 4 ) && ( iterations < 1000 ) )
   {
     y  = 2 * x * y + iy;
     x  = x2 - y2 + ix;
     x2 = x * x;
```

```
      y2 = y * y;
      iterations++;
    }
    return iterations;
}

void computerow( int index, int * data )
{
  double y = -1.5 + (double)index / ROWS;
  for( int c=0; c<COLS; c++ )
  {
    double x = -1.5 + (double)c / COLS;
    data[c] = inset( x, y );
  }
}
```

Listing 10.23 shows the code for the master process. The master process needs to set up an array large enough to store all the results from the worker processes. The master process computes the zeroth row of the output and then waits for all subsequent rows to be calculated by the other processes. The `MPI_Recv()` call takes parameters that indicate the expected type of data and an array where the data is to be stored. The call also takes parameters that identify the process where the data is to come from and takes a tag—in this case the line number—that identifies the data being sent. The final parameters are the set of nodes that should be included in the communication and a variable to hold the status.

Listing 10.23 The Master Thread Accumulates All the Results from the Worker Threads

```
int numproc, myid, rows, cols;


void masterprocess()
{
  int ** data;
  MPI_Status status;
  data = malloc( sizeof(int*) * ROWS );   // Allocate memory to store data
  data[0] = malloc( sizeof(int) * COLS );
  computerow( 0, data[0] );                 // Compute row zero
  for( int currentrow = 1; currentrow < rows; currentrow++ )
  {
    data[currentrow] = malloc( sizeof(int) * cols );
    int process = currentrow % ( numproc - 1 ) + 1;
    MPI_Recv( data[currentrow], COLS, MPI_INT, process, currentrow,
            MPI_COMM_WORLD, &status );
  }
}
```

The worker processes run the code shown in Listing 10.24. Each process computes every Nth row of the matrix and then passes this row to the master process. The main routine is also shown in this listing. This routine needs to do the normal setup and tear-down of the MPI library and then decide whether the process is the master or one of the workers.

Listing 10.24 **MPI Worker Thread and Setup Code**

```
void workerprocess()
{
  int * data, row;
  data = malloc( sizeof(int) * COLS );
  row = myid;
  while ( row <= ROWS )
  {
    computerow( row, data );
    MPI_Send( data, COLS, MPI_INT, 0, row, MPI_COMM_WORLD );
    row += numproc-1;
  }
  free( data );
}


int main( int argc, char *argv[] )
{
  MPI_Init( &argc, &argv );
  MPI_Comm_size( MPI_COMM_WORLD, &numproc );
  MPI_Comm_rank( MPI_COMM_WORLD, &myid );
  if ( myid == 0 ) { masterprocess(); } else { workerprocess(); }
  MPI_Finalize();
  return 0;
}
```

The program as written achieves little parallelism. This is for a couple of reasons. The first is that the send and receive operations are blocking. The sending processes cannot make progress until the receiving process receives the data. The receiving process compounds this by looking for the data in order.

The code could be modified to use a nonblocking send operation so that the worker processes could overlap communication with computation. Another improvement to the code would be for the master process to accept data from the workers in any order, rather than requiring the data to be received in order.

With the increase in the number of available cores, it has become appropriate to combine MPI for parallelization across nodes with OpenMP for parallelization within a node. This allows an application to use coarse-grained parallelism to scale to large numbers of nodes and then a finer degree of parallelism to scale to large numbers of cores.

MapReduce as a Strategy for Scaling

MapReduce is an algorithm that is well suited to clusters because it requires little communication and it is a relatively flexible approach so long as there are multiple parallel queries to be completed. Implementations are available in various programming languages

The MapReduce algorithm has two steps. The map step takes a problem and distributes that problem across multiple nodes. The reduce step takes the results from those nodes and combines them to provide a final result.

MapReduce works best when there is an operation to be performed on multiple sets of input data. For example, consider computing the frequency of the use of all words over a range of documents. A single thread would compute this task by reading each document and then using a map to increment the value of a counter for each word encountered in the document.

The MapReduce version of the code would perform the following two steps. In the map phase, the master thread would assign each worker thread to perform the word count on a particular document. In the reduce step, each worker thread would return the list of word frequencies for its particular document, and the master thread would combine all these into a single set of results.

From the description, it should be obvious that the algorithm could be implemented using MPI. In fact, the only difference between this and the code to compute the Mandelbrot set is that the MPI master thread did not need to tell the worker threads what to compute since this information was provided in the source code.

What makes MapReduce different from an algorithm implemented in MPI? There are two major differences.

First, MPI is a general-purpose framework for the composition of parallel problems, whereas MapReduce is an approach for a specific kind of problem. So, it may be possible to implement MapReduce-type problems in MPI, but it is not generally possible to implement all MPI problems using a MapReduce framework.

The second difference is that MPI is designed to work on a known grid of computers. MPI relies on the fact that there is a known node performing the work and that this node will at some point return the results of the computation. MapReduce is built on the basis that the nodes performing the work may not be reliable. If a node does not provide the result within a suitable time period, the master node can restart the query on a different node.

There are two characteristics of the MapReduce work that enables this restart to happen. The first is that the master node explicitly requests work from the worker nodes. So if the worker node fails, the master node can make the same request of another worker node. The second characteristic is that the nodes do not contain state. So if a worker node fails, the master node can restart from a known point and not have the problem that one of the other nodes is already using partial answers from the failed node.

MapReduce is usually implemented as a library, such as the Hadoop implementation. This library provides the functionality for distributing the work across multiple systems, restarting the work if one of the nodes fails, and so on. The advantage of providing this as a library is that improvements to the library code will be felt by all users of the library.

Grids

Possibly the simplest approach to utilizing multiple compute threads is to use a grid. A *grid* is a collection of nodes. A task can be dispatched to the grid, and at some point the results of that task will be returned to the user.

Conceptually, a grid is the task management aspect of MapReduce without the "map" and "reduce" algorithms for performing computation. A grid will typically provide much greater node management functionality than a MapReduce implementation. Node management might extend to powering down idle nodes or allocating clusters of work to co-located nodes. So, the two approaches will be broadly complementary in nature.

Transactional Memory

We have already talked about some of the complexities of implementing a functionally correct parallel application. One particular problem is that of data races. In a large program, it can be quite hard to truly eliminate all possible races. Even using data race detection tools does not guarantee that there are no further races hidden in the code.

The safe software solution is to place mutex locks around all potentially critical sections of code. The mutex locks ensure that only a single thread can access the critical variables and hence that the application will work correctly. However, mutex locks both impose a performance penalty on access to the shared variables and also work only if all accesses to the variables are protected by a common lock.

The idea of transactional memory is to attempt to address both issues. Transactional memory is really aimed at the correctness issue. If it can also make a difference to performance, that is an additional benefit rather than a critical benefit.

Transactional memory enables the developer to protect accesses to variables within a transaction. A *transaction* is a block of code that either completes successfully or fails and does not then result in any change in system state.

A common syntax for transactions has not yet been developed. One possibility is the use of the keyword `atomic` to wrap the entire transaction. Listing 10.25 shows an example of this. The transaction moves a value from one location in an array to another. The keyword `atomic` indicates that the specified amount must be moved atomically between the two locations in the array. Since transactions can fail, the `atomic` keyword must implicitly retry the transaction until it successfully completes. The critical points here are first that the transaction cannot leave the data in an unknown partially completed state and second that no other process can see a partially completed transaction. This makes the use of the keyword `atomic` appropriate.

Listing 10.25 **Accessing Multiple Accounts in a Single Transaction**

```
void move( int from, int to, int value )
{
  atomic
  {
    accounts[ from ] -= value;
```

```
    accounts[ to ] += value;
  }
}
```

Transactions will fail if any of the variables used in the transaction are modified (or potentially read) by another thread. This is where transactions can improve the safety of parallel code. If there is another modification of a variable used in a transaction outside of that transaction, the transaction will fail. It is not possible for the transaction to complete in the presence of data races. This does not stop situations where multiple threads access a variable outside of a transaction, but it does eliminate problems with the granularity of locks or potential deadlock situations.

Transactional memory can be provided either in software using a library or at the hardware level. Hardware transactional memory is the ideal. This is where during a transaction, hardware tracks any other accesses to variables used by the transaction and aborts the transaction if necessary.

Software transactional memory is provided by a library that ensures that the variables used in the transaction are accessed atomically only. As such, it tends to have a much higher implementation cost compared to hardware transactional memory. Providing transactions in software can help address the correctness issue; however, it is unlikely to do so in a way that also leads to performance gains over using any other approach.

Vectorization

Vectorization is the software optimization of using single instruction multiple data (SIMD) instructions to perform computation in parallel. Since the instructions act on multiple items of data at the same time, this is really an example of parallelism at the level of the instruction and data. As such, it can result in a significant gain in performance without the overhead associated with synchronizing and managing multiple threads.

Listing 10.26 shows that the simplest example of this is the loop. This loop adds two vectors and places the result into a third.

Listing 10.26 **Loop Amenable to SIMD Vectorization**

```
void sum( double *in1, double *in2, double *out, int length )
{
  for ( int i=0; i<length; i++ )
  {
    out[i] = in1[i] + in2[i];
  }
}
```

Using normal instructions, referred to as *single instruction single data* (SISD) instructions, each iteration of the loop would require two loads: one addition and one store operation. However, SIMD instructions act on a vector of values. A vector might hold two double-precision values or four single-precision values, and so on.

For a SIMD instruction set that handles two double-precision values in parallel, each iteration through the SIMD version of the loop performs two loads of a pair of elements each, an addition operation on that pair of elements, and a store that writes the resulting pair of elements back to memory. Consequently, the trip count around the loop will have reduced by a factor of two. Assuming the latencies of the operations remain the same, the resulting code will run twice as fast.

Most modern compilers have the facility to identify and utilize SIMD instructions, either by default or under a combination of flags. The generated code will work only on hardware that supports the instructions.

SIMD instructions complement other parallelization strategies. If the loop shown in Listing 10.26 acted on large arrays of data, multiple threads could handle the computation efficiently. However, if the arrays were small in size, the synchronization overheads may dwarf the gains from parallelization. SIMD instructions would be effective in both situations, perhaps providing a doubling of performance. However, they could potentially provide that doubling of performance even when the length of the arrays is too short for efficient parallelization.

Summary

In this chapter, we met many other approaches to parallelization. These included library-based approaches such as Threading Building Blocks, which seek to provide infrastructure for parallel applications and preprocessors such as Cilk++ that hide some of the complexity of the underlying libraries. A particularly interesting domain is how the future C and C++ language standards may include standardized support for parallelism, which would go a large way toward enabling portable code at the language-standard level. Another approach to providing parallelism is using different programming paradigms, such as functional programming languages like Haskell. This approach could potentially avoid some of the problems that make coding parallel code in C/C++ difficult.

Parallelism should not just be considered a problem to be solved within a machine. One of the more complex problems is using parallelism to compute the solutions to problems that are too large to be solved by a single system. Technologies such as MPI enable a single application to span arbitrarily many systems. The approach of using multiple systems enables other hardware features, such as bandwidth or disk, to scale with the number of processors. Algorithms such as MapReduce are an approach that allows problems to be broken down into chunks that can then be solved in parallel using many systems.

Finally, we looked at how hardware can provide more opportunities for parallelism. The CUDA approach of providing many simple cores enables a block of simple code to be executed by hundreds of threads in parallel. Transactional memory presents a possible solution for the problem of producing correct multithreaded code. SIMD instructions provide greater opportunities for instruction-level parallelism that increase performance without the requirement for multiple threads.

It would take an entire book to cover any one of these topics in depth. The objective of this chapter was to provide exposure to alternative ways of parallelizing applications. Some of these approaches might represent the ideal solution for a particular problem you are facing. The more important outcome should be a realization that it is possible to produce a parallel version of a program by changing the rules, perhaps by changing programming language or perhaps by changing the hardware used.

Concluding Remarks

This book has covered a large range of parallelization approaches and topics. The next steps are to take this knowledge and apply it to an existing or a new application. This final chapter acts as a summary of the steps necessary to successfully develop correct and scalable multithreaded applications.

Writing Parallel Applications

The key part of writing parallel applications is identifying where the parallelization will provide the most benefit for the least cost. If the application has not yet been written, then analysis is necessary to determine what work can be completed in parallel. This analysis needs to take the critical performance metrics for the application into account—is the application more concerned with throughput, or is response time more important? Both are usually important, and the question can be interpreted as whether the expected response time is sufficiently fast, in which case the threads can be assigned to providing throughput, or the response time is insufficient, in which case the threads should be assigned to reducing this.

Making an existing application run in parallel is a harder task. The first step is to profile the application to determine where the time is currently spent. The art of performance tuning is to determine a region of code where sufficient time is spent so that any improvement in that region would result in an observable performance gain for the entire application.

Identifying Tasks

The basic building block of parallelism might be called a *task*. A task can be passed to a single virtual CPU for completion. Identifying these tasks is a matter of carefully examining the profile of the application and locating the largest possible chunk of independent work.

There are two potentially conflicting constraints. The most efficient scaling will come from identifying the largest chunk of work that can be completed independently. Doing this will keep the synchronization costs to a minimum. However, the greatest scaling will be achieved by identifying the largest number of independent tasks. Consequently, the best overall scaling will result from meeting both of these criteria—identifying a large number of tasks, each of which takes a significant amount of time before it requires synchronization with other threads.

Profiles will help in discovering these tasks. There are multiple ways that the profile can be "sliced." The traditional slice is to look at the top functions, identify the function that is taking the time, and attempt to make this function parallel. Doing this might identify sections of the functions that are independent or perhaps a loop that can be executed in parallel.

However, when considering parallelizing an application, this slice of the profile may not be sufficient. The time spent in the top function could be only a small percentage of the total runtime. Therefore, it might be necessary to look at the time spent both in a function and in all the functions that it calls; this might be referred to as a function's *callee tree*, or its inclusive time. This should represent a larger amount of time, which could therefore be divided between more tasks, or provide a small set of threads with more work before they require synchronization.

Parallelization is not just about parallel computation. It is also appropriate to consider time that the code spends waiting for some external event. Take a web server as an example. It will wait until it receives a request from a remote client, and it will then send an appropriate response to the client. We have already looked at a parallel version of this where one thread waits for incoming requests while other threads service the requests that have already arrived. The performance and utilization gains come from enabling multiple threads to wait in parallel.

An application might employ multiple parallelization strategies in order to utilize the most CPU resources. Taking the web server, we already have some fundamental parallelism in responding to the incoming requests, and a further level of parallelism might be found using multiple threads to formulate each individual response.

Estimating Performance Gains

One critical aspect of parallelization is knowing the expected performance gains, usually estimated using a variant of Amdahl's law. Knowing how much work will be performed in parallel indicates how much impact it will have on the runtime. An application where half of the work could be performed in parallel has an expectation of getting at most twice as fast when parallelized. Knowing the degree of parallelism that the code can support provides a realistic expectation for the scaling of the code. If the same code scales to only eight threads, then the code can at most get about 1.8x faster when parallelized.

Understanding this scaling helps in determining which parts of the code should be targeted for parallelization. After a first parallel region has been identified and coded, the remaining serial code will probably contain further opportunities for parallelization, and these opportunities will be a more significant proportion of the remaining runtime. Hence, it is likely that parallelizing an application will be an iterative process, with each stage causing further opportunities to become more attractive.

Determining Dependencies

The largest barrier to parallelization is dependencies within the algorithm. These can be true dependencies where a result is required before the application can use that result or false dependencies where the dependency is a result of the implementation rather than the algorithm.

False dependencies are easiest to resolve. A change to the implementation will remove the dependence enabling the application to run in parallel. For example, a dependence might be broken using two arrays—one to hold the original value and the second to hold the modified value.

True dependencies come in two forms. Data-carried dependencies are where the result of a previous operation is needed before the next operation can start. Memory-carried dependencies are where the next operation relies on the results of a previous computation being available in memory.

Even if the problem is a true dependence, it need not stop all parallelism. Sometimes it is possible to use speculation to enable computation to continue even when the exact result is not yet known. At other times there may be independent work that can be completed while one thread works on a serial section.

Data Races and the Scaling Limitations of Mutex Locks

Bugs because of data races are the most obvious manifestation of a parallelization problem. These relate to updates of variables without ensuring exclusive access to the variables. These are usually resolved by adding synchronization primitives (such as mutex locks) into the code to ensure exclusive access to the variables.

Although mutex locks can be used to ensure that only a single thread has access to a resource at a time, they cannot enforce the ordering of accesses to data. An alternative approach is required if there is an ordering constraint on the accesses to shared resources. For example, if two threads need to update a variable, a mutex can ensure that they do not update the variable at the same time. However, a mutex cannot force one of the two threads to be the last to perform the update.

The problem with adding mutex locks into the code is that they serialize the access to the variables. Only a single thread can hold the lock, so if there are multiple threads that need to access the data, the application effectively runs serially because only one thread can make progress at a time. Even if requiring the mutex lock is a rare event, it can become a bottleneck if the lock is held for a long time or if there are many threads requiring access to the lock.

Locking Granularity

The granularity of a lock is how much data it protects. A lock with coarse granularity will protect a large amount of data, and a lock with fine granularity will protect a small amount of data. Although it is tempting to place locks at the finest level of granularity possible, it is not usually the best strategy. Having many locks with fine granularity tends to introduce overhead. The overhead comes from the increased amount of memory needed to hold these locks and the decreased likelihood that the locks will be cache resident when they are needed.

However, having few locks usually results in those locks becoming contended by multiple threads, which limits the scaling of the application. Therefore, the granularity of the locks is usually some kind of trade-off between a few contended locks and many uncontended locks. The appropriate balancing point will depend on the number of threads, so it may actually change if the application is run with different workloads or with different numbers of threads. Hence, it is important to test an application with both representative workloads and on a representative system with sufficient virtual CPUs.

The key to picking the optimal locking strategy is often a good grasp of the theoretical performance of the application, in comparison with the actual profile of the application. It is also important to examine the actual scaling of the application as the number of threads increases.

Parallel Code on Multicore Processors

For serial codes, there are few differences between running on a single thread of a multicore processor and running on a single CPU of a multiprocessor system. The real differences occur when running a parallel application on a multicore processor compared to running the same application on a multiprocessor system.

One of the largest problems for a multiprocessor system is that of nonuniform memory latency. An application will get the best performance if it is close to the memory where its data is held. Unfortunately, it is all too easy for an application to be migrated away from its ideal location, resulting in the application experiencing an increase in the memory latency and a corresponding drop in performance.

Although it is possible to get multicore systems that are also multiprocessor, it is common to have only a single multicore processor in the system. A single multicore processor can provide sufficient threads for many parallel tasks. A single processor system also experiences a uniform memory latency, often lower than the latency of a multiprocessor system. Migration of threads between cores of a single multicore processor has a much smaller impact than migration between processors.

However, the migration of threads between virtual CPUs on the same processor is not totally free of cost; there will be some cost if a thread migrates from a virtual CPU where it has some data held in the first-level cache to one where it does not.

Threads on the same multicore processor can communicate through shared memory, typically either the first or second level of cache. Most synchronization relies on memory operations to communicate between threads, and using memory that is resident in the on-chip caches means that the communication costs between threads are the cost of the latency to the shared cache. The latency of on-chip cache is measured in tens of cycles; memory latency is usually measured in hundreds of cycles. This low latency enables low-cost synchronization.

Many of the other issues encountered with parallel programs relate to the communication costs between the threads. For example, the cost of false sharing where multiple threads update separate items of data residing on the same cache line is the cost of migrating a cache line between caches on different processors. On a multiprocessor system, the cost of false sharing is some multiplier of memory latency. On a multicore processor, the shared cache line becomes resident in the cache, and the communication costs are substantially reduced. This means that the performance costs of false sharing can become insignificant. Similarly, the costs of true sharing are reduced; shared data becomes cache resident, and even mutex locks can become resident in the cache.

Low communication latency leads to better scaling because the overheads associated with synchronization are substantially reduced. Hence, multicore processors have a better scaling potential than multiprocessor systems.

Optimizing Programs for Multicore Processors

In some senses, the process of optimizing programs for multicore processors is no different from the process of optimizing them for single-core processors. An improvement in the performance of the serial code will still lead to a performance gain on a multicore processor. Therefore, traditional program optimization skills are still very relevant.

What has changed are the potential benefits from parallelization versus those from optimization. Suppose an application spends half of its time in a particular routine. Traditional optimizations applied to that routine might lead to a 10% gain in performance, and perhaps it might even be possible to double the performance of that particular part of the code. Ideally, the gains would come from algorithmic improvements, but they often also come from tuning to take advantage of the features of the hardware. Hardware-specific tuning tends to be high cost because there is no guarantee that it will be as effective on a different processor and, consequently, runs the risk of requiring further tuning in the future.

The other option is to parallelize the code. If this is successful, the performance of the routine with two threads could be twice that of one thread, and it may be possible to scale to four or eight threads, yielding even more impressive gains over the serial code. The potential gains from parallelization are far greater than the gains from traditional performance tuning. Although the traditional approaches are still relevant, it is best to consider parallelization for performance as early as possible.

The best approach is a probably a hybrid. It is still important to profile the serial code to ensure that there are no obvious problems with it. There is no point in using multiple threads inefficiently through either a poor choice of algorithm or a poor implementation. Once any major issues with the serial algorithm have been resolved, the work can move on to improving the scaling and performance of the parallel implementation. The final choice of where to spend developer time depends on the potential gain from the work. Could a developer get more performance through optimizing the serial code or through parallelizing the serial code?

There is one other aspect of multicore processors that causes parallelization to be a more attractive approach than serial performance tuning. The way that threads on multicore processors share the cores resources may make it more effective to use multiple threads than to try to improve the performance of a single thread.

A single thread running on an otherwise idle multicore machine may get more than its fair share of resources. Adding a second thread will reduce the available resources. However, while one of those threads is stalled, the other will again have access to the full resources of the core.

Hence, for a multicore processor, the time that a thread spends stalled actually represents time when other threads can make forward progress. The practical result of this is that there may be no benefit in throughput from eliminating all the stall cycles from every thread.

An alternative way of thinking about this is that once a multicore processor is issuing an instruction at every opportunity, there is no further benefit to be had from removing stall cycles from the threads running on the processor. Each thread will spend the same amount of time waiting to issue another instruction regardless of whether it spends that time waiting for a stall condition to resolve or just waiting while other threads issue instructions.

The end result is that multicore processors do three things that simplify the development of parallel applications:

- They provide the necessary hardware threads to run parallel applications.
- They reduce the synchronization costs of parallel applications.
- They reduce the impact of instruction stream stalls, so it becomes less critical to produce optimal code.

The Future

This book has covered a number of approaches to producing parallel applications. We have discussed the classic approaches of POSIX threads, Windows native threads, and OpenMP. We have also covered some of the emerging alternatives such as Intel's Threading Building Blocks and CUDA from Nvidia.

What is certain is that it is now critical to be familiar with writing parallel programs. Parallelism is pervasive; it is no longer possible, or desirable, to assume that increasing single-threaded performance will solve the performance issues of an application. The opportunity is there to double or quadruple application performance using multiple threads.

As a result of reading this book, you should be able to identify and use the tools that you need to write parallel programs that are functionally correct and scale well to many cores.

Multicore processors represent the perfect storm for parallel programming. They provide the developer with plenty of threads, and they reduce the impact of the traditional limitations to scaling. The low synchronization costs and costs of data sharing of multicore processors make it possible to produce applications that potentially scale to greater numbers of threads or perhaps scale on parts of the code that previously were too short to parallelize profitably.

Bibliography

This bibliography lists a set of references that provide more details on the topics covered by this book.

Books

POSIX Threads

Butenhof, David R. *Programming with POSIX Threads*. Reading, MA: Addison-Wesley, 1997.

Windows

Richter, Jeffrey M. and Nasarre, Christophe. *Windows via C/C++*. Redmond, WA: Microsoft Press, 2008.

Algorithmic Complexity

Aho, Alfred V.; Hopcroft, John E.; Ullman, Jeffrey D. *Data Structures and Algorithms*. Reading, MA: Addison-Wesley, 1983.

Sedgewick, Robert. *Algorithms*. Reading, MA: Addison-Wesley, 1988.

Computer Architecture

Patterson, David A. and Hennessy, John L. *Computer Organization and Design: The Hardware/Software Interface, Fourth Edition*. Burlington, MA: Morgan Kaufmann, 2009.

Parallel Programming

Andrews, Gregory R. *Foundations of Multithreaded, Parallel, and Distributed Programming*. Reading, MA: Addison-Wesley, 1999.

Breshears, Clay. *The Art of Concurrency: A Thread Monkey's Guide to Writing Parallel Applications*. Sebastopol, CA: O'Reilly Media, Inc., 2009.

Mattson, Timothy G.; Sanders, Beverly A.; Massingill, Berna L. *Patterns for Parallel Programming*. Boston, MA: Addison-Wesley, 2004.

OpenMP

Chapman, Barbara; Yost, Gabriele; van der Pas, Ruud. *Using OpenMP: Portable Shared Memory Parallel Programming.* Cambridge, MA: The MIT Press, 2007.

Online Resources

Hardware

AMD	*http://developer.amd.com/documentation/guides/Pages/default.aspx*
SPARC	*www.opensparc.net/opensparc-t2/index.html*
Intel	*www.intel.com/products/processor/manuals/*

Developer Tools

AMD	*http://developer.amd.com/cpu/Pages/default.aspx*
Intel	*http://software.intel.com/en-us/intel-sdp-home/*
Microsoft	*http://msdn.microsoft.com/*
Oracle	*http://developers.sun.com/*

Parallelization Approaches

Cuda	*www.nvidia.com/object/cuda_home_new.html*
MPI	*www.mpi-forum.org/*
OpenGL	*www.khronos.org/opencl/*
OpenMP	*www.openmp.org/*
PThreads	*www.opengroup.org/austin/*
TBB	*www.threadingbuildingblocks.org/*

Index

T

Multicore Application
Programming

For Windows, Linux, and
Oracle® Solaris

Developer's Library

FREE Online
Edition

Your purchase of **Multicore Application Programming** includes access to a free online edition for 45 days through the Safari Books Online subscription service. Nearly every Addison-Wesley Professional book is available online through Safari Books Online, along with more than 5,000 other technical books and videos from publishers such as Cisco Press, Exam Cram, IBM Press, O'Reilly, Prentice Hall, Que, and Sams.

SAFARI BOOKS ONLINE allows you to search for a specific answer, cut and paste code, download chapters, and stay current with emerging technologies.

Activate your FREE Online Edition at
www.informit.com/safarifree

> **STEP 1:** Enter the coupon code: UOTNZBI.

> **STEP 2:** New Safari users, complete the brief registration form.
> Safari subscribers, just log in.

If you have difficulty registering on Safari or accessing the online edition, please e-mail customer-service@safaribooksonline.com